CHARLOTTE
The Last Suffragette

Whitton-Tardif bout makes fight history

'In this cornah . . .'

See also page 1f
By Roger Appleton

'No Solid Blows!

Mayor Swings Her Fists At Tardif

By TOM KERR
of The Journal

Mayor Whitton lost her temper...

SIX-HOUR MARATHON

Council Upholds Mayor On Future Sewage Levy

Call By Campeau Nearly "Duress", Whitton Reports

By Phillip Wiltur

Election rally

Whitton threatens to 'read Riot Act'

Audience jeers mayor, chairman

By Roger Appleton

Three hundred spectators and 27 political candidates were threatened with the Riot Act and placed under police supervision as the Carleton Ward civic election meeting exploded in wild chaos Wednesday night.

The Riot Act threat came from Mrs. F. D. Richardson, the meeting chairman, and was delivered in the name of Mayor Charlotte Whitton.

Gasps of amazement from crowd

WORKS INFORMATION

Mayor 'Will Shake City's

Whither Whitton? oundations

By W. M. Arnott
Chiefs Staff Writer

Mayor Charlotte Whitton told Board of Control she will "shake this city to its foundations" when she presents to City Council an...

BY RICHARD JACKSON

JUDGE WHITTON?
Chairman Whitton?
Senator Whitton?
Even Ambassador Whitton?

The Journal's Parliamentary

Charlotte's secret weapon

'FILTHY REMARK'

Defending Good Name –Whitton

By TOM KERR
of The Journal

Mayor scares board with her toy pistol

'My Lord Mayor, if I pull your chain, will you flush?'

rt attack claims former mayor

Charlotte Whitton dies

Leading civic figure more than 20 years

By Marsha Sksee

Charlotte Runs Third

REID IN A WALK

Fogarty, Jones, Webber And Heit on Board

The Last Suffragette

Suffragette

**DAVE
MULLINGTON**

GSPH

GENERAL STORE PUBLISHING HOUSE
499 O'Brien Road, Box 415
Renfrew, Ontario, Canada K7V 4A6
Telephone 1.613.432.7697 or 1.800.465.6072
www.gsph.com

ISBN 978-1-897508-77-0

Cover, design, and layout: Magdalene Carson
Printed by Custom Printers of Renfrew Ltd., Renfrew, Ontario
Printed and bound in Canada

Library and Archives Canada Cataloguing in Publication
Mullington, Dave, 1941-
    Charlotte : the last suffragette / Dave Mullington.
ISBN 978-1-897508-77-0
    1. Whitton, Charlotte, 1896-1975. 2. Mayors--Ontario--Ottawa--
Biography. 3. Social workers--Canada--Biography. 4. Feminists--Canada--
Biography. I. Title.
FC3096.26.W5M86 2010   971.3'8403092   C2010-901415-4

Front cover:
Charlotte Whitton opens Ottawa's Community Chest campaign, September
25, 1963. (Credit: Gary Bartlett, courtesy of the Ottawa Citizen)

Back cover:
Official portrait by Robert Hyndman, City of Ottawa Archives.

To Béatrice,
with love.

Contents

Preface

I never met Charlotte Elizabeth Whitton. Although I lived in Ottawa while she was mayor and my mother was a keen supporter of hers, I was still in high school or university and had neither the time nor the interest in municipal affairs during her reign at city hall. However, I clearly remember that it was during this time that I first saw my mother involved in politics. My mother was a die-hard Whitton supporter, so whether it was during weekly afternoon bridge parties at our house, or lengthy telephone conversations with her friends across the city, she took every opportunity to promote her. I often wondered what could stir my mother to get so excited about a politician, as she cared little for provincial or federal affairs. My father, a First World War veteran and commissionaire, ignored politics altogether at the time, as did my brother Hugh and sister Nancy. However, there was no debate in our house about whom our family supported; it was Charlotte.

I remained mystified as to how this woman could hold my mother and so many others under her sway, but I had my own life to live and I didn't really care all that much at the time. After graduation I moved out of town, and then out of the country, and it was twenty years before I returned to Ottawa to work as a reporter with *The Ottawa Citizen* and found myself connecting with Charlotte once more. She was dead by then, but the mere mention of her name still earned headlines and nodding smiles from those who had witnessed her extravagant antics and championing of the "little guy." In fact, at five-foot-one, she was first and foremost a "little guy" herself, but one who had pushed aside many a "big guy" to earn her place in the nation's memory.

I should mention here that I'm not using Charlotte's first name condescendingly. For anyone to have called her anything but Charlotte during her political career, when she gained her main claim to fame as the first woman mayor of a Canadian city, would have been highly unusual. She was "Charlotte" on the campaign trail and she was "Charlotte" in the headlines. She signed her column in the *Citizen*, "Charlotte," and she called her nightly television program on CJOH "Dear Charlotte." In 1968, her longtime friend, *Toronto Star* columnist Lotta Dempsey, wrote: "All you have to say is Charlotte. Headline writers and newscasters do. And everyone from grade school children to grandfathers rocking on verandahs of old peoples' homes know who you mean." And so, throughout this book, she is simply Charlotte.

Acknowledgments

M any people helped in the preparation of this book, but in particular I want to thank my wife Béatrice, for putting up with my long, awkward hours and my restive emotions as I cobbled it together, and my brother Hugh, who like Béatrice, reviewed an early draft of this work and offered sage advice.

Paul Henry, Claire Lee, Serge Barbe, and Serge Blondin of the City of Ottawa Archives, and Mrs. Gillian Barlow of the Queen's University Archives were helpful in locating Whitton material in their collections. My fellow members of the Canadian Authors Association Centrepointe Writing Group, including Anita Miettunen, Lynn Campbell, Ramma Kamra, Molly O'Connor, and Gwen Smid, provided practical input in critiquing the Introduction. Ernie Bies of Ottawa assisted with the fact-checking, national *Globe and Mail* columnist Roy MacGregor kindly helped with my search for a publisher, and Teresa Bendal, head librarian with the Alberta Government Library in Edmonton, pointed me in the right direction for background information on Charles B. Hill.

Furthermore, I want to acknowledge the following people for the time they allowed me and the information they provided in interviews over the past few years: Fran Baldwin, Marguerite Barclay, Gillian Barlow, Ruth Bell, Claude Bennett, Lillian McCann Benoit, Bill Boehmer, Chris Brand, Dave Brown, Elizabeth Carroll, Oakley Carey, Mary Carman, Dr. James Coupland, Kathleen Derry, Marion Dewar, Pat Fulton, Garry Guzzo, Andy Haydon, Bruce Hillary, Jacquelin Holzman, Tim Kenny, Lucille Lalonde, Marjory Lindsay, Bill Luxton, Sandi Heins, Marie Henderson, Murray MacLean, Diane McIntyre, Jean Milligan, Aubrey Moodie, Pat Murray, John Nelligan, Gordon Palbiski, Bill Peacock, Helen Peart, Beatrice Ross, Audrey Philips, Teresa Smith, Phyllis Swaren, Blanche Szendrey, Gilles Tardif, Jim Watson, Vic Whittaker, John B. Whitton, Stephen Whitton, and Eleanor Wilson.

I also want to thank publisher, Tim Gordon, editor Susan Code McDougall, and art director, Magdalene Carson of General Store Publishing House.

Introduction

"**P**ut up or shut up," said *The Ottawa Journal* editorial of October 21, 1950, in effect.

Charlotte Whitton had been talking up a storm in favour of women's active involvement in political affairs for years, and now, with the civic election just over a month away, it was time that she finally did something about it. Show some leadership, it urged. Stop talking and writing about it, just do it. The newspaper approved of the few political gains women had made in recent years and now "the very able Dr. Whitton as Alderman Whitton, Controller Whitton, Mayor Whitton, Charlotte Whitton, MLA [Member of the Legislative Assembly], the Hon. Charlotte Whitton, an inspiration and example to the whole feminist cause, could be effective beyond their dreams."

It was all that the fifty-four-year-old spinster could have asked for. The editorial appeared on a Saturday and by the following Monday, Charlotte was willing to stand for city council if the conditions were right. By Tuesday evening, the newspaper reported that "a representative group of women, as yet unnamed," had formed an election committee, and Charlotte had said that she had been inundated with calls of support. The bandwagon was rolling, and Charlotte had the horses' reins firmly in hand. She would run for office and she would show those misogynistic men and those lackadaisical ladies just what a woman could do. It was something she had contemplated, something she had dreamed of, for years. Yes, a determined woman could do quite well in politics and she was going to prove it.

By Wednesday of the same week, she announced that she would run for a seat on the board of control, a sort of inner cabinet of the city council whose members were elected by voters across the city, as opposed to the aldermen who were chosen to represent individual

Women played a commanding role in Charlotte's election campaigns.
City of Ottawa Archives, MG011/CA6572

wards. There was no time for dithering, for the election was just five weeks away. However, Charlotte had a speech to give in Toronto late in the week and there was no way anyone would stop her from talking. No one ever had, and no one ever would.

So, amidst the scurrying around by her energetic but inexperienced female supporters, Charlotte took time away from her campaign to talk to the graduates of the Normal School in Ottawa on Tuesday and left for Toronto on Wednesday to present yet another address. She would be back in the national capital on the following Monday and they had better be ready, she warned her campaign team, which already was beginning to experience her authoritarian style. Minor disagreements were creating minor annoyances between the candidate and her team, but they were largely overlooked in the excitement of the moment.

For now, the women were solidly behind her. Mrs. H.G. Barber, president of the Local Council of Women in Ottawa, called a meeting of all women's groups in the city, with the intention of backing Charlotte. "The Ottawa Women's Club urges support of Dr. Whitton for board of control," president Mrs. Inez Shepard said. "No matter what our politics are, it is important to all of us to have a worthy woman representative in civic affairs," the *Journal* reported.

Meanwhile, nothing was heard in the media from the potential male candidates, aside from the usual speculation about who might run for mayor. Incumbent mayor E.A. Bourque probably would seek re-election and he might be opposed by former controllers Grenville Goodwin and/or Dr. Gerry Geldert, but all three were playing their cards close to their chests and few people really cared anyhow. Likewise with the potential candidates for board of control. Incumbent controllers Len Coulter, Dan McCann, Charles Pickering, and Paul Tardif probably would try to retain their seats and undoubtedly a few new faces would appear to challenge, but no one was saying anything publicly at the time because, well, the election was at least five weeks away and this was Ottawa. Federal politicians were the newsmakers here; city council was mostly ignored when it came to media coverage.

The postwar period was a reasonably prosperous time for Ottawa, and except for the civic elections every two years, little heed was paid to the municipal council. It was just two years earlier that Stanley Lewis had finished a thirteen-year run as mayor, a term that had been overshadowed by war and marked by inactivity at the city council table. In fact, longevity on council was an accepted fact and dullness was worth money in the bank.

There was nothing dull about Charlotte's campaign. For the first week she had relied on a rather disorganized group of close female friends, but come the second week, it was time to get serious. She told the women that she wanted a qualified, substantial campaign team that would work to exhaustion if necessary, and she wanted it at once. She also wanted a midtown campaign headquarters, and she wanted it at once, too. Otherwise, she told a stormy meeting of 130 Local Council of Women members and representatives of another ninety women's groups at the Château Laurier Hotel, she was withdrawing immediately. Enough said. Charlotte would have her midtown campaign headquarters and the LCW deposited an emergency bond valued at between $300 and $1,000. The official campaign committee was struck and the bandwagon kept rolling. Mrs. Robert Dorman was chairman, Mrs. A.E. Armstrong was vice-chairman, and thirteen other women were responsible for such areas as finance, publicity, transportation, telephone canvassing, and polling.

Prospects were looking good. Charlotte now had the support of many local women's groups — from the Elizabeth Tudor Chapter of the Imperial Order Daughters of the Empire (IODE) to the Women's Historical Society of Ottawa to local members of the Women's Press Club of Canada — and she figured that if she could attract 20,000 votes on December 4, she would win herself a seat on the board of control. As for the male voters, who cared? There were more than 20,000 women voters out there, and besides, the male candidates for controller probably would split the vote among themselves. And when someone suggested that perhaps Charlotte should have a man to chair her campaign's finance committee, she snapped back, "Naming a man would be an admission of defeat at the outset. Let's make this a women's campaign as far as chairmen are concerned." Of course she would not be opposed to receiving the votes of males, nor their financial contributions, but at least for the time being, she would focus on women for support.

The Women's Civic Campaign Committee was established and the fundraising began. "Donations from a nickel up, or even five coppers, will be accepted," Charlotte announced. Then she changed the name of her campaign team. Henceforth it would be The Charlotte Whitton for Controller Committee. That way, she told the *Journal*, men could be included. But they would have to remain in the background. "If we are successful, it will be thanks to the men as well as the women. The husbands of our hard-working conveners have had to put up with telephones exploding day and night in their hitherto peaceful homes and by now most of them have had to get used to going without breakfast unless they get it themselves. . . . We girls have got to make this campaign a partnership with the boys." The story appeared in the November 3 edition, and it was the third time in as many days that a Whitton story had appeared in the paper — always on page three and usually accompanied by a pleasant picture of the candidate — while there was rarely a mention of any possible opponents.

The *Journal* was totally supportive, as was its local rival, *The Evening Citizen*. The October 21 *Journal* editorial urging her to run for office was preceded by a lengthy article the previous day, headlined,

An original Whitton poster from her 1950 election campaign.
Photo by author

"Legal Dice Loaded Against Women in Council." It appeared under Bobbie Turcotte's byline, but it might as well have been written by Charlotte herself, for it included many of the complaints that she had written and spoken about for years. Women were required to spend a lot of time on housework, it argued, or if they were business-women, they were too tied up in their work, resulting in little time for political activities. And there was one other problem. "The hustle-bustle of public election deters a lot of otherwise willing women. They are apt to shrink from the idea of door-to-door canvassing and feel diffident about too much public speaking. And the unbroken record of defeat of every woman candidate for [city] Council to date stands as a big black barrier in their minds."

Indeed, city council was a men's club. Every mayor since the municipality was incorporated as Bytown ninety-five years earlier had been male, likewise all the aldermen and controllers. In 1921, the first year that women could seek municipal office, Mrs. J.A. Wilson had sought a seat on the board of control, but failed; likewise, in 1938, when Mrs. H.G. Barber, president of the LCW, and in 1948, when Marjory Mann had run in aldermanic races. But it was now 1950 and Charlotte was running. And Charlotte was Charlotte. There was no one else like her.

Born in the Ottawa Valley town of Renfrew, Ontario, on March 8, 1896, Charlotte was a brilliant student who excelled in all academic subjects as well as at sports. One of her numerous activities was as a regular contributor to the Saturday youth pages in *The Globe* (later *Globe and Mail*). At Queen's University in Kingston, she won both academic and athletic awards, sat on the students' council, and served as the first woman editor of the student newspaper. She then enjoyed an illustrious twenty-year career in social work. Social welfare historian Dr. Richard Splane described her as "the dominant figure in developing . . . the leading national social policy agency in its field." After a falling out with the welfare community, she turned to public speaking, consulting, and freelance writing for magazines and newspapers. After ten years at this pursuit, she turned to local politics.

Among her principal fora as a writer was the *Citizen*. By late 1950, after writing a thrice-weekly column for the paper for two years on a broad range of topics, she directed her readers' attention to the dangers of communism, or "sovietism," as she called it. "The hunger for power and prestige can prove just as virulent as that for property or wealth, and the madness of its lust can possess a Stalin just as terribly as a Hitler, Mussolini, Napoleon or Genghis Khan," she warned in a typically foreboding column on November 7. Two weeks later, she concluded an exhaustive, eighteen-part rant against the philosophy that she warned was threatening both Europe and North America.

That was the iron-fist side of Charlotte. The velvet-glove side showed itself at about the same time when she addressed the Ottawa Women's Forum on civic problems. Turning on the charm, she informed the amused delegates that her cat Rustie had advised her that she would know who her real supporters were at election time, then went on to explain her hitherto little known religious situation — her mother was a fervent Catholic while her father was a keen member of the Loyal Orange Lodge, an organization that had little liking for Catholics, francophones, Jews, or anyone else who was not an anglophile. "Where does that leave me?" she asked rhetorically. "Right in the Anglican Church. All the leftovers arrive in the Anglican Church," she smiled. The women loved it and they loved Charlotte. The Ottawa Women's Business and Professional Club announced its support for her civic candidacy, as did the Earnscliffe Chapter of the IODE, and the Fairmont section of the Women's Christian Temperance Union. The bandwagon continued to roll.

The media were only too ready to conspire with Charlotte's candidacy. To think, a woman running for civic office! What a story! What colour! Let the ink flow! On October 25, influential *Citizen* columnist Austin F. Cross penned the first of a number of glowing reports on the new candidate, and on November 11, the *Journal* featured a comely young Whitton supporter with the headline, "Blonde, beautiful and civic-minded." It told how one young businesswoman, Colleen Nolan, had joined the "First Ladies of the Order of the Needle and Thread" — Charlotte's campaign logo was the needle and thread, to represent the need for domestic repairs at city hall — while riding to work on the streetcar seated next to Mrs. Dorman, Charlotte's campaign chairman. Nolan, like so many other women caught up in the excitement, was quickly convinced of the need for a woman at the council table and immediately joined the cause.

One week later, on November 18, the *Citizen* began a three-part profile headlined, "The Whitton Story: Willing Fighter For Any Cause She Believes In." Underneath her photo, the caption read, "Dr. Charlotte Whitton, CBE [Commander, Order of the British Empire] . . . a dandy cook." Introducing the three-part series by writer Holland Cox, an editor's note advised, "Dr. Charlotte Whitton, CBE, is one of the most amazing personalities this city, and indeed this country, of ours has ever known. Her past record is eloquent testimony of this fact." The profile was no hatchet job. "No one in Canada today is better known in her chosen field of endeavour than Dr. Charlotte Whitton, CBE, and her work here is being watched in other lands where her services would be greatly valued, but she is first and always a Canadian and has turned a deaf ear to all offers."

Yes, she was some woman indeed, all five-foot-one-inch, 130 pounds of her. That was when she was watching her weight; otherwise, she added as much as ten pounds, "for she's a dandy cook and likes what she cooks. Her hair is black except for a streak of white which has been there since youth, and she keeps it to a close shingle — 'less trouble in the wind.' Her hands and feet are very small, but it is her hazel eyes — alive, changing colour with every emotion — that are her most attractive feature. They dance and sparkle with amusement, grow fierce at mention of injustice, tender and sympathetic when she comes in contact with misfortune and unhappiness." But she was much more than a short, attractive woman, Cox assured *Citizen* readers. She had been a leader in Canada's social welfare sphere, for which she received the CBE honour, and she had received two honorary doctorates from Canadian universities in recognition of her work. She definitely was a woman of substance.

Not to be outdone, the *Journal* responded four days later, describing Charlotte as nothing less than a girl-next-door domestic diva. Its headline across the top of the third page read, "Men, Bachelor Girl Charlotte (Phone 3-8392) Bakes a Tasty Cake and Can Fix Gadgets Too." Below were three photos of a cheerful, middle-aged Charlotte baking a cake. Reporter Lesley Johnstone's article began, "Civic-minded Charlotte, with her diversity of accomplishments, appeared in the role of home-maker (bachelor girl, apartment 236 Rideau Terrace, phone 3-8392) when she spoke at Stewarton Church hall yesterday . . . to the Pauline Bilsky Chapter of Hadassah." Charlotte told the Jewish women that as the eldest child in her family, she had been used to housekeeping, and every Saturday morning at about eight o'clock, she had been expected to rise and make the noontime dinner and whip up a couple of pies and cakes for the weekend meals. But, she added modestly, she had not been an accomplished student in domestic science class. Johnstone continued, "When examination time came, she stood before her little hot stove and dealt with the invalid broth while the girl next to her, whom she didn't like, played with making a gingerbread which would go to a teacher beloved by both girls. This was too much for the practical Charlotte. 'I put sulphur in her gingerbread, and the whole shooting match blew up, stove and all.'" Following a visit to the principal's office, Charlotte withdrew from domestic science class. "There must have been some prescience I was to lead a manless life, because my manual training has been of the greatest value to me. I can fix most gadgets in my home and I can still cook." That story appeared on page three.

On page sixteen of the same edition, a headline read, "Charlotte Gives Qualifications, Tells Why She Is Running for the Board." The article began, "Fit 'n' fiftyish, in a life where every birthday added to her mental stature (she's only as high as your heart), Miss Charlotte Whitton told the Pauline Bilsky Chapter of Hadassah she is like the rugby player 'who hits the line where he makes his weight count most.'" As for her election platform, she vowed to fight for more low-cost housing, a better deal for pensioners, and a new city hall.

Interestingly, neither paper found the space to profile any of the male candidates in a similar manner. The men simply ran on their platforms, limited as they were, and placed small advertisements in the papers during the last week of the election campaign. Meanwhile, in *Le Droit*, the city's only French-language newspaper, the upcoming election received scarce coverage, concentrating its support on veteran francophone controller Paul Tardif's return to the board of control.

It would be folly to say that the English-language papers patronized Charlotte to the extent that they ignored her perspective on municipal issues of the day, but certainly their coverage overwhelmingly concentrated on her femininity and her outspokenness, at least in the early weeks of the campaign. As the final week progressed, coverage was more balanced, but Charlotte was always ready with a quip or a crack, and it seemed that no matter what she said, it was news. For example, after twenty-three contenders appeared at an all-candidates meeting on November 27, the headlines next day highlighted Charlotte's plea that something be done to allow women late in their pregnancies — there were only about 100 such cases in Ottawa at the time — the opportunity to vote, possibly at special polls in the hospitals. It obviously was too late to arrange such a deal for the pregnant women, but the lone female candidate succeeded in hogging the headlines once more. Other issues of more concern to the general voter, such as allowing professional sport on Sunday or reducing the size of council, were relegated to the lower paragraphs of the newspaper reports.

When one candidate for controller, Roy Donaldson, tried to outshine her in the publicity department by choosing a diaper and safety pin as his campaign emblem to suggest that the four incumbent controllers were still in their second childhood, Charlotte upstaged him the following day by showing up at a campaign meeting bedecked in the gold buckle of her great-uncle's swordbelt on one lapel and her needle-and-thread insignia on the other. "If anybody wants to draw blood, I'm ready," Charlotte told the enthusiastic crowd. "I've been told the going will start to get rough now, and I've come prepared."

She needn't have worried. It was obvious that she had the support of almost all women voters in the city, while her six male opponents would fight it out for the remaining three seats on the board of control. It was so obvious, in fact, that candidate C.E. Pickering pleaded in a newspaper advertisement "to the women of Ottawa" that they vote for four candidates, as they were allowed to do, rather than just for Charlotte, as they seemed inclined to do.

There was a record turnout at the polls on December 4, 1950, and while some were surprised that Grenville Goodwin defeated incumbent mayor Edouard Bourque, the big news was Charlotte's dominance in the controller category. The results for controller were as follows:

Charlotte Whitton	38,405	votes
Len Coulter	31,071	
Dan McCann	25,484	
Paul Tardif	24,206	
C.E. Pickering	22,687	
Roy Donaldson	20,180	
Frank Ellis	10,988	

Charlotte led in all but three of the city's fourteen wards, and those wards were in Lowertown, the francophone domain of Paul Tardif. As a result of her first-place finish, she earned the position of deputy mayor, which meant that if anything should happen to Grenville Goodwin during his term over the next two years, Charlotte would become mayor, the first female mayor of a Canadian city. Which is how it turned out and which is why Charlotte and her explosive outbursts, her rapier wit, her outrageous gimmicks, and her high-handedness put dull, old Ottawa on the map and regularly saw her name featured in headlines from coast to coast, and even beyond.

For the next two decades, civic politics in Ottawa would never be the same, and Charlotte would be named Canada's woman newsmaker of the year six times in the span of eleven years.

PART ONE  Youth

1 "Pisces Was Rising"

Charlotte Elizabeth Whitton was born under the sign of Pisces, the fish, at 6:25 a.m. on a cold, blustery March 8, 1896, in Renfrew, Ontario. "Pisces was rising at your birth," reads a handwritten astrological report found among the voluminous personal papers Charlotte left with the Public Archives of Canada, now Library and Archives Canada. "[So] you're kind, sympathetic, benevolent and generous . . . the moon in Libra confers upon you personally a refined character . . . you will always be kindly, genial, affable and courteous, and will try to preserve a happy disposition." Those born under Pisces, astrologers say, are also often weak-willed, secretive, and vague. How wrong these phrases are! Charlotte had many good qualities, but "a refined character" she was not. And weak-willed, secretive, and vague? Definitely not!

"There will be many contradictions," the report noted more accurately, but "if I had [illegible word] pretty closely upon your actual birth time you will have the following appearance—A rather short and somewhat fleshy body, round face, a good complexion, brown hair . . . [You will be] fond of the opposite sex, yet not given to bondage; you will injure yourself more than others. You may be inclined to be both prostigal [sic] and extravagant."

The report, which comprised twenty-one legal-size pages, but was neither signed nor dated, suggested that she would find employment both socially and financially rewarding.

Charlotte was the first of eight children born to Elizabeth and John Whitton, of whom only four survived beyond early childhood. Their father worked at a variety of jobs in and around Algonquin Park during much of Charlotte's childhood, while their mother operated a boarding house on Raglan Street, the main thoroughfare through Renfrew which served, as it does today, as the town's commercial centre.

It was a time when the wood frame stores along the street were being replaced by brick buildings and the streets were lit by arc lights suspended high atop electricity poles and wired to the small generating station constructed by Renfrew pioneer A.A. Wright. The unpaved streets were muddy during the rains of spring, summer, and fall, but the high wooden sidewalks kept pedestrians' footwear and the women's ankle-length dresses relatively dry and clean. The electricity poles, meanwhile, offered a handy place to hitch one's horse while doing business along the street.

Typhoid struck the town during the summer following Charlotte's birth. That and other diseases were blamed on the dead horses, cows, hogs, and dogs that had been dumped into the Bonnechere River, which bounced and burbled down the falls and through the open farmlands along the town's western outskirts. Wisely, that December, town council voted in favour of building a proper waterworks plant which helped to alleviate health concerns.

Renfrew, a small community fifty-five miles west of Ottawa that was established in 1828 when Xavier Plaunt established a small lumber business by the side of the Bonnechere, retained the flavour of so many hinterland towns of those days. Boisterous rivermen taking a break from the logdrive on the Bonnechere whooped it up in and around the local bars and only police chief Barney McDermott and his dog Spot managed to keep a semblance of law and order. There was little infrastructure and few government services, and people learned to get by on their own. If, for example, Charlotte's father had to go north to find work, so be it. If Charlotte's mother had to take in boarders to feed her family, then that's the way it was. They would make do.

Renfrew was a town of Protestant Scots, Irish, and Englishmen, as well as Catholic French-Canadians, Irish, and Poles, and although their numbers may have been similar, their economic and social positions were not. The Scots, such as lumber tycoons Alex Barnet, James Carswell, and James Stewart, ruled the roost while the others settled for second or third best. Nevertheless, the frontier sense of community prevailed. Everyone pitched in and, for the most part, everyone got along. Even Barney McDermott, the prickliest of policemen, knew when to turn a blind eye to the illegal cockfights on Saturday nights that attracted everyone from Charlotte's father to the Methodist minister.

For her part, Charlotte could claim English, Irish, French, and Spanish ancestry, but it was her English forbears that she held in highest regard throughout her lifetime. This was mostly due to the influence of her paternal grandmother, Matilda Whitton. Charlotte was an anglophile of the first order. British royalty would be a life-long interest, and Elizabeth I, the Virgin Queen, would be her muse. At one point, she traced her ancestry back to "great-great-uncle Hum-frey" who was a bugler with the Duke of Wellington at his victory over Napoléon Bonaparte at the Battle of Waterloo in 1815.

Her English blood came from her father, a grandson of James Whitton and Elizabeth Hezeltyne. James was twenty when he married seventeen-year-old Elizabeth in Leyburn, Yorkshire, in 1840, and because times were poor in the areas of East and West Witton — the "h" was added later by some family members — the young couple emigrated to Canada. Their first stop was in Sorel, Lower Canada, but when they were defrauded by a Quebec City merchant who sold them land he didn't own, they moved on to the Kingston area and operated an inn for a few years. This was followed by a move west to a farm in Northumberland County, about halfway between Kingston and Toronto, and while James ran the farm, Charlotte's great-grandmother Elizabeth established a small creamery in the basement. The Northumberland creamery eventually proved a great success, and the area became recognized for its Brae Cheese Factory.

Charlotte's grandfather, however, had little to do with the cream-ery. And her father, an outdoorsman, had nothing to do with it at all. He ventured north to the Renfrew area as a young man and, in 1894, at the age of twenty-two, he eloped with Elizabeth Langin, age twenty-three, of nearby Carleton Place.

Elizabeth was a Catholic of Irish descent, with a bit of French and Spanish blood from further back, who had been born in Roch-ester, New York, then moved to eastern Ontario as a child with her parents, Michael and Elizabeth.

Charlotte's father, John, was a Methodist. Not surprisingly, con-sidering interfaith marriage was as popular as a skunk at a Sunday school picnic, their respective parents did not approve of the union. Nor did their churches. Thus it was that they eloped and chose the neutral, nearby town of Almonte and the neutral Anglican church for their wedding.

Charlotte, at age three.
Photo courtesy of McDougall Mill
Museum, Renfrew, Ontario

Charlotte loved her mother, but it was only in later years that she expressed any interest in her Irish roots. In those years, she would look back fondly to the "sad and pitiful words of high pride, grim grief, suffering and despair coming through my yet cheery Irish mother reciting the records of dispossession and exile from Erin; simple annals of quiet endurance and heroism as, in loneliness and dogged endeavour, strange trails were opened, crowding forests cleared, and new homes built where life went on in 'Canada West' (which some of the great aunts never could think of as the 'Ontario' of the new 'Dominion of Canada')." Nevertheless, Charlotte's undivided allegiance throughout her lifetime was to England and the Crown.

Most children begin talking when they're about a year; Charlotte began at nine months. And, as her sister Kay remarked in her unfinished biography, she never stopped talking from that point on.

As for Charlotte, she recalled her childhood as one filled with precocious activities. One of her earliest memories concerned an incident on December 31, 1899. Three-year-old Charlotte was restless in her bed that night, listening to her parents and aunts and uncles downstairs playing euchre, so she decided to play a trick on her visiting cousin, who was one month younger. "That was the moment I chose to climb out of my crib, crawl under the bearskin rug in the upstairs hall, creep, enwrapped therein, silently across and pounced upon the guileless little visitor, sleeping in his cot. His hysterics were fearful to behold, and the new century opened very painfully for me,"she recounted in one of her columns published in the *Citizen* in 1950. In another column at about the same time, she recalled the following as a four-year-old:

> What an undertaking it was to get ready for school or Sunday school, particularly since you wore better and lighter cashmere stockings that day. Next to your skin, neatly wrapped around your ankles, beneath those stockings, were the southern extremities of your "fleece-lineds." Then you pulled your stockings up straight and smooth and gartered them fast. You put on your good, firm laced boots, and then, with the family's help, your overstockings were literally hauled up over those two layers of leggings. Those overstockings had rubbers, like a pair of scows, attached. Thus, enwrapped as thoroughly as an Egyptian mummy, you traversed the two or three blocks of Renfrew's snowy streets to St. Paul's Church or the Public School, for they were, and are, beside each other, to the constant anxiety of the stained glass windows of the former. No matter what way you went, you had to pass one of the town's five brawling hotels or two liquor stores. And you were taught, very early, not to look that way, and if you did, not to mention whose father you saw, going in or coming out, if he seemed to have been hurt or needing help as he walked.

Another Whitton commentary, this time in a May 1950 edition of *The Renfrew Mercury*, praised the recently deceased Margaret Isobel Eady as one of the best teachers she had had during her school years. Miss Eady's father was a police magistrate and the grandmaster of the local Orange Lodge in the early 1900s, and Miss Eady believed in a proper upbringing. She taught more than faith and language; she taught life and character itself, Charlotte recalled.

If you wanted to go, she would read to you, hours, in the pleasant back garden of her home or have you read to her; and she would tell you that an ewe was not an "eewee" and that your Ottawa Valley "kaerds" were "cards" where polite bridge was played . . . [and] when at noon she found you jeering at a poor drunken man, propped against the school fence, she had herded you all into her room, sent Bert Campbell to buy an egg at the corner grocery, Alex Knight to bring some alcohol from the science room. Then she had broken the egg into the glass, where it cooked hard before your goggling gaze. Then you got a lesson, more enduring than strapping, on the pity of what alcohol could do to brain and body tissues.

Charlotte rarely mentioned her usually absent father, but Kay, her younger sister by eight years, was less reticent. "Father was, like his father and brother, a gay and handsome nineteenth century product and, according to Charlotte, she went to the taverns with my Mother to find Father so that the Renfrew policeman, Barney Mc-Dermott, wouldn't bring him home in a wheelbarrow, because that was Barney's unique process for sobering up the Renfrew drunks. He sometimes carried them right to bed. . . . The only time I recall Father's alcoholism was when I was about five and he was being terribly sick, which probably helped cure him. He had a tremendous appetite and was overweight, like all his family, which caused great tumult at their funerals, with heavy oak caskets involving the removal of a bay window and front doors."

But, as Charlotte recalled in a 1952 column in *Maclean's* magazine, "My father . . . was an easy, genial man. Until his death in my fortieth year, we had only two or three really stand-up rows." The worst occurred when she was sixteen, after she had participated in a high school debate on women's right to vote and to be elected to Parliament. Her father was firmly opposed to women in politics, figuring they belonged there as much as they belonged in competitive sports, which to him meant not at all. "I came home, flushed with pride and excitement, and to proclaim my hope of someday becoming a real minister at Ottawa. . . . My father's temper flared as I had rarely seen it. Like rugby, politics was for the boys and men." Charlotte had robustly disagreed.

The year 1950 was a particularly good time for public reminiscences by Charlotte, possibly because it was a time of calm introspection following the extraordinary pressures of recent years. In 1947, she lost her dearest friend and live-in companion Margaret Grier, and in 1948, there was an energy-sapping libel trial in Alberta. Perhaps she was also imagining that there would be little free time in the future, for she had expectations of a great political career, a career that might start at city hall but surely would lead to the House of Commons and probably a cabinet post in a Progressive Conservative government. In fact, examining Charlotte's speeches, writing, and behind-the-scenes political activities, it doesn't seem far-fetched to suggest that she could see herself one day as Canada's first female prime minister. At any rate, she frequently used her Saturday column of her thrice-weekly commitment to the *Citizen* as an opportunity to look back to her earlier days, especially her childhood.

For example, there was this recollection of her first visit to Ottawa as a youngster:

> I never can call our Hell's Half Acre of Confusion Square, the Plaza [later renamed Confederation Square]. I still see it as I first saw it, a frightfully train-sick child, brought down on the "local" on a special excursion of the Anglican Sunday School children from all the "stops" along the line from Renfrew to the Broad Street station. Then we were given our first ride on street cars, where we were even sicker than on the train, and then taken to Britannia, where we got sunburn on the beaches and cramps in the water and, after a perfect day of excited misery, went home, trainsick again all the way, to get over the touch of sun, the colic and chills that were all we had to show for the pennies we had saved all the year to be in on the outing.

During the school year, she excelled at both sports and academics. In 1903, when she was just seven years old, her name appeared in the *Mercury* among the students named to the class honours list. Facilities were primitive in Charlotte's time. The school lacked a gymnasium or a playing field, wood stoves kept the classrooms warm in winter, and physical education classes were limited to calisthenics in the aisles. The toilets were outdoors, but you learned to live with that back then, just as you learned to live with a lot of life's shortcomings. You simply overcame them, Charlotte would argue.

Indeed, Renfrew overcame its backwoods image for one brief, improbable year when it stood the sports world on its head. The little town of 3,000 captured headlines across North America as it produced what was then the greatest collection of hockey all-stars in the game's history. The year was 1910, and the man responsible was Renfrew railroad and mining magnate M.J. O'Brien. Charlotte was then fourteen years old and a fervent rink rat. O'Brien's success in moving mountains to ice a championship team would not be lost on the impressionable young "Lottie," as she often was called.

O'Brien, known respectfully around town as "M.J.," and to Charlotte as "Uncle Imjay," was born in Lochaber, Nova Scotia, in 1851, and arrived in Renfrew in 1880 as a railroad contractor. An imposing, heavyset man, O'Brien began making his fortune at the age of fourteen, earning ten cents for each pail of water he delivered to thirsty railway workers in Antigonish County, Nova Scotia. He continued in railroad construction and, by 1879, found himself carving out part of the Kingston and Pembroke Railway in the Renfrew area. It was here that he met his future wife, Jane Barry, and set down roots. However, that didn't stop him from obtaining railroad contracts in the Maritimes or elsewhere in Ontario. The contracting business was profitable, but it wasn't until shortly after the turn of the century that his Halifax lawyer, future prime minister Robert Borden, steered him into a deal for a silver mine at Cobalt, in northern Ontario, which eventually made him a millionaire.

Despite his wealth, which could have seen him owning a mansion in any city of his choice, O'Brien had become a Renfrew boy at heart. In 1907, he decided that it was time to put his adopted hometown, a dedicated hockey community with the Creamery Kings as its team, on the map. This coincided with the dawn of professional hockey, an era when the best players signed short-term contracts and went where the money was best. Much of that money was spent in Ottawa and Montreal where the Silver Seven and the Wanderers, respectively, regularly challenged for the Stanley Cup. Despite the odds, O'Brien and other opulent Renfrewites, such as timber tycoon Jim Barnet and industrialist and member of Parliament for Renfrew South, Tom Low, agreed to bankroll a proper Stanley Cup challenger.

Their early efforts between 1907 and 1909 were rebuffed, but by 1910, after various hockey associations folded or reorganized as the National Hockey Association, later to become the National Hockey League, the town was abuzz over local talents Bert Lindsay, Herb Jordan, and future Hall of Famers Frank and Lester Patrick. There was also Fred "Cyclone" Taylor, the most talented player of the era.

Therefore, it was no surprise that a hockey-mad tomboy like "Lottie" Whitton was often seen loitering outside the local arena after school in order to meet these stars. And Renfrew being as small as it was, it was understandable that if she didn't see them at the arena, she might well greet them as they strolled along Raglan Street, or even at her own dinner table if they happened to be boarding at her home. Thus it was that Lottie was treated to just about the best fourteenth birthday party a rinkrat could wish for — a place on the players' bench for one of the odder games in professional hockey history.

As her birthday on March 8 neared, the Creamery Kings, who soon would become better known as the Millionaires because of their excessive salaries, were achieving status as Stanley Cup contenders. Yet just a week before her birthday, the Montreal Wanderers damaged Renfrew's chances by defeating them 5–0 in Renfrew and then dashed all of Renfrew's hopes by winning the Stanley Cup against the Senators in Ottawa on March 5. However, in those days, the season did not end with the winning of the cup. There were still more games to be played, and Renfrew hosted Ottawa on Lottie's birthday.

March 8 arrived, and what a great birthday it turned out to be. Lottie was on the Renfrew bench as the home side faced off against the visiting Senators. The final score was 17–2 for the home team, with Newsy Lalonde scoring six goals, Lester Patrick four, Cyclone Taylor three, and Frank Patrick and Hay Miller with two apiece. Icing on this birthday cake saw Taylor carrying out an earlier threat by scoring a goal while skating backwards. Frank Cosentino described it in his book, *The Renfrew Millionaires: The Valley Boys of Winter 1910*:

It was late in the game, the contest had been long decided. Taylor picked up the puck in his own end and raced towards the boards cutting sharply up ice. He isolated the point men with a feint inside and moved around them. In just a few strides be was alone in on [Senators goalie Percy] LeSueur. He pivoted around, his back to the goalie and while continuing backwards, lifted the puck past the startled Ottawa net-minder! Even the Ottawa fans applauded that one!

Many years later, in a column in the *Citizen*, Charlotte recalled the thrill of that game; she also mentioned it in a brief article in *Saturday Night* magazine without mentioning her own involvement.

High school was even more enjoyable and productive for Charlotte than elementary school had been. In 1911, at age fifteen, she won the girls' senior all-round championship in sports, she was captain of her form's basketball team, and she was also the only student in Ontario that year to pass the Model School Entrance Exams with honours. When Renfrew Collegiate Institute principal N.W. Bryan organized a mock parliament that year, Charlotte played the role of Robert Borden, then leader of the official Opposition. At the commencement exercises in December, she was one of the girls who donned tartan skirts to dance a Scotch reel. But the highlight of her year occurred when classmate Clifford "Tip" Briscoe invited her to the Renfrew Fair, "and we had to pool the 50 cents we each had to spend in order to finance the venture."

Learning came easily to Charlotte. That, combined with an incredible memory and a burning desire to finish at the head of the class, allowed her to achieve outstanding academic results. When she graduated from Renfrew Collegiate in 1914, she was named the top student in her class, receiving first-class honours in Latin, French, English, mathematics, and modern history, and second-class honours in German and medieval history. She was the winner of the $250 McLaughlin Prize, the $200 registrar's award, a $50 board of education scholarship for general proficiency, and the year's "student of distinction" award from Thomas Low, industrialist, hockey fanatic, member of Parliament, and a future employer.

Also during her high school years, when she wasn't helping her father with his accounting books in Whitney during the summer, or working at Isaac Pedlow's clothing store on Raglan Street after school and on the weekends, Charlotte was one of the most frequent contributors to *The Globe's* Saturday youth page, entitled, "Circle of Young Canadians," using "Red Wing" as her pseudonym. It was in those pages that Charlotte's insatiably curious mind first revealed its depth. In 1911 alone, she wrote about Lucy Maud Montgomery, Johann Sebastian Bach, William Shakespeare, learning to swim, and plucking goose feathers. She also argued that Tecumseh, the First Nations chief who fought with the British in the War of 1812, was a legitimate Canadian hero. The following year included a review of Sir Walter Scott's *Ivanhoe*, an article about the joys of playing hockey and baseball, and, "as told by Louis Baptiste," a short essay on the fact that men loved to fish because it gave them a chance to forget their business affairs as well as their wives' "prattle" about hobble skirts, women's suffrage, and the need for the men to change the collars of their shirts. On a more serious note, she provided a lengthy explanation of wireless telegraphy to her fellow "Circleites," and mentioned that she adopted "Red Wing" as a pseudonym because that's what her fellow students called the female teacher who always wore a red tie to school.

Charlotte corresponded both publicly through the *Globe* and privately with a number of her fellow Circleite friends. Among these was "Falstaff," later recognized as Bill King, a Queen's student whom she eventually dated and who would play a significant role in her life at Queen's and beyond.

Thus we come to the time when Lottie Whitton, eighteen, renowned rink rat and Renfrew scholar, was about to launch into a new phase in her young life, a step into the ivy-covered, limestone walls of Queen's University in the distant city of Kingston.

2 From Hen Coop to Cum Laude

Immediately upon her arrival in Kingston in the fall of 1914, Charlotte was initiated into the grand order of the Hen Coop. A solid, three-storey house also known as The Residence, just off campus at 174 Earl Street, not far from downtown Kingston, the Hen Coop housed sixteen lucky Queen's girls. Meanwhile, another hundred or so unlucky girls from out of town would have to make do with often rundown neighbourhood rooming houses, often eating at the Hen Coop because of the poor conditions at their own accommodations. Indeed, the Hen Coop would prove a wonderful nest from which to fly to the many attractions and activities on campus, and a wonderful place to make close friendships, some lasting a lifetime.

By tradition, the "old girls" had to put the "youngsters" in their proper places. The latter had to learn the proper pecking order, with the senior-year girls ruling the roost, the junior-year gals on the next perch, and followed in order by "the tolerated sophomores and less-than-dust freshettes." So they gathered round the fireplace and piano in the ground floor living room, where the freshettes were encouraged to recite their own poetry, render modern verses to religious tunes, or impersonate nursery rhyme characters. When the seniors were satisfied, the party paused for "a banquet of unsurpassed excellence which so astonished the guests that it was necessary to insist upon them eating it," according to an account in the student newspaper, *The Queen's Journal*.

Just as the young ladies were beginning to feel quite comradely with the seniors, they were returned to reality by the rules of the house. If the doorbell rang, a freshette was expected to answer; if the telephone rang, a freshette was required to reply; when it was time to sit for dinner, the seniors had priority. At night, the freshettes were expected to take the coal oil lamps upstairs to light the hallways outside the second and third floor bedrooms. When one left the house, one signed out in the little black book kept at the front door by the housemother, Mrs. Norman Fraser, whose room was just to the right of the door, and signed back in on return. If a girl was escorted home by a boy, there was to be no lingering by the front door; the young gentleman was expected to leave immediately, or the ever vigilant Mrs. Fraser might intervene.

The highlight of the year was the Residence Dance, organized by the seniors-dominated house council. Once it was thought the freshettes were suitably skilled in the fine arts of dancing and etiquette, each of the girls put a Queen's boy's name in a hat and Mrs. Fraser, a friendly but worldly wise woman, would vet the names. Only decent boys were allowed in, so if a boy's name came up and he wasn't invited, you could be sure Mrs. Fraser knew a thing or two about him that she did not appreciate.

That was life at the Hen Coop. But for Charlotte, it was only a small part of her life at Queen's. A multiple-scholarship winner, she attacked her university courses and outside activities, such as sports, poetry, and drama, with her usual dynamic enthusiasm.

First, however, there was initiation into Levana, the female students' association named after the Roman goddess of the rising sun. There is no known report of Charlotte's initiation, but judging by a recollection of the Candlelight Ceremony in Charlotte's senior year, for which she was one of the organizers, it must have been a shock to the newcomers. All the freshettes were costumed and herded blindfolded into the university gymnasium, guided by the unseen hands of older students amid the screechings of wailing "ghosts," and marched round and about through cardboard catacombs. Then, still blindfolded, pitiless seniors assailed them in the open hall with threats of hideous horrors still to come and had them eat awful concoctions. Upon removing the blindfolds, the seniors had them ride around in small boys' carts, or romp about on hobby horses and perform other silly, degrading tasks. Once they survived that, the initiated were served sandwiches and coffee, an orchestra played and a Paul Jones dance ensued, to everyone's delight.

If those two initiations weren't enough, the freshettes also had

The "Hen Coop," Kingston.
Photo by author

to undergo an informal initiation within the larger male-dominated university community, for there was still antipathy by many of Queen's male students towards the co-eds. This was despite Queen's leading role among Canadian universities in its approach to women students. The university, founded in 1841 as a Presbyterian college, began in rented quarters with fifteen young men studying for the ministry. By 1870, it was one of the first universities in Canada to accept female students, and by 1876, it had allowed women to attend classes in chemistry and logic. That was not without a debate, however, for the *Queen's Journal* argued that the women's "proper sphere of action is the domestic circle," not science nor philosophy. Nevertheless, by 1877 there were eighty students being taught by six professors, and by 1912, there were 1,500 students. However, by the fall of 1916, due to the demands of the Great War, the number was down to about 600, of which almost half were female.

Thus Charlotte found herself in the right place at the right time. Having begun her freshman year in the fall of 1914, she found that what had once been a male-oriented bastion was now taking on mildly feminine airs.

Ever the one to seize an opportunity for full advantage, Charlotte broke into the previously male preserve of the campus newspaper, starting as a reporter in the fall of her second year, and later becoming one of three associate editors. In her final year, she was editor-in-chief. Similarly, in December 1916, she and her close friend Eva Coon were the first women elected to the Alma Mater Society, the students' union, which exerted a major influence on the day-to-day running of the university. Campaigning for the position, Charlotte's notice in the *Queen's Journal* reminded students that she had been poetess for the Levana Society in 1915 and was currently the prophet-historian on the Levana executive, vice-president of her graduating class, a member of the yearbook committee, secretary of the field hockey club, captain of the girls' ice hockey team, and president of Levana's ice hockey club. "Lottie rings true, she has proved herself so capable and faithful in every thing she has undertaken, that we may be sure that she will never fail her Alma Mater," the blurb read.

She breezed through the year getting top marks in her studies. It's also worth noting that despite her small size, Charlotte was known as a bruising defender in all three sports she played — field hockey, ice hockey, and basketball. She also delighted in espousing the suffragettes' call for the right to vote, a right women in Canada had obtained by 1918. In fact, thanks to her brother John Bartholomew's (J.B.) enlistment, she was allowed to vote in the December 1917 federal election due to a clause in the *Wartime Elections Act* granting the franchise to all adult family members of servicemen.

In addition to her enthusiasm and her obvious intellectual and physical talents, she was also known for her occasionally abrasive personality. Harry Campbell, her predecessor as *Journal* editor and who was then serving overseas, mentioned in an otherwise warm letter that she had been called "hard names" the previous year by schoolmates. Mabel Powell, who had recently graduated from Queen's, wrote to compliment her on the lively spirit of the college paper under her direction, but added, "Grace and I wondered if all your time was spent in scrapping."

In a 1977 interview for a book on Queen's past, Powell commented on Charlotte's ascendancy at the school. On arriving at the Hen Coop, "the first person I saw was Charlotte. She took French, English, German with me and I liked her very much and you could see that she was at the top of her class." She seemed to have a nice personality and "I liked her very much at that time, but a good many

Charlotte, centre, and the 1917 Queen's University's women's hockey team.
Charlotte Whitton Collection, Library and Archives Canada, PA-127274

people found her a bit overbearing. And anything that she was into, she wanted to domineer. She was a strong girl, and all the girls played ground hockey and she would boss them around." She had a good sense of humour, "but probably her undoing was the fact that she was a very vindictive person and she wanted a little bit of honour extended to her. . . . When she first came she was good at everything, she was a strong girl, good in athletics and everyone admired her. But as time went on, she pretty well wanted to boss things and so she was resented and she really wasn't as well liked finally. . . . People envied her ability and she knew she was an intelligent person and she knew that they did, and she got to the place where she expected that people would pay tribute to her ability."

Charlotte's sister Kay later wrote that all the girls in the Hen Coop had a nickname and Charlotte's, true to character, was "Black Minorca," after the tough, little, black-feathered chicken. A fighter and a crower.

Probably Charlotte was frustrated in that the other girls at Queen's simply failed to match her own enthusiasm, energy, and intelligence. To compensate, she expanded her friendships to include her English professor, William McNeill, and another English lecturer, Wilhelmina Gordon, the first female faculty member at Queen's and the daughter of Daniel Miner Gordon, principal of Queen's from 1902 through to 1917. Both McNeill and Gordon would remain close friends for many years afterwards. She was particularly close to Gordon, whom she saw as a role model, a woman who had broken into the academic ranks of the university's male faculty. The following excerpt from one of Charlotte's letters to "Dear Miss Gordon," dated July 5, 1917, illustrated that friendship, as well as Charlotte's manipulative tendencies. It concerned a potential move by Charlotte and three friends from the Hen Coop to a new women's residence, The Avonmore:

Elsie and I have discussed The Avonmore [and] it does not seem so terrifying to us, but we have our doubts about the other two inmates. They would be very necessarily two young ladies who could do their work at any and all moments, under any and all circumstances. Now, so far I have found but Elsie, who "fills the bill." That was why Mo decided at the very last moment to apply for a single room, swayed quite considerably by the thoughts of Final Eng. [English?] and the very "vivid" memories of "off nights," when Elsie and I were staging our capers in an entirely separate room. Mo, as I have said, decided quite suddenly on this policy of "splendid isolation" — quite swept the boulders from Elsie and me. We had a council of war, whose findings were about as follows. I told Elsie how anxious you had been that there should be some unity, as a basis in the launching of the present scheme. Now I asked her whether she'd be "game" to try it with me, as I felt that Elsie & I and Mora could not be "put up" in entirely separate quarters within the house. It was a bit of a wrench to think of poor, dreamy souled old Mo, fighting out all her moods without us to laugh and worry her back into wholesome sanity of being, but we finally decided that we might try it.

Just six days later, "Charlie," then on summer vacation in Renfrew, again wrote to "Dear Miss Gordon" about the prospects for accommodation for the following school year:

I was rather "put out" when I received your letter, at the prospect of rooming with Nell. I might risk Nell with three, and two rooms, but she is too valued a friend to risk rooming with her. She is very nervous, and cannot do the least bit of work without absolute calm. In the archives, I drove her crazy because I studied by looking straight ahead of me, in a most blankety-blank manner, I must confess. And really, Miss Gordon, Elsie and I simply have to room together if we possibly can. Yet we, too, wanted separate rooms — that was why we applied for the Farrell's and also why we were rather relieved not to get them at The Residence. I know it would be absolutely unfair to ask for two single rooms in The Avonmore, so what I would suggest — is getting Myrt Clinton in with Nell — I shall write Nell myself — and Elsie and I shall withdraw, to take rooms somewhere in the vicinity . . . You have too many sane, older girls, but you know whatever their merits (and I do like some of those youngers [sic]) Dottie, Mary, Bernice, Gladys, Jake, Gwen, Vincent Moffatt, Daisy and Mere, are not the very best nucleus in the present case. Not that Elsie and I would be so presumptuous as to offer ourselves for the leavers but with Hay, Mabel Johnson, Miriam, and Helen McLean we might try. You see, I have lived with these people . . .

It's uncertain from their exchange of letters what Gordon suggested, but whatever it was, the outcome must have been satisfactory, for Charlotte did not mention residence again in their ongoing correspondence, much of which is stored at the university's archives. Instead, her final year was consumed with studying for a pedagogical degree, editing the *Journal*, and pondering future prospects.

It was as editor of the *Queen's Journal* during the 1917–18 academic year that Charlotte, or "Lottie E. Whitton, MA," as she identified herself on the masthead, came into full bloom. She had full control of an instrument that she could shape as she wished, and a weapon that she could wield to press her concerns. It was the power of communication, a tool on which she would fall back time and again during her roller-coaster career in social work, freelance journalism, and municipal politics, as well as a popular public speaker.

Her editorship began sombrely enough, however, for the front page of the first issue of the *Journal* in the fall of 1917 was filled by the obituaries of two Queen's professors, a sober warning from the outgoing Queen's principal, Daniel Miner Gordon, about the precarious state of the university's finances, and a listing of Queen's students who had won military medals or who had been named in dispatches from the war in Europe. Also on the page was a two-year-old poem written from the trenches of Belgium, *In Flanders Fields*, by John McRae, a physician with the Canadian Expeditionary Force.

Inside, Charlotte's first editorial began in rather humdrum fashion: "Once again the clinking of coins and the heaving of sighs becomes distinctly audible in the precincts of the Old Arts [Building] and the venerable building awakens to the tread of Queen's 78th class. With the stirring of old activities into action, the *Journal* has thrilled again to life, and now makes its 45th entry into the broad light of college life." But, it reminded students, they had to get in their $1 annual subscriptions, they had to provide the paper with news items, and they had to both solicit and encourage advertisers. Only then would the six-page, twice-weekly paper continue to publish, she threatened.

Her second editorial struck a more sombre vein: "Here we are, deprived the privilege of the greater service, but granted the high boon of university education in this disturbed age. Out there, men are dying, dying to keep us here . . . Students of Queen's — think! What have we done, what have we shown . . . these then shall be the watchwords of every loyal student for this session — Seriousness, Sincerity, and Service — in work, in sport, in leisure."

It was a quiet year on campus and the calm was reflected in the paper. There were occasional lapses, such as noisy disputes over whether the university should ban initiations, or whether the women athletes should be allowed to use the university's "Q" crest, which was emblematic of the men's participation in interscholastic sports, but generally the news from overseas cast a pall over all. There was increasing coverage on the front page of the student paper concerning the Queen's students who had died or who had been badly injured in the war, and the student council debated the propriety of holding dances at such a period.

Meanwhile, Charlotte was receiving cautiously phrased letters from her brother J.B., who was serving in France as a scout with the Royal Highlanders of Canada. In February 1918, he enthused: "We are having a peach of a time around here now — not much work to do and lots of time for sports." Two months later, however, the news was grim concerning two friends: "James was badly shot up sure enough but Hill wasn't so bad just a .303 and what if it was just below the brain as long as it didn't get his brain and never knew a fellow's brains were in front of his ears but I am no doctor so I won't argue." In August, he himself would suffer a serious head wound during the battle of Amiens.

A generally gloomy mood pervaded the Queen's campus. The men were required to undergo military training, and the women took first-aid courses and knitted socks and sweaters for the soldiers in the evenings, or worked on weekends in the temporary military hospital set up in Grant Hall, cleaning beds or carrying food trays for the returned wounded. In fact, life was becoming pretty dull on campus, Charlotte grumbled in a December 5 editorial headlined: "What is wrong with Q this year?" It read, in part, "We admit, that since October, we have vainly endeavoured to answer that question, to answer it, just in our own mind, and finally we have abandoned our fruitless meditation. The old, eager, energetic life of the College is lethargic, indifferent, inactive, if existing at all. The Queen's spirit, our erstwhile boast and glory, seems to have vanished from the campus."

Yet classes went on, sports remained popular, and social life, though set back, could not be totally restrained. Charlotte, for example, had several suitors, among whom was a fellow she might have called her boyfriend.

Or perhaps she would have preferred to call him a male friend.

At any rate, William Whitaker King, who graduated with a bachelor of science degree in civil engineering in 1917 at the same time that Charlotte graduated in Arts, was enamoured with her, and it is obvious from their letters that she reciprocated, at least to a certain extent. In fact, their acquaintance dated back to Charlotte's days of penning "Red Wing" articles in the *Globe*'s youth pages, and King, under the pseudonym "Falstaff," did likewise. At Queen's, they frequently dated, talked about sports, and attended football and hockey games together. Charlotte also travelled to Toronto on the

Bill King
Queen's University yearbook, 1917

Max Boe
Queen's University yearbook, 1917

occasional weekend to visit "Bill" and his family. When Bill signed up on May 1, 1918, their letters to each other became more frequent, especially after he was commissioned overseas. But the relationship did not necessarily become more amorous. Instead, Charlotte played him like she would play so many people in her life: keeping him interested, but not letting him get too close. She was not one to lose either her head or her heart.

"Lottie I did not know till Sunday just what it was to leave behind my best friend," Bill pined on May 30 after leaving Kingston, "and so if my lucky star can find a place in the heavens and bring me through the whole game in some kind of shape I may then have one of my dreams come true. I wanted to say a lot of things to you on Sunday and why I didn't I don't know. After all Lottie I have yet to make good in this world and till I have done that or started on the road fairly well I should be satisfied to be thankful for small blessings. One must have a slightly higher aim than $25 per. I sincerely hope, Lottie that some day I may be able to tell you a lot of things which I have not done as yet."

He was not worthy. It was a line Lottie was becoming used to. Her girlfriends in Levana often said it to her, Bill often said it, and another male friend who appeared on the scene after Bill's departure, Max Boe, often said it, including in a letter he wrote on September 18, 1918:

"I'm just an ordinary student like so many others at Queen's." But, he clarified, "there are exceptions, and one that stands out in lashing burnished letters of gold at Queen's is Lottie Whitton." Two months later, just as he too was leaving for the war in Europe, he wrote, "Dear Lottie — Thou high and unapproachable one — what deity have I offended that I should be so unmercifully tossed about and always with much utter disappointment!" The letter, one of many that Charlotte kept and later left to the national archives, went on in similar vein, just as Charlotte's roommate, Elsie "Ted" Coolican, who had attended school with her since their childhood in Renfrew and who had lived with her in the Hen Coop, intoned in a May 31 missive that year over some slight: "All year I gave you cheerfully and gladly of my time and energy. All year I kept the roof over your head (by reminding you of your room rent), looked after your clothes, sent your laundry, packed your suit cases, when you went to see Bill or when you went home, and sometimes put away their contents when you returned, made your bed, reminded you to take your bath, sewed buttons on your clothes, mended the Jacob's ladder in your stockings, dressed you for the dances, bought underwear, etc, etc, for you and what did I get in return? Nothing but your daily absence from home and your nightly morbid acuteness. Even when I did my utmost to keep you in good trim for your work, by raising the windows sky high at night, you complained." Despite it all, Elsie signed off jokingly as "your loyal wife, Miraudy." Obviously Charlotte's personality was fairly well formed by this time and it was one that could flip from that of a cold-hearted, calculating woman — a five-foot-one dominatrix, no less — to that of a kind-hearted friend who could turn on the charm with a snap of the finger. Already friends and acquaintances were wondering which Charlotte they would be meeting on their next encounter.

One other activity during her final year at Queen's would have a significant influence on Charlotte's future. She dabbled in federal politics. During a brief visit home in December 1917, she assisted her former employer, drygoods merchant Isaac Pedlow, as he campaigned in Liberal colours for the federal riding of Renfrew South. Like most elections in the Renfrew area in those days, Renfrew South was a hotly contested battle between the Liberals and the Conservatives, or Unionists as they were then called. Pedlow, despite generous financial backing of his opponent, Lieutenant-Colonel Larry Martin, by M. J. O'Brien, defeated Martin by 3,184 votes to 2,667. Charlotte was learning some of the political machinations that would stand her in good stead in times to come.

Following that brief interlude, she returned to Queen's and completed her post-graduate degree in pedagogy in June 1918. Although a fine lecturer, a teacher she was not. She learned that quickly when called upon as a temporary replacement teacher for "88 hellions" in the public school at Barryvale, a small hamlet near Renfrew. Aside from that and a brief stint as a replacement teacher in Kingston, Charlotte never practised teaching, although she received the Governor General's prize for pedagogy at Queen's that year, but forever after she had only good things to say about teachers and their important role in society.

In her final editorial, Charlotte advised *Queen's Journal* readers, especially her women readers, that although life on campus was generally very pleasant, they must not ignore the real world beyond:

> Girls, yesterday, they were, today women, gazing with
> solemn eyes into that unveiled future, wherein the unerring
> finger points their place — there at the flaming forge of
> the nation builders, wherefrom the thousands of sinewed
> fighters have forever passed, slighter forms and weaker
> arms must be consecrated to the mighty task. These
> women, intent upon this shifted heritage cannot give to the
> passing fancies of the here and now, energy and thought,
> concentrated in preparation for the duties of that new
> world to be. And as with the men, so with the women,
> those who cannot see, or dream, or wish beyond their
> "pass" in English, or the music for their Science dance, can
> neither comprehend nor interpret the symbols writ upon
> the Present's dark, enveloping robe . . .

For Charlotte, it was time to move on.

PART TWO  Welfare Administrator

3 Righteousness Reigns

"Count yourself engaged," the April 1, 1918, handwritten note from Rev. John George Shearer to Charlotte advised brusquely. She was to start work with the Social Service Council of Canada on July 1, as previously discussed.

On May 24, he wrote again. "I'm sending books on child welfare and delinquency for advanced reading and *Social Welfare* will start publishing in October or November." In other words, read up on these topics and be ready to hit the ground running.

That was Rev. Shearer's no-nonsense style. Say it clearly and say it with authority. Another employer might have employed a more sympathetic approach towards a new employee, but not Shearer. He was all business, all the time, and his business was righteousness. Shearer, age fifty-eight, was opposed to alcoholic beverages, was against licentious literature, despised immorality in any shape or form, especially prostitution and obscene books, and fought race-track gambling and any type of commercial activity on Sundays. It was not for nothing that he had a reputation for being a stern, forceful leader and a fire-and-brimstone preacher. At one point, he was recognized by *Canadian Churchman* as "the mouthpiece of the social conscience of Canadian Christianity," but to Prime Minister William Lyon Mackenzie King, he was just another "professional religious agitator."

Born to conservative Scottish settlers in 1859 in the town of Bight, Canada West (now Ontario), little is known of his youth, but he had married by the time he was twenty-three — the couple remained childless — and had quit teaching to enter the Presbyterian ministry. In this position, he served in Brantford, Fort William (now Thunder Bay) and Toronto, and it was in the latter location that he saw what alcohol, gambling, and sexual immorality could do to the soul and the body.

Religion burned in his soul and sanctity oozed from his lips. In 1888, at the age of twenty-nine, he played a prominent part in the founding of the Lord's Day Alliance, a Toronto-based group of like-minded souls who wanted to shut down Ontario cities and towns one day a week to preserve the Sabbath as an "English Sunday," during which any activity beyond churchgoing was deemed unnecessary and probably immoral. "We may not want to copy the Puritans in every particular, but in their respect for righteousness, law, order, religion, and the Lord's Day, we could stand a good deal more Puritanism than we are getting," he wrote in the *Dominion Presbyterian* in 1906. He thought it scandalous that groups such as Seventh Day Adventists, Jews, and Chinese were allowed to keep their stores open on Sundays. He opposed the railway barons who wanted to run their trains on Sunday.

He had many allies in this crusade, including his co-founder in the Lord's Day Alliance, Thomas Albert Moore, an equally opinionated, though less eloquent, representative of the Methodist Church, as well as the labour movement. Later on, Quebec's Roman Catholic hierarchy would join the cause. Together, Shearer and Moore stumped Ontario, preaching moral renewal and railing against the pernicious evils of alcohol and sex, and work on Sunday. They attracted a broad spectrum of support, including the Sabbath Observance Committee in London, Ontario, which condemned social visits, milk deliveries, trains running, funerals, and bicycle riding on Sunday for pleasure. In Hamilton, city council debated the propriety of running streetcars on the holy day, and the issue was taken as far as the Privy Council in England; it ruled in favour of the trams.

As the crusade gained strength, Shearer quit the Presbyterian ministry to become the first general secretary of the national Lord's Day Alliance, an effective group that lobbied successfully for the passage of the *Lord's Day Act* in 1906. The Act banned most commercial activities on Sunday, but allowed provinces to make individual exceptions.

With this success under their belts, in 1906, Shearer and Moore formed the Moral and Social Reform Council of Canada, a federation of the Presbyterian, Methodist, Anglican, Baptist, and Congregational churches, and the Trades and Labour Congress, the Dominion Grange and Farmers Association, the Salvation Army, the Canadian Purity Education Association, the Evangelical Association of North America, and the Women's Christian Temperance Union. It equated religion with responsibility, and it stood for the abolition of poverty, the protection of children, the physical and moral health of working women, the protection of workers generally, the maintenance of Sunday as a day of rest, proper housing, care for "dependents and defectives," better recreation facilities, and international peace. It also opposed contagious diseases.

In 1913, it was renamed the Social Service Council of Canada.

The organization focused most of its attention on outlawing the sale of liquor, eliminating prostitution, or "white slavery" as it was then referred to, promoting voting rights for women, and establishing a network of local councils across the country.

Shearer and Moore led the council during its early years through their respective positions with the Presbyterian and Methodist churches, but in 1918 Shearer resigned as head of social services with the Presbyterian church in order to take on the full-time job as the first general secretary of the interdenominational SSCC. As well as his own paid appointment, he was allowed to hire one full-time staffer, at $100 per month, and this was where young Charlotte began her career in social welfare.

Barely out of Queen's, Charlotte, the tomboy-intellectual from the Ottawa Valley was going to the metropolis of Toronto. She undoubtedly was excited about this new job, and not surprisingly *The Renfrew Mercury* happily reported her success: "Miss Lottie Whitton, M.A., who graduated last year from Queen's University and who since has been pursuing further studies, has received an appointment to Rev. Dr. Shearer, in a literary capacity in connection with social service, and takes up her duties in Toronto in July." Like much of her early media coverage, it is quite possible that Charlotte wrote the press release for this item, if not the item itself. In fact, her "literary capacity" was as assistant editor and secretary to Rev. Shearer. At any rate, she had found her vocation and it was social welfare. In this field, she would achieve national, and to a lesser extent, international acclaim.

Margaret Grier,
circa 1920.
Charlotte Whitton Collec-
tion, Library and Archives
Canada, PA-126401

But first there was the mundane chore of finding lodgings in the big city. No problem, though. She soon found a room in Kappa Alpha Theta House at 3 Hoskin Avenue in midtown Toronto, a former fraternity house near the provincial legislature that was then home to thirteen other young women like herself, recent university graduates ready to make careers for themselves lest they not find husbands in the meantime. Among them was a young woman four years Charlotte's senior who worked for the Big Sisters and Girl Guides organizations. It was Margaret Grier, a quiet, gentle woman, with whom Charlotte would share the next twenty-nine years of her life.

Charlotte, however, was in Toronto to work, not to socialize, and Shearer had plenty of work for her to do. Characteristically, he was out of town when his assistant showed up for her first day on the job. He had warned her that he would be away, so it was no surprise when she found the small office in the Confederation Life Building at the corner of Yonge and Richmond empty. Wisely, she was prepared for the task of setting up the office, a task that she tackled with her usual zeal. First, there was the office organization to figure out, or rather the lack of same, for while Shearer was a spellbinding preacher, his organizational abilities were decidedly limited. And there was a lot of organizing to do. Besides, he had only been officially offered the position of general secretary on June 2 and had begun the job at the same time as Charlotte.

Charlotte was only too happy to immerse herself in her duties. Office supplies, done. Meetings to schedule, done. Memos to write, done. Her pace was fast and furious; after all, there were the provincial SSCC councils to contact and new local SSCC councils to establish. So many people to write to, so many to talk to. It was great! Meanwhile, the pressure was building on Shearer and Charlotte to produce the first copy of the monthly magazine, *Social Welfare*, on schedule for October 1, but Charlotte could stand the heat. Correction, she gloried in it. And she was proud of the fact that it was the first major publication in the slowly emerging field of professional social work. She was delighted to be at the centre of it all, a wonderful sphere where a woman could make a name and a career for herself, and possibly someday rise to the top, unlike the limited potential of the public service position she had turned down at the national archives, or the teaching positions she had been offered at St. Helen's School in Dunham, Quebec, or at Bishop Strachan School in Toronto. Life indeed was good.

It was true that Shearer was lord of the manor at the SSCC, but as his assistant, Charlotte used the contacts she was making as the foundation of what would become a cross-country network of like-minded social workers, most of whom were women.

Privately, however, she was not above grumbling about her boss. Writing to her former English professor and mentor at Queen's, Wilhelmina Gordon, after an obviously hectic day, "Charles" (one of several nicknames she used in her personal letters to close friends) whined, "Dr. Shearer is a man of sudden and undetailed decisions. I don't know whether you will understand just what I mean by that. He suddenly hits some idea and wants it carried out, entirely and immediately. No human force in existence, except sheer inactivity can convince him of the vast amount of detail involved. This I manage . . . [but] I find myself in the sickening box of having attempted and started too much, but having completed little, because I am not left to carry out what I plan." Just as one project was running smoothly, Shearer launched another. To keep up, Charlotte worked overtime at the start, but then found that the overtime was taken for granted, so she resorted to subtle tricks to sabotage Shearer's orders. "In short, I am utterly sick of the shape in which things are; sicker when I contemplate the remoteness of any probable amelioration; sickest because I am attempting that for which I am inadequate and unsuited." Unsuited? Inadequate? Surely not Charlotte! It must have been a very hectic day at the office indeed. Her letter to Gordon continued to grumble that she had had to battle Shearer to convince him to let her leave the office early, at 4 p.m., in order to volunteer at the hospital, and then once there the situation seemed even worse because of the number of people felled by the influenza pandemic that was sweeping the country.

"Two of my cases died, absolutely pitiable they were — young, strong, fit and so anxious to live," she continued to Gordon. "They simply choked to death in spite of every assistance which I could render at the time. Though I say that, it is not right for the woman 'I deserted.' She was a Jewish woman, down in the ward. It was an awful case — and I flunked. I stayed until after 12 o'clock. There were seventeen 'Yidds,' men, women and children in three rooms. They were simply incapable of looking after her. The doctors and her husband begged me to stay all night, but I was so tired and the house was awful. I did all I could then, left simple instructions and came home. The woman died for lack of proper care in the night. She was only twenty-two and left two children. I have been ashamed to speak the word 'service' ever since."

The letter was typical Charlotte: melodramatic and self-obsessed. Her overall situation was not that bleak at all. There were the happy evenings and weekends at Kappa House, especially due to the flowering friendship with Margaret Grier. There were the cheerful letters from old boyfriend Bill King about the pleasant time he was having in Sussex, England, despite the war. There was the mournful message from a dejected Max Boe, in Kingston awaiting a war posting overseas. There was the date with old friend Allen Derry to a Queen's rugby match, occasional contacts with her family, and the ever-flowing stream of letters to and from her former Queen's schoolmates.

But all these activities were just pleasant diversions for the industrious Charlotte. Not content with the office minutiae of writing letters, placing phone calls, and editing the *Social Welfare* articles, she also wrote for the magazine despite her lack of experience in the welfare field. At first, she wrote under the pseudonym "Kit of the Kitchen," but as the months passed and she took on ever more authority in both the office and the organization, she began writing under her own name, making sure that the graduate initials "M.A." always appeared.[1]

The magazine naturally concentrated on public welfare topics, but "Kit's" first column appeared in the third issue, in December 1918, and offered a report of a fictitious woman's committee meeting in "Mixton Corners." The meeting mostly comprised talk of tea parties and recipes, "Kit" noted, but one woman turned the discussion to possible Canadian representation in the United Kingdom's parliament at Westminster and this allowed "Kit" to argue that if Canada obtained representation at Westminster, then the Irish, South Africans, "Indian Hindus" and other British colonials might well seek a similar privilege. The result, "Kit" charged, would be that "the heathen Hindu will run the people of God." Whether those were Charlotte's own views at the time it's difficult to say with certainty, but considering previous mentions of "Yidds" and "Chinks" by Charlotte and her Queen's friends, and the concurrent racism of the period, it suggests that her own thoughts at least were along those lines. It also reflected Charlotte's tendency to stray into other realms, for there was no effort to suggest any link between constitutional change in the British Empire to the welfare situation in Canada, which of course was the purpose of the magazine.

Nevertheless, by the end of 1918, she could look back on a successful first six months in her new career. The SSCC office was running efficiently, *Social Welfare* was appearing on time, and Shearer was establishing more local councils across the country.

On the personal side, her father was still working in Whitney in a variety of jobs, ranging from butcher and fire ranger to professional

---

1   The "M.A." was permissible because Charlotte had earned a greater than seventy-five per cent average in her three years of Arts studies, which was the academic requirement for a master's at Queen's at that time. Within a couple of years, Queen's would follow the rules already set by other Canadian universities and determine that a master of arts degree was a post-graduate course. Nevertheless, Charlotte attached "M.A." to her name for the rest of her life.

Charlotte's grandmother,
Matilda Carr Whitton,
circa 1900.
Charlotte Whitton Collection,
Library and Archives Canada, PA-
114480

fisherman, her mother was still running the boarding house in Renfrew, siblings Kay and Stephen were in high school, and brother J.B. was serving in France with the Royal Highlanders and apparently having a grand time, although his censored letters left just a little doubt as to his safety. Of the Queen's girlfriends, "Mo" was still moaning over the fact that she had lost the Levana Association presidency to another girl because Charlotte and other friends hadn't supported her, while "Mary" in Morewood, Ontario, suggested, "You and Dave would not make a eugenic match, dearly beloved, so just don't honk along the high road of life by mistake! Wait for Bill, in preference." The ever-reliable "Elsie" in Renfrew confided that she and her mother had gone all the way to Ottawa by train to buy some clothes, but warned Charlotte not to tell her old boss, Renfrew clothing store merchant Isaac E. Pedlow, because if the irascible old retailer heard about it, he'd send her over an outfit and charge it to her father, who would be unhappy with the bill and even unhappier with Elsie.

On a serious note, there was belated word from France that J.B. had been injured in the Canadian advance on Amiens in August, and late in December, her beloved grandmother, Matilda Carr Whitton,

died at the age of eighty-two. Charlotte had always had a special fond-
ness for her father's mother, particularly during her youth when her
mother was occupied with raising the younger children and Grandmother Whitton enthused little "Carlotte" with the glories of England,
in particular the sixteenth-century reign of the first Queen Elizabeth.

Grandmother Whitton was "a cold, reserved woman, rather hard
than charitable; dignified to the point of snobbery; independent to
domination; critical to severity, but so really deeply passionate, far
within," which Charlotte wrote to Wilhelmina Gordon, thanking
her for her card of condolence. Grandmother Whitton wasn't warm
and cuddly like Grandmother Langin, her mother's Irish mother,
Charlotte continued, and she had a fierce temper that could erupt
at any moment, but "With Grandmother our [family's English] traditions seem to have died. She was the last who had really lived
them; the last who had known Norwich and York and 'the Mead-
ows, Snape, and Kinlock Hollan.'" Not to worry, however, for Charlotte would remain an ardent anglophile for the rest of her life, and
Queen Elizabeth I would be her permanent heroine and ultimate
role model.

The news of J.B.'s injury arrived in piecemeal fashion. In October, in a censored letter from France, he had mentioned that he
was "down the line with a cold, or something, but don't squeak." It
was only weeks later that she learned he had been treated for a serious head wound in August, and it was only after the war ended in
November 1918 that she learned her brother had recovered sufficiently from the wound to return to the front and was one of the first
ten Canadian troops to enter the recaptured town of Mons on November 10, the second last day of the war. "The young beggar never
told us, simply said he had worn the new trench boots I had sent
him," Charlotte wrote to Gordon.

One other letter arrived in Charlotte's mailbox near the end of
1918; it was from Bill King, who was serving overseas as a lieuten-
ant with the Canadian Engineers. "Lottie dear, you are no fool but I
guess I have been the fool through and through and have no excuse
to offer." There is no record of what Charlotte had written to him,
but his contrite reply appears to have been a response to Charlotte's
rejection of a more romantic relationship. The bloom of this once
rosy relationship definitely had faded.

Wilhelmina Gordon was pleased. Now that Charlotte had thrown cold water on Bill King's romantic intentions, the little lassie could put her mind to more important things, such as a scholarship to Bryn Maur women's college outside Philadelphia, or perhaps even to Somerville College at Oxford University in England, where she could work on that thesis she had been considering, tentatively entitled, "The Province of Quebec and the Dominion of Canada — an attempt to estimate the contribution of Lower Canada to the Canadian Nationality; and to interpret the oldest colony to the rest of its family." You are an intelligent young woman and you must think of your career, the thirty-three-year-old spinster wrote her younger friend on May 2, 1919, well aware that Charlotte was torn between continuing her studies or establishing her career. The previous autumn she had penned such thoughts to Gordon, noting that while she was keen on attending Bryn Maur, it would have been selfish to think only of herself when she should be thinking of helping J.B. finance his own education at Queen's once he had returned from the war and perhaps assisting the future college studies of her other brother, Stephen, and her sister, Kay, both then attending Renfrew Collegiate. On the other hand, she noted, "If I wait, I am afraid. I know is it worth it? I search and seek and ask; dream to waken and the deeper the thought, the more pain the waking. But one thing, I have made up my mind. I won't stick my job. Please don't mention this as I can't very probably leave it until next June, but whatever I do, I am going Maur fairly sure now. I am fairly afraid to turn the corner to which I have now come."

Gordon was only too anxious that Charlotte would turn that corner. She continued, in her May 2 letter: "You know that when a man is humble and says he is not worthy it makes you feel like a woman. And yet you are both young, and you would never be really happy if you jumped into matrimony before you made an effort to satisfy the other side of him. I'm relieved to find that Bill is willing to wait." Three weeks later, Gordon offered further matronly advice: "You would be well to be out of Bill's way a bit. Not that you are apt to be passion's slave, but juxtaposition and importunity are tremendous forces."

She needn't have worried, for by this time Bill King's ardor had been snuffed out and his rare letters to Charlotte after his return from Europe were simply those of a former boyfriend.

J.B.'s letters, on the other hand, concerned money, not friend-ship. Writing to his older sister in April 1919, he said he planned to work as a forest ranger for a year to raise money for his Queen's tuition, but in the meantime, having just completed his overseas military service, he was short of cash. A loan of $200 would be most welcome, he suggested, for "You see Lottie I only have one change of shirts and underwear and I have to get a trunk, rain-coat a couple of pairs of boots and all kinds of small things." Mother would help, he continued, but she was having a difficult enough time as it was just keeping the boarding house going. Father, in Whitney, was cash-strapped and unlikely to assist. "Please write soon and tell me your [sic] not sore because really you know I am doing what is square. So long, J.B."

His next letter, dated May 15, was more positive. Fishing in the Whitney area was excellent, and he thought she should plan a sum-mer holiday there. Besides, "You've got Dad dead wrong when you say he's lazy, he certainly is not lazy but he put himself badly in the hole when he was living high and it takes all he makes to keep him up now."

Indeed, John Whitton, Charlotte's father, had fallen into a finan-cial hole. Although he held a range of jobs, including part-time mag-istrate for the Whitney-Algongquin Park-Nipissing district, he rarely sent money home to his wife and family in Renfrew. About the only time he returned home, according to the children's accounts, was during the winter when the northland froze up. A big bear of a man, standing about six-foot-four and weighing close to 300 pounds, he spent most of his paycheque on alcohol, which may well be why Charlotte was a temperance advocate most of her life. When he fi-nally returned to Renfrew for good in 1926, her father had barely enough funds to open a small grocery store in town.

Charlotte loved the work at the Social Service Council of Canada, and she revelled in its complexity. She ran the office, she edited the monthly magazine, she answered queries from across the country, she sat on several of its standing committees, and she attended na-tional conferences. As if that wasn't enough, she gave evening courses on "Municipal Law and Life" during 1919 and 1920 to the Toronto Council of Jewish Women for $5 a lecture, and from time to time she lectured on social work at both the University of Toronto and McGill University in Montreal. She also frequently spoke to women's groups across the country on welfare matters.

She increased her literary contributions to *Social Welfare*, the only national welfare magazine in Canada at the time, and accordingly her prominence among welfare authorities increased, even though she was still a relatively new face in the field. Among her subjects were child welfare, "women's right to power," the national debt, working conditions in general, social problems, immigration, and racial assimilation. In fact, there seemed no subject that she was not prepared to expound upon.

As for immigration and new Canadians, she commented in a June 1919 article, "It is well to leave the discussion of the racial question to the last, for here indeed one skates upon thin ice." The previous national census in 1911 showed that of Canada's 7.2 million population, 3.9 million people were of British extraction, 2 million French, 390,000 German, 170,000 Scandinavian, 129,000 Austro-Hungarian, 105,000 Indian, 75,000 Jewish, 54,000 Dutch, 45,000 Italian, 43,000 Russian, 33,000 Polish, 27,000 Chinese, 16,000 "Negroes," 9,000 Belgian and 9,000 Japanese. In other words, Charlotte concluded, the 5.9 million of British and French stock were trying to assimilate 1.3 million others, "composed of widely differing beliefs and customs. In many, many cases, too, especially in the case of the Chinese immigrant, the foreigner is an inferior type of his own race."

Charlotte, the rugged hockey player from days gone by, was about to skate on thin ice. She acknowledged that Canada was a young country with wide open spaces that needed immigrants to prosper, but its immigration policy must be based on the "careful selection" of immigrants. Already there was enough division in the country between the English and the French, especially between Quebec and the other eight provinces. Although "the great body of the French-Canadians are a quiet, pastoral, peace- and home-loving people," there were people beyond the Quebec borders who were outraged at Quebec's opposition to the proposed conscription of soldiers for the First World War and, much to Charlotte's consternation, some of Quebec's more fiery leaders were dead set against British imperialism and allegiance to the Crown. The province, she advised her readers, "has a peculiar anachronism of feudalism, a development of Church and State alliance, strengthened by the isolation of a conquered nationality in the medium of conquerors."

Perhaps the thin ice she was skating on was starting to crack, for she refrained from addressing the more controversial issues of Oriental and East European immigration until another day in another place.

Having the podium of *Social Welfare* in which to air her views was satisfying, but she was anxious to achieve far more than that. For example, when Rev. Shearer was too ill to address the Social Service Council's national conference in Montreal in January 1920, Charlotte, by now the associate editor of the magazine, happily replaced him, speaking on "The responsibility for the illegitimate child." The problem, as Charlotte saw it, was that too many immigrant women of low mental ability had borne children outside of marriage. Many were working as domestics in rural areas and were becoming a drain on the country due to the expense of raising the children, she argued, so immigration rules should be tightened. Once again she presented herself as an authority on social work, and she was accepted as such. In fact, the speech was covered by the *Globe*, which may not have been surprising considering the fact that since the previous year Charlotte had been a leading member of the Canadian Women's Press Club, due to her editorial position with *Social Welfare*.

The press, and the *Globe* in particular, were especially attentive to Charlotte's utterances, as illustrated by a July 19 report in the paper's social pages that began: "In the ranks of Toronto's young women there is perhaps no one who is doing more for her country's weal that Miss Charlotte Whitton, B.A. [*sic*] of the Social Service Council of Canada, who recently returned from a trip to the West. Gifted both as a writer and a speaker, and combining with a wide knowledge of social problems a broad vision and sound judgment, Miss Whitton is steadily coming to the front, and her comments on Western conditions, as seen during her attendance at the annual meeting of the National Council of Women in Calgary, and at the annual meeting of the National Women's Institutes in Edmonton, and throughout a tour in the interests of her own work, are worthy of consideration."

Charlotte was definitely getting around. The Social Service Council here, other national women's groups there, and still the office to run, reports to present, surveys to be undertaken, talks to be given, connections to make. It might have seemed overwhelming to others, but Charlotte handled it with cool efficiency. Besides, where others saw only the trees, that is, their immediate provincial or local welfare concerns, Charlotte saw the forest — the national picture — as well as the trees, the leaves, the branches, and the roots.

Consequently, when the federal government's newly created Department of Pensions and National Health convened a national conference on child welfare in Ottawa in October 1920, mere months after establishing its own Child Welfare Division, the associate editor of *Social Welfare* was front and centre when some 180 delegates representing 114 mostly philanthropic agencies sat down to discuss the place of children in a postwar world. The result of the meeting was the establishment of the Canadian National Council on Child Welfare, soon to be renamed the Canadian Council on Child Welfare, and later the Canadian Council on Child Welfare and the Family, the Canadian Welfare Council, and, eventually, the Canadian Council on Social Development, as it is known today. Its honourary secretary from the start was Miss Charlotte Whitton.

The new council had no office and no paid staff — aside from Charlotte's $500 annual honorarium — but like the Social Service Council, it had plenty of ideas. Six committees were established, covering child hygiene, child workers, special needs children, education, recreation, and defective/dependent/neglected/delinquent children, and Charlotte kept its records from her office in the Social Service Council. It also received an annual grant of $5,000 from the Department of Health for the dissemination of informative child-rearing brochures and pamphlets, which Charlotte was in charge of distributing.

As men withdrew from her social circle, Charlotte's attachment to Margaret Grier grew closer. By 1920, they had moved out of Kappa House and several blocks north into a house at 106 Admiral Avenue with a woman named Adeline. She seems to have been a silent partner, for there does not appear to be even one letter from her amongst the voluminous correspondence Charlotte left to the national archives. Grier, on the other hand, was a regular correspondent when "Dear Old Lot" was on the road. On April 16, 1920, for example, she wrote, in part, to Charlotte who was attending a welfare convention in New Orleans: "Dear Old Lot, I've got to burble about my troubles to someone — why are you so far away . . . When you come home this time, young woman, I'm going to have nothing to do with you beyond cool civilities morning and evening. I'm sick of this empty life business when you go chasing around to your old meetings."

Three days later, another letter from Grier: "Dear Old Lot, There are so many good reasons why I should write to you this time that I don't even have to look up an excuse before digging in. Last Saturday Lot I was even more convinced than ever that you are a wonderful girl. To think of your remembering the 18th my dear in the midst of all the scurry of getting off and then to send flowers! Well words fail — but the roses (sunset) are lovely and I have brought three down to the office with me so that I can see them in the glory of unfolding. It always seems such a pity to waste things at home, though of course Saturday and Sunday were no waste. I spent nearly all of yesterday at home just going out to Church and to the Convent for vespers. Thanks for your letters Lottie dear, you don't know how I miss you for you see everything is just the same monotonous old routine here and you have interesting things happening."

On June 11, Grier began another letter, "Silly to write soon after you're gone and when you'll be back before I could even get an answer but I just have to tell someone how I miss you and you are the safest confidante, I guess!" On January 26, 1921, the friendship was still flowering as Grier gushed, "Dear Darling, Just two nights gone and I'm so lonesome. I could cry whenever I stop to think for a minute. Of course to make matters worse I had to go down to your office this noon to get the card to take into the Business Women's Club and it is dreadful to go there when you aren't around. Oh Lawrie dear, Im [sic] just about crazy all the time you are away from me . . ."

Early in 1922, Charlotte received an offer she found impossible to refuse. It meant concentrating on something other than social work, but the challenge was simply irresistible. Welfare work would have to be pushed aside — temporarily, as it turned out — for broader possibilities. Nevertheless, she felt impelled to write a typically long, melodramatic farewell for *Social Welfare*. It began:

The rifting of relationships extending over a very full and pleasurable period of life cannot but carry wrenches and regrets that somewhat blur the vision of the new land into which the wayfarer journeys. And as I leave the circle of silent, unseen acquaintances, whom I have known for four years through *Social Welfare*, it is with a keen premonition of impending loneliness, and a sense of withdrawing from a large group of spirit friends, whose minds and thoughts have met mine regularly for four years, much as one meets daily some unknown person on the street, until one feels that surely each should greet each. . . . *Social Welfare* has been a large factor in my life and into it have I written many thoughts and statements . . .

And so, with my farewell to it, I make my farewell, also of you and you and you, reader friends, dimly seen and touched through the distances but kinship of the printed page . . .

4 A Whiff of Parliamentary Air

" **M**iss Whitton Goes to Ottawa," read the front-page headline of *The Renfrew Mercury* on March 29, 1922, noting that the town's former top student had just been hired as "confidential secretary" to the town's leading politician, member of Parliament Thomas A. Low.

"Miss C.E. Whitton goes to Ottawa," echoed the headline on page sixteen of *The Globe* on the same day. In yet another glowing reference to Charlotte in the women's pages, *The Globe* reported, "Miss Charlotte E. Whitton, M.A., well known in social service circles in Toronto on account of the excellent work she has done during the last four years as Secretary to the Social Service Council of Canada and as Editor of *Social Welfare*, has accepted the position of confidential secretary to Hon. Thomas A. Low, Minister without portfolio in the Federal Government." (In a separate report on the same page, Agnes Macphail, who in 1921 had become the first woman elected to Canada's Parliament, told how lonely it was being the lone female in the 235-seat House of Commons. It was very intimidating, Macphail said, and she wondered if she would even have the courage to speak in the House.)

Curmudgeonly Mackenzie King was the newly installed prime minister and austere, scholarly Arthur Meighen had replaced Robert Borden as leader of the Conservative Party, which made him the leader of the Opposition. The main issues of the day included postwar recovery, trade tariffs, and the Liberals' desire for more autonomy from the United Kingdom.

Tom Low's invitation to Charlotte surprised many acquainted with the stubborn politics of the Upper Ottawa Valley and of Renfrew South in particular. Many felt it odd that Low, a lifelong Liberal, would hire Charlotte, whose father was a known Conservative and whose own views leaned toward a right-wing agenda. Yet he was well acquainted with her abilities, having presented her with the Thomas A. Low "student of distinction" medal when she graduated from Renfrew Collegiate. He also undoubtedly had heard of her effective office management at the SSCC. Similarly, Charlotte was quite familiar with Low and the internal politics of Renfrew South, having helped her old boss, store owner Isaac Pedlow, win the seat for the Liberals in 1917.

Tom Low

There is little record of Charlotte's political activities during this phase in her life, but because of her position as Tom Low's private secretary, one can imagine that she was well aware of his political and departmental affairs. Her sister Kay wrote in her unpublished biography of Charlotte that Charlotte often sat in the public gallery of the House of Commons when her minister attended, and back at the minister's office, Charlotte treated Low "in a possessive, motherly way. She had a mat outside the door of his office, and before you could come in, you had to wipe your feet, no matter who you were. If you attempted to come in without wiping your feet, she would usher you out and say you had to shake all soil off your shoes."

Thomas Andrew Low was a rags-to-riches business success story. He was born in Quebec City in 1871 and arrived in Renfrew as a poor, but ambitious teenager in 1889. He first worked for Renfrew lumber baron Martin Russell, who, incidentally, was said to have strolled about his workplace with $1,000 bills in the pockets of his overalls; however, within four years, Low had earned enough money to buy a partnership in a small sawmill on the Bonnechere River with another area man, John Knight. That mill soon burned down, but Low survived the setback and by about the turn of the century he had become one of the town's leading businessmen.

As a sideline to his business empire, and with the support of M.J. O'Brien, Isaac Pedlow, and others, Low was elected member of Parliament for Renfrew South in 1908 and served for three years as a low-profile backbencher. He stood aside in 1911 to leave a seat vacant for defeated cabinet minister George Graham, and in 1917, he watched from the sidelines as Pedlow won the seat for the Liberals. He was returned in 1921 after Pedlow stepped down.

The 1921 election was held on December 6, but as early as September 8, Tom Low was on Mackenzie King's doorstep seeking a cabinet role if the Liberals won as expected, King confided to his diary. Another diary entry, for October 22, noted that Low had joined King for lunch that day and again raised the question of a cabinet post. Again King was cagey, saying it was premature to name a cabinet before he had won the election. Once the election was won, however, Low was the first to call on the new prime minister. "He offered his services in a nice way, but I made no commitments," King wrote in his diary. By the end of the month, King had decided on his cabinet and while Low was included, the prime minister had concluded that he was too much of an intellectual lightweight to handle the defence portfolio he sought. "I decided to take him in without portfolio on understanding he would look after work of organization in our province & for the party, this he promised to do. He seemed pleased."

Tom Low hated it, Charlotte would write many years later. He detested being known as a "Minister without portfolio," and he disliked being shunted aside with odd-job assignments. But at least it was a step in the door to the inner cabinet sanctum, and he could always hope that his stature would rise. So it was with his new assistant when she arrived in his office on March 28, 1922, for her first day on the new job. A private secretary's role was not something she had dreamed of as she worked for and won all those academic honours at Renfrew Collegiate and Queen's University, yet it was a foot in the door to national politics — something she had toyed with while playing Conservative leader Robert Borden in a high school debate several ago — and she was ready to pay her dues.

Quickly, she learned the rules of the lowly political assistant: pay attention to your constituents' concerns, know the party line, keep your boss happy and well informed and, most important of all, keep a keen ear and a sharp eye out for behind-the-scenes developments in the political capital as well as back home in the constituency. It was in the latter that Low was particularly susceptible, for Renfrew County politics were among the toughest, rawest in the nation. Even within his own Liberal riding association, Low had to keep his back to the wall. However, watching it all intently from the sidelines was his bright and ambitious young parliamentary secretary.

Low's first year back in the House passed almost unnoticed. He spoke only once, in June, and although he began by praising the Liberal budget and its proposal to lower freight rates for farmers, his comments led into an area that was near and dear to Charlotte's heart and quite possibly were proposed by Charlotte herself— immigration. "What the seas are to England the railways are to our Canadian West," Low told the House, and while the country needed and wanted thousands of immigrants to settle the western provinces, it would be better for all if the skin of the newcomers was of a particular hue. "No doubt there is a certain class of immigrants we do not want to see coming into the country," he said, without naming that class, but added that the most desirable newcomers would be former Canadians lured back from the United States, as well as Britons, Americans, and Scandinavians. Perhaps not coincidentally, Charlotte had written the following in a paper published in the previous year by the Social Service Council of Canada: "No question is more clamant; no national problem so related to the revival of this nation's prosperity as the settlement of this country's unoccupied lands by desirable immigrants, carefully selected, and judiciously and scientifically aided in their undertakings." Healthy Europeans were especially welcome if they could afford to pay their own way, she had written. What were to be avoided were the "feeble-minds," or mentally challenged, who not only added little to their new country but threatened its very intellectual capacities in the long run by breeding more than the rest of the population. This view she shared at the time with other advocates of eugenics, the now disgraced ideology that argued the human race could be improved by selective childbearing and segregating the mentally and physically weak. Among the many prominent Canadians who seriously considered such views were Mackenzie King and Helen MacMurchy, chief of the federal health department's child welfare division.

At any rate, when King decided to shuffle his cabinet in March 1923, Tom Low asked for the immigration portfolio, even though he had shown no interest in the subject aside from his comment in the House the previous year. King said no, instead naming the Renfrew South MP as his Minister of Trade and Commerce; remaining as Low's private secretary was Miss Charlotte Whitton.

Tariff issues were the hot issues of the day, and there was debate even within King's cabinet as to whether the government should grant a preference to British goods over other imports. Low and some other senior ministers were opposed to the preferential rates in order to protect local farmers' markets, while King wanted to appease the British somewhat since he was seeking greater autonomy for Canada. All of this likely interested Charlotte, but there is no record in her own files or in the department's files of her actual involvement in the controversy. About the only thing known about her political activities at this period is found in a letter she mailed to a Queen's friend in August in which she recounted her busy life — arranging press conferences for the minister and scheduling his tour of the western provinces in the fall, as well as her off-hours work with the Queen's Alumnae Association and the Canadian Council on Child Welfare.

As for Tom Low, he kept an extremely low profile in the House in 1923, not speaking once, according to Hansard. However, he was re-elected in September, and in December, the prime minister handed him the uninspiring assignment of arranging for the cabinet's official photo, in addition to his duties as a minister of the Crown.

The following year was a more positive one for both Low and Charlotte. He was front and centre as cabinet discussed such weighty issues as international shipping rates, deepening the St. Lawrence River, the cost of livestock shipments overseas, and the expense of marketing facilities in the United Kingdom for Canadian products, and he spoke frequently in the House. Charlotte enjoyed the perks of parliamentary privilege when she joined the minister and his family on a European trade mission.

The trip was a wonder for the wide-eyed young woman from Renfrew. At the end of the first day, July 12, she observed in her diary, "We are oil burning, and the ship cast an incredibly dirty undercurrent discernable even in the filth of New York harbour . . . sea beautiful & boat riding like a swan. But oh the people. If it weren't that the tribes are lost, I imagine every Gentile would have been crowded off. And the garb! Never again shall I worry about clothes for a transatlantic trip . . . Nice lunch, good dinner for which everyone dressed. Tea nice. Danced after dinner in lounge, played mah jong. Dancing remarkably conservative except for one or two lounge lizards . . . If only Grandma could have seen England once more . . ."

July 14 [aboard the White Star Line's luxury liner S.S. *Homeric*] . . . Some bizarre outfits — one orange & purple affair looked like an Oddfellows installation . . . Disgusting dancing by some. Some of the younger girls quite obviously without corsets, girdles, brassieres or "retainers" of any kind but two or three lounge lizards . . . Bill [Low, the Minister's son] a good dancer but Jean [Plante, a family friend] says he does not hold you tightly enough. Mr. Low says they are not allowed to dance that way at home."

July 15 [aboard ship]: "Walked three quarters of a mile and wrote several letters. Feeling great, so rested. Think must try to finish my poem on wheat started last fall. Woman on boat I want to speak to — wonder who she is . . . Must drop Max [Boe] a line poor lad! I really must give some time to Wembley . . . [where she would be giving a public address on Canada Day at the British Empire Exhibition].

The vessel arrived in Southampton on July 18, and the first stop was London and a brief stay at the fashionable Ritz Hotel. Strolling the streets of London with the Lows, she pitied a woman with "poor gnarled, reddened hands" scrubbing steps near the British parliament and she commented that Canada's House of Commons was a finer building than its United Kingdom counterpart. She viewed a painting of Elizabeth Tudor and wrote: "She is beautiful as I believe she was, her gold-red hair, crisping about her crown, the beautifully shaped hands showing clearly, as she holds out her Coronation ring to the petitioning Parliament, clad in robes of wondrous colours . . ."

Within days, Charlotte, Low's wife Mary, his son Bill, and Jean Plante began a tour of western Europe as the minister involved himself in trade discussions in London. The small touring party visited the Hague on August 5, Brussels on the 6th and 7th; on the 8th, they inspected the First World War battlefields along the Belgian–French border, and on the 10th, they were in Paris. They returned briefly to London, only to be back on the Continent by the 18th.

August 19, Geneva: Shared a compartment with the frankest Englishwoman of the demi-monde I ever met. She does enjoy life—drank a bottle of graves [*sic*] as though she were eating a blueberry.

Milan, Rome, and Florence followed in quick succession.

August 27, Florence [after buying a lapis lazuli gem for Margaret Grier]: I do miss her—I want to turn to her a hundred times every day. She will so understand how I feel. Paid far too much but it'll be her present.

Then back to London by the end of the month and a quick tour north to Scotland by way of the Yorkshire Dales, the ancestral home of the Whittons. Finally, a short speech on the topic, "The Social Background in Canada," before a distinguished audience at the British Empire Exhibition at Wembley, a brief attendance at a Buckingham Palace garden party with the minister and his wife, and then home to Canada aboard the Canadian Pacific's elegant *Empress of Scotland*.

In October 1924, Low was re-elected in Renfrew South despite the opposition of M.J. O'Brien and Isaac Pedlow, both of whom were now solidly in the Tory fold. Mackenzie King retained Low as his Minister of Trade and Commerce, but not without reservation: "Low came to see me about some matters. He spoke of being fond of campaigning, the truth is he carries an exaggerated 'ego,' is an almost impossible man for others to get on with, and may break down completely one of these days."

King, who was overworking himself due to the illness of some of his senior ministers, was growing increasingly impatient with Low. "[He] is in a listless helpless condition . . . I had to speak firmly to Low before the Cabinet to get him to take in hand the conference on trade with the West Indies for which he has primarily responsible. He tried to shift it onto [immigration and colonization minister James] Robb then onto me," King grumbled to his diary on March 28. Then, in mid-summer, King's cabinet was split over whether or not he should call an election in the fall. Low and some others were strongly in favour, but King had serious reservations. He called in each of his cabinet ministers separately and questioned them as to their chances of raising sufficient election campaign funds. In his diary, he noted, "Low is the greatest failure of all. Spoke of one source [of funds] which [George] Graham says quite impossible & illegal, and on [sic] other source he had only a suggestion to offer but nothing arranged or thought out. He is having a joint debate with [Conservative MP Sir Henry] Drayton at a picnic tomorrow—another evidence of his love of notoriety."

One month later, King spoke to Toronto industrialist Vincent Massey and suggested that if Massey was a successful Liberal candidate in the expected fall election, he would hand him the trade and commerce portfolio and send Low to the Senate. Low must have learned of this, for on September 2, King acknowledged to his diary that "Low has been working hard." But it was too late. King was determined to move Low out of the cabinet and into the Senate, and told him so on September 4. To punctuate his impatience with Low, who was also the Liberals' senior political organizer for Ontario, King stopped him from distributing the party's campaign literature and handed this task to veteran Liberal backroom adviser, Senator Andrew Haydon of Ottawa, a close friend of Charlotte's.

The October 29, 1925, election spelled the end of Tom Low's political career. It was his first defeat in five federal elections, and he was unseated by the Conservative candidate, Dr. Jim Maloney of Eganville, a small town twenty miles west of Renfrew. Maloney had the personal and financial backing of M.J. O'Brien, the latter to the tune of $10,000, as well as the support of Isaac Pedlow, the former Liberal member of Parliament for the riding, who spoke at Tory rallies and erected posters across the riding lambasting Low and the Liberals for a host of political sins.

King's Liberals won the election, but King lost his own seat in North York. He was not a happy man, and he was particularly unhappy with his Ontario organizer: "Low has been a sinister figure, an incompetent bungler throughout, a curious combination of good nature good intentions and bad judgment great conceit and bull headedness or obstinacy [*sic*]. He has cost the Administration a lot." Low presumably didn't pick up on King's negative vibes, for two days after his leader had penned those cutting remarks, Low was in King's office pleading to stay on as minister by seeking election in a safe by-election beyond Renfrew South. The answer, not surprisingly, was no. Ever the optimist, Low sent King a basket of flowers for Christmas. It did him no good. King had decided that Low would never again be in his cabinet, and early in 1926, he told him to stop his fundraising efforts on behalf of the Liberals.

Tom Low died on February 9, 1931. Death was attributed to a cold and complications, *The Globe* reported, and on hearing the news, King turned to his diary: "Low was a loyal & true friend and though he was not a success as a Minister had personal qualities which won him many friends. It was a real shock to learn of his death."

Two days later, King visited the Low home where his ex-minister's body was waked: "It was a scene of genuine and great sorrow . . . Mrs. Low looked very old & worn & broken. She said to me that Tom loved me dearly . . ." He saw that Low's son Billy, twenty-three, was shaken by the death, and Tom's younger brother sadly recounted how Tom as a young man had raised him when both their parents had died. Tom's widow, Mary, told King that Tom never failed to return from trips abroad without gifts for all the family. Alas, at the end he had been stricken by erysipelas, a skin disease that spread over his face, perhaps the reason for leaving the casket closed.

As a postscript to Tom Low's life, King noted in his diary in December 1931, some ten months after his former minister's death, that he had spoken to Low's son Billy and had learned that Tom Low had left considerable debts behind, some of which were "political borrowings."

Political borrowings were not the only debts Low left behind, apparently. Joan Finnigan, the prolific Ottawa Valley writer who published a number of oral histories told to her by Valley oldtimers, wrote that Low was involved in a stock scandal shortly before his death and his name "is in bad odour to this day in the Valley and many stories are told of his mysterious death." Rumours of bank failures and stock market swindling—there's even a tale that Tom Low scooted off to South America with his loot and the reason his casket was closed at the wake was because it contained someone else's body—are rife in the Valley, but then stories like that are part and parcel of Ottawa Valley lore.

Even in 2009, some long-time Renfrew residents said there remained a foul odour to Tom Low's name, but the town square on Raglan Street, the land for which Low donated in 1918, remains named after him.

Surprisingly, for someone who left behind so many words on so many subjects, Charlotte left few comments or recollections of her time as Tom Low's parliamentary secretary. Nevertheless, the four-year political detour with Low stood her in good stead in the years to come. It had been an excellent apprenticeship in the internal workings of government and, just as important, it had provided influential political and public service contacts that would be useful in the years ahead.

Charlotte may have moved quietly in the corridors of power as Low's assistant, but away from his office, and sometimes from within, she maintained a busy extracurricular life travelling, speaking to women's groups on a variety of topics and, above all, remaining involved with social work. She kept in touch with her former associates at the Social Service Council of Canada and broadened her network of contacts in the Canadian Council on Child Welfare. Due to the CCCW's pitifully low budget of $5,000, she carried out the council's correspondence from her apartment and her parliamentary office.

By this time, she had earned a reputation among women's groups, such as the National Council of Women and the Women's Institute, as a leading welfare spokeswoman and a fascinating speaker. In June 1926, the Ontario branch of the influential Imperial Order Daughters of the Empire, a philanthropic group of women with affiliates across the country, asked her to lead a lobbying effort concerning the provincial government's proposed legislation regarding the "feebleminded," which she of course accepted. Later in the month, the IODE's national chapter presented her with a life membership to show its appreciation of her efforts, and within a few years, the National Council of Women invited her to convene its child welfare committee in whatever spare time she could find. Meanwhile, she frequently and successfully urged the various women's groups to lobby the federal government to continue its annual grant to the CCCW.

It was also during her time as Tom Low's secretary that she developed especially close relationships with more senior women in the feminist and welfare fields, especially Emily Murphy of Edmonton and Helen Reid of Montreal. Murphy, who was by then in her fifties, had become the first woman magistrate in the British Empire in 1916, but she was better known by her pseudonym, Janey Canuck, under which she wrote a number of books about the Canadian west. Under her own name, she wrote the *The Black Candle*, an exposé of the drug trade, with special emphasis on Western Canada and Chinese immigrants' involvement in the trade, which was published in 1922. Later in the decade, Murphy became one of the "Famous Five" who succeeded in pushing the Persons Case all the way to the Privy Council in London, where that august British body ruled that women were indeed "persons" and therefore were eligible for nomination to the Canadian Senate.

However, it was in her role as a vice-president of the Social Service Council of Canada that she came to know Charlotte. After Charlotte was named Tom Low's private secretary, Murphy congratulated her: "My dear Miss Whitton, Your new job as Lowe's [*sic*] secretary will add bumps to your phrenological chart, even if your head has little room for more bumps . . . [this] is going to be a very vital loss to the council. We had come to look upon you as an indispensable part of the machinery, and I know that Dr. Shearer was planning to lay even more responsibility upon you . . . At any rate, lassie, I am always happy to hear of your success and well being, for you may take it from me, that no young girl in Canada is as well known and as widely beloved as you."

In a similar motherly manner, Helen Reid, vice-president of the Canadian Council on Child Welfare, took young Charlotte under her wing. When Charlotte returned from Europe in September 1924, Reid wrote to her protégée: "Welcome home again, Little Wanderer! I was so pleased to get your Genoa letter and I had [it] framed — a really vivid picture of your travelling around Europe gaping at the

Slavs! A wonderful first experience and when taken alone even more interesting and rich and thrilling!"

It was another in a lengthy list of letters that Charlotte and Reid exchanged, for it was at this period that the two, along with Ella Thorburn, CCCW president, appeared to run the organization pretty much on their own.

Reid had impeccable credentials. After graduating with first-class honours in modern languages in 1889 as one of the first female students at McGill University, she studied in Germany and Italy before returning to Montreal where she eventually became director of the Montreal School of Social Work. She was also a member of the IODE, the Victorian Order of Nurses, the Red Cross, the wartime Canadian Patriotic Fund, and other volunteer organizations. She served on government committees and published studies on welfare, health, and immigration topics, and in her spare time, she translated, wrote poetry, and travelled widely.

Reid had as broad a perspective on social welfare matters as Charlotte, and they shared a strong sense of ownership when it came to child welfare. When prominent British parliamentarian Margaret Bondfield visited Canada on a fact-finding mission in 1924 to look at the condition of immigrant British children and unmarried women in this country, they did their utmost to make sure that she did not undercut the CCCW's unofficial authority in that area. Similarly, when Dr. Helen MacMurchy, director of the Department of Health's child welfare division, suggested that the CCCW sponsor one of the division's public speaking engagements in Ottawa, she was told very plainly that the council was quite capable of deciding where it should spend its limited budget.

Reid and Charlotte were convinced that the CCCW needed a full-time staff person and an office of its own, and there was little doubt who they had in mind for the position. Reid hinted as much in the fall of 1924, but Charlotte, still employed by Tom Low, was not yet prepared to gamble her government sinecure for an uncertain future with the poorly funded council. Charlotte had seen other national organizations struggling under similar constraints and wanted nothing to do with it. Reid was patient, but in December she broached the subject again: "And what about you? You indicated to me pretty definitely after my insistence that you could &

would come to us after this session of Parliament in a $3000 a year salary . . . If we can't get you, we must get someone else or close up. **We want you!!!"**

Still Charlotte held out, although she was impressed by Reid's fundraising effort. Undeterred, Reid asked the CCCW executive in March for permission to hire Charlotte, but the executive postponed its decision.

When Rev. Shearer died in Toronto on March 25, 1925, the wind went out of the sails of the Social Service Council of Canada and it seemed highly likely that if Charlotte was going to go anywhere in social welfare in Canada, it would be with the CCCW. In July of that year, while still with Tom Low, Charlotte complained to Reid about the constant pressure she was under, especially in regard to a CCCW campaign to publish a series of pamphlets on prenatal care: "This lusty Council infant is too heavy to hold every day after your day's work. I am scribbling this in bed at ten Saturday night for Miss Dixon to type. I have been at [Low's parliamentary] office on West Indian trade until dinner—I do most of the Council work at this hour and in this way, so please do not think when your queries are not answered early, or my information seems slow in going forward, that it denotes negligence or the like. It's just that I am [*sic*] 'driven' beyond twenty-four hours that day and had no twenty-fifth hour for the Council."

Reid replied reassuringly that she was doing a magnificent job. "I suppose I might as well arrange to write you daily! Are we in **love**? Why! Yes! Why not?" she added facetiously.

Although Charlotte frequently complained of being overworked by her parliamentary duties and by the demands of the child welfare council, she still found time for her alma mater. She chaired the Queen's Alumnae Association's fundraising committee between 1922 and 1925, and this resulted in the opening of the four-storey, sixty-bed women's dormitory named Ban Righ (Gaelic for "wife of the king") Hall in November 1925. Its completion, after fifteen years' effort on the QAA's part, was due in large part to Charlotte's bargaining ability with the architect to keep costs down and her fundraising prowess, as well as last-minute financial support from the aforementioned Senator Andrew Haydon of Ottawa. Earlier, in 1923, she was among several Queen's graduates invited to join the selection committee for the school's new chancellor, and later that year, Queen's principal R. Bruce Taylor asked her help in obtaining an interview with Tom Low so he could lobby the minister for the appointment of a Queen's professor to the National Research Council. One year later, Taylor thanked her for Dr. A.L. Clark's appointment to the council. Undoubtedly in return, she was able to get favourable attention for the entry of her siblings, J.B. and Kay, to Queen's; her third sibling, Stephen, would attend the university later. In 1928, Charlotte was elected to the university's board of governors.

She had one other important career-enhancing interest during her time with Tom Low. She was involved with some of Ottawa's most influential women, including the wife of the governor general, in forming a private club for women. The Chelsea Club became the female equivalent of the city's Rideau Club, the male-only bastion founded by John A. Macdonald, Georges-Etienne Cartier, and other leading politicians in 1865 and which was located on Wellington Street immediately opposite the Parliament Buildings. The more modest Chelsea Club was established in a three-storey house several blocks south of Wellington on Metcalfe Street; the author of the club's 1925 constitution was Charlotte Whitton.

As for Charlotte's very private personal life, Margaret Grier soon found a job in Ottawa after Charlotte moved to the capital, and together they moved into a small Centretown apartment. Later, as Charlotte's career advanced and Margaret's position as the assistant secretary of the Canadian Association for the Prevention of Consumption and Other Forms of Tuberculosis (later renamed the Canadian Tuberculosis Association and eventually the Canadian Lung Association) remained comfortably stable, they moved into a modest third-storey flat on the eastern edges of tony Sandy Hill. Although there was nothing to suggest that the two women's relationship was a sexual one, there's no doubt from their correspondence that they and their close friends considered them "a couple," with Margaret handling the homemaker role and Charlotte that of the main breadwinner.

Meanwhile, the men in Charlotte's life refused to disappear and she continued corresponding with them. In May 1922, humble Dr.

Max Boe had written from Medicine Hat, Alberta, that although he was then working with another doctor in a medical practice, "I haven't really accomplished very much in the last two years," while he had heard she had achieved "brilliant accomplishments." In October of that year, Bill King, now president of his own civil engineering firm in the Toronto area, wrote in similar vein: "Sorry my acquaintance has caused you so much irritation and humiliation. Lottie your letter of condescension while it contains certain facts is absolutely wrong in its conclusions, although after meeting you on Saturday for a moment certain facts were driven home."

On December 27, 1923, Boe wrote once more: "Lottie, I've wanted you, since college days. I cannot say it was a 'falling intensely in love' more a great admiration and a wonderful sense of good comradeship, an understanding beyond all common ken, that induced the desire, and don't you think that leads where we would go? Geo. Kelly and I were speaking on the subject once in England, and he said when your name was mentioned, he'd be afraid (I may be mistaken in the word) to marry someone that was cleverer or knew more than he did. I thought it was more a case of one man's manhood matched with womanhood, so to speak—yet he caused me much thought; especially the fact that you overestimate me so much . . . I'm afraid I fall far short of your estimate . . . it's time I decided to marry now or never; I'm 30 years but still a child at times . . . That's all I have to offer Lottie, with whatever the future holds, but it's yours for the acquiescing. Please let me know Lottie, With sincere wishes, Max R.B."

When she hadn't replied by January 21, he wired her at the parliamentary office: "Please relieve the tension send a favorable reply if possible." Her reply by telegraph the next day read: "Have been in and out of city constantly this month, and leaving again tomorrow or Thursday. Shall write this week, from here or Montreal. Received letter and wire, and appreciate both—C.W." The last mention of Boe in her archived files is the note she wrote during her European junket: "Must drop Max a line poor lad!"

The men in her family also riled Charlotte on occasion. In February 1924, just after she had fended off Max Boe's pleadings, her brother J.B. raised her wrath by asking for a loan so he could buy a suit for his graduation. She replied in full dudgeon:

At Christmas, and when I was down [to Queen's], I pleaded with you, not to drive ahead on that dress suit proposition. I asked you to be a little less selfish, and do what others were doing for you, go without something, and rent an outfit, even if it did not fit you, like an Adonis. I thought you were doing [*sic*] to do this. Instead of which, you have evidently been leading mother a dog's life, and what I did not know, have been demanding extra money all year and grousing like a kid, because you did not get it . . . I tell you J.B., you'll know when you start earning, what it costs one, oneself to send $110.00 a month off regularly as clock work [*sic*] to some one [*sic*] else. I cannot say though that I was surprised at what you have done. You are absolutely headstrong, and selfish, and I often feel sorry to think, of the lessons life will drive home, and which you will try not to learn . . . But, I told you at Christmas, and I told you again in Kingston, with K, there, that if you could find the means to provide yourself with the outlay of some hundred dollars for the Science dance, you could jolly well do the same for the rest of the year, and for your fees . . . I have not been mean ever with any of you, to the limit of my means, and I was not going to bight [*sic*] this time, either . . . So I am done, as I told you, I would be, from the time you went on with this dress suit proposition. I have done my best and have gone without a new dress, and so am staying at home from the Governor-General's Drawing Room. But from this moment I'll serve myself, and you can scratch as I did, and find your way to raise the rest of the cash you need this year. I told you that if you couldn't go to the Science dance, in a rented suit, and could raise the means to float one, and all that goes with it, you could hustle. You took the choice, and you can stay with it. Try your hand at financing your own bank for a while.

And we'll talk business from now on. You may just remember for future reference, that the money you have had has just been a loan . . . As far as cash goes, you had a double barrelled warning, twice, and you took your choice, so from now on, you can count me out.

For once, however, a man spoke back to Charlotte. Unlike Bill King and Max Boe, J.B. was her brother, not a spurned boyfriend. He had also seen action overseas during the First World War, where he had suffered a serious head wound; he would not be messed with so easily. Especially as her missive arrived while he was preparing for his final examinations in engineering. He replied two days later:

> Dear Lottie: That was a great letter to receive at this time of my course . . . As far as I am concerned for myself, the rest of the course could go; but I think of Mother occasionally and also of the kids. It will be great for Steve to meet my profs if I quit now, I am sure. You probably think you have handed me a "knock-out," maybe you have as far as college is concerned; but what of Mother, you will shorten her life — or worse, by doing this. You know where she is headed for as well as I do and yet you'll pull such a stunt. I wish I had followed my own inclinations when I came home and got a job; instead of trusting you to see me thru [sic]. I haven't been "demanding" extra money all year. I ask for money when I was broke and I wasn't broke because I was "whooping it up." I was at social evenings up till Christmas, the Dumbells and about a dozen movies. This was my first formal dance since I came here . . . Well as far as I am concerned we are thru [sic]. You may think it worth while to square yourself with Mother tho [sic].
>
> Thank you greatly for yielding your first claim, when you know damn well it would take at least two weeks to negotiate a loan if possible at all.
>
> Don't worry about getting your lawyers, when I have the money you'll get it; till then not even a lawyer can take blood from a stone.
>
> J.B.

Ten days later, Charlotte's father wrote to her from Whitney in his own strong, unpolished manner:

Dear Daughter

Your Mother has become reconciled by now over the fuss that has been over J.B. I thought for a few days that it would affect her mind as J.B. certainly was going to quit and come home at once it certainly kept the wires hot for a couple of days then he was able to negotiate a loan of $100.00 from some one in Kingston from whom or how we do not know however he is sure of getting enough to carry him until May. So that has eased your Mother's mind for the present and I do hope that there never will be an occasion for such a rumpus again.

He admonished her for writing to her brother just as he was studying for exams and suggested that it would be her fault if he failed and decided against returning to Queen's. "Another thing it has done it has made Steve give up the notion of going at all as he absolutely says that if he ever goes it will be on his own money or not at all." He emphasized, however, that the scrap was between J.B. and Charlotte and that he and his wife did not want to get involved.

"Please give my best regards to Margaret with kind & best wishes to yourself. Your affectionet [*sic*] Father, J.E. Whitton."

5 Dust-up in Geneva

Just as Tom Low's parliamentary career was nosediving and finally crashing with his defeat in the October 29, 1925, election, Charlotte's career in social welfare was about to take off. Undoubtedly sensing Low's downfall, she discarded the hometown politician like a smelly sock when a new opportunity arose at the annual general meeting of the Canadian Council on Child Welfare in Ottawa in late September. Helen Reid had done her job well, not only convincing the council's governing board of the urgency to hire its first, full-time executive secretary, but also convincing Charlotte to seek the position.

The board needed little convincing as to timing or as to who the new director should be. With barely a hint of discussion, the choice was Charlotte, the young woman who had been stitching the umbrella organization together from the loose threads of its various member organizations since its inception in 1921. As president, Ella Thorburn noted in her summation of the conference that the meeting of representatives from nineteen national organizations, sixteen civic groups, and 191 individuals had "proved an outstanding success in every way, thanks to the untiring effort expended in preparation on the part of its Honourary Secretary, Miss Charlotte Whitton. Great things for the future of the council were heralded by the decision at the final business meeting of the session to employ a full-time paid secretary."

However, no sooner had Charlotte accepted the position — effective November 1 — than her career took another turn. This time it was in the international sphere. Early in October, just days after the CCCW annual meeting concluded, she learned from her former history professor at Queen's, Dr. Oscar Douglas Skelton, who was then King's under secretary of state for external affairs, that there were moves afoot at the League of Nations to invite Canada to propose a candidate for a seat on the child welfare committee of the League's

Advisory Commission on the Traffic in Women and Children. The advisory commission, after pressure from the United States, had agreed rather reluctantly to accept one representative from the Americas to sit on its child welfare panel, so it had sent out the call for nominations from Canada, the United States, and South America. Skelton advised Charlotte about this on October 3, and two days later, she wrote thanking him for receiving her and Ella Thorburn at his office that same week to discuss the matter.

Then the manoeuvring began. The League had inadvertently suggested that the Social Service Council of Canada, Charlotte's former employer, propose Canada's candidate. Charlotte, however, was adamant that her current organization, the CCCW, should make the choice, and she said as much to Skelton. She also advised an old acquaintance, Grace Abbott, head of the United States Children's Bureau in Washington, that Skelton agreed with her, and that "he would do what was possible to have the League Council minute amended so that the Child Welfare Council and not the Social Service Council should be asked to make the Canadian nomination." She further suggested to Abbott that the United States, Canada, and South America should press for three representatives, or assessors, on the committee instead of just one.

On October 8, she went one step further. She appealed directly to the influential general secretary of the International Association for the Promotion of Child Welfare in Brussels, who was a member of the League's commission, to support her position that the Americas deserved three assessors rather than one. How could "three essentially distinct people" be represented by only one person, she asked. Ignoring the fact that the Central and South American countries differed as much as Canada did from the United States, she argued, "I think that this request is a just one and I think that it is also very essential to the success of the Commission that these widely different sections of North and South America should be given the opportunity of making a contribution to the League. I am sure that the Commission will lose much if, by the representation of only one part of this hemisphere, it is deprived of contact with the very significant child welfare development in the other two sections."

Two days later she wrote Skelton again, warning that if Canada and the United States didn't move fast on this issue, the South Americans might offer a candidate and the League might accept that person as the sole representative of the Americas. She also complained that the Social Service Council of Canada was now rudderless, following the March 27 death of its longtime leader, Rev. Shearer.

On October 14, almost two weeks after she had learned of the proposed appointment, Charlotte received a letter from the assistant secretary of the SSCC, Marjorie Bradford, in Toronto, saying that she had just received a notice from Geneva about the appointment and was asking Charlotte to "please enlighten me as to the meaning of all this." Charlotte replied curtly that "through some error in the office here," the information about the candidacy had not been forwarded to the SSCC. However, after another ten days, Bradford, still awaiting the official notice from Ottawa, wrote Charlotte again: "Would it be troubling you too much to ask you to ascertain from [External Affairs] whether those papers are now being purposely withheld pending possible re-arrangements, or are they still straying somewhere in the mails?" Charlotte's response: Copies have been made and will be sent in the near future.

Obviously, and with good reason, Bradford felt the SSCC was being sidetracked by the CCCW, so Charlotte tried to placate her somewhat by suggesting that both Canadian organizations propose three candidates each, and let External Affairs choose Canada's nominee to the League panel. In the meantime, she further undercut the SSCC by writing to W.A. Riddell, head of Canada's advisory office at the League and a man answerable to her friend Skelton, explaining why the CCCW was more important than the SSCC.

Her manoeuvring was just getting started, for as it became obvious later on, her prime goal was to have herself nominated as Canada's representative on the League's child welfare committee. As the fall colours turned, the race for the Canadian nomination heated up. On November 4, Charlotte issued a letter to CCCW officials advising them of the League request and added that the SSCC had "asked for our co-operation in this matter," which was stretching the truth somewhat. They were also asked to provide the names of three candidates for the nomination.

The results began arriving soon after. Judge Emily Murphy of Edmonton voted, in order of preference, for Charlotte Whitton and Ella Thorburn of Ottawa and Mrs. P.E. Marchand of Montreal. Helen

Reid's candidates were Charlotte, social worker Howard Falk of Montreal, and suffragist Mrs. Adelaide Plumptre of Toronto. Mrs. Jessie Stewart, an acquaintance of Charlotte's who was the grande dame of the Ottawa Valley town of Perth and a leading official with the IODE, named only Charlotte. Meanwhile, Bradford wrote Charlotte again on November 6 to say that the SSCC was still in the dark, officially, because it had received nothing in writing from the League nor from External Affairs. "Please drop me a line . . ." she pleaded. Finally, on November 10, Bradford sent out her request for nominations from the SSCC's member organizations.

The results were in near the end of the month. From the CCCW, there were fourteen votes for Whitton, six for Reid, four for Thorburn, three each for Murphy and Marchand, and single mentions for ten others. On the SSCC side, Charlotte was again the frontrunner, followed by five others. Combining the results, the two organizations advised External Affairs of their three nominees — Charlotte, Helen Reid, and former Winnipeg juvenile court judge D.B. Harkness, in that order. On December 14, after the League had agreed to accept one assessor each from Canada, the United States, and South America, Skelton advised "My dear Miss Whitton" that she had been approved as Canada's assessor on the League's child welfare committee.

She quickly patched up her differences with Riddell, Canada's chief representative at the League, and at about the same time she received a welcoming letter from Dame Rachel Crowdy, an Englishwoman who headed the League's advisory commission, now renamed the Social and Opium Questions Section, and who also was secretary of the child welfare committee. "I feel I must write a personal word to say how very delighted I am that we are going to have you on the Child Welfare Committee. I have always heard a great deal of your work and remember very clearly the one occasion on which we met in Geneva some years ago. I hope you will find it possible to come to the next meeting of the Committee on March 22nd, and that I may avail myself both then and at any time of all the knowledge and experience you have acquired."

Meanwhile, despite this flurry of interest in the League's committee, Charlotte did not neglect her duties as the new, full-time executive secretary of the CCCW. In early December, she moved into a one-room office on the fourth floor of the seven-storey Plaza Building in downtown Ottawa, just two blocks east of Parliament Hill, where the tenants included a broad range of private businesses and government and non-government agencies. The Japanese consulate shared the second floor with other tenants, the American trade commission was on the third, as was the Tuberculosis Association of Canada, Margaret Grier's employer. Sharing the fourth floor with the CCCW were an oil company representative, a grocery wholesaler, a contractor, an architect, a jeweller, and the Italian consulate-general. Across the hall from Charlotte's office was Florence Ryan's hairdressing salon.

It was a modest new beginning for the Canadian Council on Child Welfare, an organization that had been set up in 1920 as a clearinghouse for information concerning child welfare and which had operated on a shoestring budget since its start, supported mainly by an annual $5,000 federal government grant. Now, with an annual budget of approximately $10,000, it could afford a permanent executive, a part-time secretary whom it would share with the TB Association, and the purchase of second-hand furniture that had been discarded by the federal government. Charlotte's $3,500 salary roughly matched her pay while with Low; her part-time secretary would be paid $1,200 a year. Also, $500 was budgeted for travelling, $600 for rent, and smaller amounts were listed for various items such as printing costs, stationery, and research. On the revenue side, there was the $5,000 federal grant, a substantial contribution from the private sector, and organizational memberships.

Despite its meager finances and its penny-poor office space, the CCCW quickly gained respect as the leading privately run child welfare organization in the country, overshadowing the Social Service Council and frequently eclipsing the federal health department's child welfare division, which was led by Dr. Helen MacMurchy, the eugenics-preaching former "Inspector of the Feebleminded" in Ontario. What could not be budgeted for, in dollars and cents, was Charlotte's zealous effort to push the council's views, as well as her personal opinions, on all matters affecting child welfare. (It was purely coincidental, of course, that Charlotte shared her "C.W." initials with child welfare, a subject that commanded her thoughts and actions for two decades.)

She began 1926 in fine form, writing all nine provincial justice ministers on January 5, requesting information on their juvenile delinquency laws and then, after consulting W.L. Scott of Ottawa, a lawyer and prominent authority on child welfare legislation, produced a pamphlet which she then sent back to the provincial ministries for fact-checking. It was then printed as a CCCW pamphlet, although the council had done little but piece together the contributions of others.

Similarly, on January 7, she wrote Dr. A. Grant Fleming of Montreal, convener of the CCCW's hygiene section, proposing that the council use an Ontario leaflet as the basis for an informative pamphlet that would be sent to prenatal mothers across the country, and hoped that he could interest an insurance company to sponsor its printing and distribution. As a manager, fiscal conservatism was always in the back of Charlotte's methodical mind.

As if all these activities and public speaking engagements across the country were not enough to occupy her time, Charlotte was also preparing to attend her first meeting of the League of Nations' child welfare committee. It would be her inaugural step onto the world stage and she wanted to ensure that it would not be a faltering one. To do so, she arrived in Europe one week before the League meetings in order to visit Italy for a week-long inspection of the new child welfare setup there. Her partner Margaret Grier had also arranged a European tour at the same time on behalf of the Tuberculosis Association of Canada. Grier would study the effects of sunlight on the treatment of TB patients while Charlotte was attending the League meetings. Afterwards, they would spend six weeks travelling around Europe as Charlotte inspected various child care institutions; together they found plenty of time for sightseeing.

It was also at this time that Grier made out her will and named Charlotte her sole executor and bequeathed all her possessions to her dearest friend and flatmate.

Charlotte continued a running correspondence with Julia Lathrop of the United States Children's Bureau during the month of February as they prepared for Geneva; she also kept in close contact with John Joseph Kelso, Ontario's superintendent of neglected and dependent children and one of the pioneers of child welfare in Canada. It was obvious that she was gearing up for a battle with the

European-dominated child welfare committee, and while Lathrop was keen on a set-to, Kelso advised caution. Among the issues to be dealt with was the committee's plan to have a League convention, or treaty, on child immigration that would see the host country pay the costs of returning immigrant children to their homelands if they were to be repatriated. That was fine for countries like France and England, which sent their children overseas, Charlotte argued, but certainly was unfair for the host nations, such as Canada and the United States, which accepted them.

So, just prior to the start of the Geneva meetings on March 22, the rookie committee member from Canada made clear her position. She also made it clear that she wasn't there to be a wallflower, for she presented a list of ten additional items that she wanted placed on the agenda, which undoubtedly rattled a few of the old-guard panel members, a number of whom were titled European personages. These items included the causes of maternal mortality, malnutrition, the custody of young offenders, the treatment of "feeblemindeds," school curricula, visiting teachers, the education of crippled children, and the necessity of providing an education based on religion and morals. Once the meetings began, she battled successfully to postpone for a year the distribution among member nations of a questionnaire on national child welfare laws, arguing that it didn't relate to Canada because of our constitutional system. In this country, child welfare was a provincial matter and consequently there was no simple, single national response to questions about child welfare laws. Instead, each province went its own way with its own set of rules and regulations, and this was a point Charlotte found difficult to impress on European minds.

She did not accomplish much in her first appearance on the world stage, but then she was not likely to due to the complex organization that was the League of Nations. There were three senior components to the League: the Assembly, the Council, and the Secretariat. The Assembly was made up of representatives of all member states and met once a year; the Council was composed of permanent and temporary member states and dealt with international disputes at its thrice yearly meetings; the Secretariat was the bureaucracy. The League also included numerous commissions and committees, which studied different aspects of international affairs, and these were answerable to both the council and the assembly. Among them was the child welfare committee on which Charlotte sat, which itself was a sub-committee of the Social Questions Section. To further complicate an already complex maze, the child welfare committee established its own subcommittees, two of which Charlotte was chosen to join. One was a legal subcommittee, established only after Charlotte and Julia Lathrop of the U.S. raised such a fuss over the child immigration questionnaire, and the other was a subcommittee on the protection of life and health in early infancy.

After the March meeting, Canadian diplomat W.A. Riddell wrote a personal message from Geneva to CCCW president Ella Thorburn in which he concluded, "You will be pleased to learn that Miss Whitton has proved what we all expected — an excellent assessor on the Child Welfare Committee. I have heard nothing but the highest praise of her work, in spite of the fact that she got a lot of her own way, after a hard struggle. I am very pleased that she has been appointed to the Legal Sub-Committee . . . We are looking forward to seeing her again in Geneva at the time of the Labour Conference. My wife also had the pleasure of seeing her in Florence last month."

Obviously the rough-hewn, prickly gal from the Ottawa Valley had shown those stuffy European nobles a thing or two about bureaucratic in-fighting.

Following her League meetings and her European fact-finding/holiday tour with Grier, Charlotte returned to Ottawa in May and resumed her role with the CCCW. But with the confidence of international experience behind her, she acted more independently than previously. The frequent correspondence with vice-president Helen Reid practically ceased and there was less consultation with Ella Thorburn.

Charlotte began processing the mountain of statistics she had received from the provincial justice ministers in response to her January request, for her aim was to provide important CCCW input into the reworking of Ontario's *Children's Protection Act*. To do so, she used yet another Queen's University contact, Ontario attorney general William Folger Nickle, as her key intermediary with the provincial cabinet.

Nickle was the brother-in-law of her mentor at Queen's, Wilhelmina Gordon, chair of the university's board of governors, and a member with Charlotte of the Queen's committee that nominated the university's new chancellor in 1923. A Kingston lawyer, he had been an alderman and mayor of the city and, for six years beginning in 1911, served as the Conservative member of Parliament for the Lake Ontario city. Since 1923, he had been member of the Legislative Assembly for Kingston and provincial attorney general. Now she was dispensing advice to him as he was becoming acquainted with social welfare issues while his department wrestled with revamping the *Children's Protection Act*.

First she recommended that he hire Ottawa lawyer W.L. Scott to draft the new act, since Scott had already drafted the province's *Juvenile Delinquent Act* and was a past-president of the Ontario Children's Aid Society. Then she urged him to hire other of her child welfare colleagues, such as J.J. Kelso and Robert Mills of Toronto, on a temporary basis, and when the draft was completed, he should call on still more of her contacts, such as CCCW president Ella Thorburn and the rector of her Anglican parish in Renfrew, Canon William Quartermaine, for comment.

She continued a frequent correspondence with Nickle, but in December 1925, she had second thoughts about her advisory letters so addressed this message to his home, rather than his government office. "Just in case you're sending my letters to your office files, I would suggest that you remove a couple of personal letters, particularly the long one. If these ever went to the 'open files' where anyone in the Department might see them, and my opinion of some of the changes came to the knowledge of the Commission, I am afraid we would be in a rather bad position for co-operation." Even she realized that some of her comments were intemperate. From then on, many of her letters to provincial and federal politicians were marked "personal and confidential."

Passage of the *Children's Protection Act* languished as the year 1926 progressed, so Charlotte continued to lobby for the changes she sought. She also campaigned for improved schooling conditions for handicapped children, promoted CCCW issues in the pages of the council's quarterly newsletter, *Canadian Welfare*, and addressed women's groups in several Alberta cities during a speaking tour in August.

The unfinished fight at the League of Nations, however, was an itch she could not scratch away. Her pen ran non-stop since the last session of the child welfare committee in March, with letters flying back and forth between Charlotte and welfare officials in Canada, the United States and the United Kingdom, along with correspondence to leading Canadian politicians and bureaucrats. Her correspondence was flowing so robustly that occasionally mistakes were made, such as the time one of her letters to Julia Lathrop in Washington was inadvertently sent to Dame Rachel Crowdy in Geneva, which included personal photos. Despite minor miscues like that, Charlotte did make some headway in her campaign for child welfare improvements at Geneva, but even more notable was the fact that she raised her own profile within the League.

One of the first to hear from her following the Geneva meetings was Frederick Charles Blair, Canada's assistant deputy minister of immigration. In 1924, he had been largely responsible for rewriting Canada's immigration laws and while doing so had given serious attention to Charlotte's earlier writings on the topic. Now, writing from Basle, Switzerland, in April prior to her tour of England, she again raised the complaint that the Europeans did not understand Canada's situation as a haven for orphaned or needy children, most of whom were brought here by private emigration agencies based in Britain. "Confidentially, I may say that I feel that there is a 'dead set' of misrepresentation, etc., of our immigration law, regulations etc., in some of the European countries, and in the United Kingdom, I imagine, though I have not been there yet. I have had great pleasure in explaining that we have the best system of family and unaccompanied women immigration in the world. Italy is certainly 'annoyed' with us — that much to our credit anyway."

To Crowdy, secretary of the League's child welfare committee, she complained in July that the monocole-wearing Sir Austen Chamberlain, former Chancellor of the Exchequer, 1925 Nobel Peace Prize winner and brother of future British prime minister Neville Chamberlain, had misrepresented the committee's activities when, as rapporteur to the League's Council in June, he suggested that the committee had overstepped its mandate by dealing with such issues as the legal, health, or economic aspects of child welfare which were handled by other League committees. "I think myself though that in view of this report of Sir Austen, we should have a definite statement of our scope of work for the next agenda. We feel here that child welfare is essentially a field for international study and action along certain lines. I am sure that if we were to draw up a statement of why and what we think is so, in this connection, it would be more satisfactory to the Committee and the Council of the League." She also informed Crowdy that letting the League's prison commission, rather than its child welfare committee, study the future of juvenile courts "is entirely repugnant to our practice, legislation, and fundamental principles in the work on this side [of the Atlantic Ocean]."

Shortly after she had written to Crowdy and Lathrop about Chamberlain's "error," she received replies from both women agreeing that she had a point, but it really wasn't worth having a major confrontation over. "Frankly I very much regret that he should have written such a report, and do not feel it was really justified," Crowdy wrote, but added that the child welfare committee had been making progress in recent years despite opposition from those higher up the League's bureaucratic ladder.

But Charlotte would not let go. In August she wrote to Dame Katherine Furse in London, the British delegate on the child welfare committee, suggesting that the female members of the committee meet privately before the following year's meeting to iron out their own agenda. Furse agreed. Later in the month, Charlotte appealed to the acting Canadian prime minister, Sir Henry Drayton, that he advise his senior officials at Geneva to raise the minimum-age-for-prisons issue at the next meeting of the Assembly, the League's senior body, in September. He agreed to do so.

Pleased with herself, she couldn't help but inform lawyer W.L. Scott of her success: "I thought you would be interested in the enclosed copy of a letter from Sir Henry Drayton [to his officials in Geneva], which is self-explanatory, beyond the fact that I brought the matter to his attention personally."

Scott replied: "The letter is admirably worded, and I am inclined to think that you must have been responsible for a draft." (Charlotte frequently drafted replies for more senior officials even before she had informed them of the topic on which they would be commenting.)

Meanwhile, Furse wrote Charlotte in October to inform her that Chamberlain's report to the League's Council had been forwarded to the Assembly and had run into some opposition in the senior forum. The result, for the time being, was a stalemate over how broadly the child welfare committee's mandate extended, so in that respect Charlotte had at least tied the contest of wills with Chamberlain and those of like mind. And she was heartened near the end of the year when she attended a meeting of twenty-three Canadians who had served at the League of Nations and listened to their advice on dealing with the Europeans; their recommendation for dealing with the snotty Europeans was simple: "Treat 'em rough."

(At the time, the Liberals under Mackenzie King had returned to office after a brief Conservative reign. Undersecretary of State for External Affairs O.D. Skelton was anxious to promote Canada's growing autonomy from the United Kingdom.)

Charlotte had little time for a personal life in 1926. She missed the official opening in April of the Chelsea Club by Lady Byng of Vimy, wife of the governor general, and quite possibly the graduation of her sister Kay, who received a bachelor of arts from Queen's, for she never mentioned the latter ceremony.

She did, however, attend a tea party with Margaret Grier in July at the Shortts' residence in affluent Rockcliffe Park Village, next to Ottawa. This invitation again reflected her attachment to Queen's University, as well as her growing connections to Canada's senior public servants. As O.D. Skelton recounted in his diary, the host of the party was Dr. Adam Shortt, Dominion Archivist, a former economics and political science professor at Queen's, and the acclaimed founder of the federal civil service. Among the guests were Queen's economics assistant professor William Mackintosh and his daughter Margaret, as well as Skelton and his wife Isabel. Skelton had been Charlotte's history professor when she arrived at Queen's in 1914, but on this day, it was she who was in the driver's seat, for she drove him and his wife home in her car after the party.

6 A Lust for the Lurid

I n 1927, Charlotte, on behalf of the Canadian Council on Child
Welfare, began child welfare surveys across Canada, a move that
would raise the profiles of both her organization and herself nationally and leave politicians and social workers from coast to coast
trembling in her wake. In most of the surveys, completed between
1927 and the early 1930s, her modus operandi was simple: hear
about a problem, cajole the locals into inviting you to investigate,
collect as many statistics and alarming anecdotes as possible, write
up your observations and conclusions in as forceful a manner as
possible, recommend a complete overhaul of the system in place,
trumpet your most devastating findings to the media, and then, as
the public and media were in an uproar, suggest replacing many of
the local officials who had let the situation deteriorate by bringing
in trained social workers of your own choosing. The latter, because
at the time only McGill and the University of Toronto had schools
of social work, inevitably came from Central Canada.

This was partially the case with her first urban survey. Early in
1927, the Rotary Club of Vancouver realized that the city had a serious childcare problem on its hands. The aged waterfront building
on Wall Street housing some 200 wards of the Children's Aid Society, aged between six and eighteen was, in the words of one Rotarian,
"a shocking fire-trap!" and its atmosphere was "cold and cheerless."
Nearby was a so-called "baby cottage" operated by the CAS for its
wards aged from two to six years, and it, too, was in disrepair. It was
obvious something had to be done, and the Rotarians were ready to
help, but they could not do it all by themselves. Although they were
prepared to allocate a $22,000 charitable fund towards the construc-
tion of a new building that would house some 400 children between
six and eighteen, the estimated cost of such a structure was in the
range of $500,000, well beyond their ability to pay. It was obvious

the municipal and provincial governments would have to be approached for support, while the Rotarians hoped to collect a further $200,000 through fundraising efforts by themselves and other service clubs in the city.

First, however, the Rotarians wanted to discuss the matter with someone properly trained in social work. So, in the absence of any professional social workers in Vancouver, they turned to known professionals in the United States. The latter, in turn, referred them to the Canadian Council on Child Welfare and its executive secretary, Charlotte Whitton.

Charlotte jumped at the opportunity and was soon in Vancouver discussing the issue with the Rotarians. Her conclusion came quickly: a full-scale survey was needed. The Rotarians agreed, and they hired the CCCW to conduct it for a $4,000 fee, a considerable amount at the time.

Soon after, Charlotte had her survey team in place. She chose Robert Mills, director of the Toronto Children's Aid Society and former director of Toronto's social welfare division, as her chief consultant. He was assisted by three women from separate Toronto social agencies: Margaret Nairn, Vera Moberley, and Leila O'Gorman. Charlotte, meanwhile, maintained overall control and wrote the concluding ninety-two-page report. Her findings, released in the fall, recommended a new, larger building to house the six-to-eighteen-year-olds and new housing for the younger children; that the CAS sell its valuable waterfront location and move to a less expensive area of the city; and that it replace its unqualified staff with trained social workers. The province did not escape her scrutiny either. She recommended that British Columbia should reorganize its welfare department and staff it with professionals; that it establish a "Family Agency" to act as a child-placing service for neglected children; that it provide properly trained case workers for unmarried mothers; and that it remove children from institutions as much as possible and place them in foster families.

The province and city responded favourably to Charlotte's recommendations, and monies were raised for the CAS to get its new buildings and a new manager whom Charlotte had recommended, Laura Holland of Toronto. Holland, a trained nurse and social worker who would become a lifelong friend of Charlotte's, had been chief of Toronto's municipal health division when she was hired as British Columbia's first professional social worker. Charlotte also persuaded Montreal social worker Howard Falk to run Vancouver's Council of Social Agencies, as well as several other trained social workers to move west to take up provincial government positions.

The inquiry had been short and sharp, and its co-ordinator, Charlotte, received numerous accolades for the subsequent results.

She followed up this success the following year with two more surveys: Manitoba's Royal Commission on Social Welfare and a child welfare survey in New Brunswick. Both surveys attracted attention, but it was the latter that truly demonstrated Charlotte's ruthless determination to bring about change. Charlotte used the poor, ill-educated people of New Brunswick to further the CCCW's reputation and the children as "a device" for her own purposes. According to Sharon Myers, whose 2004 doctoral thesis for the University of New Brunswick examined the study in detail, "Whitton knew the child was a device when she conjured the sub-standard child; she knew the child was a device when she called on [Elizabeth] King to elevate the lurid and sensational. The product that resulted — the endangered child — was a handy thing, an object of service to Whitton's political agenda." It was "as concerned with its own reputation and welfare as it was with children's."

There was no question in 1928 that New Brunswick was a "have-not" province and its welfare setup was a mishmash of philanthropic organizations each doing its own thing. These amateurs, either through service clubs, women's groups or churches, reflected the divisions across the province, both religious (Catholics versus Protestants) and linguistic (Anglophones versus Francophone Acadians). But many informed people in the province recognized that there was a serious child welfare problem and they willingly listened to Charlotte's call for action.

As Myers recounted, Huilota Dykeman, provincial director of public nursing and New Brunswick's representative on the CCCW board, was in favour of inviting the CCCW to carry out a provincial survey, but first she and Charlotte had to drum up support. So in September and October of 1927, they toured the province together, meeting with small groups in various towns and cities and holding

*Charlotte,
August 1928.*

Jules Alexander Caston-
guay, Charlotte Whitton
Collection, Library and Archives Canada, PA-137535

a public meeting in Saint John, the province's most populous city, which attracted the interest of various parties, especially that of the local Kiwanis Club. "Part fact, part fiction, fiercely grounded in classical techniques of persuasive rhetoric, Whitton's message was clear: New Brunswick children were not up to snuff, neither by national nor international 'standards'," Myers maintained.

It was agreed; a survey was needed and the Saint John Kiwanis Club offered to pick up the tab, to the tune of $600. With the contract in hand, Charlotte turned to a relatively new CCCW staff member, Elizabeth King, to lead the survey.

King was a native New Brunswicker who had graduated with a master of arts degree from Acadia University in Wolfville, Nova Scotia. She had been an investigator with Ontario's Mother's Allowance Commission prior to joining the CCCW and had assisted Charlotte in her Manitoba work.

Charlotte, ever mindful of the need for and the power of publicity, advised King by letter on November 3, 1928:

I think it would be well for you to get some photographs of some of the worst places, especially in St. John, Moncton and Fredericton. It is going to be hard to awaken New Brunswick out of its complacency. If you have a camera try your hand at some of the worst cases you find anywhere, but especially in these cities. If not, make a bargain with one of the photographers of each place to get a few pictures which we can use. This sounds like very primitive muck-raking but I do not think your native province will respond to much else . . .

Emboldened by her superior, King replied two days later:

Have you a fiery and thunderous plan for propaganda to arouse these indifferent lethargic old New Brunswickers? They don't seem to realize that they are almost a relic of the back ages — and if they did they wouldn't care. Their chief aversion is spending a cent more than they have to. Anything as long as it does not call for money . . .

Replying on November 7 from Winnipeg where she still was participating in Manitoba's Royal Commission, Charlotte offered this further crisp advice: "Verify all the lurid stories that you get and we shall use them. It is the only thing to stir New Brunswickers."

And so it came to pass. Once King began her two-month field investigation in October, she followed Charlotte's "muckraking" orders to the letter. Accordingly, she reported on absent and/or abusive fathers, immoral or "feebleminded" unwed mothers, and malnourished, poorly clothed, illiterate children in shockingly wretched home conditions. She visited twenty-eight communities in all fifteen counties, interviewed 206 "interested persons," visited three institutions, and personally spoke to ninety-eight of the families she included in her report.

Among the dozens of cases King detailed, along with some moralizing, were the following:

Case #57: Jane R., pregnant and an illegitimate child herself, was an unwed mother of two, aged six months and four years. When she appeared before a magistrate to swear who the father of her latest, unborn child was, she asked to postpone the hearing until the child was born so that she would have a better idea who the father might have been. Eventually she gave the names of nine men, any one of whom might have been the father of her child, and said three Indians whose names she did not know were also implicated.

Case #59: A widower who had been released from an insane asylum was living with his son, 15, and daughter, 13. On one stormy winter night, the two teenagers were seen half-dressed hauling wood with oxen. Another time, the girl was observed ploughing the frozen farm ground in her bare feet. When the widower was arrested, his son testified that "he slept on the floor at night with no bedding, and with nine dogs around him to keep him warm."

Case #62: A ten-year-old boy with club feet was called "Rolling Johnie" by many people because of his ungainly gait. Welfare officials offered to admit him to hospital for corrective surgery, but his parents refused, saying, "The Lord made him that way and must have meant him to remain so."

Case #166: A boy was regularly sent out to make money for the family by selling papers, begging or stealing. "If he went home at night without any funds, he was forced to sleep in a packing box in a nearby warehouse. The outcome was that the boy died of pneumonia."

Case #201: A family living in a rural district included the two parents, neither of whom worked, and four children between two and twelve years old. "They occupy a log hut, with just a hole to crawl in, and the children have no bed or covers to sleep in and have to sit by the fire to keep warm."

Case #258: Eight-year-old John had been forced to leave home by his mother some time ago and she had since married a man who was not John's father. John's father wanted nothing to do with John. So John was taken in "by an old woman of doubtful reputation whom we will call Susan. She has no home, nor has she the means of providing for John."

Nothing, it seemed, was right with children's welfare in New Brunswick.

To make sure New Brunswickers got the point, Charlotte advised King to provide the local press with "interesting generalities, but nothing that will give away the survey."

Not surprisingly, some New Brunswickers criticized the inviting of "outsiders" to investigate and comment on the province's child welfare picture, despite the fact that Charlotte had set up an advisory committee that included representatives of the Central Welfare Council of New Brunswick, the Saint John Kiwanis Club, and the Saint John Board of Trade. Strongest among her critics was Ella Paint, a woman who battled her on the letters page of the *Evening Times-Globe* in Saint John and in at least one public meeting. Paint's criticism stung Charlotte so much that when she received an anonymous letter from a Saint John address, Charlotte threatened to drive over and confront the resident, whom she suspected was Paint.

Charlotte's concluding 200-plus-page report blasted the provincial government for not having a superintendent of neglected children as required under the provincial *Children's Protection Act*, shot holes through the province's existing child welfare laws, and fired off incendiary rounds at the lack of treatment for juvenile offenders, the ignoring of school attendance rules, and the neglect in enforcing minimum age working laws. It was so explosive that the provincial government could not ignore it.

Based on his background, one might have thought that Premier John Baxter would have been more accommodating. Here was a man whose father had deserted the family when Baxter was two years old, and who had quit school at fourteen to work in a dry goods store then as an accountant for a butcher in his quest to obtain a law degree (shades of Charlotte, who had worked in Isaac Pedlow's dry goods store in Renfrew and who had done the books for her father's butchery in Whitney to help pay for her education at Queen's). Baxter had other priorities, however, including expanding the Maritime provinces' rights within Confederation. In addition, he was afraid of offending the more conservative elements in his party and the province. Instead, he privately urged Charlotte to get a positive reaction to her report from her self-appointed advisory committee, as it would be that much easier to sell New Brunswickers on a decision approved by New Brunswickers, rather than something conceived by "outsiders."

And so it was done.

Baxter introduced a revised *Children's Protection Act* in 1930, but Charlotte was greatly displeased. The new law would put authority for children's welfare in the province's hands, rather than in those of the privately run Children's Aid Society, as per her wishes. Although the legislation was passed on April 10, 1930, as the legislature adjourned, Baxter failed to send it to the lieutenant-governor for royal assent, so it never went into effect.

"In the end," Myers concluded, "Whitton had control of neither the premier nor the [advisory] revision committee, the community nor even her own proposal. New Brunswickers appeared quite comfortable abandoning Whitton's philosophy and evolving amendments which may not have made sense to the [CCCW], but made sense to some members of their community." In effect, Charlotte had struck out.

Despite this setback, the CCCW under Charlotte undertook similar, though often less extensive and less controversial, surveys during the late 1920s and early 1930s. These included surveys in Hamilton (1928); Ottawa (1929–31); Montreal, Fredericton, and Saskatoon (1930); Calgary and Kingston (1931); Regina and Brandon (1932); Halifax (1933); and Winnipeg (1934); as well as reports for British Columbia, Ontario, Quebec, Nova Scotia, and Prince Edward Island (1930). The result was that when it came to child welfare, the CCCW's and Charlotte's reputation topped the list.

Her reputation was rising, but she also was attracting growing opposition from some professional social workers, even more so from the non-professionals who had been dismissed or demoted as a result of her surveys. From both ends of the country, complaints surfaced that she was parachuting Central Canadians into positions of authority.

Some professionals, meanwhile, were concerned over her growing dominance in the social welfare field and what they considered her empire building. This belief was underscored when, in 1929, the Canadian Council on Child Welfare changed its name to the Canadian Council on Child and Family Welfare (CCCFW) and expanded its research field to include just about everything concerning the family, including movie censorship and alcoholism. At the same time, Charlotte was promoted from executive secretary to executive director, and the council moved to larger office space in a house at 245 Cooper Street, several blocks south of Parliament Hill, which it shared with the IODE. The house was just a five-minute stroll from the Chelsea Club at 236 Metcalfe Street, of which Charlotte was a co-founder and one of its most prominent members.

Despite the muted rumblings of opposition to her autocratic ways, Charlotte was riding high in her social welfare domain. The CCCW, with four employees in addition to Charlotte, was busy publishing pamphlets, managing surveys, and promoting the cause of child welfare across Canada. Charlotte was also in demand for speaking engagements in both Canada and the United States. Then, after some hard bargaining in 1928, she accepted the additional role of part-time convener of the National Council of Women's child welfare committee, a position similar to her role as the IODE's child welfare committee convener. She seemed to be everywhere — a nor'easter belting through the Maritimes, a tornado touching down in Ottawa, a Chinook chasing through Calgary, and a southwest Pacific gale crashing onto the shores of British Columbia.

"I would like to attend the Toronto conference since I've been away from Ontario so long," Charlotte wrote Barbara Blackstock of the National Council of Women in April 1929, "but an emergency has arisen, which may take me there suddenly any day this week . . . I am nearly desperate with needs in all parts of the Country and no one to fill them."

On July 16, she advised an English social worker whom she hoped to place in a Canadian job: "I had thought I might run over to Devon [England] in August or September, but recent developments here have lead [sic] to a request from the prominent Family Organizations in Canada that our Council expand to become the Canadian Council on Child and Family Welfare. This would mean practically doubling our organization, its staff, and responsibility, under my general direction. If this is to be done it will mean the heaviest kind of work for months and I do not see that I could get away." That was written after she had returned from visits to Canada's east and west coasts.

During the same period, she used her active involvement in the Council of Women, the IODE, the Canadian Association of Social Workers, and the Canadian Council on the Immigration of Women to establish an unofficial network or web of agencies that would support each other and the CCCW. For example, she urged the other groups to lobby the federal government for continued funding of the CCCW, and she got the Council of Women to support her activities at the League of Nations. Indicative of her ability to pull strings, she suggested that the National Council of Women ask the IODE if she could represent the latter on the former's executive council; another time, she recommended that the National Council of Women and the IODE hold their annual general meetings in the same city in two consecutive weeks so that members like herself, who belonged to both groups, could attend both meetings.

Despite her recognition as a leading Canadian authority on welfare, she still bridled at any hint of criticism. Thus, when a Regina woman wrote that the CCCW had done nothing to assist British children sent to Canada by British emigration societies and that the federal government had acted in 1924 only after the British parliamentary panel led by Margaret Bondfield had complained, Charlotte shot back: "Our Council has been fighting steadily at this question since 1920. Also, before Miss Bondfield was ever appointed to come out here we were largely instrumental in having Ontario and four other provinces enact juvenile immigration protective legislation, Ontario passing its legislation the session of 1924 . . . We were extremely anxious for an inquiry and were partly responsible for the agitation which resulted in the Bondfield Commission. It is not the Canadian Child Welfare agencies but the apathy of the Canadian public which is responsible for the situation in this problem."

All this activity meant that Charlotte had to put her League of Nations activities on the back burner; however, the stove was still lighted and the pot was still bubbling in 1928. Her rookie year at Geneva in 1926 had been both eye opening and controversial for Charlotte, and her second, in 1927, was only slightly less so. She had spoken to seven of the ten items on the child welfare committee's agenda, and in doing so had managed to take another shot at the monocle-wearing British aristocrat, Austen Chamberlain, for his impertinence in suggesting that the child welfare committee stick to its limited mandate. She also continued her opposition to a draft ruling that host countries should pay for immigrant children's repatriation, called for a full statistical breakdown of individual countries' age-of-consent laws, and presented a CCCW publication, *The White List*, which graded the wholesomeness of movies. Generally, though, she concentrated her energies on CCCW activities in Canada, such as her various surveys.

In January 1928, however, her attention was drawn back to the League. She asked the chair of the child welfare committee, Dame Crowdy, if the scheduled March 19 start to the annual ten-day meeting in Geneva could be pushed back to allow her to combine the committee meeting with a planned personal European tour. Impossible, replied Crowdy. The notice to some two dozen committee members had been approved a year earlier and could not be changed. In February, Charlotte complained to friends that the March meeting would interfere with her work in Saskatchewan and besides, crossing the stormy North Atlantic by ocean liner in March would be a gut-wrenching experience that she preferred to avoid. Nevertheless, she arrived on time and succeeded in postponing a committee report on illegitimate children for one year because she claimed it did not properly reflect the situation in Canada.

There was one other serious disagreement between the Charlotte and the League committee in 1928. It involved an offer from the American Child Hygiene Association to fund a $5,000 international study on neglected children. The dispute centred on who should conduct it, i.e. someone from an English-speaking country or someone from a "Latin" nation. As Charlotte later informed her U.S. confidante, Julia Lathrop, who had not attended the Geneva meeting due to illness, "We fought continuously with the Latins. The French delegation was determined to get hold of the U.S. cash, backed Mlle. L. Chaptal of the French delegation. The 'White speaking races' which includes [*sic*] Denmark and Germany are determined that this will not be the case. We feel that this study must be made by a British or North American worker. It would upset the apple cart to tell anybody over there just what we feel."

The annual meeting had been somewhat successful, she told Lathrop, because she had been able to force the postponement of a survey on illegitimate children, and the committee had approved the U.S.-funded neglected-child study as well as a study of the treatment of children by juvenile courts. Unsatisfied with this success, however, Charlotte suggested to Lathrop that they approach a few like-thinking delegates on the committee before the official meetings so that they could "get some co-ordination in this unwieldy group."

Lathrop replied, "Your letter was encouraging though not in itself exactly buoyant! To know that you have been on the spot and have triumphed over one or two Nordics as well as a few Latins is delightful."

But the battle with Léontine Chaptal was just shaping up. Her main issue with Chaptal was that the Frenchwoman, like most European officials at the time, believed that child welfare should be the domain of visiting nurses, rather than social workers. North American social workers, on the other hand, felt that they should control the welfare of children. Underlying these points was the fact that Charlotte wanted to be involved; no one was more aware than her of the importance of statistics to shape a study's final results. Therefore, if anyone was going to play with statistics, she wanted to be part of the action.

There was little Charlotte could do at the League to prevent Chaptal's selection as survey manager, for the European votes on the child welfare committee easily outnumbered those from North America, even if the British sided with the latter, as they occasionally did. So Charlotte turned to other efforts. On September 4, 1928, just as she was starting Manitoba's Royal Commission on Child Welfare, she wrote to Bascom Johnston of the American Child Hygiene Association, suggesting that his group withdraw its sponsorship of Chaptal's survey.

Johnston replied that the association was having second thoughts about the survey, but admitted that the offer had been made and accepted, and that there was little his organization could do about it. Similarly, Lathrop suggested she be patient and give Chaptal a chance. Unsatisfied, Charlotte urged Johnston to prod the League committee to ensure that the study would be done "by a person and under the supervision of a Committee competent to line up the study along the principles and practices on which we want information." Someone like her friend, Miss J.I. Wall, an English child welfare official, would do the job properly, she suggested. But the issue already had been decided in Chaptal's favour. She also wrote to W.A. Riddell, Canada's chief representative at the League, saying that with Chaptal's nomination as survey leader confirmed, she was having second thoughts about the benefits of Canada's participation in the League's child welfare committee. "As far as I am concerned, I am now quite satisfied that this study would be of such little value to us in Canada that I am not in the least interested in being associated with it."

Perhaps not, but that would not stop her from talking and writing about it. In October, she complained again to committee chair Crowdy that the statistics Chaptal wanted from Canada were almost impossible to assemble, since child welfare was a provincial prerogative, rather than a federal one, as in Europe. She also drafted a sharply worded, three-page letter on legal-sized paper to Crowdy complaining of a host of issues, but wisely ran it by her friends Lathrop, Grace Abbott, and O.D. Skelton before putting in the mail. Once again, her friends advised patience on her part, and the letter, which she had hoped the Americans would co-sign, was not sent. Abbott noted, "I feel that the European habit of saying disagreeable things very sweetly — which irritates me more than anything else — would make them feel that it was a harsh letter!! — Not that they don't deserve it."

In December 1928, as the Manitoba and New Brunswick surveys were wrapping up, Charlotte sought an interview with Skelton over the League survey issue, but he politely passed her off to his understudy, Lester B. Pearson, who treated her with admirable diplomatic coolness.

The following year was much the same as far as relations between Charlotte and the League's committee were concerned. Again her request to change the date of the annual meeting was rejected, and she continued to complain about the difficulty of amassing the information Chaptal required from the nine provincial governments.

Also, Chaptal was planning to visit Canada and the United States in connection with her survey, and Charlotte was expected to be her principal hostess while in this country. Undoubtedly miffed by Charlotte's lack of co-operation, Chaptal had no communication with her until July when she wrote that she had arrived in Montreal and would be in Ottawa the following week, where she would be staying at the Chelsea Club. Fine, Charlotte replied, she would be in town all next week, "and shall be glad to be of service to you then." However, as there really was not much to see nor many people to visit in Ottawa, Chaptal would be better off scheduling her time elsewhere in Canada. Accordingly, Chaptal's visit to Ottawa was brief and her itinerary concentrated instead on Montreal, Toronto, Sudbury, Winnipeg, and Quebec City. At the end of her tour, she informed Charlotte that she would be returning through Ottawa at 5 a.m. in order to make train connections for her return voyage overseas, so it was not necessary that they confer again in Canada.

That was fine with Charlotte, for by then she was fully occupied in the expansion and name change of the Canadian Council on Child Welfare to the Canadian Council of Child and Family Welfare, with all its added responsibilities. As for the League and its child welfare committee, Charlotte wanted to resign her assessorship and only stayed on at the request of the Canadian government, which was using the position as a weapon in its ongoing battle for autonomy from Britain on the international stage. Nevertheless, she missed all of the committee's annual meetings between 1929 and 1933.

Summing up her experience at the League in a letter to Riddell in June 1930, Charlotte warned that if the League did not do something to change the Social Questions Section that included the child welfare committee, "There is a grave danger that persons and agencies who have been associated with the most progressive developments in modern social work on this Continent and elsewhere cannot risk having their names and efforts associated with the work and publications for which the Section and Committee are responsible. Quite frankly I do not feel that there is, in the entire personnel of the section one thoroughly qualified, informed, and competent official with any precise general knowledge of the field of child welfare and general social work."

Riddell replied, "It is much more difficult to prescribe a remedy, however, than to diagnose a complaint. I have sometimes thought that it was a doubtful policy for the assessors from North America to absent themselves from the meetings. The Europeans are always here, and naturally are more likely to have their way when they are unopposed." He also informed her that although he had recommended her as a possible successor to Crowdy as committee secretary, the head of the League's bureaucracy, Sir Eric Drummond, vetoed the recommendation because of her "propaganda" for social workers. "He agreed with me that you had great ability, but stated that it was not the kind of ability that he wishes to have represented in a Chief of Section."

Thus was Charlotte's career at the League of Nations returned to the back burner, only this time the fire in the stove was dying out.

Despite all this activity in the years 1927 through 1931, Charlotte managed to find time for her personal life. For example, in the fall of 1928, amidst the Manitoba Royal Commission, the New Brunswick survey, and her ongoing row with the League committee, she and Margaret Grier moved into a two-storey, two-bedroom apartment on Rideau Terrace in New Edinburgh, immediately adjacent to the more upscale village of Rockcliffe Park. It was an apartment they would share until Grier's death in 1947, and in which Charlotte would reside until the mid-1960s. At about the same time, Charlotte bought a new car, a 1927 Marmon sedan for $1,900, but she was involved in a collision almost before the paint was dry. The insurance company sent her $23.35 for damages, due to "car travelling at excessive speed, ripped mud guard." It was just one of a number of minor traffic accidents in which she would be involved in the coming years.

The following year, she was chosen president of the Ottawa University Women's Club in May and admitted as a member to the Renfrew Golf Club in July. In December, she and Ella Thorburn began promoting a booklet they had written and self-published on the Memorial Chamber in the Peace Tower.

As well, after being elected to Queen's University's board of governors in 1928, she became a member of the board's search committee for a new principal. In 1930, she was involved in an internal committee battle against her old friend W.F. Nickle, chairman of the board of governors, and others on the board over limits on the principal's authority. Partly as a result of the argument, Nickle resigned as chairman in the fall.

One other item of note from this period was a three-page, typed letter she wrote to Miss Gladys Potts of the London-based Society for Overseas Development of British Women in which she divulged yet again her deep affinity for Britain despite the shortsightedness of certain of its emigration officials: "Personally, as a Britisher who feels her obligations to the Empire more strongly possibly than those to her own country, I feel that one of the greatest menaces in Canada to the British connection, is the attitude in migration circles at the present time" of those officials in Britain. She concluded the letter with a postscript: "Please consider this letter as a personal note from one Britisher interested in Empire settlement to another engaged therein."

All in all, this period was a fine time for Charlotte. She had taken over direction of the Canadian Council on Child Welfare and had seen it expand to become the Canadian Council on Child and Family Welfare. She had begun her child welfare surveys, she was a popular speaker across the country, and she had made her mark on the international scene with her performance at the League of Nations. The years to come would prove to be even better.

7 Tough Love Advised

F or many, the dark days of the Depression, touched off by the Wall Street stock market crash of October 29, 1929, was the worst disaster of their lifetimes. Businesses failed, farms folded, unemployment rose, family quarrels worsened, parental desertion rates increased, children suffered. Unemployment was high in Ontario and Quebec, but even worse in the Maritime provinces hit by poor fishing and industrial strikes. On the Prairies, the situation was dire, as drought had transformed the area into a giant dust bowl, while British Columbia was awash in strikes and unrest. Governments at all levels across the nation and around the world were scrambling, often desperately, for solutions. In Ottawa, Prime Minister R.B. Bennett, the corpulent corporate lawyer from Calgary, was stymied for an adequate response.

Amidst this maelstrom of misery, Charlotte thrived. Never had the need for social workers seemed greater, never was the quest for new ideas more urgent. It was an opportunity she would not ignore, and once again her organization, the newly renamed Canadian Council on Child and Family Welfare, stepped up to the plate.

Early in 1931, when it was obvious that Bennett and his Conservative government were unable to solve the crisis, the CCCFW called a national conference, which attracted representatives of federal and provincial governments and member agencies from across the country. Behind closed doors, the delegates hammered out nineteen recommendations they hoped might overcome the nightmare that was unfolding. Chief among the recommendations was a plan to put the unemployed to work on public works projects, such as building roads, replacing slums with improved housing, and eliminating railway crossings by constructing overpasses. As well, they suggested settling unemployed men on new farms, or in other cases sending them back to their hometowns if they had gone elsewhere for work or handouts. For unemployed young women, they suggested hostels be built to train them for domestic service.

Bennett was in a nearly impossible position. Having taken office after defeating Mackenzie King's Liberals in the July 1930 election, he, like many national leaders, was confounded by the global crisis. In his first year in office, he raised tariffs on imported goods to help Canadian manufacturers and producers, and he handed out $20 million to the provinces for unemployment relief, but these measures had little effect. The situation worsened and the suffering of his fellow countrymen was not the sort the self-made millionaire was familiar with.

R.B. Bennett was born in Hopewell Hill, a small community on New Brunswick's southern shore, on July 3, 1870. His father traced his ancestry back through a line of shipbuilders, and his mother's family were of United Empire Loyalist stock, settlers who left the Thirteen Colonies after they declared independence from Britain in 1776 so as to continue living under the Union Jack.

"As a boy, 'Dickie' Bennett did not care for playing games like other children. He was a serious, studious type, and his mother, who had been a school-teacher, helped and encouraged him to understand and appreciate learning," wrote H. Estelle Scott in a favourable sketch in 1935.

Bennett's mother wanted him to be a schoolteacher like herself, and at seventeen, he found himself armed with a teacher's certificate in charge of a small rural school. At twenty-three, he quit teaching to study law at Dalhousie University, during which time he befriended a fellow student named Jennie Shirreff and her brother Harry.

Upon graduation, Bennett became a junior partner in a Chatham, New Brunswick, law firm. Bennett also taught Sunday school, lectured at the Temperance Hall, and was elected to Chatham town council. In 1897, he moved to Calgary and joined the prominent law firm of Conservative senator James A. Lougheed. Within a year, he was a member of the Legislative Assembly of the Northwest Territories — Alberta, like Saskatchewan, received provincial status only in 1905 — and remained an MLA, off and on, until 1911, when he became a member of Parliament for Calgary. In the meantime, his law practice and real estate dealings in Calgary profited nicely, making Bennett well-to-do.

Jennie, however, moved to Boston after graduation to work as a nurse. She befriended the daughter of Ottawa-area matchstick tycoon E.B. Eddy and then wed Eddy after his first wife died. When Eddy himself died in 1906, Jennie inherited his business empire. By 1911, however, when Bennett was just starting his parliamentary career in Ottawa, the Eddy business was failing, so Jennie asked Bennett for advice, which he gladly provided. When both Jennie and her brother died a few years later, Bennett inherited a large share of the business, which recovered and became a major industry in the region for decades afterwards.

Despite these business interests, R.B. Bennett lived for politics and pursued it with a passion. His reward came in 1921 when the Conservatives, led by Arthur Meighen, defeated the Liberals under Mackenzie King, and Meighen named Bennett as his justice minister. Unfortunately that success was short-lived, for King's Liberals were returned to power in December of that year. It was a tumultuous time in Canadian politics, and Bennett served briefly as finance minister in 1926, during another brief Meighen government, before King once again regained power. Meighen stepped down as Conservative leader in 1927 and was replaced by Bennett, who defeated King in 1930 to become prime minister.

Like King, Bennett was a bachelor. He did not avoid women; he just had no time for romance. He was described as shy, religious, and deeply devoted to the memory of his mother, for whom he had a carillon installed in his church in Calgary. He was also very close to his sister Mildred and to his long-time secretary, Alice Millar. He also communicated frequently with another like-minded female, Charlotte Whitton.

Theirs was a platonic friendship. Kindred bachelors, each with his or her own lofty goals and needs, they were the perfect odd couple, for they shared conservative ideas and lived unostentatious but comfortable lives despite the Depression. It was not surprising, then, that as Bennett was desperately trying to deal with the economic crisis, his thoughts turned to Charlotte.

A few years earlier, in 1927, when as executive director of the CCCW she had asked if he would allow his name to stand as a patron of the council, the new Tory leader cheerfully accepted and, he noted, "recalled old memories of that exceedingly able Private

Secretary who gave such service to her Chief [Trade and Commerce Minister Thomas Low] and who is now giving even greater service to an even greater cause."

Now she could do such service for her country, he decided in late spring of 1932. He suggested that she tour Western Canada and report back to him on the situation there. Charlotte, of course, was willing and able.

The CCCFW could hardly afford to allow her three months' leave for the mission for, as she noted in a general mailing to potential donors the previous year, the $10,000 received from the federal government, the $6,000 from the life insurance companies of Canada, and the $1,000 from the army and navy veterans' associations were proving inadequate for the organization's increasing workload. She and the CCCFW had been busy in the intervening two years with surveys across the country, and by now, she was conducting investigations in Ottawa and Calgary.

The Ottawa study began early in the year and involved the setting up of a Community Chest, the forerunner of today's United Way. In the fall of 1931, Charlotte heard that the city's loosely knit Council of Social Agencies (CSA) was considering the joint fundraising effort, for until then the agencies' individual efforts had been relatively unsuccessful, considering the magnitude of the Depression. She quickly offered the CCCFW's support because, as she told the CSA, her organization had a wealth of experience in that sort of thing.

Charlotte also advised the editor of the *Ottawa Journal*, P.D. Ross, in a "personal and confidential" letter dated November 19, that the CSA would be making a big mistake by rushing to a decision without proper technical advice and allowing the city's politicians to dictate its makeup, "which will undoubtedly lead to the most undesirable mixing of private charity and municipal politics." There was to be a public meeting on the issue the following Friday so, "[to] this end I had taken the liberty of jotting down a few lines which might be of use to one of your editors if you deemed the situation worthy of consideration." However she reminded him of the confidentiality of this letter, because "naturally I did not want to bring our organization into the picture at this stage, or make an appeal myself at this time, because it would hamper us from full usefulness in the developments."

On the same day, she sent a similar letter to the editor of the *Ottawa Citizen*, Harry Southam, along with an article she wanted him to run prior to the Friday meeting, advising him that she would be sending more articles for Saturday's pages. Not surprisingly, both men ran favourable editorials in the following days. To push matters further, Charlotte wrote Southam the following week to suggest he print four more of her articles on the subject and, if he wished to send a reporter to interview her, she would prepare the questions and answers for the reporter. Instead he made do with a lengthy editorial praising the CSA for its decision to invite "scientific preparation" and "the skilled guidance of some one thoroughly familiar with the fundamental principles and techniques" to organize its planned survey.

With the local media in hand, Charlotte then turned her attention to Colonel W.E. Weld, the CSA's secretary. A major study by trained personnel was needed, she advised him, and she was prepared to undertake the study at once. The CSA quickly accepted the offer, and she got to work immediately. Although the city of 130,000 and its social agencies were clearly divided along religious and linguistic lines, the situation was not nearly as dire in the national capital as Charlotte had found it in New Brunswick. However, it still was not good. She found that forty per cent of the population was dependent on federal government jobs, but many of those were low-paying, clerical and secretarial positions that were as temporary as the government sittings of the day. As well, in recent years, the number of private charities had ballooned from a half dozen to about thirty, resulting in considerable duplication. What the report avoided, though, was the "lurid muckraking" that had been so evident in the New Brunswick report. One could suppose that the fact the author lived in the city may have influenced its tone.

Her 115-page report in May 1932, entitled, "One Campaign but Three Chests," called for a single "Financial Federation," or Community Chest, whose funds would be split along religious lines, that is, between Protestant, Catholic, and Jewish communities. There would be one massive joint fundraiser per year in the city and the proceeds would be divided among the CSA's sixty-two individual agencies. Those agencies in turn would allot their spending along religious lines roughly paralleling the percentage of population and wealth of the three religious groupings. She also recommended, without explanation, that hospitals should make unwed mothers pay for their children's births, while married women would continue to receive the service freely. Her report was eagerly accepted.

In Calgary, she contacted the managing editor of the *Herald*, C.R. Haydon, in January 1932, and suggested that the CCCFW be invited to organize a survey leading to the establishment of a Community Chest in that city. She also wrote Mrs. Harold Riley of the Calgary Council on Child and Family Welfare with the same suggestion, adding that she planned to be in that city in June as part of her western tour for Bennett. She was confident "we could give you a pretty good job at very little cost." She added that a colleague, Ethel Parker, had just completed a similar survey in Victoria and would be in Calgary in June as well to discuss a possible survey.

Charlotte was under no misapprehension as to the enormity of the economic and human crisis when she began her western tour for Bennett in June 1932. In March, for example, she broadcast an appeal on an Ottawa radio station calling on residents to support a new women's workshop that took in sewing and knitting orders. The workshop convenor was prominent socialite Mrs. A.J. Freiman, wife of the leading department store owner in town and national president of the Jewish women's group, Hadassah in Canada. The treasurer was Mrs. H.B. (Ella) Thorburn, past-president of the CCCFW and by then involved in a range of charitable activities in the capital. The important point about the workshop, Charlotte stressed, was that it was meant "to provide employment, not relief; work and payment, not charity, for a large group of women, upon whom the present depression has laid a heavy burden. In those rooms, you will find quiet, efficient service, along lines of almost perfect business organization." Although a few of the women were accepting government relief cheques, most "represent a group who, with heroic courage, are determined that they will not go on relief, either public or private, until every last avenue of other means of support has been explored." The women were paid between $2 and $2.50 per week for their part-time work, compared to the $4 per day Charlotte paid her personal secretary, Mrs. J. Sullivan, to type her speeches and other personal correspondence.

She continued in her Ottawa radio appeal: "Now is the time of greatest need, just when winter fuel and clothing have depleted meager savings and spring work has not yet opened up. It has been a time of long, long wearying days and weeks and months. Small signs that are hopeful are breaking; good times are not around the corner, not for many months yet, but there are some hopes of 1932 closing with more encouragement than it has opened. Through these months we must hold the fort, all of us, as those who have suffered most, the unemployed themselves have held it, in all these weary months."

In April, she forwarded a lengthy memo to Bennett outlining her views about his government's make-work projects. Surprisingly, for someone who abhorred giving welfare payments to healthy men, she suggested that it was better to give straight relief than pay for unnecessary public works. "A work relief programme is about twice as expensive as reasonable home relief for the same number of families. Therefore, while the greater value of relief work over relief is recognized, if funds are limited and the need great, urgency and economy may require careful consideration of whether more aid cannot be extended to a greater number of persons, by a well organized system of family relief, than a system of 'made' relief work," she advised. (During this period, she often underlined many of the statements in her various reports.)

She further recommended that due to their experience, relief agencies should dole out the relief funds and — Bennett must have loved this part — that the major funding should come from provincial and municipal coffers rather than from the federal government. To buttress her argument against make-work relief projects, she reached back for historical analogies, referring to France's "ateliers nationaux" program, in existence since 1848, and Britain's 1905 royal commission on relief. The latter produced a fifty-nine-volume report which concluded that make-work projects were a total failure when it came to solving an economic crisis.

She concluded by suggesting that Bennett had two options when it came to relief: he could provide government funding for all health and social assistance measures, or he could be tough and limit funding to the truly needy. "It is submitted that along the second path lies not only the one line of development which the resources of the Canadian community can support, but also the way that sound social statesmanship would select."

With her opinions already set and armed with a letter from Bennett to the western premiers seeking their co-operation with her survey — "You undoubtedly know Miss Whitton, if not personally, by reputation. She probably is the most capable woman engaged in social welfare in the Dominion" — she began her survey on June 15 in Winnipeg. Next day, in an eleven-page, handwritten letter from her temporary accommodation at the upscale Alexandra Hotel, she warned Bennett that there was growing unease in Winnipeg as "a better class" of citizen was joining the unemployed on the breadlines and they were beginning to organize public protests. Communist agitators, meanwhile, were also stirring up demonstrations of their own. To counteract any future troubles, she suggested he follow up an idea mentioned to her by James Richardson, the wealthy Winnipeg grain exporter, financier, and chancellor of Queen's University, to put all able-bodied unemployed men in mobile work camps and have them cut roadside weeds, clear wheat fields and clean Crown lands as they moved north from the provincial capital. "The Militia Dept [sic] could provide tents and camp kitchens, i.e. organization run along military lines; the men be fed and given some pay, and I suggest 'assigning' part of it, as in the army, against their winter maintenance."

At one point she referred to these camps as "concentration camps," but that was well before the term had the abhorrent connotation of Hitler's death camps.

While she stayed at the finest hotels when she visited the major centres, her lodgings were much more modest in the smaller towns and villages that she visited by car or train, ranging from humble inns to private homes. Most of her travel was done in the comfort of a Canadian Pacific Railway train, but there were days when she was chauffeured over dusty, bone-crunching, potholed back roads that must have been exceedingly exhausting on the mind as well as on the body. On June 20, for example, she was driven 265 miles by a volunteer and stopped at several towns and villages along the way, usually meeting and questioning a mayor, or a reeve, or a public health nurse about local conditions. Three days later, her itinerary included the following small Saskatchewan communities: Milestone, Lang, Yellow Grass, Weyburn, Estevan, Bienfait, Trossachs, Radville, Ceylon, and Pangman. Her files at the national archives contain

a map of Western Canada with her route marked in colour, leading south from Winnipeg in a near oval pattern through southern
Manitoba and Saskatchewan, north to Regina, west to Calgary, down
through southern Alberta and British Columbia, north through the
Okanagan, west to Vancouver and Victoria, north through Vancouver Island, a boat trip further north to Prince Rupert, then by train
to Edmonton, with a detour northwest to Dawson Creek, then east
through northern Alberta, Saskatchewan, and Manitoba, and south
to Winnipeg, before returning to Ottawa.

The story was much the same no matter where she went. Unemployment was high, the municipalities were overburdened by the
number of requests for relief they received, and a disproportionate
amount of relief funds allegedly were going to new settlers or lazy
transients seeking easy charity. For example, Reddy MacLean, municipal clerk of the town of Souris, Manitoba, population 1,400,
complained that "foreigners" — i.e. recently arrived settlers — were
receiving half the town's relief funds, while district nurse Miss Pater-
son said that although there was little malnutrition, she had "found
quite a tendency growing among people to demand more in way of
relief, hospital aid, medical supplies, etc." Wealthy Scottish-Cana-
dian farmer John Hume, who spent his winters in the United States
or Ontario, argued caustically that "The western farmer is where he
is, because he spent before he earned. The eastern farmer always
earns before he spends." In Swan River, the public health nurse told
her the "foreign" settlers never had it so good because they were receiving more in relief than they ever earned through their farms, and
in Dauphin she heard that most of the part-time relief work went
to Ruthenians, from Eastern Europe, because Ruthenians comprised
the majority in the town and controlled the town council and its
relief effort.

In Manitoba's southwest region, the area of the province hardest
hit by drought, she contemptuously described "white trash pockets"
of squatters eking out a bare living as they had done even in good
times. She also found "the breed," or mixed-blood Métis families
living on the edge of Indian reservations who received no support
from the Department of Indian Affairs and who failed to fit in with
the "white" community, preferring odd jobs, "making brew," and allowing their women to work as prostitutes. "Inheriting with their red

blood, its fatal tendency to tuberculosis, and by their habits of life developing others of our most contagious and loathsome diseases, they become a menace to much of the life and health they touch," she complained. She concluded that the fourfold problem for rural Manitoba included (1) shiftless, often "mentally defective," white-trash settlers; (2) "the breeds"; (3) new settlers trying unsuccessfully to farm poor land; and (4) recent Old Country settlers trying to work good farmland, but held back by taxes, mortgages, and equipment costs.

In Saskatchewan, the worst hit of the provinces because of the drought, the public school nurse in Weyburn, Miss Morton, told her that the families of those on welfare were better off than those working part-time, because the former were receiving more money than the latter. She said many families on welfare had told her it was the best winter they had ever had because they were receiving relief payments. In Swift Current, she listened as J. Furness, the relief commissioner, spoke about the 1913 drought and how many who had received relief payments then had never repaid them. Except for the Mennonite sect, who were self-sufficient, the area's farmers had foolishly bought too much land and too much machinery on credit and now were paying the cost. In Estevan, she heard that the local miners had been on strike, or had been laid off, and that communist agitators were stirring up protests.

The picture was much the same as she moved across Alberta. In Lethbridge, as in other communities, the unemployed miners established a social club, but the talk, as they played cards or billiards, was about the future and whether they should adopt peaceful means to improve their lot, or follow the communists in taking more direct action. On July 3, writing a seven-page interim report to Bennett from Medicine Hat, she acknowledged many prairie cities were unable to afford relief payments for their unemployed residents, but "I would suggest that you do nothing further to relieve them of their legitimate local burdens unless you do much more, that is take over entirely the Employment and Unemployment Relief Administration." She also mentioned that "the transient problem is getting quite out of hand," and that she had stayed one night at the luxurious resort at Banff and had found that the staff outnumbered the guests. (She, Margaret Grier, and other members of the Canadian Women's Press

Club stayed one night at the resort as guests of the Canadian Pacific Railway, which also partly sponsored the club's June 28–30 convention at the Hotel Palliser, in Calgary, where Bennett had a private suite.)

The situation was different in British Columbia, where she spent almost a month, travelling by train, car, and boat. There was still a fair amount of seasonal work in lumbering, mining, and fishing, but the problem, as always for B.C., was the warm climate which acted as magnet for young people from the rest of Canada seeking the easy life. In Penticton, the government agent in charge of relief, Mr. Dewdney, told her the unemployed were "living like kings," and there was nothing the city could do because the relief rate had been set by the province. The provincial government, meanwhile, was unable to meet the challenge, and there was graft and corruption up and down the length of the province. At Alert Bay, on the northern coast, the secretary of the Conservative Party association, Mr. Todd, said that people with the right connections to the provincial government were hired as foremen in the work camps, and there were occasions where there was one foreman for as few as three or four workers. Elsewhere, lumber companies linked to the provincial government were renting their unused lumber camps to the province as work camps for the unemployed for the then-astronomical price of $7,000 a year. Then there was the case of the Prince Rupert druggist who bought camp beds in Edmonton for $2.10 each and sold them to the province for $6.50 apiece. Or the situation in Mission Camp, where 104 carpenters were on the payroll, but when she visited, only four were found working.

The stories of graft and corruption amid all the hardship never seemed to end in British Columbia, as Charlotte carefully noted on loose pieces of paper as she scrambled from one unhappy community to another. However, on July 31, while taking a train from Prince Rupert to Edmonton, she cheerfully jotted to Bennett: "By the way, I got up at 6:30 on a cold morning to hear you open the Imperial Conference . . . Your splendid address came through wonderfully well, your voice was vibrant, strong, unmistakably yours and having heard and seen you speak. I could almost imagine the outthrust chin, and frowning intensity which accomplished that delivery . . ." She said she had spent almost a month in British Columbia, but she had not taken her planned holiday because "I found things too upsetting." The provincial government under Premier Simon Fraser Tolmie was not functioning properly, the municipalities were desperate, and everyone was blaming the federal government.

"Indicative of the extravagance and carelessness which characterized the setting-up of the [relief] camps," she noted, "is the claim voiced in quarters that are undoubtedly well-informed that the set-up and equipment averaged $88.00 per man, as compared with $6.00 per man in the Ontario set-up and a slightly higher figure in Manitoba." As in the other provinces, welfare payments for the unemployed varied greatly from municipality to municipality. For example, the average relief funds per family per month over a three-month period in B.C. in 1932 were as follows: New Westminster — $39.40; Burnaby — $32.56; Victoria — $30.80; Vancouver — $16.50 for groceries only; Nanaimo — $15.00; Richmond — $7.28; West Vancouver — $6.

The news was much the same as she wound her way back east through the northern prairies. However, as the crisis in Ottawa worsened, Bennett called her home for a briefing in mid-August, cutting off the northern Ontario leg of her survey because he himself was planning a western tour in the very near future.

Back in Ottawa in mid-September, she submitted her expense account, which totalled $2,518.20. It was based on a living allowance of $15 per day plus other expenses, such as bus fares and car rentals. She also offered, if Bennett wished, to survey the rest of the country. That offer seems to have been lost in government red tape, for it was never acted upon. In the meantime, she returned to her CCCFW office on September 15 and promised that her report would be coming shortly.

She was true to her word. A lot of the 295-page report appears verbatim from notes she had taken along the way; however, it is supported by copious statistics and background papers provided by the provinces and municipalities visited. Not surprisingly, it attacked "foreigners," communists and excessive graft in British Columbia, but is dulled by stilted language and massive amounts of statistics that were open to broad interpretation. Innuendoes from unnamed "confidential" or "influential" sources as well as named officials are laced throughout.

Among her recommendations was the establishment of two or three large-scale camps for unemployed males in the hinterlands of northern Ontario and northern Quebec. They would be the responsibility of the Department of Labour, but would be run on military lines by military personnel. They would comprise only unmarried men at the start, but as the camps became established, unemployed married males and their families could be included. "I believe in the Province of Ontario I could settle fifty thousand men in two years, and have a quarter of a million men serving them. I believe the whole three hundred thousand could get their winter warmth and their food where they were working," she advised. The federal government would have to supply the camp for the first year only, for "by the end of the second year I would sort out the sheep from the goats." Capable settlers would be given forty acres of land to develop, and if they did well, they would receive another forty acres the following and each successive year, so long as they worked it to proper advantage. At the end of fifteen years of successful production, the tenant should be given the land free of charge.

She also recommended that Bennett set up a national registration and classification system for the nation's unemployed and issue personal identification cards "in the nature of a passport" for them. There would be three classes of unemployed males: (a) those between eighteen and twenty-five; (b) the sick, handicapped or chronically ill whose benefits were covered fully by the provinces; and (c) able-bodied transient males over twenty-five years of age who would be drafted into "concentration camps . . . in areas where constructive works can be undertaken." The latter would be under semi-military discipline, given three meals a day, paid a small allowance for essentials, and credited with a small amount of "assigned pay," which they would receive at a future date.

Unemployed women, she noted, were not a threat to the nation's stability because they usually could find domestic work or remain with their families. Consequently, she offered no advice in their regard.

In October, Bennett's government introduced legislation establishing military-run camps across the country for the unemployed. Admission was voluntary, but if single, unemployed males did not attend, they would be ineligible for relief payments. If they did enter the camps, basic room and board was provided and they would be paid just twenty cents a day.

The news at the CCCFW on her return was not good. Revenue was down, expenses were up, a deficit threatened. It was not what the financial conservative wanted to hear. Spending cuts had to be made, and efficiencies had to be introduced. On September 23, she complained in a letter to Howard Falk of the Vancouver Council of Social Agencies that she still had to complete her report to Bennett and "I feel much like a hen that has hatched out a whole flock of eagles and is now running for cover under any barn in sight."

Contributions from member agencies across the country had declined precipitously. In Winnipeg, for example, James Richardson had the previous year paid the full $1,200 provincial fee from his own pocket, but "he cannot do this again this year." He had said he would try to raise money from other Winnipeg businessmen, but he was not optimistic. Similarly in Toronto, a loyal CCCFW director reported raising only small amounts, such as $10, from his fellow businessmen. Consequently, Charlotte told Falk, she was forced to lay off the CCCFW's shipping clerk and its librarian, and feared more cuts would be necessary.

Amidst this financial pressure, the council received an invoice from the Bell Telephone Company in Ottawa that lighted the firecracker that was Charlotte, by now well known for her petty tantrums. The invoice totalled $13.25 and covered long distance calls to Vancouver, Hamilton, and Renfrew. There must be some error, she wrote Bell. Especially concerning the collect call from Vancouver, which she had taken at home, but which she was charging to the CCCFW. She had been told she would be charged $4.75 for the first three minutes and $1.50 for each additional minute, so she had planned accordingly to limit the call to less than three minutes. She continued:

> Because of the warning I had received, I also asked two friends to be present when I telephoned. I had my own watch on the desk before me and they had theirs. I was called to the telephone and Central said that Vancouver was calling and wished me to pay the charges. I said I

would do so and it was fully three minutes after that, before the party came on the wire. I spoke to my friends and asked them to time this because I would likely be billed for the time lost. The party to whom I wanted to speak came on the wire. I had taken the precaution of writing down what I was going to say and had timed it to within the three minutes easily. I spoke to Mr. Falk, the Executive Director of the Vancouver Social Agencies, saying at once that I had only three minutes, that therefore he could not speak to me at length, but would he telegraph me on the business which I was referring to him. He did not say four sentences to me and we concluded the call. My two friends and I compared our watches and each of us had the separate record that the conversation took two and three-quarter minutes . . . I wrote down what I said before I started to talk and I had taken the precaution of having these two friends check on the time. Certainly if this is the toll that is to be charged for two and three-quarter minutes conversation to Vancouver, it is the last time that we shall attempt any use of long distance with any of our agencies.

Four more paragraphs followed, detailing previous long-distance calls and prices charged; in sum, her letter got a speedy reaction from the company. Bell's district manager in Ottawa admitted that the corporate giant had erred on the Renfrew charge and in this case the company would accept her word on the timing of the Vancouver call. He granted her a $2.50 credit.

As the year ran out, Charlotte had one last salvo at what she considered wasteful spending of taxpayers' dollars. It concerned city hall's donation of Christmas hampers to the poor, which she considered unnecessary largesse on the City of Ottawa's part.

Nineteen thirty-two was an important year for the executive director of the CCCFW, but not necessarily remarkable, for more achievements and more honours were in store.

On the personal side, it was just another busy year for the whirlwind that was Charlotte. In January, she attended a meeting of the Ottawa committee of the National Council of Education, of which she was a member, but she sent her regrets to the left-of-centre Canadian Radio League that was forming and which would soon successfully lobby Bennett to establish the Canadian Broadcasting Corporation. In February, she found time to compose a speech for Mrs. Jessie Stewart, former national president of the IODE, to the group's Guelph chapter, and in the same month she was admitted as a member to the influential Toronto Ladies Club. Later in the year she joined the Renfrew Golf Club.

She was sidelined for three weeks in February and March with a nasty case of influenza, and in May, as she was completing work on a proposed Community Chest for Ottawa. She also wrote a short history of a church in Whitney, Ontario, where she had spent summers with her father and brothers during her college years. In June, she accepted an advisory, part-time role with the child welfare committee of the International Labour Organization in Geneva.

Despite her reputation for orderliness and efficiency, however, there were occasions when she would slip up in her personal affairs. In October, she wrote Mrs. Jessie Stewart's personal secretary to advise her that she, Charlotte, had mistakenly deposited some Standard Oil shares in Mrs. Stewart's name with her broker, rather than in her own name, and she would appreciate it if the secretary could straighten out the difficulty.

It had been a trying time for Charlotte, financially, for her investments, like everyone else's, were rocked by the stock market collapse. Not that she was heavily invested, but it hurt just the same. In 1931, two of the companies she had invested in, Greenshields and Company and W.A. Stanford Limited, declared bankruptcy, and in 1932, her $715 worth of shares in Bishop Bethune College in Oshawa became worthless when the college announced that it was broke. These were lessons the ever-penny-pinching Charlotte would take to heart.

Her interest in Bay Street had begun as early as 1927 when she received an information sheet from Donald I. McLeod of McLeod Young Weir stockbrokers about two prospective investments. In April, she bought three shares in Hayes Wheels & Forgings and three shares of Stanford's preferred shares through him. She bought and sold a number of other stocks during the year and showed a certain amount of financial acumen in that she was allowed to buy on margin. As well, she invested $500 in a private fund organized by Dr. C.M. Hincks, medical director of the CCCW-affiliated Canadian National Committee for Mental Hygiene, which had been placed in the trust of Montreal millionaire and philanthropist J.W. McConnell, who owned the Saint Lawrence Sugar Refineries Ltd. McConnell had promised Hincks and his associates that he would invest it safely, but if there were any losses, he would cover them.

"I am quite satisfied with the legal document which you have given me. Let us hope that it proves a real 'sugar plum'," Charlotte wrote the Toronto-based Hincks. It was. Two years later, nine months before the stock market crash, McConnell wrote Hincks that he was sending a cheque for $57,180. Furthermore, he warned, "the market for some time has been irregular and rather uncertain . . . The various participants may now wish to invest the funds due them in some permanent security, or they may have other use for the cash . . . I hope the results may be found satisfactory to yourself and your friends." Hincks then forwarded a cheque to Charlotte for $2,020.35 — a pleasant profit on her $500 investment. The "marvelous enclosure" made her day, she told Hincks.

Most of her personal stock choices comprised a motley group of companies, including, in 1928 alone, Fraser Power, Canadian Pacific Railway, International Nickel, Kroger Grocery, Cosmos Cotton, and National Grocers, as well as the previously mentioned Hayes Wheels and Stanford preferred. Also, on the advice of a cousin involved in Calgary's oil and gas industry, Col. James Lowery, she nibbled away at shares in Alberta-based Home Oil and, in mid-1929, in Lowery Oil. Because stock prices at the time were trading at astronomical records, many of her purchases included just a fraction of one share. Her trading, in character, was cautiously conservative.

Still, the market crash stung just as much as if she had invested heavily. One year after the crash, in October 1930, the newly renamed McLeod Young Harris & Scott brokerage informed her that it could not accept her request to transfer Margaret Grier's account to hers, because of lack of collateral in Grier's account. Charlotte argued in vain that Grier's losses were due to the firm's bad advice and therefore she should not be penalized, but the company remained adamant. Months later, the National Trust Company of Toronto was handling her account, rather than McLeod, Young.

It had been a busy, productive, but very tiring year for Charlotte, so it is perhaps not surprising that in December 1932 she wrote a friend in Toronto requesting the name of the publisher of a book on the monastic life.

A period of silent humility in a distant monastery—preposterous as it seemed, in Charlotte's case—was not in the works, however, for her profile in the welfare sphere and in the national political arena continued to pick up steam as 1933 began. Instead, she made do with a brief, much-needed holiday in Bermuda in early January, for, as she told a Toronto friend, "I was utterly exhausted with the combination of circumstances that I have been facing all autumn." Indeed, like all organizations and institutions in Canada, the CCCFW was feeling the negative effects of the still worsening Depression.

Of immediate concern was the CCCFW's funding. Member organizations were slow in sending in their contributions and the federal government had reduced its annual $10,000 grant by ten per cent. Yet the financial crisis meant the council's eight divisions were trying to handle a larger workload. On January 28, she appealed to Bennett to restore the ten per cent reduction his government had introduced. This request followed a letter she sent to him one week earlier, requesting an interview to discuss the following issues: that he call a national conference on unemployment relief, that he hire a couple of her "thoroughly experienced and qualified workers" as federal relief advisers in Eastern and Western Canada respectively, and that he listen to her opposition to the use of relief funds for medical care, more administrative staff, or low-income pensioners. There is no record of the request being granted, but on February 2, she sent Bennett a short note thanking him for restoring the full $10,000 annual grant.

Satisfied with that, she applied in April to the funding ministry, the Department of Pensions and National Health, for a further $5,000; however, when that was rebuffed, she appealed to Bennett, also unsuccessfully. Incidentally, Charlotte's $3,500 salary at the Council remained the same as it had been since the heady days of 1928, as did those of her three-person staff. Considering the times, it was adequate indeed, comparable in 2009 terms to approximately $63,000.

As autumn 1933 arrived, Charlotte once more appealed to Bennett for more funding. This time, however, his government had a different solution. She was informed in September by Dr. Robert Wodehouse, deputy minister for Pensions and National Health, Margaret Grier's former boss at the Canadian Tuberculosis Association, and her next-door neighbour at McGregor Lake, that the department was considering transferring its child hygiene division to the CCCFW; along with it would go the division's annual $13,000 budget. The timing, Wodehouse informed her, coincided with the retirement of the division's chief since 1920, Dr. Helen MacMurchy. Charlotte, who had rejected the government's offer to replace MacMurchy as division chief, told him she would deliver the offer to the Council's board of governors at its next meeting, early the following year.

She also forwarded the following message to the embattled prime minister in December from a Saskatoon acquaintance: "But what could any one do without our great leader Mr. Bennett? Even when I was very ill and weak they brought the radio to my room so that I did not miss any of his great speeches. If Canada rejects him at the next election she will deserve the fate that will be sure to befall her."

Bennett would reward Charlotte for her faithful support in 1934.

Nineteen thirty-three was as turbulent a year in Charlotte's private life as any previous one, and while there were the usual highs and lows, such as minor car accidents and petty disputes over small, day-to-day affairs, one occurrence affected her more than most. Margaret Grier became ill.

Ever-dependable Margaret, the housekeeper, the listening post, the travelling companion. When Charlotte visited Toronto on a business trip, Margaret often accompanied her and shared her room at the Toronto Ladies' Club. When Charlotte attended the Canadian Women's Press Club's week-long convention in Calgary in 1932, Margaret shared her suite at the Palliser Hotel. Margaret kept the home fires burning as Charlotte raced back and forth across the country, either supporting the Council's provincial and local organizations, handling odd assignments for Bennett, or giving talks to all manner of women's groups. If anyone was waiting for Charlotte when she returned to Ottawa by train, it was Margaret.

Charlotte's sister, Kay, described Margaret as fair-haired with blue-grey eyes, a woman who was always controlled and always seemed interested in what others were doing. "Whenever Charlotte 'erupted,' Margaret was there to counsel patience and the grace of humility," Kay wrote in her unpublished biography. When they moved to their Rideau Terrace apartment, it was Margaret who decorated the place with carved walnut and brocade furniture from her own family's home, and it was Margaret who transformed a bedroom into a study for Charlotte, "who treasured every scrap of paper."

Grier was hospitalized briefly in March with stomach problems, but the seriousness of her illness became evident in April when she was rushed back to hospital for emergency surgery. "I have spent most of my time at the hospital and have had very little sleep so I am in no shape to write," Charlotte wrote to *Winnipeg Free Press* newspaper columnist Kennethe Haig on April 5. "I was allowed in yesterday for a short time . . . She is conscious, but suffering a great deal and speaking a little."

Typically, Charlotte's time was so taken up with her myriad affairs during the year that she had to turn down a request from the Montreal Business and Professional Women's Club to start an Ottawa chapter, and she had to refuse an offer to join the prestigious editorial board of *Encyclopedia Canadiana* (now *The Canadian Encyclopedia*).

On the other hand, there was still time for speeches, as she indicated in her curriculum vitae, which she circulated amongst Canadian Clubs across the country. The CV noted that in addition to her full-time position with the CCCFW and her part-time activity with the League of Nations, she was on the national executives of the Employment Service Council of Canada, the Canadian Council on the Immigration of Women, the Canadian Association of Social Workers, the Social Service Council of Canada, the Church of England in Canada's council on social service, the IODE, and the Canadian Women's Press Club. She was also a member of the Board of Trustees of Queen's University.

Grier recovered somewhat, but she remained too weak to return to work. On June 5, Charlotte wrote once again to Haig: "I have waited and waited, hoping that I would get at least ten minutes in which I might write a personal note to you, but these things no longer happen to me. Life seems to have become increasingly hectic and so I have at last decided to dictate a note to thank you for all your kindness in reference to Margaret and for your inquiry. I have her up in a cabin now at McGregor Lake. This involves a twenty-four mile drive for me morning and evening and I think it may be the last straw . . . I hope that things will ease off within the next two or three weeks; if so you may hear from me in the long deferred letter; if not you will likely hear about me for I shall likely be confined in one of the homes for the deranged."

Shortly afterwards, Charlotte wrote to a Toronto friend, the city's chief public health nurse, Edna Moore, to say that Grier's condition seemed to be worsening. Grier had tried to help her boss, Robert Wodehouse, with a federal health conference that his department was planning in Ottawa, but "had a rather bad emotional smash up which put her back in bed for a couple of days. She is terrified of the conference, but on the other hand, Dr. Laidlaw says she should face it," that she had to get over her psychological fears. "She is positive she will crack up during the conference and he says that after all there are lots worse things you could do than just cry." To help her friend, Charlotte pleaded with Moore, who would be attending the conference, to keep Grier company during the meetings and help her with the layout of the tables at the official lunches and dinners "which are the fears she seems to feel the most."

There was little improvement in Grier's condition in July, as Charlotte informed a cousin living in Toronto. Twice Grier had tried returning to work, but both times had retreated home, unable to bear the strain. Medication failed to solve her suffering, and her doctors feared that there was little hope of recovery. By August, however, the situation had improved, for Charlotte advised her cousin that although Grier's nervous system "seems shot completely to pieces . . . she is now making a very determined effort to take over her responsibilities again in full and we are doing our very utmost to see that she stages a come-back. Her own chief has re-arranged his work so that he will take her Quebec field work in September and this will eliminate the necessity of travelling which she could not face. She will therefore, just have to tackle the office for the first few weeks and I am confident that with slow going she will come back."

Quite probably an important factor in Grier's partial recovery was the opportunity to pass a very relaxed summer at a cottage on McGregor Lake, a short distance north of Ottawa, which Charlotte had purchased from Wodehouse in the spring. McGregor is one of many small lakes nestled amongst the thickly forested Gatineau Hills on the north side of the Ottawa River. The lakes then and now provide summer homes to many senior public servants as well as leading Ottawa businessmen and professionals. The cottage was next door to Wodehouse's own summer residence, and it was where Charlotte often would bring her out-of-town women friends for a relaxing week or weekend.

Charlotte's real estate dealings also extended to inquiring about a "badly deteriorated" house in Renfrew that she was considering buying for her mother and, eventually, for herself. But, as she advised the general manager of the Bank of Nova Scotia in Ottawa in May, she did not want anyone in Renfrew to know about her interest at that point, presumably because the owners would raise the price. She asked the bank manager to make discreet inquiries through his contacts in Renfrew, and when she heard that the asking price was more than $7,000, she replied that she would not go above $4,000, particularly as it needed repairs estimated at about $1,000. She made no purchase that year, but three years later, in 1937, she bought two undeveloped properties on Lorne Street, near the centre of town, for $200 apiece.

It's not known how much she paid for the McGregor Lake cottage, but what is known is that she took out a $900 mortgage on it in 1933, that the annual municipal tax was $5.94, and that the school tax was $3.75, for a total tax bill of a mere $9.69.

One other incident of note that year was a brief correspondence Charlotte had with a male admirer writing from Victoria, British Columbia — O.A. Bass, the deputy attorney general of British Columbia. A truly kindred soulmate to Charlotte's hard-hearted approach to Depression-era relief, Bass blasted "vote-seeking politicians [for] enabling the sponging, loafing and indolent to feed on the industrious and thrifty . . .

Yes, we have no bananas today, that is, we have as you say "an unique election" in British Columbia, and also as you say "B.C. has always been different." That is what the fellow says to the girl that he is courting. She's not a bit "different" but she swallows the bait. The hen that has been laying all these social welfare, paternal, maternal, spoonfeeding and wet-nursing eggs has brought out a very assorted brood of chicks, but has omitted to teach them how to become self-supporting. Hence the "unique" election in B.C., which has been "different" in encouraging the laying and hatching of these eggs and now has the useless chicks to keep, and was the first to plaster the statute books with sloppy, maudlin legislation encouraging the shiftless not only to remain so, but to make a good thing out of it. (I very nearly perpetrated a split infinitive on you).

And now, Charlotte, Dear, I'm going to ask you to do something, or rather not to do it (and don't get angry, as it is only in an advisory sense): Don't write your signature in a slanting-dicular [*sic*] manner. Write it straight in a line with the rest of the letter. If you will consult your book on *Character in Calligraphy* you will see what I mean.

It is unnecessary to put on paper how much I like you, but you can guess.

Yours as here — 2 — 4, [signed O.A. Bass]

Possibly embarrassed, Charlotte replied weeks later that she had been travelling on business in the Maritimes when the letter had arrived at her office and it had "almost demoralized my staff in my absence. It is much appreciated. I must get hold of that book on handwriting and see what Freudian instincts are concealed beneath my slanting signature." She said she was happy to hear that he had won re-election and added, "I do not know when I shall be out [to British Columbia] but I do hope that I shall be able to crank a crab or lobster with you then."

8 Harems, Opium and "Chile Sauce"

"That-a-girl! Press Club here 'bursting' with pride and reflected glory," wrote newspaper columnist Lotta Dempsey Richardson in a brief note from Edmonton.

"Heartiest congratulations from Mrs. Cooper and myself," read the telegram from the Toronto-based general manager of the Motion Picture Exhibitors and Distribution of Canada, John A. Cooper.

"Senator Dandurand telephoned long distance from Montreal to congratulate . . . and to add how warmly he would 'admit' and welcome Mlle. Charlotte to the Order of the Senate of Canada," read the note from the senator's staff.

Dandurand, Cooper, and Richardson were among many to congratulate Charlotte on the latest news, her inclusion in the 1934 New Year's honours list as a recipient of the Order of the British Empire. She had been named a Commander of the Order, and for the rest of her life, she could, and would, attach the letters "CBE" after her name. It was the first of many honours that she would collect in the years ahead.

"It is the second highest rank open in the Order and carries with [it] the likelihood of promotion to the 'Dame Commander,'" Charlotte cheerfully informed her friend Howard Falk of the Vancouver Council of Social Agencies. She provided more details about the honour and added: "I have had a very nice letter from [Opposition Leader] MacKenzie [*sic*] King while Senator Dandurand called me long distance." Senator Raoul Dandurand then headed the Canadian mission to the League of Nations.

In the next edition of *Saturday Night* magazine, writer Mary Agnes Pease enthused to readers, "All her life, and she is still young, Charlotte Whitton has been a glamorous person . . . In the past year, in order to find out for herself the actual conditions of families living in the outlying regions of Western Canada, she went into the northern part of the Peace River district, the drought areas in Northern Saskatchewan, the coastal islands of British Columbia, and the Crow's Nest Coal country. She is impelled by higher motives than the desire for gain, and, in consequence, is loved, trusted and respected by people in every walk of life."

She was honoured at the January meeting of the Ottawa branch of the Queen's Alumnae Association, praised by her fellow members at the Ottawa branch of the Press Women's Club, and was the belle of her birthday banquet at Hotel Renfrew on March 8, with her mother proudly joining her at the head table. Asked to speak at the banquet, Charlotte waxed eloquently about feeling very humble over the honour Bennett had arranged and happy to have been raised in a lovely town like Renfrew, which held so many warm memories, such as the picnics on Pinnacle Hill where she entertained her young friends by reciting ancient Greek poetry, or passing the "haunted house" on Raglan Street, or working in Isaac Pedlow's store, where she experienced the benefits of accuracy, responsibility, and punctuality.

She was flattered by the attention, particularly by the positive press she was receiving. She also was becoming more attentive to her image, as shown by the following note to the editor of *The Canadian Magazine*: "Everyone has objected violently to my use of a photograph that was taken in an annoyed mood several years ago. I have had another taken this morning, still in an annoyed mood. It is an effect the photographers have on me, but I hope to send you [a better] one tomorrow."

Although she rarely fussed about her personal appearance, she improved on her already impressive résumé by stretching the facts somewhat by promoting herself from "associate editor" of *Social Welfare* magazine to "joint editor" between the years 1918 and 1922, when the late Rev. Shearer was *the* editor. The résumé, however, correctly informed the media that she then belonged to three prominent women's clubs, in Ottawa (the Chelsea), Montreal (the Themis), and Toronto (The Toronto Ladies' Club), and that she was a member of the Rideau Badminton and Ottawa Ski clubs in the national capital.

At the office, by then named "Council House," there was much work to be done. The annual general meeting of the CCCFW to be held in Hamilton in April had to be organized, yet before that, she had to meet with the Council's executive board.

Among the major issues to be discussed was the federal government's offer to transfer its child welfare division to the CCCFW on a one-year trial basis. The transfer was first proposed by the deputy minister of pensions and health, Robert Wodehouse, and approved by R.B. Bennett. But it was not without opposition from some social welfare and health groups, such as the Canadian Social Hygiene Council and the Canadian Medical Association, who viewed it as a further power grab by the CCCFW.

Not so, argued Charlotte in a long letter to *Saturday Night* editor B.K. Sandwell, which she marked "personal." It was merely a wise, cost-cutting measure by Bennett. Besides, the health department's child welfare division under the aging Dr. MacMurchy had done very little about child welfare compared to the CCCFW's efforts in recent years. "In respect to the transfer of the Child Welfare Division, the situation is this: For several years, as many perhaps as six, Dr. MacMurchy's work, as known to the provinces and the co-operating agencies, has been only apparent. I hope nothing will force our office to reveal exactly in what state it was at the present time of transfer. Her last fine piece of work I would date as her maternal mortality study of 1927, which we shall now revive and press."

She said MacMurchy's total annual budget was only $12,000, and of that half went to MacMurchy in salary ($4,500) and travelling expenses ($1,500). The CCCFW's budget, on the other hand, had grown from $5,600 in 1926 to roughly $35,000 in 1933, due to an annual $10,000 grant from the federal government and $8,000 in funding from the country's life insurance companies; the rest came from member organizations and private sources. So, she argued, the government was saving some $6,000 from MacMurchy's salary and travel costs, while it would move the remaining $6,000 from the child welfare division's budget to the CCCFW.

Using the same argument, she similarly persuaded the CCCFW's board of governors to accept the division's transfer at an executive meeting in February attended by seven of the twelve governors. At another board meeting in March, again with just over half the board present, she was given a pay raise to $4,000, up from $3,500, and approval to once again attend the League of Nations' committee meetings in Geneva in April, as well as time to tour child care institutions in England afterwards. The only sour notes at the March meeting, as far as Charlotte was concerned, involved the board's refusal of her request to represent the Council on the Fair Trade Council of Canada and resignation of the representative of the National Council of Women on the CCCFW board, Mrs. H.J. Cody, in protest over the transfer of the child welfare division to the CCCFW.

Again, faint charges of empire-building were voiced in some welfare circles, but Charlotte was so busy and so determined to get her way that she completely ignored them.

Geneva beckoned. Although Charlotte had not attended a child welfare committee meeting of the League of Nations since 1928, due to her frustration with the European-dominated body, she had maintained her assessorship in the committee as a result of pressure from the federal government. Now, in 1934, she was ready to return. In fact, unlike the situation in 1932 when she wanted to resign from the committee, and was dissuaded from doing so by W.A. Riddell, Canada's senior officer in Geneva, she looked forward to stepping back into the ring, like a boxer making a comeback after a brief retirement.

It looked like a heavyweight match was shaping up, for she sparred throughout 1933 with League officials from afar. She argued that the committee's spring schedule meant rough sea crossings for the North American delegations, that the draft of Léontine Chaptal's survey report improperly reflected Canada's position on neglected children, and that Canada got the short end of the stick when it was denied permanent delegate status on the advisory commission of women and children in favour of Turkey, India, and Chile.

"Since Canada lacks harems I can understand her losing the seat given to Turkey on our Commission, and since she does not grow opium extensively nor marry her children at eight years of age, I can understand India also getting representation, but for the life of me I cannot understand why we should lose out to Chile, especially when as far as I know, their original assessor took very little interest in the Commission and Chile herself I think is seriously in arrears in her dues to the League. Possibly we do not use enough 'Chile sauce' or perhaps it is too much in our work with the League Council,"

Charlotte wrote under-secretary of state O.D. Skelton after he informed her of the decision in October.

At the same time, she wrote Riddell, threatening once more to quit the League committee, but he, in turn, chided her bluntly: "It is possible that Mlle. Colin [the French delegate on the committee] may not have helped us with the Rapporteur on account of the fact that you and she have not always seen eye to eye, but I have no confirmation of this. I think the fact that you had not attended a meeting of the Committee since 1928 naturally told against us in the final result . . . I know that you were very busy with other work and found it impossible to come this year. You must, however, realise the difficulty of convincing child welfare enthusiasts in Geneva that this explains your absence from the last five sessions."

That was in late 1933. Now, in 1934, bygones were bygones. Charlotte was leaving Depression-ridden Canada and her hard-working four-woman office staff for another bout of international diplomacy amid the quiet luxury of the Swiss city, which she once described as "a comfortable city . . . Even the swans on the Lake of Geneva have each their own straw baskets, and in the cold days of the early spring solicitous officials of the Parks Branch may be seen gently guiding the beautiful birds towards the shelters along the banks . . . Everywhere there is neatness, order, planning, thrift, and the air of an intensely rationalistic approach to life," although "she lacks that sense of eternity which clings about London and Rome, and that air of living intensely for the day which permeates the very trees and flowers of the Champs Elysées."

It was a lovely getaway, but she could not totally forget or ignore the cares of home and office. There was always Margaret's health to worry about, and the occasional unpleasantness with a certain office staffer to ponder.

The following excerpts from letters she addressed to Grier in Ottawa during her trip portray her mixed emotions during this period:

March 28, the Admiral Beatty Hotel, Saint John, N.B.:

Dearest Putty,

I do hope that you were not as lonesome last night as
one little black pup, who sniffled all over his basket until

he was afraid what the porter would think. I just felt circumstances had put iron bars about you to keep you from being with me, when I saw those gates close behind us yesterday. O! Putty! I miss you dreadfully—you have been a dear, dear worry to me so long.

Wasn't everyone nice to me? Miss Smellie gave me such a nice bottle of eau de cologne; the flowers were so lovely. Mary Burnham's wee chicken is so perky on his shelf, he'll make me feel good on Easter morning. "Life Begins at Forty" & the sweetest red compact you ever saw to go with my new evening dress. Mr. Hackett was on the train and took me to dinner. Fraser Elliott was on & drove me to the hotel & gave me lunch. Jim McKenna took me to dinner. The president of the Harbour Board of Trade has called the CPR and told them they are to give me a cabin with bath. Mr. Dunnamie, the managing editor of the paper, has written the British United Press to look after me well & get me tickets to any unusual function while I am over . . . I'll write from Halifax,

Love on love Putty, Rags.

March 30 (Good Friday), aboard the Canadian Pacific Railway's *Duchess of York* ocean liner:

Dear Mardie,

I am on board and sailing on a Bay of Fundy that is so preternaturally calm as to be almost ominous . . . Everything is orderly and not filthy like the Halifax docks. The Saint John people were really very nice to me. I got roses, sweat [*sic*] peas, and spring flowers from them, including some gorgeous white iris . . . Mr. Wright had my tabled fixed up with him and a nice Irishman. They say the sea will cut up as soon as the sun sets, so I may not be compos mentis, Halifax. But after the pressure of recent days I have never had as calm and pleasant a "get off" from the dock. They [*sic*] are only forty cabin passengers and few look interesting. But the boat, as you know, is beautifully

laid out and very graceful, she keeps her unshapely
posterior out of sight . . . My very best of Easter love to my
"hot cross" bunny, Rags.

March 31, aboard the *Duchess of York*:

Dearest,

Just getting out of Halifax and want to catch the mail.

Thanks for the lovely flowers — my fifth so I am
sending them to the frig to cheer me later. Nice card from
the Robinsons, a luncheon party with the Junior Leaguers,
and a two pound box of candy here, with no card from
anyone sent from Ottawa, and a really very nice telegram
from 'R.B.' [Bennett]. Wasn't that nice of him.

Weather has been gorgeous & even two of mine ancient
enemies in Halifax charming & gracious to me. I go now
for a cocktail with two shipmates — one from Aberdeen
and one from Belfast — nice men both . . .

April 6, aboard ship:

Dear Putty,

Here we are riding towards Scotland and how we had two
bouncing days! Last night I was sure the ship would break
in two and I was planning what I would take — a box of
candy for food, my hot water bottle full of cold water, my
blankets and my little bottle of brandy. Once the ship just
whined from stem to stern with the whack she got.

I have stayed in bed until 6 p.m. every day but one . . .
The stewardess said I looked like a little pup up in the
corner of my berth, crowded away from everyone when
she came in. The men kept me full of cocktails — said it
would keep me afloat — and it seemed to do so. The first
three days were fine but these last! I do not know whether
it would be better to be seasick or to have this "dead head"
I have. I must be rested but I seem deader than ever. I have
had three nightmares about [CCCFW staffer Agnes Baird].
She is worrying me stiff . . .

Lying in my bunk I have kept thinking of my red cat, & I see her all snuggled in, down among the greens in her own bed with just the curls showing. Then I sleep and dream we are at college & you're in one of your cry babies." I hate to tell you how often I dream that now — about once a week . . . Well, dee, I'm going whoopy just writing so much. So here's off & love on love, Sharl.

April 8, Paris:

Dear Mardie,

Oh! What a forty-eight hours since I last wrote you — You may never see your dog again, so I felt under absolute obligation to write.

The *Duchess* certainly rolled more abominably and abdominally than even your best performances arriving at Glasgow nearly 24 hours late. [There was a wild party on board the ship on the final night of the voyage] and lounge steward, Mrs. MacKay and I alone kept sober — we took only one cocktail & two liqueurs but the others! It was the best party since the *Ascania* though. Then three of the men, like me, had to leave the boat at Glasgow — she was so late — we dashed to get our train & in the rush Houghton, a very nice Englishman, as my nice Irish Mr. Patterson said, I being "the most popular man's lady & the most unpopular ladies' lady afloat with my five boyfriends" was supposed to have a party. By dinner, my five boyfriends had collected four more unattached men, so when we went to the lounge it was too much. I insisted they gather up three lone women and then Mrs. Allan MacKay of Montreal (Percy Cowans of MacDougall & Cowans' daughter married to Cairine Wilson's nephew) came up from the hold like me . . . I am going out of France with 58 francs & I think I'll come back by Spain to avoid this land, though I believe I would like the French better if they spoke English more clearly! I have no more paper so good night, dear Putty. I had to write you much love, Sharl.

April 11, Hotel Richemond, Geneva:

Dear wee Putty,

Oh! Do I miss you, you little crosspatch! I'd be glad even to have you scratch me how. It's awful to come again to places where you have been with me. I miss you so much, more at the Richmond [*sic*]. Oh! We must have the next trip together — that's how much good it's doing me to have gotten away from you.

It seems incredible that I have been here three days and have no time yet to write you, though these sessions have been interminable and intolerable . . . Persia, China and Turkey are "messy" additions to the League Committee, while Chile is a weak sister. But India is splendid. They have sent Mrs. Siberian, a splendid Hindu woman, a graduate of Oxford . . . and wears the most gorgeous "togas" and jewels . . . When I think of what I could do with the money it's cost to bring me here, I could yell . . . We wrangle all day and Monday night I had dinner with the British: last night, Dr. Ekstrand [of Sweden] had a most interesting "Souper Suedois" — his wife is a charming Russian . . . What my figure will be I do not know. [Various hosts] serve you everything and you just float in wine & liqueurs. The Belgians had a "sherry" on Monday. The Riddells are having an "evening" for me on Monday.

I shall hope to write you a long letter tomorrow. It's very late now, I am weary & I do miss you every day. Sharpie.

April 13, Geneva:

Dear Putty,

I dreamed I saw seven cats fighting in the runway to Mrs. Thorburn's garage while I was on the way to Church. Tell her that I hope she is in no such difficulties either in the Public Welfare Board or with my staff as to require my prayers — the only interpretation that I can put upon my vision.

I am so busy between sessions and entertainment that I am not able at all to get at my letters — and those for flowers and books are added to my C.B.E. arrears . . . The Polish delegate and I have become quite confreres though neither one knows what the other one says. [She also struck up friendly relations with the Hungarian delegate and once the League meetings were over she planned to tour England at the end of the month, as well as visit Ireland.] It is incredible that five times I have been over and never slept a night in Ireland. Oh Puddy! It's no use — we've got to do something — win a ticket in the Irish sweepstakes or something to get you over — and I haven't even bought a ticket! . . . I am really much too tired to enjoy anything myself, and certainly this ten days in the tower of Babel is as bad as a trip west. It's Baird, darn her, who is mostly responsible. Every night, just as I get half asleep I begin to worry about that situation . . . Much love to you, Deewee, & to the wee house, Rags.

April 15, Geneva:

Dear Pussy,

Three weeks ago today you went out to the Shortts, looking like a thunder cloud while your poor puppy was chasing his tail with your tin cans and two bottles tied to it. Two weeks ago today I lay tossing in the cradle of the deep! A week ago today, I was rushing from London to Dover at this hour. Today I am sitting with my windows open, unto the most glorious sunshine with the little leaves bursting from the twigs of the trees & the [illegible word] of Mont Blanc simply brilliant across the lake . . . Much, much love Dee, and be a strong cat soon. Sharl.

In an April 21 letter, Charlotte told Grier about the "perfectly ripping reception" the Riddells had hosted for her on the sixteenth, as well as a three-hour luncheon given by Count Curton de Wiart in Geneva on the seventeenth, and another reception on the eighteenth. Then it was off to Rome for a meeting of the League's cinema committee, which she had joined, and a conference on world movies which Italian leader Benito Mussolini attended. The dictator kept his foreign guests waiting ninety minutes, she noted, and then "a great door opened and the Minister of Education, the Governor of Rome & Mussolini were projected into the room. It is the only verb suitable. They simply bounded in, and into their seats, everyone shouting and giving the Fascist salute. Mussolini is much shorter than I thought and looks like a darker, more determined Mr. Meighen with an undershot jaw. He moves almost in mechanical jerks . . ."

She found time to visit child-care institutions in Rome and Turin before returning to Paris at the end of the month. Writing Grier from Paris on the twenty-eighth, she remarked: "Unfortunately every single day but one has been spent in solid work, and the evening of that day, I worked until 11 p.m. . . . I long for my little house both in Rockcliffe and at the Lake, and my cat 'Fresette'." The following night she was staying at the prestigious Forum Club in London and recounting how an Englishman whom she had met on the *Duchess of York*, Mr. Houghton, had invited her to lunch.

May 4 was a very special day for Charlotte. "Dear Puddy, I'm all in a dither! Where have I been? Over half an hour in private residence with the Prince of Wales — all by myself — I am not yet conscious. I feel I made a blithering ass of myself but he was very nice, anyway, and such a flock of questions he asked me. Nearly died, and once called him 'Your Majesty' when I meant to say 'His Majesty your father.' I only hope I did not say, 'Your Majesty, his father.' I do not seem conscious yet . . ."

More letters followed as she toured southwestern England and Wales, apologizing in one that "Everything is so high and exchange so bad, that I have been very short of cash and can buy very little. I am bringing you only trifles. I wish I had saved and bought you one decent thing." But she would be home shortly and she was looking forward to purchasing a new car in which she could drive Grier around town and to their McGregor Lake getaway. "Oh! I shall be excited to be home again, even if it means that cawing gang of envious crows again. I have some strong eagle friends. Much love, Sharl."

And what of the League's child welfare committee meetings? Apparently they did not accomplish much, for Charlotte hardly mentioned them to Grier, noting only the "wrangling all day" in the "tower of Babel." At the same time, there were no major controversies and the threatened battle with Léontine Chaptal never occurred. As well, she would later acknowledge that the joint meetings of the child welfare committee and the committee on the traffic in women and children had "marked a very definite advance in the development of greater co-operative control in the unfortunate conditions of white slave traffic in the Far-East, China and Persia having been invited to participate in these deliberations." In fact, shortly after she returned to Canada, Charlotte received a very warm greeting from Dr. Eric Ekstrand, the Swedish director of the Social Questions Section, who wrote to say, "how highly I have appreciated the interesting account you have given of the work done at the session of the Child Welfare Committee at Geneva . . . May I take this opportunity to tell you what you have already heard here on several occasions, how highly your presence was appreciated by all the members of the Committee as well as by the Secretariat. Your intimate knowledge of the questions dealt with by the Committee and your constructive mind contributed in a very noticeable degree to the work. I therefore certainly hope that you will not fail to come back for next year's meeting."

After the cocktail parties and the hobnobbing with the European nobles on the League committees in Geneva and Rome, Charlotte returned to Canada, where the country was struggling with the worsening Depression. The prairie provinces were still drought-stricken, unemployment across the nation was as bad as ever, and many of the men in the army-run work camps were becoming more restive.

At the CCCFW's annual meeting in Hamilton in May, Charlotte laid it on the line. More and more was demanded of her organization, but financial and personnel resources were not keeping pace. Communities across the country were seeking the council's advice and support, but her limited staff had been run ragged and were unable to handle the workload despite the addition of two new assistants, Muriel Tucker and Marjorie Bradford. (The latter was the same woman with whom Charlotte had exchanged terse, testy letters in 1928 when Bradford was at the Social Service Council of Canada and Charlotte was seeking the assessor's role at the League of Nations.) Nevertheless, she added, one of the council's seven divisions — the leisure and education committee — had managed to establish a national council on education, and the council itself had accepted the transfer of the health department's child welfare division on a one-year trial basis.

Besides, she continued, "Looking out upon the whole sea of social work and public welfare in Canada today, it is only a man of little perception who would fail to realize that we are in the very vortex of most significant changes and developments, which have concentrated what would ordinarily have been the experience of decades into a score or two of months. As social work and intelligent citizenship are able to give the answer, will the future character of this country, its institutions and perhaps ultimately even its form to be determined, and, as in any field of human endeavour, the discovery and development of fundamental principles and their successful application centre about the necessity of personnel, adequate in training *and* experience, to take the leadership in stimulating more effective organization and administration." Her solution was to hire and train more social workers who would gather more information, analyze it and make recommendations. Also, if the money was available, centres should be opened to provide short-term courses for untrained public welfare workers, and social workers from Britain should be hired to provide further instruction here.

In the meantime, however, the CCCFW was having difficulty finding a council president, for the likely candidate, Montreal *Gazette* publisher and president of the Montreal Council of Social Agencies, Philip Fisher, like many of his fellow board members, could not find the time from his own harried business affairs to properly oversee Charlotte's running of the organization. As well, there was the constant problem of arranging suitable dates and locations for the board to meet, due to the fact its directors were based across Canada and rail travel, rather than air, was still the norm. Consequently, it was not unusual to have less than a third of the board in attendance for their meetings. For example, for the September board meeting in Toronto, only seven members attended, all from Toronto. Similarly, at the board meeting one month later in Montreal, only seven members attended, all from that city.

It is obvious in hindsight that the council had overstretched itself, and Charlotte was feeling the pressure. "We have had so much difficulty this year," she wrote board member Margaret Nairn in early September, "in many ways that if it had been possible for me to leave the Council without bringing about its disruption at the time I would have done so at any time within the last eight months. I am only now beginning to get the situation steadied again, but I have to go to Winnipeg this week for nearly a month's work and shall have to return in November." This was about the same time that Marjorie Bradford joined her staff while others departed. Also, she had to raise some $9,000 from private sources to meet her annual budget requirement, which obviously was another major concern.

Once she was in Winnipeg, the pressure continued. As she confided to Grier in a letter, her council headquarters was in disarray, the medical profession continued its opposition to her takeover of the child welfare division from the federal government, friends working in the Manitoba government were threatened with the loss of their jobs due to a reorganization, she was having trouble lining up hosts for a visiting British lecturer whom she had invited to Canada, she feared the handyman at McGregor Lake had not cleared the shoreline and, to top it off, the bathroom in her expensive room in the Fort Garry Hotel had flooded that day. "Oh! Pussy!! It's pretty awful! It's been long and tough and I have fought on, and this fells me . . . Oh! Mardie! I can't go on, I just can't, and I don't know what to do. I hate my job and I have no other, & God! How I hate the Medical Association & that stupid nursing group seeing their future go before their eyes, sits and does nothing but follow!"

The following day, September 16, she wrote Grier that she was working from breakfast to midnight "and with teeth that have never stopped aching. My patience ebbs as they do."

It only got worse. She was ordered to bed by her doctor in early October for ten days because of an infection in her arm from poison ivy, and near the end of November, Bradford, who had just joined the staff in September as Charlotte's assistant, or stand-in in her absence, threw caution to the wind and unburdened her own concerns to her new boss. She wrote that one of her associates refused to cooperate with the general direction they were headed in and threatened to air her concerns to the CCCFW's board of governors:

Miss Bennett [another colleague] tells me confidentially (and this information is for your private information alone and I know you will not refer to it) that although you gained a technical victory at the last annual meeting of the division, some of the men went home disaffected and did quite a bit of talking among nurses and others . . .

Now the only thing that remains to be done is to put in a personal bill for over time for three sleepless nights, when I have tossed on my downy couch over this mess. I have suffered from palpitation of the heart, and all sorts of internal disorganization and I assure you that I will certainly welcome it if you will stay home for the next eight months and not make any surveys and not have any emergencies. One of these days I am going to sit down and write you a confidential report too . . .

Amid these growing professional problems, Charlotte's blood pressure had elevated a few more notches when she learned that a federal customs officer had charged Grier an import duty on books that she, Charlotte, had received as gifts upon her departure for Geneva in March. She had mailed the books to Grier while aboard the *Duchess of York* and felt she should not have been required to pay the import tax. As was her wont when it came to battling minor officials, Charlotte went over the tax collector's head and took her complaint directly to the Collector of National Revenue, F.H. Journeaux. She was after the clerk's head, but in the end received only Journeaux's apology and the return of the customs duty paid.

There were other instances in 1934 when she was outraged, such as a summer dispute with Robert Wodehouse over the property line dividing their McGregor Lake properties, or the fact that her brother J.B. had taken her 1927 six-cylinder, 17.3-horsepower Essex Coupe back to Renfrew in July before she had had a chance to advise her co-owner, Grier, that she had sold it to him. But these were mere trifles in the pressure-cooker life she was leading.

Just as she had curiously ended 1933 by requesting a book on monastic life, in December 1934, she enigmatically had the office secretary enclose a ten-cent coupon from Rice Krispies in a letter to the Kellogg's cereals company in London, Ontario, requesting a copy of *Mother Goose Stories*.

9 Bowing Out

Nineteen thirty-five was a fairly calm period for Charlotte, for a
change. Her organization shortened its name, Canadian Council of Child and Family Welfare, to a more manageable Canadian
Welfare Council, but its purpose remained the same, and Charlotte
continued to write lengthy policy statements which were released in
pamphlet form and distributed as "a statement issued by the Board
of Governors." She also provided Bennett with unsolicited advice
from time to time.

In February, for example, she advised the prime minister in a
seven-page missive, entitled, "National Relief Plan Urgently Needed,"
that it was the responsibility of the federal government to solve the
seemingly never-ending Depression. However, as she had done previously, she argued that his government should merely oversee the
provinces' efforts in dealing with the problem, rather than introduce
a plan of its own for which it would be held accountable. Her temporary solution was for Ottawa to set up a federal advisory council
to ensure that the provinces were handling relief expenditures properly. Further, she advised, in her customary bureaucratic bafflegab
when writing reports or memoranda:

> The effective treatment of unemployment need today
> involves the stabilization of employment, decasualization
> of the labor supply, adequate minimum remuneration
> for employment, and such practical measures as the
> stimulation of works programmes, controlled settlement,
> slum clearance, and the movement of labour to fields
> in which it can find employment and become self-
> sustaining. These measures are all an integral part of better
> social planning for the community, together with the
> introduction on a sound actuarial basis of contributory

unemployment insurance in applicable industries and other like measures of an equitable nature to meet dependency from various uncontrollable but assessable causes.

The advisory council would establish rough guidelines for relief payments, which would allow for local exceptions, and if the provinces and municipalities did not follow those standards, then the federal government should cut off their funding, she argued.

Apparently Bennett was not listening this time, as the call for an advisory council went unheeded. As one might expect, Bennett was receiving advice from all corners. And, to worsen the crisis, the unemployed nationwide were growing increasingly restless. Most vociferous were those men in the army-run relief camps of British Columbia who had formed the communist-dominated Relief Camp Workers Union. B.C. Premier Duff Pattullo and Vancouver mayor Gerald McGeer flooded Ottawa with lengthy telegrams and letters, calling for a full investigation of the camps, but their pleas went unheeded, at least during the first couple of months of 1935.

Bennett, the bachelor millionaire from Calgary who lived in a luxurious seven-room suite at the Château Laurier Hotel while in Ottawa, worked at his own leisurely pace. In January 1935, he had launched his own version of Franklin Roosevelt's successful New Deal, which Roosevelt had introduced two years earlier when ten million Americans were unemployed. In five radio broadcasts over ten days, Bennett uncharacteristically renounced "the old order" of laissez-faire capitalism and decided that federal government regulation and control of the economy were in fact needed. He charged that unnamed "unscrupulous and greedy" persons had used faults in the capitalist system to enrich themselves while others suffered, and, with an eye on an upcoming fall election, he told Canadians that he and his Conservative Party would right those wrongs. He vowed to introduce an unemployment insurance plan, a minimum wage, and laws limiting working hours. He also promised to rewrite the rules concerning old age pensions and health and accident insurance.

The drumbeat of protest, however, continued to grow louder. In March, the Workers Unity League, the parent organization of the Relief Camp Workers Union, met in Kamloops to plot a massive walkout from the British Columbia camps on April 4 so as to attend a rally in Vancouver. Led by Toronto-born Arthur "Slim" Evans, a longtime communist labour leader, they called for a thirty-hour work week, a fifty-cent-an-hour minimum wage, an end to military control of the camps, elected camp committees, and the repeal of Section 98 of the Criminal Code, which banned "unlawful associations" and which was aimed primarily at the Communist Party of Canada. Meanwhile, Bennett suffered a heart seizure on March 7, sidelining him for a month, during which time his cabinet under acting prime minister Sir George Perley ordered a royal commission to survey conditions in the relief camps.

It was a case of too little, too late. Some 1,500 men from the camps arrived in Vancouver over the next two months and, on June 3, after causing numerous disturbances and demonstrations in the city, decided to take their protest to Ottawa. Boarding freight trains — the railways let them ride free atop the boxcars — they picked up "recruits" as they travelled east and the "On-to-Ottawa" trek attracted popular support all along the way. However, when the trekkers reached Regina on June 14, numbering some 2,000 and threatening to attract thousands more when they passed through Winnipeg and Toronto, Bennett, having recovered from his heart seizure, put his foot down. He ordered the railways to stop providing free rides and he ordered the RCMP to stop the strikers from moving any further east.

In an effort to ease tensions, he invited an eight-man delegation to Ottawa for direct talks while the rest of the trekkers remained in Regina, sustained by three meals a day, paid for by a benevolent government at twenty cents a meal.

The June 22 meeting between Bennett and Evans and their respective associates did not go well. Evans demanded "work and wages" for his men; Bennett said that was not affordable. The argument continued for some time, but was memorable for Bennett calling Evans an embezzler and Evans calling Bennett a liar. The meeting concluded with neither side giving an inch and the trek committee retiring to Regina, travelling first-class on the CPR at government expense.

Back in Regina on the 26th, Evans tried to continue the trek by road, rather than by rail, but again the RCMP was ordered to block all traffic heading east. Also, a new, temporary relief camp was set up outside Regina to hold the trekkers until they could be returned to their starting point. Evans called for a truce, suggesting his comrades would return home voluntarily, but the government was done with bargaining; the men would be sent to the camp and then returned home according to the government's schedule.

On July 1, the trek committee organized a public meeting in downtown Regina to protest the latter order, but the police arrived en masse to arrest Evans and other trek leaders, and a riot ensued. One policeman was killed, dozens of individuals were injured, 130 were arrested, and the trek was finally halted. Those trekkers not arrested in the riot were forced home by train at the government's expense.

Bennett had won the battle, but lost the war when he was soundly defeated in the October 14, 1935, election by Mackenzie King's Liberals. He was done in by "Bennett buggies" (cars hauled by horses because their owners could not afford gasoline), "Bennett neighbourhoods" (slums), and long, lean years led by a portly prime minister who seemed to live in an ivory tower like a medieval despot, far removed from the cares of ordinary citizens. The fact that he spent much of his time in his comfortable suite at the Château Laurier Hotel and dressed like a proper English gentleman did not help his image, despite the fact that in private he was a reasonably generous man, doling out small amounts of money to thousands of individuals and institutions who sought his assistance. The Conservative Party was to remain out of office in Ottawa for the next twenty-eight years.

Charlotte, meanwhile, who had recommended creation of relief camps to Bennett in her confidential 1932 report on Western Canada, kept a low profile. Coincidentally, on June 20, as Bennett was tracking the trekkers' activities from his suite in the Château Laurier, Charlotte was attending a meeting of the Canadian Women's Press Club on the hotel's ground floor and, according to a CWPC report, demonstrating the proper protocol for curtseying before the governor general and his wife — a slight bend of the knees with the left toe at the heel of the right foot — prior to a CWPC visit to the vice-regal residence at Rideau Hall.

Perhaps due to financial reasons, she did not attend the League of Nations committee meetings in 1935, concentrating instead on the newly renamed Canadian Welfare Council. Still hard-pressed financially, the CWC was working on an annual budget of $40,000, and to oversee its eight divisions, Charlotte had to rely on only five full-time directors and two part-timers, as well as an office clerk-secretary. The divisions included Maternal and Child Hygiene, Child Protection, French-speaking Services, Family Welfare, Delinquency Services, Leisure Time Activities, Community Organization, and Public Welfare Administration; each division had its own volunteer committee overseeing its affairs.

In a rambling report published in May, which she entitled, "Canadian Cavalcade 1920–1935," Charlotte called for "the entire scientific reorganization of our cluttered social services, and their coordination to meet the need of social security within the economic capacity of the country to provide. Statesmanship of the highest order, and wise intelligent executive administration alone can bring our people out of their need," she argued. Only a national enquiry would do, and the enquirers would include federal, provincial, and voluntary sector representatives. This proposal, too, went unheeded by the beleaguered Bennett.

In December, after the Liberals had taken office, there was another "statement issued by the Board of Governors, Canadian Welfare Council," obviously authored by Charlotte:

As the late autumn merges into winter, and Canadians enter the seventh year of seriously slackened employment and resultant social need, one element in the situation demands recognition beyond all others, and that is this. A condition which has persisted, with such slight fundamental variation, over more than half a decade, must cease to be described or regarded as an emergency or temporary state of affairs, and must be grappled with for what it is — a profound and prolonged tremor of our whole economic and social system which in turn has caused certain displacements in our employment opportunity and structure.

Her solution, once again, was a broad-based advisory council that would introduce national standards for relief payments and see that they were enforced.

Mackenzie King was listening. According to his diary for January 8, 1936, he was working on a proposed National Employment Commission, which would include an advisory committee. "[Labour Minister Norman] Rogers had a memo proposed by Charlotte Whitton, an excellent piece of work, but that seemed all. I decided to send for Bernard Rose of Montreal to help in preparation of this material," he wrote. It was not the first time he had been impressed with Charlotte. In July 1934, after she had written a well-crafted memorial to the late Liberal senator Andrew Haydon, then opposition leader King acknowledged to his diary: ". . . an exceptional fine and very just tribute. I phoned [O.D.] Skelton to find out if he or his wife had not written it. He gives the credit to Miss Whitton but I am sure they both gave it many of its finishing touches."

Charlotte, incidentally, had been so proud of her Haydon memorial that she had had a hundred copies printed and sent to Haydon's friends. In December 1934, King, who was among the recipients, had written her personally: "I should just like to say that a more beautiful or worthy tribute could not have been written . . . I have read nothing in the course of this year which has given me a like measure of satisfaction. In style of exposition and utterance generally, it has all the dignity and true proportion of classical tributes which have endured for centuries."

It was always thus with Charlotte; people treated her with accolades or brickbats, rarely with neutrality. In February 1936, for example, the lieutenant-governor of Ontario informed her that he had made enquiries concerning an unstated issue and found that the provincial health officers from Alberta, Saskatchewan, Manitoba, New Brunswick, Nova Scotia, and Prince Edward Island, as well as the Canadian Medical Association, all of whom were still smarting from the CWC's 1932 takeover of the Child Welfare Division from the health department, had complained to him about the lack of co-operation they received from the CWC. The following month, however, J.H. Brace, president of the prestigious Empire Club in Toronto, remarked in his introduction of Charlotte as guest speaker:

Today we have with us Miss Charlotte Whitton, C.B.E., a citizen of Ottawa — I think I could say a citizen of Canada, of Geneva, in fact, a world renowned citizen. Last evening when speaking to a friend who I think knows Miss Whitton very well, he passed the remark that we would have as our guest speaker today the Canadian with the most brilliant brain we could find. He made no inference as to that being one only amongst the ladies; he threw in the professional and business people, the artists, the scientists, and scholars, and even the politicians.

Obviously the change of government had not affected Charlotte's reputation as one of Canada's most influential welfare experts, and probably the leader in her field at that time. In fact, six months after King established his National Employment Commission in May 1936, Charlotte was among the experts whose temporary services were sought and obtained. She was allowed four months' leave from the CWC to head up the NEC's aid co-ordination division, a body that was to study the extent of federal aid to the unemployed and recommend ways it could be handled more efficiently.

Her report, released in March 1937, was apologetic, for she claimed there simply had not been enough time available to prepare a proper presentation. Her "unfinished" report was 195 pages in length. She had hardly got started, it seemed.

Indeed, it had been a busy time for Charlotte. In between two tiring trans-Atlantic crossings to attend League of Nations committee meetings in February and April 1936, her father passed away on March 23, sending her home to Renfrew where she immediately took on the role of executor of his intestate estate. In the fall, she wrote an eleven-part series of articles on welfare topics for the *Financial Post*, in which she again stressed the need to rein in "the millstone of relief." Then, early in 1937, she resigned from the Canadian Association of Social Workers when it questioned her academic qualifications for membership.

It was the death of her father at age sixty-five, however, that once again focused the spotlight on Charlotte's strained ties with her family. Some years earlier, John Whitton had moved back to Renfrew from Whitney to join his wife Elizabeth, where he established a fruit and vegetable shop on Raglan Street and an animal hides trade a couple of blocks away. Neither was

*John Whitton, Charlotte's
father, 1936.*
A.L. Handford photo, Library and
Archives Canada, PA-126402

particularly profitable, for when he died from a heart attack in the local barbershop, his personal assets totalled only $2,812.05, while his liabilities were $1,726.62. His business assets and liabilities were similarly minimal.

None of the Whitton children was living in Renfrew at the time. Charlotte, age forty, was in Ottawa; J.B., thirty-seven, had a temporary provincial government job in Barry's Bay; Kay, thirty-three, was working for an advertising agency in Toronto; and Stephen, thirty-one, was nearing graduation with a bachelor of commerce degree from Queen's University.

All of John's children returned home for the funeral, as Kay recalled in her unfinished biography of her sister:

[Charlotte] got to Renfrew before two o'clock and, because she was leaving immediately after the funeral for League of Nations conferences in Paris and Geneva (she explained that to nearly everyone who came in the front door in the next two days) she rushed up to Pembroke [the seat of Renfrew county council] to apply to have herself named administratrix because she was positive Father had no will, and Mother had never heard of one. Big Sister had managed to call a funeral director and order a special oak casket because Father had reduced to 300 pounds. My Younger Brother had been visiting with Frank [Kay's husband, Frank Ryan] and me in Toronto when the word came in late afternoon of Father's death. We drove all night in the pouring rain and around the detours caused by a severe earthquake at Cornwall. When we came to Mother's house after a 5 a.m. to 8 a.m. sleep, Charlotte was off and running. The funeral director asked my Big Brother, "Where is your sister?" "Out counting hides at the warehouse, and after that at the lawyer's," he answered. I never saw Big Brother so mad.

Every night of the wake my Big Sister and her friend, Margaret Grier, carried all the flowers out of the parlour to the summer kitchen and, as soon as they went to bed, my brothers and I would carry them all back until I got hay fever. The brothers were sitting up all night because my Mother threatened to keep "the wake" herself if the men of the house weren't red-blooded and faithful. Of course the brothers played poker and ate a lot and fell asleep, but everything was fairly peaceful until Big Sister came down early and saw the flowers. "You're just trying to spoil the funeral leaving the flowers in this hot room," she stormed.

She and Margaret took the flowers out again the next night and the brothers brought them right back in, because they didn't want to sit up all night without flowers.

"It's too lonesome at night without flowers," said my Big Brother.

Before we left for church, all the ladies were given an Aspirin to soothe their nerves and get them back to the house to get ready for the party after the funeral.

In an interview with the author in 2007, John Bartholomew Whitton Jr., J.B.'s son and co-executor of his aunt Charlotte's estate, described his grandfather as "a giant of a man," who killed his own cattle by taking an axe or a hammer into the pasture, grabbing the beasts by the horns, and clubbing them to death. John B. Jr.

explained that on the morning of his grandfather's death, the deceased had gone to see his banker about a business loan, explaining that he needed a third truck, because the two trucks often used by his two sons to drive to Montreal and back for fresh fruit for the store were inadequate. After a "strong argument" with the banker and the latter's refusal to grant him the loan, John Whitton went to his local barber for a more sympathetic ear. The barber left his shop temporarily for unknown reasons and when he returned he found John Whitton slumped dead in his chair.

Incidentally, Kay did not describe her father's post-funeral wake, which, given the household toil and turmoil at the time, must have been a most interesting affair.

Returning to Geneva in mid-April 1937, shortly after submitting her preliminary National Employment Commission report to Mackenzie King, Charlotte gamely volunteered to serve on the World Committee on Nutrition, as well as the Child Welfare Committee, accepted the chairmanship of a new committee on child placements in families, and took on the added responsibility of *rapporteur* (official reporter) of the Advisory Committee on Social Questions, a panel on which she had sat as a full delegate since 1935 due to pressure applied by the Bennett government.

Her standing at the League had improved immeasurably since the early battles of the late 1920s, and so too had Charlotte's view of the League and its activities. In an undated six-page review written at the time, she acknowledged that the international body had failed in some of its major objectives, especially in not protecting Ethiopia from Mussolini's invasion in 1936, but reported that the Social Questions section had achieved much progress. "Its session completed, the Committee's members disperse to four Continents; some go to the oldest states of recorded civilization, some to the youngest, but all are united in their common effort to contribute of the best of their accumulated experience, to the end that health may be better, labour happier, and the living of life richer for all peoples upon earth," she wrote.

The situation was not as rosy in Canada, however. In March, she informed the president of the Canadian Association of Social Workers, B.W. Heise, that she had not renewed her membership in the association because the group had refused to nominate her for a role with the National Employment Commission in 1936 because "I was not a qualified social worker . . . that I could not be trusted; that I was a politician; that I was anathema to the King Administration; that I was certainly unacceptable to the Honourable the Minister of Welfare for Ontario, etc. and so forth, in the same saga of vilification, of which I have heard many cantos among certain groups, largely centred in Toronto." Heise admitted she had powerful enemies in the CASW who had tried to cancel her membership in the association because she had never obtained proper academic accreditation in social work, but added that the CASW board wanted her to stay on.

There were also serious problems at the Canadian Welfare Council. Marjorie Bradford, the acting executive director who three years earlier had complained of exhaustion trying to emulate Charlotte's dizzying pace, wrote again in May 1937 to Charlotte, then in London after the League meetings to attend the coronation of George VI, with several items of bad news. Helen Reid, Charlotte's former mentor and a mainstay of the CWC from its start in 1920, was in serious condition in a Montreal hospital after having a breast removed due to spreading cancer; another mainstay, Ella Thorburn, was losing interest; her close friend and colleague, Ethel Parker, had rejected an offer to be promoted to a divisional chairmanship; and other officials were being less than co-operative. "Do you like the sound of my monkey wrench tinkering with all your precious machinery? If you think I am having a good time just can that idea right now," she added bluntly. Further, CWC president, John Hackett of Montreal, announced his intention to stand down at the upcoming annual general meeting because he did not agree with all of the CWC's policies, and Montreal *Gazette* publisher Philip Fisher, a longtime board member, would decline the presidency because he planned on taking a year-long sabbatical from all professional activities.

Apparently undismayed, Charlotte accepted an extension of her posting with the National Employment Commission so as to complete her unfinished report from March. She eventually submitted an exhaustive report in December.

By the fall of 1937, however, it was obvious to all concerned that drastic measures were needed to resuscitate the CWC. And no one knew it better than Charlotte. Still on leave from the CWC until October, she informed Frank Stapleford of Toronto, who was expected to accept the council's presidency at the annual general meeting on September 22, that she realized the gravity of the situation, so suggested a two- or three-month freeze on all CWC activities, during which time she would conduct a full review of the council's operations. She would then report to a small "technical committee" composed of Stapleford and several others, who in turn would report to the full board of governors. Within days, Stapleford replied that the board had agreed to raise her pay, but her idea of reviewing her own agency was a non-starter.

Stung by this unexpected rejection, Charlotte sat down on September 24 and wrote Stapleford a stinging, four-page, handwritten response:

> I do not think that any member of the Board can possibly know fully how intolerable and unstable the Council's basic structure is, and has been in all these recent years. For at least five years I have worked in constant awareness of it, never able to extricate myself from immediate pressure for its righting. Office setup is improved but shaky, and requires more consistent routine and procedures. Good senior executive staff are neither directed nor utilized as they should be because work has headed up too intensively in me, and even more so, because of the pressure of circumstances, in Miss Bradford not only during my leave but long before because of my frequent absence. Pressure of work and time has simply meant lack of opportunity for regular planning and conference. In this situation, I do not think we can attract, nor do I think we can retain, good executive assistants . . .

She had offered the best leadership she was capable of, but:

> I absolutely lack the physical strength, the mental and spiritual resources to step back into the situation as it exists today, and take up, as though it were yesterday, the day to day routine of Council's responsibility, without the substantial reconsideration by the Board and, I hope, reorganization that I deem essential.

The Canadian Welfare Council was the third most important thing in her life, after the Anglican church and Queen's University, she continued.

> [So] I am therefore asking you and the Board to allow me to file my resignation, effective at your discretion, and in any case not later than the close of the present fiscal year, March 31st, 1938. I shall return to duty, at my old salary, waiting only ten days or a fortnight longer here to wind up my duties more completely in view of the changed situation . . . I ask you to accept my word that I am doing this only because I am not capable of accepting and discharging successfully the heavy duties of Council executive director without the prior review and re-orientation that I feel must face anyone who will tackle that post . . . I have no definite plans for the immediate future at all and am rather resting myself on God's mercy for the more distant future.

Then she had second thoughts, for atop the first page is marked: "Not sent."

She returned to the office on schedule in October and it was practically business as usual, or at least as normal as it could be with a whirling dervish like Charlotte in command.

Problems. There were problems aplenty, Marjorie Bradford noted in a September 29, 1937, report that she wrote while ill at home. Reports from Saskatoon and Winnipeg surveys were overdue, because the temporary women hired to write them were incapable of meeting their deadlines, while a third report on a Hamilton survey was late because the woman who carried out the survey went on vacation before completing her work. Bradford continued:

> Sorry about lateness of reports, but I've pretty much run the office alone during summer, due holidays, tonsils, etc . . . I do not want you to worry simply because I have decided to stay at home. I am really feeling no worse, but this seems to be the only way to overcome the complaint, whatever it is. I suppose you know that Muriel is away today, Miss Clark yesterday and today and Miss Heidman is not back yet. I will

talk to you at any time if you want to come here, provided you are not afraid of being infected with something.

She also reminded Charlotte that she was expected to write the CWC submission to the Rowell-Sirois Royal Commission on federal-provincial relations, due in the following spring.

Back in the executive director's chair at Council House in October 1937, Charlotte immediately got down to business. Her main priority was to re-assert her authority, for the board of governors, alarmed by what they had heard about CWC mismanagement at their annual meeting in September, had established a "committee of future policy" to guide the CWC out of its apparent confusion. Charlotte was not opposed to the committee, but she did inform committee chair Robert Mills that she wanted to replace Bradford on the panel now that she was back. A compromise was reached whereby both women sat on the committee, but not before CWC president Stapleford suggested diplomatically that she should be less autocratic and allow her staff "lots of elbow room to fully express themselves and use whatever initiative they may have."

Charlotte undoubtedly was a control freak — another of her early moves upon her return was a major staff shuffle — and among her major failings was an inability to concentrate on her main occupation. Thus, as she was pulling the CWC back into shape and preparing a brief for the Rowell-Sirois Royal Commission, she was also occasionally lecturing at the schools of social work at McGill University and at the University of Toronto and stepping up her involvement in fundraising for her alma mater, Queen's University. "I am such a bird of passage that I would advise never taking the trouble of coming down to the office until you have found whether I am in Toronto or Timbuctoo or Ottawa," she advised the Renfrew lawyer in December who was handling a lease on her mother's house.

Then there was the League of Nations. She had fought fiercely to obtain her assessor's seat on the child welfare committee in 1926, she had battled with variable results against stuffy European nobility in her early days on the panel, she had ignored it totally for a few years, but in recent years she had returned to Geneva, had taken on more roles in the international body, and had seen her profile raised to a point of prominence. But once again the tide turned and her spirits were dashed, as she made clear in frequent correspondence to Margaret from Geneva in April 1938.

"Things are hectic, worse and worse . . ." she wrote on April 21 as the committee meetings were getting under way. The League was becoming "a cluster of the little powers," she scoffed in another letter three days later. The Irish Free State and Yugoslavia had been admitted to membership, and Japan, which had invaded Manchuria in 1931 without serious repercussions, continued to be represented at the League even though other delegates did their best to ignore the Japanese envoys. "The whole atmosphere is one of futility," she complained. Meanwhile, she still had not received the CWC memorandum from Bradford that she had requested prior to her departure. To top it off, Bradford had announced plans to take off all of July and August for her summer vacation, even though everyone at the CWC was stressed out due to the organizational workload.

"How I wish to get clear of it all, live humbly and happily. How I am longing to get back to you and the Lake! I am so tired," she sighed, signing off. "Much, much love to my rock of ages and greetings to my indifferent red pussy [cat Rustie]. Charl."[2]

One week later, she was battling a touch of influenza and her humour had not improved. "We drag on and on," she grouched to Grier from Geneva, and because the meetings had been extended a few days to complete committee business, it meant sailing home on Friday the 13th of May—an unhappy omen for the superstitious Charlotte—and probably the loss of a planned week's vacation at McGregor Lake. Also, the fact that the overdue memo finally received from Bradford needed extensive revision did little to brighten her disposition.

In the end, Charlotte's view of the League of Nations can be summed up by a congratulatory telegram she sent to famed Canadian suffragette, writer and lecturer, Nellie McClung, on her appointment to the League in 1938: "Good luck, though you will be sickeningly disillusioned."

It was in such a foul mood that Charlotte returned to an embattled, testy CWC Council House in late May 1938. Sitting on her desk was a fifteen-page memo dated May 17 from Bradford, written

---

2 Throughout her personal correspondence, Charlotte signed off with a variety of names, including "Charl," "Sharl," and "Sharlie."

in Bradford's typical no-nonsense style, although it obviously was proffered with a disillusioned heart.

"I have felt less than the dust around here since last September. I have been a lady of uncertain status and I have not felt disposed to curry favor or take anyone's friendship for granted beyond a point of sincere conviction. But somewhere in your letter you said I held you up to contempt among the staff." Not so, Bradford wrote. In fact, when word leaked out among her colleagues about Charlotte's staff reorganization the previous fall, she had not known a thing about it, even though she had been Charlotte's principal assistant and temporary stand-in off and on for three years. She had pretended that she had known about it all along, "and that everything was hunky-dory . . . Miss Query wept in my office for a long time — chiefly from hurt feelings because she had been shunted to filing without even the courtesy of discussing it with her . . . I think the morale of the staff was seriously impaired by the way you went about it all — and certainly my morale has remained in bits all winter." Or at least as low as it was after the spat they had had months earlier when Bradford found her coat sitting in the wastebasket and "I wanted to ask you why you hadn't unscrewed my fire place as well!"

She continued: "When I took over to let you go to the National Employment Commission, I did so with grave misgivings and extreme reluctance. Do you know it is a tradition in our organization from long before I came here that whenever you return after a few weeks' trip there always has to be an explosion and a ripping of someone or more up the back before everything settles down peaceably again?" As for her perceived "demotion" in last fall's shakeup, "Do you know I had the curse for practically three weeks after I learned of my supposed disloyalty?" When things went wrong, "Muriel gets headaches, you get poison ivy and I get the curse."

Oh, and one other thing, she advised her boss. The Rowell-Sirois Royal Commission was asking why the CWC submission was late.

Bradford's memo was effective. Charlotte, writing to CWC president Stapleford on May 25, informed him that she had returned home a few days earlier and "reached the office Monday [the 23rd] to be faced immediately with a cloud of arrows from all directions, the largest of which was the instruction to appear before the Rowell Commission this afternoon" to present the council's case for its role in a renewed federal-provincial partnership. Always quick with a quip or an extended commentary, she confidently spoke on the CWC's submission which was co-authored by herself and six CWC governors and which recommended, among other things, that people who lived in hinterland communities where there was little chance of finding work should be moved to built up areas where work was available.

Despite the animosity and the turbulence, Charlotte weathered the storm at Council House and continued to rule throughout the rest of 1938. She still spoke on behalf of the CWC, and when the media wanted a reaction to welfare-related news of the day from a welfare leader, they inevitably turned to Charlotte. In December, for example, when the Canadian Press news service sought her reaction to a story from England concerning the purchase of infants from unwed mothers or poor married couples, she was quick to confirm that similar "adoption brokers" were active in Canada, despite the best efforts of organizations such as the CWC or the Children's Aid Societies. In at least one unnamed Canadian city she had heard that cards had been placed in windows offering babies for sale at $35 per child. This was later confirmed to have happened in Montreal. The story was played down at the time, but almost ten years later, Charlotte's name would be headline news across Canada concerning a so-called "child-trafficking" controversy in Alberta.

The immediate storm clouds did not dissipate, and 1939 would prove a watershed year in Charlotte's relations with the CWC. The governing board, which in the early years of the council had rubber-stamped most of Charlotte's initiatives, was stepping up its own authority and clamping down on hers. In January, Stapleford wrote to inform her in no uncertain terms that it was her responsibility to raise funds for the welfare council in Toronto, not his. For Charlotte, the situation was becoming untenable. She sat down on February 4 and composed a lengthy resignation letter to Stapleford.. This time, she put it in the mail. Excerpts follow:

Dear Mr. President,

I have not wanted to write this letter, but after long and careful deliberation, somewhat induced, I admit, by the peremptory and repeated advice of my doctor, I feel that I must, in justice to the Council and myself.

For nearly a year now I have felt that the contribution which I could make to the Canadian Welfare Council was not adequate to its needs in the present stage of its development. I would be insulting the intelligence of the Board and denying my own were I to pass over as of little account what I have been able to do for the Council and through the Council in my nineteen years of association — thirteen of them full-time — with it. But partly because it has grown out of a mere conference in 1920 to its present stage with no change in its executive officer, it seems to lack a certain integration in its membership, and that corporate responsibility in its Board, through which its permanence alone may be assured. I do not know whether it is because my particular capacity may lie along other lines, or because for so long I lacked any other technical assistants, and consequently too many of the things expected of the Council rested upon me and had to be done by me, and within time limits, or not at all . . .

Whatever the explanation, I have felt for some time that the consolidation of the Council's structure and finance was the most urgent task before its Board and its executive staff and, try as I would, I could not extricate myself from the day to day needs of my office and urgent demands of agencies and communities, and of Council members themselves, for services that could not be denied. In twelve years of full-time operation the Council's budget has expanded tenfold and yet its immediate present and its future have never seemed to be so ill assured . . . Therefore, I do not feel that any question of special leave would be practicable in the present instance, nor do I feel that it would be just to Miss Bradford particularly, or those who will carry on in the Council. My post should not be held open but should be filled as soon as possible for the work to be done is staggering as it is . . .

Therefore, with the deepest regrets, and the sense of severing what has been in real truth a large part of my life's interest and work, I would ask you to present my resignation to the Board of Governors . . . My contract requires three months' notice. I would have liked to be released by the end of the Council year, and in any case shall conclude this year's programme and report. I would like to be released, if possible, not later than April 30th, and, providing the Board is prepared to face the possibility of some period of enforced leave in that interval, I shall do what I can to clean up business in which my contribution may be useful.

I have no other plans, no prospect of any other line of service or activity. I shall have to choose that later for it is necessary that I continue in so called "paid employment." But this immediate action I am taking in the light of the past and present and leaving the future to find itself.

One final thing I would like to say. I do not think there are more than two members of the Board who realize the volume of work and the pressure and nature of the responsibilities with which recent years have surrounded the post of your director, and any assistant to the director. Because Miss Bradford's devotion to her work has been beyond all praise, it has been possible to weather the times so far and to such extent as we have. It will not be possible for you to think of having her carry on, even temporarily, without other and additional staff of at least equal calibre and experience with her own. You have some admirably capable and loyal junior staff in the Council, who, inadequately remunerated through the years, have given generous and unstinted service. They too should be protected, and the pace and pressure of their work be lightened. I would ask special thought and consideration in the plans of the Board on their behalf and Miss Bradford's.

With deep gratitude for the partnership of these past years, and my fervent hope for the Council's good future, I remain, yours sincerely,

[signed Charlotte Whitton]

Hold on, Stapleford replied immediately. The situation was bad, feelings were hurt, everyone was feeling a touch angry, but that was no reason to resign after all she had done for the council. "I think you are attaching too much importance to the present financial situation," he argued. After all, every organization had its highs and lows and this just happened to be a particularly low point in the council's history. Take an extended vacation of a couple of months and free your mind from the strains of the office, he advised.

"The job as it now is was built up by you and fits like an old glove. I could not conceive of any work which would give you more of the kind of thing that you want than your present one. I quite realize that you cannot keep going at your present pace. It has been a marvel that you have stood it so long . . . If you left the Council there is no one who could be secured who could keep up the diversified activities which you have carried on. There would inevitably be a big drop."

She deserved leave with full pay, he told her, but added that if she did not have a quick change of mind, he would have to present her resignation to the full board of governors at its next meeting in seven days.

Charlotte replied on February 9: "I did not answer your very kind letter at once because I naturally want to think it over again." She did think it over again but remained adamant; the resignation letter would go before the full board. It was on the board's agenda on February 13, and rejected. Instead, she was granted several months' leave of absence for health reasons.

It was a swell vacation—the first true holiday she had had in years. She left Council House on April 30, and it was an immediate case of out-of-sight, out-of-mind, like a child leaving school at the end of the academic year. As quick as a light switch, Charlotte, the eternal Anglophile, was tingling with anticipation because the upcoming visit to Ottawa of George VI and his queen consort, Elizabeth, was just days away. Ah, the excitement! Royalty! The word was reverence itself in Charlotte's mind, and while Elizabeth Tudor would always be the major mentor in her mind, contemporary royals held an exceedingly warm spot in her heart.

Perhaps it had begun in 1901, when the Duke and Duchess of York, later to become George V and Queen Mary, had passed through Renfrew on their Canadian tour and grandmother Matilda Carr Whitton, a Briton to the core, had led a bright five-year-old girl to see the Royal Couple appear on the platform at the rear of the train during a whistle stop. More likely it was during her impressionable teenage years at Renfrew Collegiate and Queen's University that this mania for "the Crown" developed. Whatever the case, it had fully entrapped

Charlotte by 1934 when she found herself trembling and practically speechless before the Prince of Wales in a private audience at Buckingham Palace. Then there was the coronation in 1937 when his brother, the Duke of York, became King George VI, following the 1936 abdication crisis, and Charlotte, despite the many problems at the Canadian Welfare Council, found time to detour to London after the League of Nations meetings to watch the coronation procession from a vantage point at Canada House. She had wept "as, in all the panoply of monarchy, King George VI and his gloriously appareled Queen Elizabeth rode by, their robes of state and the Royal regalia beautiful and precious beyond imagining."

Then, like a stroke from a friendly fairy's wand, the Royal Couple was in Ottawa and there was Charlotte, standing in the crowd outside the home of the governor general on May 11, 1939, admiring as the king sat erect in the royal landau with his beautiful queen as they proceeded to Parliament Hill for official ceremonies.

But it only got better, as she recalled years later in a composition she entitled *Royal Remembrances*:

We had guests both in town and at the lake. So, of course, I got poison ivy, one of the finest of my many premium visitations. I had been bidden to the Royal Garden Party [at Rideau Hall]. Thither I went, my arms dripping but swathed in shoulder length kid gloves, a cloth coat thrown over my shoulders to ward off the chill of that May day. We took up our positions just at the top of the stairs, where Their Majesties were to meet, traversing with Their Excellencies, [Governor General] Lord and Lady Tweedsmuir, each their sides of the square along which their guests had gathered."

The king cut the first piece of cake, then:

[that] long-time servant of the Crown, [the governor general's principal aide-de-camp Henry] Willis-O'Connor, came towards us, a list in his hand.

That was all the notice we had that the privilege of presentation was to be ours. I had time only to shed my coat on to the ground, curtsy and look up into the darkest blue eyes I have ever seen, of Her Majesty Queen Elizabeth, clothed in the most indescribably exquisitely soft shade of peachbloom, hat and gown, and gloves, shoes and pearls all matching, and with a diamond maple leaf as her shoulder knot.

Again I garbled what I would say and went on being incoherent as Her Majesty asked me really intelligent questions about our welfare services and Lady Tweedsmuir tried to help me out. How I envied Senator Cairine Wilson who, presented just before me, had said, "Your Majesty honours us by wearing our emblem today." I remember in what a friendly family fashion Her Majesty replied, "Oh! Yes, Queen Mary lent me that . . ."

The next day, jammed against a pillar at the Château, my decorations seeming as large as cowbells, I tried to share in the ceremonial unveiling of the War Memorial, where my brother stood in the Veterans' Guard, but I saw only the back of a tall and talkative man in front of me. Even he, however, was silent as the King's final solemn words of dedication came over the loud speaker: "Without freedom there can be no enduring peace, and without peace no enduring freedom."

Charlotte watched solemnly from the sidelines on May 14 as the king and queen departed Ottawa by train at Union Station and "took part of our hearts away."

The vacation continued. Long, lazy summer days at McGregor Lake ensued as Charlotte and Margaret occasionally welcomed women friends from across Canada and the United States — most of them involved in social work — while at other times they just chatted to each other by the fireside, or rowed the flat-bottomed boat they called *Moucher*, and trolled for trout or bass on the calm, cool lake, or else watched as Rustie the cat hunted mice in the pine cottage they called Wensleylea, after Wensleydale in Yorkshire, England, ancestral home of the Whitton family. It was the first time Charlotte fully enjoyed the pleasures of this hideaway in the Gatineau Hills, seemingly far removed from the demands in Ottawa.

It was also a time when she could put her handywoman skills to use. The previous year she had purchased $900 worth of pine lumber which she now used to build singlehandedly a small cabin that she would use only for writing. It was a small A-frame hut fit for a short person, with only a desk and chair and a small cot for furniture, but the window looked out through the maple saplings towards the lake and proved in later years to be the site where Charlotte did much of her writing. It measured just over ten feet square, while inside it was nine feet six inches high at its apex and six feet, six inches at the side walls.

The summer was memorable for Charlotte for at least one other reason: She became a doctor. An honorary doctor of civil law, that is. In August, she and one other woman, Miss Edith Russell of the University of Toronto's nursing department, were among thirteen to receive the honour from the University of King's College in Halifax. From then on, if she wished, she could sign her name Dr. Charlotte Whitton.

It was a gloriously relaxing summer, during which time she also had a two-storey house built for her mother on her Lorne Avenue properties in Renfrew, at a cost of $5,700.

Come September, however, she began to set aside her "idle" ways, beginning with a speaking engagement at the Canadian Women's Club in Toronto. She also returned to her office at Council House.

She hadn't changed, despite the extended vacation. Nor had the CWC's administration improved. In fact, with the resignation of Marjorie Bradford in August, there were further financial and administrative concerns. In mid-November, Charlotte complained to Nora Lea, a Toronto welfare official with whom she had been friends since Queen's, that recent appointments of welfare officials across the country were poorly considered. Replied Lea: "What concerns me far more than any of the above in regard to your letter was the very evident indication that you are driving yourself too hard," that she had again taken on too heavy a workload. Other friends told her the same thing, and it was true; she was unable to slow down, and she was burning out quickly.

She was on the road again in January 1940, with welfare meetings and/or speaking engagements in Montreal, New York City, and Washington, followed by another round in Toronto, Winnipeg, and

British Columbia. "I am so tired before I start that I cringe when I look at my itinerary," she wrote one friend, Marcella Penzel of Little Rock, Arkansas, in late December 1939.

Sure enough, on March 8, 1940, her forty-fourth birthday, she advised CWC president Stapleford, "I have come to the end of the road and it has to be faced. I do not feel that, as the non-voting executive officer of this Council, I should be left longer carrying the impossible responsibilities left upon me . . . The situation has grown progressively hopeless since early January . . . Before Christmas, my doctor told me I was back where I was before my leave, and warned me, warnings since repeated, that I was likely to 'crack up' with no warning . . . (As a matter of fact, I am writing this for dictation at 2:45 A.M., the tenth sleepless night I have had in a row) . . . I know, now, that I should never have reconsidered my resignation, and that the sooner matters are brought to a real head the earlier the hope of a responsible group and structure arising from the Council's ashes."

Somehow, Stapleford convinced her to stay on, but just one month later, she received another unhappy shock in the form of a letter from the Queen's University registrar, Jean Royce: "I am sorry to have to tell you that the election of Trustees by Graduates has resulted in the election of Dr. W.C. Clark and Dr. Alexander Macphail." In other words, she had not been re-elected to the board after twelve years of faithful, unstinting service to her beloved alma mater. On a lighter note, one board member hoped she would be re-elected in the future, for otherwise he would have no one to quarrel with at board meetings.

With the outbreak of the Second World War in September 1939, the Canadian government and national non-governmental agencies turned their efforts to the war effort. Charlotte was particularly interested in having British children brought to safe havens in Canada for the duration. She had a good relationship with Zoë Puxley, Britain's assistant under-secretary for public health whose department was responsible for the care of children and colleague at the League of Nations. At first Puxley wanted to keep children in Britain despite the war, but as the Luftwaffe pounded British cities, she decided that they would be better off sent overseas temporarily and Canada, as a member of the Commonwealth, was an obvious choice.

Charlotte, who earlier had opposed the acceptance of European child refugees, most of whom were Jewish and whose evacuation was supported by the Canadian National Committee on Refugees under Cairine Wilson, now welcomed the British youngsters. Some 1,500 children arrived from England during the summer of 1940, but the program was quickly cancelled in September when seventy-seven of the young evacuees drowned when their ship, SS *City of Benares*, was sunk by a U-boat while crossing the Atlantic.

Although it was obvious that a parting of the ways for Charlotte and the CWC was imminent, she stayed on at Council House during 1940 and 1941, keeping the office running, writing memos, attending conferences, and speaking to welfare and women's groups across the country. She also kept in touch with a friend in the insurance industry who suggested that she should consider insurance sales as her next career.

In the meantime, she wrote a booklet for the IODE, entitled *God's Good Tide*, that appeared in March 1941 and concerned two topics that interested her most — herself and her English roots. Promoted by the IODE, of which she was still a member of the national executive, it was reprinted four times that year with proceeds going towards the Order's war effort.

The book received good reviews, and so did Charlotte when in October she was awarded an honorary doctor of laws degree, this time from Queen's University. She "has made a place for herself not only in Canada, but throughout this continent, in the organizing of Social Service work to the greater benefit of those who are in need," Principal Robert Charles Wallace asserted while conferring the honour. True to form, and a portent of things to come, she protested when told that there were not enough academic gowns for everyone at the graduation ceremony, so all graduates would have to appear in civilian clothes. Flustered but adamant, Charlotte sought out and obtained an academic-looking gown from the Anglican church and proudly wore it to the ceremony.

Finally, after several false starts, Charlotte and the CWC agreed on a termination date, December 31, 1941. After sixteen years as executive director of the organization she had nurtured from birth, the maternal strings were to be cut, but there were no tears. "Following our conversation in Montreal yesterday, this is my formal confirmation of my request to have my resignation take effect on December the 31st, after which date I would have no connection or responsibility towards

the Council or office," she wrote Philip Fisher, the new CWC president. She acknowledged that she had submitted her resignation in
the spring of 1939, had threatened to quit in 1940, had again offered
her resignation in April 1941, and once more in September, but this
time it was for keeps. And it was. The CWC board met on November
24 and approved the request. Her social welfare career was kaput, or
so it seemed.

Before she closed the door on the CWC, Charlotte had to have the
last word. Her message to the board, which she entitled "Signing Off,"
ran to twenty pages. An excerpt:

> Your retiring director deems it obligatory to relieve the in-
> coming director of any responsibility for sins of omission or
> commission marring the first three-quarters of the Council's
> twenty-second year of operation, April 1 to December 31,
> 1941 . . .
>
> It but remains for me to thank you once again for the
> years of partnership and opportunity during which we have
> been privileged to be of some service to Canada through
> service to the Canadian Welfare Council, and to record my
> gratitude for the warm and generous recognition recorded by
> the Board for such part as it has been vouchsafed me to play
> therein . . .
>
> As the contribution to human history of this compara-
> tively small and young country will be limited only by her
> own stature, so I believe the contribution of the Canadian
> Welfare Council to Canada's life to be limited only by the
> vision, courage and determination of its Board of Governors.
> For a generation now confidence in its potential work in
> this nation's life has been a lode star as it has been a driving
> power in my own life. May I then be forgiven the trespass, if
> I close this last report on a somewhat personal note, and the
> prayer that you with whom Council's destinies now rest will
> deem it, and Canada, not unworthy of the obligation which
> the service you should give it imposes.

PART THREE  Freelancer

10 A Woman of Leisure

After her resignation from the Canadian Welfare Council at the end of 1941, Charlotte spent the rest of the decade as a woman of leisure. But for Charlotte, "leisure" meant professional speaking and writing assignments and consulting when she pleased and as she pleased. There were no more worries about dealing with unhappy employees and no more concerns about answering to a board of governors that increasingly questioned her decisions. Yet she still had to earn a living. She also had to provide moral support for an increasingly ill Margaret, but she could do it on her own schedule and she could do as much or as little as she pleased. Being Charlotte, though, meant there was more emphasis on the "much" than on the "little." Thus, the 1940s were a merry-go-round of independent engagements, interrupted by idyllic summer days at McGregor Lake, or relaxing in the comfortable two-storey apartment she shared with Margaret in New Edinburgh.

McGregor Lake was Charlotte's escape valve, her release from the pressure cooker she invariably placed herself in. It was a chance to don old work pants held up by suspenders, to get out a hammer or saw and to patch things up; it was a chance to climb into the solid wooden rowboat *Moucher* and go bass fishing in a quiet corner of the lake, and to read by lamplight well into the night. There was more time for visitors, more time for Margaret, more time for their cat Rustie, more time for contemplation. There was more time, period.

The lake was just over twenty-five miles north of Ottawa, yet light years from the rigid, civilized world of the national capital. There was no electricity in the 1940s, and few cottages. There wasn't even a navigable road into her well forested, one-acre property; she had to row *Moucher* across the lake to reach it. Squirrels, groundhogs, and deer loitered about the place, while amongst the maple, wild apple, and chokecherry trees that grew close to the cottage flew robins, kingfishers, phoebes, vireos, waxwings, goldfinch, grosbeaks, bobolinks, and rare tanagers. Ducks swam on the lake in front of the cottage, and the odd bear poked a curious nose onto her property from time to time. At one point, she counted 138 different varieties of wildflowers.

For last-minute purchases, she rowed across the lake, got into her car, and drove the seven miles of gravel road to Perkins Mills, now Val des Monts, and J.W. Burke's general store. If an experienced handyman was needed, there was always Oakley Carey to call upon, or if he wasn't available, there was "the Frenchman," Alcide, who charged what she considered an outrageous $7.50 for an ordinary household task. (When she complained to Alcide's wife, the woman explained, "But Alcide, he's a man," and therefore worth more than the $6.50 Charlotte normally paid his wife for similar caretaker duties.) When the plumbing failed one year, Charlotte took a plumbing course in Ottawa and thereafter handled those repairs herself.

The warm, welcoming interior of the post-and-beam pine cottage consisted of a large open room with a fireplace and wicker chairs in the centre, a buffalo hide on one wall, and bookshelves of mystery stories, novels, and nature studies. Along one side of the main room were two bedrooms, the dividing wall for which reached only part way to the ceiling — the better to chat between the rooms as she and her guests talked themselves to sleep. Each of the two rooms held two beds, and two couches were available in the main room for more visitors.

Later on, Charlotte would build her own boathouse and include two more beds that sat on floorboards just a metre above the normally clear, cold lake.

In the A-frame writing cabin she called "The Work House," there was only a small cot and a metre-high oak writing desk and chair.

Among her neighbours on the lake in the 1940s, in addition to Robert Wodehouse and his family next door, was the Poy family whose daughter, Adrienne, later became well known as a journalist and ultimately a governor general of Canada. (In her 2006 autobiography, *Heart Matters*, Adrienne Clarkson proudly related the tale of her mother catching "the largest pike that anyone had ever seen on McGregor Lake.") Other summer residents included Col. Henry

Charlotte's "Work House" at McGregor Lake.
Photo by author

Bankhead of the United States Legation (now Embassy) in Ottawa, whose niece, Broadway star Tellulah Bankhead, visited from time to time; Montreal Canadiens star Aurel Joliet; and the Oblates of Mary Immaculate, a Roman Catholic order of priests who owned a large summer retreat on the other side of the lake from Charlotte.

Dr. Jim Coupland, a retired Ottawa dentist living in Almonte, Ontario, recalled in an interview that Charlotte was well known around the lake as a keen handywoman, an ardent fisherman, and a frequent hostess to a broad selection of women. She was also a great cook, and when Coupland, who was then just a youth, and his friend Tim Kenny did odd jobs for her about the cottage, she paid them with delicious cherry pies and captivating tales.

"We'd say, 'Miss Whitton, tell us that story . . . Tell us about the time [in the early 1930s] you were in Vancouver.' Well, she went underground with the police in Chinatown in Vancouver and came up three blocks later, you see, at a Chinese restaurant and as she came up the stairs — and she could be very dramatic — she said 'I felt feint, I thought I was losing my head because everything was cloudy.' Well it turns out there was a lot of steam from whatever they were cooking, and she realized what happened was that the woks were causing the steaming and the whole wall was a mass of cockroaches, and as the steam went out the cockroaches rushed up the wall and when it subsided they came back down." Apparently that was the end of her underground investigations.

"Charlotte liked to amplify, [and] like some politicians, you could believe sixty or seventy per cent because she could make a good story," Coupland added.

Tim Kenny recalled times when he had to take out his motor-boat to rescue Charlotte and her passengers aboard her rowboat after it had been pushed by strong winds to the far end of the lake and threatened to capsize. Her little rowboat might have been incapable of making its way through the rough waves, but she remained in command as she directed young Kenny towards her cottage. Also, he recalled, when the cottagers around the lake decided to form a protective association in 1945, Charlotte was their first president. "Charlotte wasn't noted for being very quiet; she was very outspoken," he remarked wryly.

One of her frequent visitors was more generous. Kennethe Haig, a columnist with the *Winnipeg Free Press*, wrote in 1941:

This woman, who holds two honorary doctorates . . . has dynamic physical energy to uphold the brilliance of her intellect. To her intellectual power is added a devastating wit, and to her analytical ability a constructive imagination. Audiences sway beneath her hand. Her occasional verse has color and cadence; her prose the breadth and sweep that flows from the long-loved currents of English literature. There is the cottage by Lake MacGregor [*sic*] and a canoe that glides as one with her, unafraid, sure about the gleaming waters. There are the long talks of men and women and books and places, broken by gales of laughter that dance with the moonlight and bring the pines crowding closer . . .

Mary Carman, a senior federal public servant who inherited Charlotte's McGregor Lake property from her father Grant, who purchased it from Charlotte in 1966, and continues to maintain it, has kept such Whitton memorabilia as a "Conservation Pledge," as well as a framed poem seeking protection against "ghoulies and ghosties and long-legged beasties" and a bluntly worded rhyme in the bath-room against excessive use of the gasoline pump: "It takes a lot of gasoline to bring this water here, of course we like to keep clean, but don't run us dry, my dear; and if you do, dear, D..., if you ever come again." The Conservation Pledge, which hung on the main room wall, reads: "I give my pledge as a Canadian to save and faithfully to defend from waste the natural resources of my country, its soil and minerals, its forests, waters and wildlife."

Charlotte was indeed a conservationist before the term became popular. She lobbied the Quebec Association for the Protection of Fish and Game to improve fishing in the small lake, and she success-fully battled the provincial highways ministry to save a small forested area called Brady's Bush from destruction due to a road widening. When a robin landed on her cottage porch with an injured wing, she collected worms for three days for the bird's four fledglings, she recalled once in a newspaper column.

Haig wrote that Charlotte claimed her soul would rest at McGregor Lake after her death. Mary Carman said, "Her spirit is here . . . just the quietness, which is probably the antithesis of what people thought of her. My guess is that when she was up here, she was a very different person than when she was at a council table as-serting her dominance over men."

No sooner was Charlotte out the door of the CWC than she was on the road earning her keep by talking. On January 12, 1942, less than two weeks after her resignation went into effect, she was in Buffalo, New York, addressing the local Council of Social Agencies; later that month she was in Chicago, speaking to that city's social agencies council. In April, she toured the U.S. Midwest, speaking in Chicago again, as well as in major cities in Nebraska, Arkansas, Mis-souri, Tennessee, and Iowa. Her topics ranged from Canada's social services setup to Canada's war effort, the latter topic of great interest to Americans for they had only recently declared war themselves fol-lowing the December 7, 1941, bombing of Pearl Harbor in Hawaii.

The summer of 1942 provided something of a lull in the storm that was Charlotte, for she found time to complete a history of the Ottawa River timber industry from her hideaway in the Gatineau Hills — A Hundred Years A-Fellin' — but in the fall she was back on the road. The federal government's Wartime Information Board, of which her brother-in-law, Frank Ryan, was a director, sponsored her tour of Western Canada, an exhausting journey by train, boat, and automobile that included twenty-five appearances in twelve British Columbia communities, ten appointments in three Alberta cities, fourteen talks in five Saskatchewan towns, and eleven dates in six Manitoba municipalities. She could talk about whatever she pleased on behalf of Canada's war effort, a board spokesman advised her in writing, but she was reminded that she was not speaking on behalf of the board, despite its financial support.

Charlotte was often called upon by the media for a comment, and inevitably she received a good press reception from her predominantly female interviewers. In Vancouver, for example, Ada McGeer of the CBC advised her in writing exactly what ten questions she planned to ask in her interview. "They may not be what you want at all. If this is the case, put any words you like into my mouth . . . I know from the packed meetings that you have had here that people would be very glad to have some message from you. (May I suggest that you mention in your message as a good conclusion: 'We shall bend our backs to the struggle, sacrifice and suffering, but when the battle is won, men will see that the future state will be bound to honour not only considerations of territorial but of individual and social integrity.')" Charlotte, a lifelong member of the Canadian Women's Press Club, always had an easy ride with the distaff side of the media, but it's unlikely she used McGeer's suggested phraseology in the interview. She had no difficulty whatsoever in finding words of her own choosing.

As the Second World War wound down, her thoughts increasingly turned back to social work, and so her talks in Michigan or Pennsylvania or Illinois in 1943 included the following topics: "The problems of youth in the post-war world," "War's impact and our post-war plans," and "Women and the future of family life." Similarly, in 1944 and 1945, her topics included "Working today and planning tomorrow," "The public school in the democratic state," and "Today's children in tomorrow's world."

After the war, she continued to speak throughout North America, and though the number of her talks declined due to other priorities, her audience expanded as men's clubs, such as Rotary, Kiwanis or the Life Insurance Institute of Canada, heard her out. Such was the demand that in September 1945, she politely declined an invitation to speak to the Rotary Club of Montreal, because "jobs have piled on jobs and trips on trips. I have Philadelphia, Washington, Chicago, Detroit and Des Moines now right upon me."

Surprisingly, copies of her many speeches that she left with the national archives show that the prepared addresses were fairly long-winded, repetitive, and dull. The fact that they were so well received suggests she likely interspersed her addresses with off-the-cuff asides such as random recollections of her unruly childhood in Renfrew, or her underground activities in Vancouver.

As the decade neared its end, her addresses increasingly turned towards more feminist themes, such as the role of women in politics and the undervalued work of predominantly women's careers, such as teaching and nursing. Despite her strong feminist leanings, she was not opposed to the postwar situation in Canada, whereby returning soldiers reclaimed their jobs in industry, often replacing the women who had held those jobs in their absence. The latter returned to their homes as wives and mothers, and Charlotte, who thought that that was fine for married women, rarely mentioned the fact. Single women like her, on the other hand, should be allowed to keep their jobs and should be paid just as much as men doing the same work, she argued.

While speaking was good for her soul — the applause undoubtedly was nourishing for her hungry ego — and the pay (often about $100 a speech in the United States, but considerably less in Canada) fed her purse, it was not enough to sustain her financially. Freelance writing provided a broader dimension for her inquisitive mind, and meant added income. And write she did! During the 1940s she wrote two books, worked on others, and frequently contributed articles to national magazines, such as *Maclean's, Saturday Night,* and *Chatelaine.*

Like public speaking, writing was not a new venture for her. As a teenager she had written articles for the *Globe*'s youth page, as a university student she had edited the student paper, as an early member of the Canadian Women's Press Club she had published some of her poetry in a club booklet entitled *Verse and Reverse,* and as executive director of the CWC she had written countless reports, memoranda, and letters. She had also written a twelve-part weekly series for the *Financial Post*, in 1936, on Canada's social climate.

Her 172-page history of the Ottawa Valley timber trade was sponsored by Ottawa Valley timber magnate David Gillies. Not surprisingly, the Gillies name featured prominently in the story, but while deferential to the Gillies family, it was also a lively, informed tale of the trade as a whole, carefully catching the raw quality of the men and their times. However, when it came to analyzing the role of the timber tycoons, she was almost rapturous with her choice of words for her patron and his contemporaries, who "have seen, often with clearer vision than the people themselves, the inter-relationship of protected growth, wise and temperate cutting, planned distribution and assured marketing. To the industry must go considerable gratitude for the conservation policies of the last half century."

Many would disagree with those words — "rapacious" comes to mind as a possible description for some in the forest industry at the time — but then Charlotte always knew when to flatter and when to flatten.

Another book-length manuscript she worked on intermittently between 1943 and 1948 was a biography of James Armstrong Richardson, the late Winnipeg business tycoon. He had been a member of the CWC's board of governors during the 1930s and sat with Charlotte on the Queen's University's Board of Governors until his death in 1939.

While that work took up considerable time and effort on her part, she also earned a respectable income from consulting on social issues.

The first to call on her social work expertise was the new leader of the opposition, John Bracken, in the spring of 1943. Bracken, who had just won the leadership of the newly renamed Progressive Conservative Party in December 1942, sought her advice in regard to a recently published report by Leonard Marsh, a McGill University professor and a member of the federal government's committee to study postwar reconstruction. In his report, which is considered a classic in Canadian social welfare literature, Marsh reviewed the full slate of provincial and federal social security laws in Canada and recommended a broad series of proposals that if implemented would turn the country into a welfare state. Bracken, who had served as premier of Manitoba for two decades until turning to federal politics, knew little about the national welfare picture and relied heavily on Charlotte to provide a Conservative viewpoint on the issue.

To the surprise of few, Charlotte went on the offensive. Marsh's recommendations would bankrupt the nation, she charged. Marsh's ideas paralleled those of his former associate at the London School of Economics, Sir William Beveridge, who in the fall of 1942 had released the Beveridge Report, which was seen as the blueprint for the United Kingdom's post-war welfare state. Marsh called for a "national minimum" standard to eliminate poverty and provide a decent living for all disadvantaged Canadians. To pay for this, he advised the federal government to introduce a personal contributory system, similar to today's employment insurance program.

"The basic criticism of the proposals," Charlotte argued scornfully in her report to Bracken, was that Marsh was trying to implement Beveridge's policies in Canada when the two countries, the United Kingdom and Canada, were very different and "all the elements of the Canadian situation demand the evolution of realistic measures, grounded deep in the character of this country and its people . . . This calls for knowledge and love of this land, inventive imagination and courage." She attacked Marsh's report as being restricted only to social insurance and social assistance, while what was needed was an umbrella-type of administration for what she termed "social utilities," such as education, health services, and child welfare. While Marsh called for a universal social security setup, where everyone who could contribute would, and everyone would be eligible for support in times of need, Charlotte wanted to restrict eligibility to those truly in need. The rest could look after themselves, as far as she was concerned.

In the long run, many of Marsh's recommendations were implemented, and Bracken mostly ignored her advice, but Charlotte nevertheless published her findings in book form, entitled *Dawn of Ampler Life*, in late 1943. She attracted more media coverage at the time than the unassuming Marsh, who, incidentally, had asked her in January to review some sections of his report before it was finalized. She had rejected his offer, informing him that she would be analyzing his report for Bracken and possibly commenting publicly on it. At the same time, she remarked pointedly that she had offered her consulting services to three federal departments since her departure from the CWC, and all three offers had been ignored.

No sooner was *Dawn of Ampler Life* in the hands of her publisher, Macmillan of Canada, than Charlotte was at work on another consulting contract. This time, the newly elected Conservative government in Ontario under George Drew hired her to review the administrative setup of its public welfare ministry and recommend changes. She accomplished that complex task in just three months and produced a 190-page, statistics-filled report that recommended twenty-two administrative changes and blamed the previous Liberal government for poorly administering the department.

She followed that up in December with another provincial report concerning a girls' reformatory in the town of Cobourg, about midway between Kingston and Toronto. The home for delinquent girls had been the scene of a violent attack in September in which four girls in the Pink Dormitory unsuccessfully tried to escape by overpowering the night supervisor, grabbing her keys, and fleeing. A ministry official investigated the situation and found that this was only the latest in a series of fights, vandalism, theft, and escape attempts at the home since 1937, the year it had been moved from Galt.

Charlotte's report to the provincial secretary, George Dunbar, recommended a major personnel overhaul, and just as she had done with the public welfare ministry report, she suggested which of her social work friends or acquaintances should be hired for the new positions. In one instance, she named Nora Lea, her former aide at the CWC and an occasional visitor to McGregor Lake.

Her Cobourg report was not important so much for what it recommended, but rather for the fact that it illustrated once more Charlotte's inclination to manipulate others to fit her own values and ideals. For example, she advised Dunbar to go public about the situation and blame it all on the previous Liberal administration: "I strongly advise, therefore, that you make this Report of mine public, as soon as possible saying, in effect, 'Upon taking my portfolio, I was immediately faced with severe criticisms about the care of delinquent girls in the Cobourg unit of the Provincial Training School. I visited the School and was sufficiently concerned at once, to attempt to get back the Galt property, and, failing in that, to push forward the preparation of another unit as quickly as priorities allowed us. However, I felt the whole situation needed reviewing and I therefore arranged for an over-all Report."'

As ministry officials dragged their feet on the report's recommendations, and Dunbar seemed to have lost interest as the months passed, Charlotte wrote to Dunbar on May 16 advising him that she had spoken to a writer with the *Canadian Home Journal* — "the recognized organ of the Women's Institutes," she explained — and arranged for her to write a press release on the report, as well as to put a positive spin on the girls' reformatory issue for the *Journal*. Further, "I would suggest that this summary of Mrs. [Rica Maclean] Farquaharson's should be mimeographed, mailed to all the dailies and weeklies in Ontario, and a copy given to the Canadian Press . . . I think it would be a good idea to release it without comment, then judge public reaction and develop policy reacting thereto where the criticism proves constructive."

In the meantime, she spoke out against the federal government's plan to introduce mothers' allowances, gave speeches in Pennsylvania, Illinois, and Canada's western provinces, became involved in a petition to block the rezoning of a property neighbouring her mother's home in Renfrew, toyed with the idea of seeking election to the House of Commons carrying the Conservative banner. Why not, she teased reporters from the Saskatoon *Star-Phoenix* and the Toronto *Daily Star*. a woman's point of view was needed in the House of Commons to direct attention to the nation's social needs. (Women represented only two of the 243 ridings that year.)

At about the same time, she mentioned in a personal letter to Frank Stapleford, former president of the CWC, that her parliamentary prospects seemed good. "Now, if I follow through, get elected at Ottawa, and become Minister without Portfolio and Chairman of the Assistance and Utilities Board, we'll all go places . . ."

The Tories seemed willing to have her. In April 1944, the national director of the Progressive Conservative Party, Richard Bell, invited her to sit on the board of a new fundraising committee. Bell, who came from an old Ottawa-area family and represented Ottawa West in the Commons, explained that the campaign would be aimed at seeking small donations from across the country "to offset the constant cry of the C.C.F. [Co-operative Commonwealth Federation, a forerunner of the New Democratic Party] that this party gets its money from powerful financial interests and is, therefore, at the mercy of such groups."

Charlotte gave Bell's offer considerable thought, but at the end of July she rejected it because Tory leader Bracken had just come out in favour of universal mothers' allowances, which she had opposed, just as he had ignored many of the recommendations included in her 1943 report to him. For Charlotte, in mid-1944, Ontario Tories were good, federal Tories were bad; both provincial and federal Liberals were bad. The other parties were inconsequential.

Two other projects in the mid-1940s consumed much of Charlotte's time. The first was the proposed biography of James A. Richardson, the second was a multi-year fundraising project for the Anglican church. Both projects gained and suffered from Charlotte's involvement.

At the time, Richardson's name was pure gold among the Canadian establishment; he was a colossus in Western Canada. For decades prior to his death in 1939 and afterwards, James Richardson and Sons of Winnipeg operated leading brokerages in both the grain industry and the stock market. He was president of Western Canada Airways, which he founded in 1926; sat on the boards of many leading Canadian firms, such as the CPR, Canadian Bank of Commerce, National Trust, Great-West Life Assurance and Canadian Vickers; and was president of the Winnipeg Grain Exchange. As well, he succeeded former prime minister Robert L. Borden as chancellor of Queen's University between 1929 and 1939, a period during which Charlotte also sat on Queen's board of governors. Richardson was a valued benefactor of Queen's, and Richardson Stadium, home of the university's Golden Gaels football team, was named after his brother George who was killed in the First World War.

James Richardson was also the one who had suggested to Charlotte creation of rural work camps for unemployed men during the Depression, a controversial scheme that she embellished and persuaded R.B. Bennett to introduce in 1932.

Richardson's wife, Muriel Sprague Richardson, succeeded her husband as president of his conglomerate on his death. Therefore, it was perhaps not surprising that Charlotte, still on Queen's board of governors, argued that Mrs. Richardson should be elected to take her husband's seat at the board, "knowing the tremendous amount of money that is held by women who have inherited large estates in Canada." Mrs. Richardson, in turn, approached Charlotte in late 1942 when she sought someone to write her husband's biography.

At the start of this new relationship, all was peace and light between the two women, the brainy, stubborn Charlotte and the wealthy, stubborn "Mrs. Richardson," as Charlotte referred to her new patron. In December 1943, as Charlotte was winding up her report on Ontario's public welfare department and starting her Cobourg reformatory study, Richardson advised Charlotte in writing that she was lining up interviewees that Charlotte should consult for the biography, but noted that she should not talk to William Nickle, the former Ontario cabinet minister who had grown up with James Richardson in Kingston and served with him on the Queen's board. "You and I see W.F. Nickle differently, a fact that I realized when you were here last," she warned, without explanation. No problem, Charlotte replied, this will be my portrait of James Richardson, not someone else's.

By April 1944, it appeared that Mrs. Richardson was having second thoughts about her decision to ask Charlotte to write the biography, according to a voluminous file in Charlotte's records at the national archives:

> Several angles which you presented merit discussion and
> I wish you were here to clarify and enlarge upon some of
> the points raised . . . I realize that your Irish blood may
> be stirred to fighting pitch by what you are uncovering in
> Ottawa now regarding Canadian Airways but my opinion is
> that the biography should not be marred by recriminations
> or by a too-detailed disclosure of the dishonesty and
> shortcomings of other men. These belong to another book,
> "The History of Commercial Aviation in Canada," which
> may not be written for many years.

(The issue concerned the federal government's decision in 1936 to establish its own national airline, Trans-Canada Airlines, now Air Canada, instead of supporting Richardson's bid to expand Western

Airways to become the national carrier. In 1999, Douglas & McIntyre publishers printed *Doublecross: The Inside Story of James Richardson and Canadian Airways*, by Shirley Render.)

Mrs. Richardson continued:

> You will need to have all the facts, however, and I hope you will not stop short of getting them but I think you should try to present the truth adequately without going much below the surface. If you go too far down in the writing, the muddy waters stirred up will overflow and one chapter of your book will be out of alignment. That is the way I feel at present but I hope my slant does not curb your investigation nor your enthusiasm. If you do not agree with my point of view, we can talk it over later and agree on what may be the limit of your revelations . . .

In June, Richardson informed "Dear Dr. Whitton" that she had hired Alice MacKay, former editor of the Hudson's Bay Company's distinguished company magazine *The Beaver*, to do some research for the biography based on James Richardson's airline business, and added, "I pass it on for your consideration and you can let me know if you would like Alice to rough out a chapter on air activities." Without comment, Charlotte continued with the project while continuing to speak far and wide as a private consultant and considered offers of a career as a politician.

By December, she eagerly wrote "Dear Mrs. R." that she had collected a shipping terminal full of research material and "I am getting more and more warmed with the way my pieces are falling into shape. Margaret [Grier] always laughs at the way I work at a jigsaw puzzle. She picks out her straight edges and fills out the frame. Then she starts filling in. I get all sorts of little piles, each hoarded up, of similar colours, etc. — she says looking like an idiot's flowerbed — and then I start and lift them all in great pieces into the pattern which I have had in my mind's eye. I am feeling very happy about all my separate hoards . . . I have blocked out 1945 pretty clearly and much of my postage is going, declining speeches. I am only going to take a few, now and then, to keep certain of my U.S.A. contacts."

By January 1945, however, her writing was not going well. "Tore up 3000 words last week but got about 750 that may survive," she wrote MacKay. "I turn from grain to history, from the family to the air and decide next time I try any biography it will be about a synthetic baby who entered a hermit's cell and lived there from the age of three months."

The research was going well, the biography was not. "If at the moment you were to take and look through my material you would be convinced it was an economic and political history of the Canadian West in five volumes from some animadversions on the [United Empire] Loyalist settlements and a few comments on the history of aviation and the moral deterioration of the Canadian political scene in the last twenty years," she wrote Richardson in June from McGregor Lake. As autumn arrived, Richardson too was having doubts. "I do feel incapable of making all the decisions that you seem to want until I either have your manuscript or an opportunity to talk it over with you . . ."

They did speak, but nothing was resolved, and by this point, Charlotte was becoming seriously involved in the Anglican church's fundraising program, she was considering a contract offer from the IODE to study child welfare in Alberta, and she had resumed her speaking appearances in the U.S. and Canada. In October, she found time for a quick visit to friends in England.

Nevertheless, in late January 1946, Charlotte contacted two publishers, Ryerson Press and Macmillan of Canada, informing them optimistically that her manuscript was almost complete and she would like to have it in published form and reviewers' hands by November 2 at the latest, in time for the Christmas sales season. "We want to have this book widely read and to have it in the finest product to leave a Canadian publishing house in many a day." Sales were assured, she noted, because Richardson would buy at least a thousand copies for her employees and other sales were a given. Meanwhile, she mailed her manuscript to Winnipeg for Richardson's approval.

Approval was not imminent. MacKay, acting as Richardson's editor, returned it with numerous corrections and suggestions, as well as an offer to Charlotte to move temporarily to Winnipeg while Richardson reviewed it herself. Charlotte accepted the offer briefly, but by early April she was back in Ottawa, even more frustrated than before. That's it, I'm quitting, she wrote Richardson.

"I am writing this letter now to ask for the just dealing between us as two mature women, who, I hope respect each other, and have had no difference of opinion as to what each wished greatly to do but have differed in judgment as to whether it had been done . . . Of my first draft I have cut over 10,000 words net; some of those to which you objected, others less essential sections in the Kingston and local history and the detailed treatment of grain handling. Of the 85,000 words now here, from 50,000 to 60,000 are re-written; the balance is largely unchanged." She had been working sixteen-hour days on the project recently, she informed Richardson, and now she was being told that Richardson had not even read her manuscript, but had had someone to read it for her. Please read the manuscript yourself, she pleaded.

Richardson was taken aback by the impertinence. "To have 'scathing, disparaging and contemptuous' applied to my simple words was a severe jolt but, fortunately, a fleeting one, because I so quickly recalled the conversation and, with it, my reasons for saying that when the amended manuscript arrived 'I would read it or have it read for me.' That, as I had already made clear to you, was exactly what I had done in regard to the original manuscript."

Ensconced as president of the James A. Richardson & Sons conglomerate, Richardson was preoccupied with running a handful of businesses, and besides, she had other, more knowledgeable people to read Charlotte's literary work for her. "Naturally, I would like to meet your wishes and I shall be most happy to accede to your request to read it first myself if you are, in turn, prepared to wait indefinitely for my comment and for its 'second reading' by Jim [her son] and Mr. Laughton [a senior employee]. I cannot promise more than this."

Slightly humbled, Charlotte responded: "Dear Mrs. Richardson; May I thank you for your letter . . . I feel somewhat relieved." And, by the way, she really didn't mind waiting until Richardson had read it through and she didn't even mind if others read it.

At about the same time, she received informal reviews from men to whom she had forwarded copies of her manuscript. A.E. Kerr, president of Dalhousie University in Halifax, said he'd read sections of the work and "continued until I had actually read most of your typescript . . . I am sure that Mrs. Richardson will feel deeply indebted to you." D.C. Coleman, Montreal-based chairman and president of the CPR, wrote: ". . . having read it with deep interest and profound satisfaction . . . I congratulate you on the results of your exhaustive research into family and business records, which results you have presented in a most attractive and impressive style . . ."

Charlotte remained glum. She still had not heard back from Richardson by June 7, so suggested to her patron that she would return the $1,500 already paid "and destroy everything that I have done. To suggest that this would not cause me real financial embarrassment is nonsense; it would but not beyond my managing; there are compensations however in the greater peace of mind of not having been paid for something that has been a failure and is of no use to anyone."

She continued: "I have finished my work in the field for the [Anglican] Advance for about ten weeks and am turning now to some hard work and earning this next six weeks; when you plan a year as a self-employed woman, you get to keep grain coming to the mill from some source the months you planned to be grinding. I hope you had a pleasant holiday, that the exams dealt well with [Richardson's younger children] George and Kathleen, that [daughter] Agnes is back, [son] Jimmie on the mark as usual and the summer ambles pleasantly with you all."

Finally, on August 14, Richardson informed Charlotte that she had read the entire manuscript and had found some errors, but "The gravest error you have made, if you value my opinion at all, is your persistent claim to copyright . . . Admittedly our arrangement was unbusinesslike. There was no formal written contract at any time but there is more than enough in our correspondence — in your letters more than mine — to establish beyond argument the basis of the agreement under which the manuscript was produced . . . I would, however, be glad to receive a statement of your account to date. I hope you are having a good summer."

Citing precedents, Charlotte disagreed about the copyright. She was confident it belonged to her. Nevertheless, she was willing to work it out with Richardson, and Richardson, in October, agreed to read the manuscript one more time before rejecting it.

Two days before Christmas 1946, Charlotte informed Richardson that she was on her way to Alberta for an IODE survey and had no more time to spare for the biography. She had set aside most of 1946 for the project, she explained, but now she had to earn income elsewhere.

The two strong-willed women continued their verbal sparring over a legal termination into 1947, three years since they had begun the project, and in April Charlotte wrote that her two copies of the manuscript would be sent as soon as Margaret Grier could find time.

Grier, in addition to being unwell, was dealing with the recent death of her brother and a cousin, and her sister's serious illness. Charlotte, on the other hand, was becoming more involved in the IODE'S child welfare survey in Alberta. The biography was put aside and no final decision was made at that point.

In the meantime, Charlotte also had volunteered an increasing amount of her time for the Anglican Advance Appeal.

It was yet another example of her strong ties to the Anglican Church of England in Canada, renamed the Anglican Church of Canada in 1955. Those ties reached back to her baptism in St. Paul's church in Renfrew, wavered gently during her college years, and then flowered when she joined the Social Service Council of Canada in 1918. In 1921, at the age of twenty-five, she was lecturing at the church's summer school at Lake Couchiching, Ontario, and in May of the following year the *Globe* reported on her talk to the Anglican women of Toronto: "It was a great array of eloquent facts and a vast amount of enthusiasm that Miss Charlotte Whitton, the speaker of the evening, brought to bear upon a memorable address on 'The Social Opportunities of the Church.'" She had warned her audience about the inroads that "pagan rationalism" was making on society and called instead for the preservation of the home and wholesome family life.

By the 1940s, she was a frequent contributor to the church's magazine, *The Bulletin*, in which she tailored many of her welfare theories with a religious touch. In October 1942, she spoke from the pulpit of the cathedrals in Vancouver and Victoria, both named Christ Church.

In November 1944, as she was still discussing plans for the Richardson biography with Mrs. Richardson, the Anglican primate, the Rt. Rev. Derwyn Trevor Owen, invited her to sit on a newly formed national church committee that would consider a four- or five-year fundraising project. She would be one of only four women on the committee, which included all of the Anglican bishops of Canada, seventeen clergy, and twenty-two laymen. Naturally she accepted the challenge.

As she struggled through the summer of 1945 on the Richardson biography, she considered a request from the general secretary of the Anglican Advance Appeal, Dean Robert Waterman of Hamilton, to carry out a three-point mission for the Appeal, namely (1) the rehabilitation of the church in war-torn Europe, (2) the organization of working women in the Canadian church, and (3) the collection of Canada's population statistics broken down so that the church would know who was Anglican and how much money they might be called on to contribute. Naturally she accepted.

In a lengthy memorandum to Waterman, she urged that the Appeal should be more than a fundraiser; it should also seek the reawakening of church members in their faith and ensure that women played a major role in the campaign, including positions on the budget allocation and interpretation committees, as well as on the executive committee. "I am convinced that nothing but a great revitalizing of spiritual power will save our Christian civilization," she warned.

The project did not begin well. In November, Charlotte complained that very little was being done and that certain executive members were hampering the project because they refused to invite leading businessmen onto their panel because they were afraid they would be overshadowed by their higher profile advisers. As well, her recommendation of a lay person to chair the executive committee, Bank of Canada governor Graham Towers, was similarly ignored. Towers, incidentally, was a neighbour of Charlotte's in Ottawa and the younger brother of her longtime friend Grace Towers.

As 1946 arrived, she had had enough. Writing to the primate on January 2, she stressed:

> It is with a very heavy heart indeed that I make this my
> first letter of 1946. It should have gone many months
> ago. But I have stayed on the Appeal Committee in the

hope that, against mounting evidence to the contrary, such experience, knowledge of Canada, familiarity with the laity, especially the women, as I had, might be of use in what I deem this nation's greatest need — a courageous return to the truths of this Church and a clergy and laity, unselfishly and inspiringly living the proof of the Christian surrender. Against every type of rejection of effort and in the face of an indefiniteness against which every ounce of my experience called out in misgiving, I have tried to be of service, only to learn, later, time and again, and from outside the Committee, that such and such action had been taken, such a person named here, or there, etc . . .

It left her no option; she had to resign.

To emphasize her unhappiness, she mailed copies of her letter to a number of committee members with whom she was on good terms. The response was immediate.

We share your disappointment, Rt. Rev. A.L. Fleming ("Archibald the Arctic") replied.

"Thank you for letting me read the Atomic Bomb you dropped into the Toronto nest," wrote Dean Luxton, bishop of London, Ontario. "I think it will do a world of good. It isn't the primate's Church or Waterman's; its [sic] your Church, & you can't resign from it . . . I believe that you can affect the whole future of the Church across Canada. And be a bit thick-skinned about some of our bishops. Some of them are asleep & frozen and they will blow cold on anything you or I may do!"

By January 22, she had reconsidered. She advised Waterman that although she was busy with her professional speaking, writing, and consulting contracts, she could still find a bit of time to organize the working women of the church while Mrs. R.E. Wodehouse, her next-door neighbour at McGregor Lake, could organize the church's married women. Then, a full month after she had written him, Owen, answered: "I think the whole story is too complicated to try to write about. I should like to have a talk with you on the subject, if you will be so kind . . ."

As her ardour for the Richardson biography cooled, her efforts for the Appeal picked up. She toured Quebec and the Atlantic provinces in the summer of 1946, and Western Canada from September to early November, speaking to women's church groups, organizing them, proselytizing to them, and revitalizing them as an important part of the Anglican church, despite the lack of support from a number of bishops and other clergy. When the church synod met in November, she reported in the church yearbook: "It was a vigorous Synod and a confident Synod. It seemed to be pervaded by some indefinable sense and awareness of a task given it and by a surge of urgency in apprehending and discharging this duty and destiny . . . In the brief span of ten days the life of the Church passed in review, a mighty organism, concerned with the lives and living of one out of every six or seven Canadians . . ." Also, Mrs. Wodehouse was chosen as the first woman ever to sit in the synod.

Charlotte then turned her attention to Alberta. The Anglican Advance Appeal, like the Richardson biography, was moved aside, to be fussed over another day.

11 **"Uncle Charlie" and "Babies for Export"**

I t began calmly and quietly enough, like so many of the major crises in Charlotte's life. An old friend, Daisy Marshall of Edmonton,
wrote to ask for Charlotte's advice. The Alberta chapter of the IODE
was considering a survey into welfare in the province and sought
someone to conduct it. The provincial government had carried out
its own study, the Henwood Commission of 1943, but there were
widespread rumblings that it was merely a whitewash of the ruling Social Credit Party's administration. What the IODE wanted was
an outsider's perspective, so they turned to Charlotte, recognized by
many as the foremost authority on welfare in Canada and a woman
with solid IODE credentials.

The time was March 1945, and Charlotte was in the midst of
writing her biography of James A. Richardson and considering running for Parliament. She would also soon be deeply involved in the
Anglican Advance Appeal. She simply did not have time for another
assignment, she advised Marshall. However, she did recommend several social welfare experts, especially her friend Laura Holland, and
further advised Marshall to talk directly to Premier Ernest Manning
in order to get his government's co-operation with the study team.

The conservatively minded women of the IODE were not looking for a fight with their provincial government. They merely sought
to learn the true picture of public welfare in the province, and if
there were shortcomings, they were prepared to support improvements through their own fundraising.

Like other IODE chapters, the Alberta branch was better known
for its quiet, behind-the-scenes charitable activities and its socials,
where women in flower-bedecked hats and long white gloves gathered to sip tea and enjoy polite conversation. Radical it was not.

(Begun in 1900 in Montreal as a patriotic organization of women, the Order shortened its name to just IODE in the 1970s; it continues to promote social service, citizenship, and patriotism. In 1924, Charlotte was honoured with a lifetime membership due to her efforts on its behalf, and in 1930, she set up the Elizabeth Tudor Chapter in Ottawa for working women like herself and which she named after her life-long role model, Elizabeth I.)

Unfortunately for the IODE, Laura Holland, then a special adviser on social welfare to the government of British Columbia, was not available. Fortunately for the IODE, Charlotte became available. She agreed to the assignment in October 1945, but only if she could start in May of the following year, giving her time to complete the expected Richardson biography and to begin work on the Anglican fundraising project. No problem, Marshall replied. In the meantime, Marshall spoke to Premier Manning and received assurances of government co-operation.

With her usual thoroughness, Charlotte began planning her survey in the summer of 1946, arranging for nine other welfare experts from outside the province to join her; field work would begin in January 1947. Each of the experts would look at a particular area of the province's welfare administration and would submit individual reports to Charlotte, who would oversee the final report to the IODE. Among the areas studied were child care and protection, care of the aged, the chronically ill and the infirm, Catholic charities, juvenile delinquency, public welfare, and Mormon welfare services.

Everything seemed in order during the fall of 1946 as Charlotte was making final preparations for the field work, but then a letter arrived in November from the provincial health and welfare minister, Dr. Wallace Cross, informing the IODE that his department would not co-operate with Charlotte, nor her people. His department had heard enough from the Henwood Commission three years earlier, so if she wanted more information, she would have to collect it herself. Furthermore, he warned his staff not to provide any information to Charlotte or her experts.

Cross's challenge merely invigorated Charlotte, who until then had been showing signs of exhaustion, as a result of problems with the Richardson biography and the Anglican fund-raising project. A showdown loomed.

Writing to Marshall, Charlotte complained: "I can hardly fathom that the Honourable Mr. Manning would have seen and subscribed to this letter. It is a letter that, in its concept and tone, is entirely Fascist and quite undemocratic. It is true neither in statute nor in fact, that public welfare and child welfare are solely the purview of the Government." They were the public's responsibility, she argued.

"We had never any intention of stirring up a revolution," Marshall responded, but nevertheless advised Charlotte to do what she had to do, assuring her of the IODE's full support.

Charlotte's group temporarily averted a confrontation with Cross and the provincial government by obtaining much of their information from social agencies, church and community groups, and municipal governments, as well as from the 118 IODE chapters in fifty Alberta communities. She also wrote to a host of welfare officials and friends in the United States, seeking their help in uncovering sinister cases of neglect concerning Alberta children who had been adopted and sent there. Undoubtedly sensing danger, Manning and Cross, as well as Alberta's child welfare superintendent, Charles Hill, agreed to meet with Charlotte and the IODE.

Little was accomplished. The government saw Charlotte as a pesky outsider butting into Alberta's affairs; Charlotte regarded the Social Credit government as social neanderthals.

Despite the roadblocks thrown in its way, the IODE-sponsored survey was completed in just four months, with the thoroughness and efficiency expected of Charlotte. It was a 200-page bombshell. Using explosive terms like "export of" and "trafficking in babies," it criticized practically every aspect of Alberta's welfare setup, but was especially outspoken over the foreign adoptions of Alberta orphans and the harsh conditions in which juvenile delinquents found themselves. It also reported that foster children were often placed in homes where they were forced to work for their keep. In general, the child welfare branch ignored accepted child-protection practices. The child welfare superintendent's powers were "without any parallel in any enactment in the study's knowledge except one in Hitler's Germany and certain provisions in the code of the Soviet Union."

The report was not made public at the time, but some of its most controversial findings were leaked. In fact, Charlotte herself spent much of April 1947 speaking about the report's findings to service clubs and IODE chapters throughout the province.

The situation received further notoriety in the following month when the *Calgary Herald* published a graphically illustrated series of fourteen articles entitled "Alberta Children in Iron Cages," with the subheadline, "Youngsters Penned Up Like Animals In 'Detention' Home at Edmonton." The newspaper reported that delinquent boys were held in damp, gloomy cells where the odour was "like the monkey house at the zoo," as well as many other shortcomings in the provincial welfare system. Much of the series was based on Charlotte's report, which had not yet been released officially. The province was in an uproar and the scandal made headlines across the nation.

The official release for Charlotte's report was set for July 24, but on July 23, the Manning government stole the IODE's thunder by announcing that a royal commission would be established to examine the welfare ministry's child welfare branch. This only served to whet the media's appetite, as illustrated by *Time* magazine, on August 4, 1947, when it reported that "chunky Charlotte Whitton . . . one of the best-known social workers in Canada . . . [had] issued a smashing summary . . . [that] found fault with almost every phase of the Alberta welfare system." The Canadian Press news service quoted an obviously rattled Cross as saying: "She is just a human talking machine. She is limited in what she says only by her own disregard for the truth. Nothing we can do can stop her from talking. All she has ever done is talk. She has never had any responsibility for child welfare administration."

Charlotte considered suing Cross for libel, but felt she had more important things to do. At any rate, it was Cross's subordinate, child welfare superintendent Charles B. Hill, whom she really went after.

"Uncle Charlie," as he was fondly referred to by many Albertans at the time, had been with Alberta's child welfare branch for some thirty years and was said to have placed more than 30,000 children in adoptive or foster homes. Like everyone else in the provincial welfare ministry at the time, he had had no technical training in social work. He more or less ran his office practically by the seat of his pants. Other provinces might have required extensive paperwork before allowing their children to be adopted, but not "Uncle Charlie."

For him, love was all that mattered. As he told *The Toronto Star* in December 1944: "Toss your scientific approach to baby adoption out the window. It's a lot of baloney . . . I feel that I'm right in believing that in the case of a healthy baby, all that matters is love . . . As for the foster-parents, I just look them over and decide if they're capable of really loving the child."

Also called "the baby man," his office was lined with photographs of "his" children, and each Christmas, the balding, chubby father figure would make the rounds of various Edmonton child-care institutions in a Santa Claus costume. He said he had never taken a holiday in thirty years, preferring instead to look after the children in his care.

Charlotte drew a different picture of "Uncle Charlie." In her report, entitled "Welfare in Alberta," she described numerous cases in which Hill not only had paid little attention to where the adopted children were going, but also that his office had done little to follow up their reception in their new homes. "In fact placements have been reported from Anchorage to Guatemala, from the nearby states of Montana and Washington to Porto [sic] Rico, with wealth rather than any other human consideration apparently the determining factor . . ." She also claimed that while American adoptive parents usually travelled to Alberta to choose their adoptees, some merely applied by letter and were accepted.

In August, the *Winnipeg Free Press* ran a seven-part series based on Charlotte's report, which it viewed as "a document of first rate national significance, which will be read throughout Canada by all those interested in the great problem of social welfare."

The Manning government maintained a discreet silence for the time being, leaving it up to its royal commission to get to the bottom of things. Heading the three-man commission was Alberta's chief justice, William Robinson Howson, assisted by Calgary judge J.W. Macdonald and Lethbridge judge E.B. Feir. Edmonton lawyer Bruce Smith was the province's chief counsel, while George Steer, another prominent Edmonton lawyer, represented Charlotte and the IODE.

Howson, a former leader of the Alberta Liberal Party, began his hearings on August 13 and almost immediately adjourned them until November 24.

In the meantime, Charlotte continued an on-again, off-again correspondence with Mrs. Richardson over Mr. Richardson's biography, was involved in a smaller squabble with the Anglican Advance Appeal over who should speak for women in the church — Mrs. Wodehouse's Women's Auxiliary or shared authority with Charlotte's working women's group — and agreed to organize a major fundraising campaign for Queen's University in the following year. She was contacted by *New Liberty* magazine writer Harold Dingman about an article he planned to write concerning her Alberta report. Furthermore, she had been slowed by a slipped disc in her back during the summer and was caused more personal worry when Margaret Grier took a turn for the worse in October and had to be rushed to hospital for an emergency abdominal operation.

It seemed like a repeat of the late 1930s again, as events spun out of Charlotte's control. A breakdown seemed imminent.

It only got worse. She had to cancel a scheduled fall speaking tour of Western Canada in order to testify at the royal commission, resulting in a substantial loss of earnings, and when the hearings resumed on November 24, as star witness, she became the target of government lawyer Smith's bitter cross-examination. The heated hearings also meant the loss of valued time away from an increasingly ailing Grier, as Charlotte shuttled back and forth across the country between Edmonton and Ottawa. When Dingman sent her a draft of his report for *New Liberty*, she glanced through it, made a few notations, and returned it to him without much thought.

Her mind was more on Grier than on Alberta, and she wrote Grier lengthy letters every night from her room in Macdonald Hotel. Smith "is inclined to be unpleasant," she said after her first day, during which she had testified for three hours. The following night, however, her mood was more relaxed: "The sunrises here are beautiful, especially from my room on the fifth floor looking out over the curving Saskatchewan [River] with the south side spread out and far beyond. All night the lights pierce and glimmer in the darkness. At dawn a faint lemon light breaks along the horizon and warms to gold, and then suddenly the sheer gold is suffused with rose and mauve which bank and break into the clearest blue . . . I can easily understand the Walkyrie and the longing of the Norse warriors to ride the crests of such beauty forever."

Margaret Grier and her cousin, John M. Jellett, undated.
Charlotte Whitton Collection, Library and Archives Canada, PA-127275

The lengthy letters to Grier continued, in part:

November 27: Dearest . . . my trial goes on and grows no more pleasant. The next time that some one wants to save a province it isn't going to be me; I guarantee that. Today they say the hearings will last three months . . . Rags.

November 28: Dear, dear Mardie . . . I believe that I am in for the worst experience of my existence and I do wish I could get your courage and strength but I do know that I am fighting evil, and in the end this must come right . . . I do not know how long it will go on but I do know that I am fed to the teeth . . . Charl.

November 29: Dear Mardie . . . O, but I want to go home and I want just to be home with you and Rustie and the fire going and a nice soft snow falling outside . . . Sharl.

November 30: Dear Mardie . . . This is awful here. I get nowhere but to the court and back here to work. I have had to refuse all invitations even if I did feel like them. And it gets worse. I guess I'll just make Ottawa for Christmas and nothing more . . . Love on love and Keep on Keeping on, Charl.

Grier may have lapsed into a coma then, for there was only one more letter to her, which in all likelihood she did not get the chance to read.

December 7: Dearest: This is a pink note to go with all your nice pink things; you are always so charming in bed — of course you are anywhere — but with your pale pinks and greens, you are especially so. All you need to give the picture of perfect tranquility is "Rustie."

Today, I had hoped to be with you, but I guess it was all right not to go as all the planes are grounded in the East and I would have been caught . . . I guess the snowflakes are beginning to fall softly now in the way I always like to think of Grandma Whitton telling us as Mother Goose plucked them off the geese we had seen flying south as the leaves turned.

I did not get down to Calgary so I shall not have seen Agnes [MacLeod] nor will she bring you word of me but I shall hope to follow east so closely upon her that it will not make much difference. And it will take the Mounted Police to get me away from you again. I know they are all good to you, but you need me — and how I need you. I went to early Eucharist and prayed for some of the strength being given to me going to you. My love to you, Sharlie.

Margaret Grier, fifty-five, died two days later, on the morning of Tuesday, December 9, 1947, in Ottawa's Civic Hospital. The cause of death was abdominal cancer.

Charlotte was shattered.

Charlotte, the audacious tomboy from Renfrew, the domineering student leader at Queen's University, the autocratic crusader at the Canadian Welfare Council, was overcome with grief. Margaret, her most intimate companion for more than a quarter-century, was dead. Margaret, who had stood by her through thick and through thin, who had always been there when she needed a sympathetic ear or a neat, tidy home, was gone. Gone, too, were the wonderful times with Margaret, the travels to Europe, the restful holidays at McGregor Lake, the warm conversations by the cozy fireside at the apartment. Grier was much more than just a flatmate for Charlotte. Their lives had been intertwined from the day in 1918 when Charlotte moved into Kappa House in Toronto. They had shared an apartment on Toronto's Admiral Avenue, moved to Ottawa together in 1922, and since enjoyed a long, happy cohabitation at 236C Rideau Terrace.

Margaret, as Charlotte's sister Kay would write later, was the only person who succeeded in telling Charlotte to shut up. Although Grier had a mind of her own, her personality was greatly overshadowed by her more extroverted companion. She also had had a career of her own. During the 1930s, she was active with the St. John's Ambulance Association, then in 1941, she was hired as an executive assistant in Department of Labour with special responsibility for dealing with wartime nurseries. At the time of her death, she was assigned to the reception of working women emigrants from Europe. Away from work, she was a member of the Elizabeth Tudor chapter of the IODE, a former president of the Ottawa branch of the Canadian Women's Press Club, and, with Charlotte, a regular member of St. Alban's the Martyr Anglican church in Ottawa. In the same vein, she had close family connections to the Anglican church. Her aunt, Mother Hannah Grier Coome, was the founder of the Canadian order of the Sisterhood of St. John the Divine, and her surviving sister, Reverend Mother Dora, was the order's second superior. She was related through a cousin's marriage to the Anglican Primate of Canada, the Most Rev. Trevor Owen.

In her will, she left her entire estate to Charlotte, which amounted to a bank balance of $10,828.17.

Just days before Grier died, Grace Towers visited Grier in hospital and informed Charlotte later that one of her friend's last utterances was: "Comfort my Charlotte, Grace; she'll need it, oh, how she'll need it."

Indeed, more bad news was in the offing for Charlotte, but first there was the question of Grier's funeral and burial, as well as the ongoing royal commission to contend with. The latter compassionately agreed to Charlotte's lawyer's request to postpone her further cross-examination, for, as George Steer argued, "She feels a moral obligation to this friend to go East and look after her burial; apparently there is no one else to whom she can appeal to do it."

Temporarily excused, Charlotte headed home to arrange Grier's funeral and entombment in a vault until her remains could be buried in the spring. Charlotte had chosen a gravesite in Renfrew's Thompsonville Cemetery, immediately adjacent to a site Charlotte had chosen for her own grave.

Undoubtedly Charlotte was looking forward to a period of peace and quiet, of solace from friends and heartfelt sympathies from acquaintances, a chance to rest up for her return to Edmonton and a further grilling from the province's counsel. It was not to be.

On December 15, 1947, less than a week after Grier's death, some 200,000 copies of the December 27 issue of *New Liberty* magazine arrived on Canadian newsstands, including 18,000 in Alberta, emblazoned with the dramatic headline: "Babies for Export, Alberta's Tragic Traffic in Babies." Citing some of the most controversial details from Charlotte's report, writer Harold Dingman's article began: "One of the blackest and ugliest chapters in the development of modern governments has been written against the province of Alberta. It is the unparalleled story of a government trafficking in illegitimate babies, exporting them to foreign homes; and the further story of unjustifiably harsh and delinquent care of Alberta's very young and very old. At these extremes of life bureaucracy and tyranny rules. It is a humiliating story, one that has defamed a proud and resourceful people."

Illustrating the story were five grisly drawings, including one showing a large, blood-red hand with what appeared to be talons reaching towards a small, thin woman with a baby, and another showing a child being handed to an obese woman while in the background a man slouched over a table, a glass at hand and seemingly drunk.

The Manning government reacted immediately. On December 16, it called on Dingman and the Toronto-based publisher of *New*

Liberty, Jack Kent Cooke, to appear before it to answer to a complaint of contempt. Forewarned that the RCMP were set to escort them to Edmonton if they did not go on their own accord, both men fled across the border to New York State and out of the Mounties' reach. On January 5, the two were charged with two counts each of contempt of the commission and libel against Charles Hill. Cooke also was charged with advising an Edmonton newsdealer to ignore the provincial government's demand that all Alberta newsdealers suspend sales of the December 27 issue of the magazine.

Returning to Edmonton early in the new year, Charlotte was once again on the stand, defending her reputation against the verbal onslaught of Crown counsel Smith. In the meantime, she had begun a diary-type scrapbook of letters to the late Margaret Grier, addressing Grier nightly as if she were still alive and they were having a chat across the kitchen table. The letters, which eventually filled two large notebooks and which Charlotte entitled *Molly Mugwump Makes Believe*, reflected an aching sense of loss and a stabbing sense of guilt for having taken her closest friend for granted through all their years together.[3] Inevitably, they also reflected Charlotte's mental state as the royal commission continued.

The following are brief excerpts from the first few letters:

December 31, 1947: Dearest: This will be the first of the New — and Empty — Years in which I shall go on alone. It is late New Year's Eve and I am on the train to Edmonton — but your spirit would know that you have been so close and yet so indefinably unattainable ever since you went. We have lived so in each other's lives and thoughts, all these years . . . We must just go on being with each other. Because I cannot see you in the withdrawn way where your spirit soars free is surely no reason why we can't still go on: it will be easier for me more quickly to find the path if you stay close and I try to keep you close. But I must not burden you here as I have this thirty years with my selfish woes and needs . . .

---

3   Charlotte later arranged with the national archives to keep these scrapbooks private for long after her death. They were not made available to the public until 1999.

Oh! Mardie, Mardie, how can I go on? Ours wasn't love; it was a knitting together of mind and spirit; it was something given to few of God: there wasn't anything silly or weak or slavering: it was just that our minds and spirits marched so together that we were the same in two different bodies. And here in the body sent, mine stays, numb and bewildered while yours soars far away. You will keep me close though, won't you . . .

Why should I not write you always as I did? So I am writing you here as I have reached Edmonton for the next stage in this disgraceful travesty that has so ruined this year and kept me from you . . .

Here the dreadful work of the commission opened, a dessicated, ailing, bitter, prejudiced, politically appointed Chief Justice presiding with no experience in Commission work, no knowledge of our field . . the whole procedure viciously and vindictely [sic] directed to me . . .

January 4, 1948 (Edmonton): Mardie, it's awful out here. I hate this city anyway . . . I have been here since Friday and not one of my so-called friends has called. I spent yesterday and this morning with Mr. Steer who for some reason is being particularly short and nasty with me. I went to Early Service and the Dean didn't bother speaking though I know him well. The company I should have had I did not get . . .

There is no soul mate now, Mardie, whom to pour out everything just as it came and know that I would always be understood, always right no matter what the world thought. I can't go on without you and to think with this horrible province and this rotten case that all this year that was to be your last I was away more than in any of our years together, more meshed and inconsiderate and selfish and withheld from you . . . And Mardie, it's not worth it: its' [sic] not worth one soft thread of that silky baby fine hair of yours that was so fine even when white. They are acting like demons: ignorant people with power. Its' [sic] so like Fascist Italy or Nazi Germany that it scares me . . .

January 5: Mardie dear, Once again, just you and I together alone tonight . . . [the commission] is stirring all Canada now and directing attention to how irregular and fantastic as much of government has become here . . . Now I only want to finish this, get my affairs and yours in order, and couldn't care how soon I join you. Home Oil [in which she had an investment] is sky-rocketing — $6.50 today and a 25¢ dividend. And I don't care at all.

January 8: Dear Mardie, Again another day: again the empty mail box in the hotel where nearly always there was the letter from you . . .

January 10: . . . My work is done and in all being there are only you and I together again. I cannot tell you how some peace or rest or sense of safety has come to me yesterday and today. Was it that you really were there yesterday, so close. I could almost feel you brush my untidy hair back off my forehead as you would do when you passed me working at my desk at night as you would say good night and go down to your room . . .

January 11: . . . I want so to get there [the Ottawa apartment] myself, to den up, like the beaten heartsick pup, I am, and there lie, wherever my mistress has lain and so have something of rest and peace again. You always called me "Rags" and said I was a natural little puppy. I am all instinct my sense of loss and longing . . . [anxious to leave] this horrid, hollow, materialistic, young and indifferent province . . .

January 12: This has been a good day though . . . this morning I was jittery . . . The day's horoscope in the paper told me not to relax . . . Then as my cross-exam began, I grabbed your baby ring under my Queen's ring and I said "Oh! Mardie, you are always with me. Now, come, my unseen guardian from the unknown land, parry their strokes." And I put a small "M" on my pad and every question I looked at it, and I would keep hanging on to your ring. And, Mardie, I never lost my head, in fact, I got too impertinent I think . . .

January 14: I have to go [on] with this [case] but then I think I shall drop all this sort of thing and try to write quietly and live quietly. What does it matter? We are speeding along to the crash of our civilization. The U.S.A. today has released a memorandum anticipating an atomic and bacteriological war by 1953 and Canada lying directly between the United States and the U.S.S.R . . .

January 15: Everywhere there are alarums. Britain, weary, is moving out of Palestine for March 1. Gandhi is again starving himself to save a warring India. Darling you sleep well. Come close and walk beside me and get me back home to where your spirit dwells. Love on love, do wrap me in yours, Sharl.

January 20: This inexpressibly lousy province and this inexpressibly lousy Bruce Smith, their counsel, who was ashamed to do it directly, have "conspired" together to issue a summons to me to appear along with Harold Dingman and Jack Cooke in this libel action . . .

Indeed, the province had subpoenaed Charlotte and several others, including *New Liberty* staff and IODE members, to testify at the trial which was to begin April 5. By this time, Dingman and Cooke had returned to Canada and agreed to travel to Edmonton to face the charges. Supported by media across the country and defended by leading Toronto lawyer Joseph Sedgwick, their defence was based partly on freedom of the press. Sedgwick argued that the trial should have been held in Ontario, where *New Liberty* was published, rather than in Alberta.

Supporting them in the House of Commons was a tall, lanky Conservative backbencher from Saskatchewan, John Diefenbaker. Referring to "'the proceedings now under way in Alberta," Diefenbaker thundered on January 29, "Without freedom of the press, there can be no parliamentary institutions. There can be no freedom of the press under autocracy, nor can there be autocracy so long as there is freedom of the press."

Just two days earlier, the province changed the charges against Dingman and Cooke and included Charlotte in the mix. All three were then charged with conspiracy to publish a defamatory libel, and Cooke faced the additional charge of inciting to publish a defamatory libel, due to his telegram to an Edmonton newsdealer advising him to sell the magazine despite the province's ban. Charlotte's alleged offence was that she had seen Dingman's article in advance and had given her approval, as shown by the handwritten notes she had added to the draft manuscript while on the train in late November.

She returned to Ottawa at the end of January to work on the Anglican Advance Appeal and to terminate the Richardson biography contract, but on March 24 the Mounties came calling. As the *Edmonton Bulletin* reported that day, Sgt. S. Glencross of the RCMP knocked on her apartment door three times that morning, each time unsuccessfully trying to serve her with papers to appear in court. The first time, she "received him hospitably . . . and was more than willing to discuss anything but service of notice. He hesitated to force the document on her, and left in full retreat, to return within an hour for a second attempt." Alas, she was at church, so when he returned the third time and she refused the notice again, he tucked it under her door. "Carefully stepping over it, like a door-mat, when she leaves or enters her home, Dr. Whitton hasn't so much as glanced at the document, and doesn't know exactly what it sets out."

Meanwhile, she was preoccupied with Grier's affairs, which included making arrangements with the Sisters of St. John the Divine to embroider church vestments for St. Alban's Church in Grier's honour. In her nightly musings in *Mugwump*, however, she confided that she was ready to go to jail over her Alberta report, even though "this horrible province is going to kill me . . . I know I am right. I know that children are suffering and as I wrote the Rev. Mother [Grier's sister] today, I have to remember it was centuries after her ashes floated down the Seine that Joan of Arc was canonized."

Nevertheless, she showed up in Edmonton with her co-accused for the trial start on April 5. Local newspapers ran front-page photographs of a smiling, confident group of defendants. Charlotte was fashionably dressed in a Persian lamb coat and black suit, heavy silver locket and an IODE pin, all topped off by a black hat that featured a long, grey feather, "one that waved and bobbed with every nod of the head." Dingman and Cooke were attired in fashionable business suits. The courtroom was packed. As Charlotte would relate later in *Mugwump*, "scroungy Abe Miller and contemptible Jimmie Frawley," the welfare deputy minister and the lawyer for the attorney general respectively, were sitting at the prosecutor's table. There was also "a drab array of malefactors" who had been chosen for possible jury duty on other cases before the court.

Judge J. Boyd McBride called the court to order. The charges were read and, after some legal bickering among the lawyers, counsel for the province announced that it was not ready to proceed with the charges. McBride looked down sternly on Charlotte and her two co-accused and dismissed all but one of the charges.

The remaining charge was against Cooke for incitement. It, too, was dismissed a few days later.

"We did not know what it meant as everyone crowded around us. It was so sudden. So ignominious, the court adjourned. Everyone celebrated," she wrote in *Mugwump*. "It has been a terrific week, my dear."

12  A Woman on the Line

"**D**r. Whitton," for the moment, was the toast of the nation, the embattled little welfare worker who had thumbed her nose at the big, bad, backward government of Alberta and had come out a winner. At the same time, Cooke was the darling of the Canadian media for standing strong for press freedom.

Congratulatory messages from all parts of the country overflowed Charlotte's mailbox and one of the most effusive responses came in May, after Charlotte spoke to a women's group in London, Ontario. F. Beatrice Taylor of the *Free Press* gushed over "Canada's Joan of Arc doing staunch battle in the cause of freedom . . . has emerged from the fiery ordeal of a conspiracy charge wearing, not only her discharge, but her wonted high courage and devastating wit . . . London women, proud of this brilliant and indomitable member of their sex . . . rediscovered a little woman with tiny feet in Cinderella slippers, an enormous mind, an illumined rhetoric, which is at the same time practical and factual, an Irish roll in her voice and a lance permanently tilted in a good cause . . . What every woman knows about 'Lottie' Whitton is that she will not fail them."

Meanwhile, the royal commission hearings continued, although the courtroom no longer was packed and the media coverage had moved off the front pages. Howson, the chairman, was temporarily hospitalized due to a heart condition, causing a further adjournment, but when the hearings reopened, the commission heard from "Uncle Charlie" Hill, the province's child welfare superintendent.

Roman Catholic, married, and with children of his own, Hill disputed many of the statements in Charlotte's report. He testified that, just prior to the meeting between Charlotte, Cross, and himself at the outset of her survey, an unnamed friend had told him about overhearing Charlotte tell her IODE friends in an Edmonton hotel that she "wanted to get all the publicity they could and they wanted to get Mr. Hill." He conceded that there might have been some shortcomings in his adoption system, but suggested adoption was like marriage: "If we were blessed with foresight we might do some things differently."

On June 26, 1948, the royal commission quietly concluded its hearings; its report would be released in December.

As for the Richardson biography, Charlotte and Mrs. Richardson reached an amicable agreement at about the same time; Richardson would get the final manuscript and all of Charlotte's drafts, and Charlotte would be paid for her work. The manuscript would be assigned, unpublished, to the Richardson company vault in Winnipeg.

The six months leading up to the release of the report gave Charlotte time to regroup. She resumed her speaking career, criss-crossing the country addressing service, social, and church groups in an effort to raise funds for both the Anglican Advance Appeal and an addition to the women's residence at Queen's University. The AAA was doing well, she learned, having received $3.4 million in pledges by May 1948, but the Queen's project, for which she was being paid as a consultant, was less satisfactory; she concluded her involvement with it in early December due to what she considered interference from the university's board of governors. She was pleased to accept another honorary doctorate, her third, from an old intellectual soulmate from her Queen's days, Watson Kirkconnell, the newly installed president of Acadia University in Wolfville, Nova Scotia. She also gave fleeting thought to running as a Conservative candidate in the following federal election.

However, as she recorded in *Mugwump*, her personal life was in its usual state of disarray. A friend from college days, Agnes MacLeod, had moved into her apartment earlier in the year then abruptly moved out, only to be replaced by another friend named Margaret, who had to be delivered to a distant Ontario nursing home after she threatened suicide "hourly." This happened in October, the same month Charlotte escaped serious injury when she crashed her car on a curve while speeding between speaking engagements along a highway in central Ontario. Then, just after Christmas, her brother

WOMAN ON THE LINE

J.B. informed her that their brother Stephen, whom she knew had been drinking heavily, had only about two more years to live due to neurological problems.

There also was an acrimonious, long-running dispute over the vestments she had ordered from the Anglican nuns in memory of Grier.

In the early days after Grier's death, Charlotte had arranged with the Sisters of St. John the Divine to make "the most perfect and exquisite piece of work which The Sisterhood has ever made," an amice, a stole, and a chasuble with a Tudor rose woven onto it for the priest at St. Alban's. It was to be ready for a special All Hallows' Eve service the following October. Within weeks, however, the nuns informed her that they were too busy with previous orders, so had referred her to Beatrice Smith of Toronto. Smith, a homemaker, had been happy to take on the work in January, but by March informed Charlotte that there were complications. The special material Charlotte sought would have to be imported from the United States at an estimated cost of $175, but Canada's customs rules at the time limited imported goods to only $10 per person. It was to be the first of numerous unpleasantries between Charlotte and Smith.

Charlotte was not amused, and threatened to sue the seamstress. The All Hallows' Eve deadline approached and it was becoming obvious that the vestment would not be available on time.

Charlotte was livid. Some 240 invitations had gone out, various organizations had changed the dates of their meetings so their members could attend, a special radio hookup had been arranged so that Grier's ailing sister, Sister Dora, could listen in from the Toronto area, and more than twenty out-of-town friends were expected at the service. "This is now all a tragic fiasco, a disgraceful and regrettable association forever with the name of Margaret Grier, the worst is that I shall have to put notices in the papers and on the radio to advise those who have heard the announcement at their meetings," Charlotte wrote to Smith on October 13.

Disagreements between the two women continued, and letters were exchanged every few days during the rest of 1948 and less frequently during 1949, as even the Sisters of St. John failed to mediate the issue. Charges and countercharges and threats of lawsuits hurtled between the two women with increasing venom. Their relationship deteriorated to the point where they did not even trust each other enough to turn over to a neutral banker the embroidery material on the one hand and the payment on the other without having one of the Sisters oversee the exchange.

Finally, in May 1949, as she was preparing for a holiday in Europe with her friend Laura Holland, Charlotte received a note from the woman hired to replace Smith, May Ricciardelli, indicating that she had taken over the assignment and hoped to have the vestments ready by the following Easter, more than two years after the purchase was first agreed upon. She met the new deadline, but unfortunately for Charlotte, St. Alban's no longer needed the vestments. Similarly, Trinity College in Toronto, where Grier had studied, rejected Charlotte's offer of the vestments, informing her that vestments were never worn in the college chapel. However, in March 1951, three years after the whole affair began, Trinity College accepted "this magnificent gift."

On December 30, 1948, the Alberta Royal Commission on Child Welfare released its report, bringing both good and bad tidings for Charlotte. It agreed with many of the recommendations in her IODE report, but it condemned her penchant for overstatement and for fudging some of her facts. It praised Charles Hill as an experienced, able administrator with an "almost fanatical devotion" to his job, but found that he had taken on too much and needed help with his administrative duties. Among its thirty-odd recommendations, it called for an end to adoptions from outside the province and for the hiring of trained welfare workers for the welfare department, as Charlotte had recommended. It also agreed with Charlotte that the department should co-operate with private, non-profit groups, and that it should decentralize its services. As for some of the charges in her report or in Dingman's article, it complained, "There was not a shred of evidence to indicate that any Alberta child had been involved in a 'black market' in babies, nor that the minister of public welfare or any of his officials had any information to that effect." Further, it suggested that "if the language of the [IODE] Report had been used more scrupulously towards the avoidance of over-statement and had been more specific with regard to instances which were intended to illustrate principles, the matter complained of could have been much more easily dealt with."

For Charlotte, the commission's criticisms were like water off a duck's back, or a snowfall in August. After the trepidation caused by the criminal charges in April and the exhilaration at their dismissal, the royal commission's findings were anticlimactic.

Meanwhile, welfare minister Cross informed the legislature that the government would implement the commission's proposed reforms only if they felt they were warranted; thus far, nothing was deemed warranted. In the end, the Alberta branch of the IODE no longer involved itself in controversial issues, Charles Hill received $5,000 from his libel suit against the *Calgary Herald*, and the provincial government waited a full decade before hiring its first fully trained professional social worker.

Overall, the IODE and the royal commission reports had almost no effect on the Alberta government. Charles Hill remained superintendent of child welfare until his retirement in 1956, Dr. Cross continued as Alberta welfare minister until he retired in 1959, and Ernest Manning stayed on as premier until he retired in 1968, at which time he was appointed to the Senate by Prime Minister Pierre Elliott Trudeau. In 1961, the Navy League Cadet Corps in Edmonton was named after "Uncle Charlie," who died in 1972. Dr. Cross, who died the following year, had the Cross Cancer Institute in the Alberta capital named in his honour.

For Charlotte, 1949 was a fairly restful year, another "time-out" in her frantic career, a time for new challenges, and a time to rub salt in some old wounds. In January, she began yet another round of talks across Canada on a myriad of subjects, and she concluded her involvement with the Anglican Advance Appeal, but not without stressing once again how the male church hierarchy was overlooking the potential of its female parishioners. She also showed her displeasure with Queen's University's board of governors by erasing the university from her list of beneficiaries. In a letter to the acting director of the school's endowment committee, she blamed the governors for the under-performing fundraising campaign, suggesting that what was needed was something like an electric shock to get their "car"started, but they "do not want ignition; they do not want explosions; they do not want high gear; they would rather run a wheel-barrow they can rundle [*sic*] than a high-powered machine that they cannot control and run around a playground or two they know instead of driving the dynamic organism that is Queen's across the national consciousness of this country." Charlotte, of course, would have been the sparkplug to fire their engine, if only they had given her the chance.

Her speaking engagements between January and March 1949 included stops in North Bay, Sudbury, Port Arthur and Fort William (now Thunder Bay) in Ontario; Winnipeg, Manitoba; Biggar, Saskatoon, Prince Albert, North Battleford, Moose Jaw and Regina, Saskatchewan; Calgary and Medicine Hat, Alberta; and Vancouver, Victoria, Chilliwack, Nanaimo, Port Alberni, Kamloops, Vernon, Kelowna, Penticton, Trail, and Rossland in British Columbia. She spoke to Women's Canadian Clubs in the larger centres, which sponsored her visits, while she spoke to business and professional women's groups, IODE chapters, and even school councils and afternoon teas in the smaller centres.

Nor had she forgotten Margaret Grier. Although the entries in *Molly Mugwump* were becoming less frequent, she continued to describe her activities and her sorrow at Grier's absence.

> **March 27**: Dearest . . . I can actually feel the wafting of your presence by. I get the fragrance of the "Blue Grass" or "Apple Blossom" that you so loved and your gentle fingers just "tip" me, touch perhaps my throbbing temples or tickle my neck, as you would . . . [I dreamed the other night] we both were . . . lying together in my bed, joshing as we often did when we had "breakfast in bed" on Sunday . . . I dream of those happy weekends when Stella [a friend] would come down and Annie [their housekeeper] give you both "bed breakfasts" and I'd flit about from one to the other with my coffee when I had come in from Church . . . Mardie, I am going to work. I am going to write. I'm going to do the best things yet done in Canadian writing. You just see that I do and they'll be "in memory of Margaret."

> **April 3**: Dearest, Do you remember the sheer joy we had together as I introduced you to modern Irish poetry, to

Yeats and Synge and the Irish singers? . . . Thursday night
I had dinner with Johnny Diefenbaker and nice Stuart
Garson joined us — you know the Minister of Justice who
was premier of Manitoba and who I disliked.

There were a few more entries in early April, and on April 23,
while visiting a friend's farm in southern Ontario, she once more
poured out her heart. She was "tired and broken" at Easter and
"choked and cried most of Holy Week," and could not go through
with her planned day-long visit to Grier's grave on Good Friday despite her best intentions. The one bright spot in her life at the moment, she noted, was that the Home Oil Company had made $1.5
million in the previous financial quarter and was paying a quarterly
dividend of 25 cents.

The next entry came three weeks later and described how she had
attended a wedding and a funeral and how much she had missed
Grier on both occasions. She also wrote that in her new will, she
had removed Queen's University from her list of beneficiaries and
replaced it with the Grier-Whitton Foundation at Acadia University,
a program offering bursaries limited to Anglican female students.

In the fall, she was off to Europe for a four-month vacation with
Laura Holland. To pay for the holiday, she wrote a twice-weekly column in the *Ottawa Citizen*, describing everything from the discom-
fort of flying to the thrill of revisiting her ancestral Yorkshire village,
from the ancient history of Norway to attending a war-crimes trial
in Germany. The writing in her "Offshore" series ranged from the
lyrical and the whimsical to the vapid and the banal — occasionally
it seemed that she was merely regurgitating local travel brochures. It
was not her finest writing, but then she was penning her thoughts
as she and Holland scurried across Britain and the Continent at a
time when international travel for the masses was just getting off the
ground. The writing also reflected Charlotte's great love of all things
English, her shock at finding the first vestiges of multiculturalism in
London, her distress at the advance of socialism, and her pity for the
residents of the war-torn cities of both England and Germany.

While travelling in northern England, she warned *Citizen* readers
"that a social revolution of incredible extent has been long in course
in these Islands and is now moving inexorably to its predestined

climax. It has not been violent, but it has been, and is, no less grim . . . In all this, the real power appears to have slipped from the old, solid strata . . ." Frustrated when she was informed there were no vacancies at the Maid's Head Inn in her ancestral Yorkshire Dales, she complained that "the old inns are passing in this strange, different England and the hotel staff can be as curt and casual as any in Toronto in Exhibition week or in Detroit or Chicago, all year round."

In Strasbourg, France, she and Holland attended meetings of the assembly of the future European Union. She observed: "This Assembly of the United States of Europe presages either the birth of a political entity–the 'USE'–which, will, (and at no very indefinite future date), prove as potent a force as the USA; or, it will mark the last and defeated effort of the old world to arrest the deterioration and decay of the rich civilization of Europe and the West."

In Frankfurt, Germany, "sheer misery" was everywhere, and to illustrate food shortages, she wrote of trading two of her dry biscuits for one sweet biscuit with a French occupation soldier during a train trip; it was the only thing she had to eat that day between breakfast and supper. In Hamburg, formerly the third busiest port in the world after London and New York, "A strange sense of unreality lays hold of one. The slow patient silence of these people contrasts, strangely, terribly, with memories of the efficient, industrious, purposeful and perfectly organized Germany of those years before Hitler, those later Twenties, when the bands played in Munich and the sun shone on the ancient mellowed roofs of Rothemburg-am-Tauger. If any man still doubts that modern warfare is insane barbarism, a few hours of Hamburg should suffice to sicken and sorrow him with awfulness of scientific conflict."

There was also a food shortage in Norway, but in Denmark there were meals consisting of "soups in plates the size of bathtubs, the terrific Danish *smorre brod* — bread, cheese, sausage, egg, salad, cold meat, fish, what-have-you, followed by a 'hot' dish of meat equal to a two weeks' ration in Britain, potatoes, etc., etc., and then an ice with fruit, cream and meringue." In Sweden, a good meal included "the multiple smorgasbord or series of *hors d'oeuvre* [sic], each a cold meal in itself; then the *'varmratt',* a lavish hot course, probably followed by nothing but cheese, but also by the world's most excellently satisfying coffee."

She had gained sixteen pounds, she confessed to her *Citizen* readers in early October, as she had eaten heartily throughout much of her trip. It had been a depressing journey, nonetheless, and nowhere was it more depressing than in England, where economic conditions "are wearing down a people already 'stretched' to exhaustion by the war's long struggle."

Happily back home in Ottawa in mid-October, after a trans-Atlantic flight and a train trip from Montreal, she enthused about once more seeing "the autumn woods . . . in madder riot for, all along the way, the crimson sumachs lighted the carnival with flaming torches, while wild fowl wheeled and settled and rose again in migrating flights. The pulp piles of Hull obtruded and then we came upon the magnificence of the Ottawa, flowing from the horizon to the horizon as we crossed the Alexandra Bridge [from Hull to Ottawa], and the Canal locks carried the eye upward to Nepean Heights. Surely there is no capital in the world whose buildings crown a more majestic cliff nor whose towers thrust upward from greater beauty than these glowing maples and golden birch climbing from the timber-dotted waters to these grey stone piles."

The "Offshore" series must have been well received, for the *Citizen* paid her to continue her column for another two months, during which time she delved into English history more deeply. Eventually, on December 24, she wrote her final "Offshore" column, entitled, "And So, Goodbye For Now." It concluded: "And now I am home, in my own Ottawa Valley; and it is Christmas Eve of 1949, the last Christmas of this century's tragic first fifty years. The moon shines down on silvered roofs and trees and roads and, in the stillness of the night, the bells below the hill are ringing, their echoes mounting clearly: 'Peace on Earth and mercy mild.'"

Peace would come to Charlotte in 1950, but only for so long. She had arranged to write a six-day-a-week column for Thomson Dailies, beginning on January 2, as well as a separate thrice-weekly column for the *Citizen* beginning on January 3. Because that did not occupy enough of her time, she began, simultaneously, a third column in March for the Halifax *Chronicle-Herald*. Each of the columns was different, although occasionally the themes would overlap.

The weekly *Chronicle-Herald* articles generally concerned welfare topics, the Thomson columns, entitled "A Woman On The Line," dealt with subjects mainly of concern to women, while the *Citizen* column, entitled "On Thinking It Over," was a potpourri of politics, philosophy, local affairs, and personal reminiscences. It was a prodigious output and one that would have scared off most writers, but Charlotte handled it with relative ease. She had enough time that, in April, she took on another IODE venture in addition to the columns.

The Thomson columns were primarily for women about women, but the range was so broad that only a few topics received regular attention. These included women's suffrage, the role of working women, health issues and the importance of and the shortage of nursing, the importance of good teachers, the lack of affordable housing, the neglect of the aged, and the need for better child care. She also dealt on occasion with national politics, international affairs, and society's growing preoccupation with alcohol and sex.

Fortunately, she leavened her pessimistic opinions with personal anecdotes, such as the time as a child she was chased by a goat she foolishly challenged in an open pasture, or the fact that although her two abstemious grandmothers — English on her father's side, Irish on her mother's — could not stand each other, they could temper their mutual dislike over a wee sip — English port for one and Irish gin for the other — when they were forced together at funerals and such.

Similarly, her *Citizen* columns covered a broad range of topics, but perhaps the most notable feature of all the columns was Charlotte's concern that the world in general was in dire straits since the Korean War had begun, the Liberals were in power in Ottawa, and the capital's municipal politicians were utterly incapable of properly running the city. It was in the *Citizen*, too, that she wrote her eighteen-part series on the dangers of communism. She could be dogmatic on Tuesday and belligerent on Thursday, but her longer Saturday columns generally tended to reminiscences of Renfrew, life at McGregor Lake, or the "fact" that cats do laugh.

"I aver that cats do laugh," she wrote on August 5, "not frequently but with the same quiet dignity which characterizes most, if not some of the most important, things they do. My cats, Christopher Columbus and Rustie, both laughed on occasion; I have snapshots which prove it . . ."

Life indeed was pleasant for Charlotte in 1950, for the newspaper columns provided financial security, her voice was still heard when it came to welfare matters, and she found sufficient time to travel about the country on speaking engagements, or to pass a relaxed summer at McGregor Lake. For once, the pressure was off.

That changed in late October, however, when an editorial in the *Ottawa Journal* challenged her to run for civic office. Never one to avoid a challenge, she not only ran for a seat on the board of control, but received the most votes of any of the dozens of candidates seeking seats on the new council. She was about to begin the most exciting time of her life.

PART FOUR

Politician

13 The Lady Controller Fights Back

Thirty-two men and one woman sat down at the council table on January 2, 1951, as Mayor Grenville Goodwin greeted his fellow councillors in his inaugural address. In his typical bland style, he remarked that some former councillors were no longer at the table, either due to retirement or defeat at the polls the previous month, while others had been elected to replace them. The city's future looked promising.

As for the newcomers:

First and foremost among these, we greet Dr. Charlotte Whitton, one of the foremost authorities on social problems in all Canada and whose great and recognized talents should be of exceptional value to this Council in dealing with all such matters . . . We greet her warmly as a talented colleague but also as an outstanding woman. And, in doing so, we would like Dr. Whitton and all the women of Ottawa to know that we are happy that the wholly masculine nature of this Council has at last come to an end. Dr. Whitton's presence among us is a real indication of the awakening interest in civic affairs by the women of Ottawa and I am sure her election is a tribute to the good judgment and soundness of the electors as well as to Dr. Whitton herself.

After dealing with a few formalities, the thirty-two men and Charlotte rose from their desks, each of which had been decorated with a rose provided by Charlotte's election campaign committee, and joined the packed audience as they adjourned to the Coliseum

Grenville Goodwin,
Mayor of Ottawa, 1951.

building at Lansdowne Park for the traditional post-inaugural reception. For Charlotte, it was a case of "so far, so good."

It had been an exciting election campaign followed by a resounding victory on December 4, in which she had topped the seven-candidate poll for the four controller positions. *The Ottawa Journal,* which had challenged her to run back in October, concluded:

> Miss Whitton made the perfect candidate . . . She spoke
> admirably, whether in person or on the radio, and there
> was meat in her speeches, there were quotable bits, there
> were humor and philosophy, there were ideas, there
> was evidence of study, of experience, of a splendid grasp
> of public questions, or a keen and enquiring mind . . .
> Controller Whitton, so abounding in energy, so resourceful
> in ideas, now has to prove that she can co-operate
> with men in a common task of government, that she
> has a practical and realistic mind. She has a wonderful
> opportunity, and 38,405 people [her vote total] are
> cheering for her."

Also complimentary was her church rector, Rev. Lionel Bruce of St. Alban the Martyr. Just after her victory, Bruce had offered her the prestigious left front pew for use during Sunday services, a pew once reserved for Sir John A. Macdonald, Canada's first prime minister, and his wife, Lady Agnes Macdonald. The offer was happily accepted.

Mayor Goodwin was a man she could work with. Calm, soft-spoken, and balding, father of four, a warden in the United Church and owner of Goodwin Optical Company, he had served as a controller for six years in the 1940s before unsuccessfully seeking the mayoralty for the first time in 1948 against Edouard Bourque. Like most of his predecessors as mayor of Ottawa during the first half of the twentieth century, Goodwin favoured low property taxes and healthy infusions of federal government assistance. (Former controller Charles Pickering once claimed that Ottawa's longest serving mayor, Stanley Lewis, who held office between 1936 and 1948, was able to do so because he lived by a simple tenet: Avoid mistakes by doing nothing. Indicative of this was the fact that the city had gone without a city hall since 1931 when the former building was destroyed by fire. Council meetings were held in the school board's headquarters, and civic offices were scattered among downtown office buildings.)

Goodwin headed council and chaired the board of control, which consisted of himself and four controllers. This was council's inner cabinet, and its members were elected by voters across the city, as opposed to the aldermen, who were chosen by residents of their particular wards.

The board of control saw the real action, as major policy items were discussed here first and only later submitted to the full council for final approval. Within the board, each controller had his/her own "portfolio," or departmental interest, but recommendations to the council came from the full board rather than the individual controller from whose department the item came.

Joining Goodwin, fifty-two, and Charlotte, fifty-four, on the board were Leonard Coulter, a forty-eight-year-old druggist with ten years' council experience; Paul Tardif, a forty-year-old paint store manager with eight years on council; and Daniel McCann, a sixty-two-year-old retired federal government printer and longtime union leader who had been on council as either an alderman or a controller, off and on, for just over two decades.

All of the men were used to working together in a fairly collegial atmosphere, but that was about to change. Charlotte's admission to the board was like letting a hungry pitbull loose into a kennel of calm collies, or loosing an irritable porcupine on a slow, crowded elevator.

The first hint of trouble arose in a post-election caucus held prior to their official inauguration on January 2. The discussion concerned who should be the acting mayor in Goodwin's absence — Len Coulter, who had held this position under Bourque, or Charlotte, whose votes easily overshadowed second-place-finisher Coulter. "There was, and is, a very considerable feeling on board of control and city council that one of the male members of the board should act as deputy to Mayor-Elect Grenville Goodwin," the *Citizen* reported. "Regrettable as it may seem, some members of council have been prepared to arrange matters so that the lady controller wouldn't get to be deputy mayor." The "lady controller" fought back, however, and when the puff of dust settled, Charlotte was accepted as acting mayor.

The meeting might have turned into a verbal donnybrook had the results been different, for board members also had to decide on their portfolios. At the time, the four portfolios included finance, public works, waterworks, and "fire and light" (the fire department and the hydro commission). No one wanted the last department, because it was deemed fairly inconsequential, but since Coulter had held the finance portfolio, McCann the works assignment and Tardif the waterworks duties in the previous administration, it seemed obvious to some that the "lady controller" and board rookie would accept the fire and light portfolio.

Of course, Charlotte would accept no such insignificant responsibility. So before the fireworks exploded, the board decided to establish a new portfolio dear to Charlotte's heart, called social utilities, the same title she had recommended to opposition leader John Bracken back in 1943. It combined a broad range of people-oriented civic departments and agencies that included health, recreation and social services, and was by far the broadest of all the portfolios. "Fire and light" was added to her duties for good measure.

Although a newcomer to the board and to council, Charlotte made it clear that she was not going to sit primly, listening and learning on the job. From the start she was embroiled in a series of controversies, some minor and some that would drag on for months. Two

Charlotte changes gears during a farm tractor competition, October 1952.

Richard Thibault photo,
Charlotte Whitton Collection,
Library and Archives Canada,
e016783841

items in particular raised her dander. One concerned recreation, the other the Civic Hospital.

At her first meeting of the Ottawa Recreation Commission — an entrenched, arm's length agency on which the mayor and one controller sat as part of the seven-person board — she gamely suggested that the commission should be integrated into the city budget through the council-controlled parks and playgrounds committee, thereby giving council full control over the ORC's budget. At the time, the ORC passed its own budget and then expected, and previously received with few questions asked, council's approval. The problem, so far as Charlotte was concerned, was that its spending was unnecessarily high. She was also particularly displeased with the fact that the men hired to supervise city playgrounds — usually retired or off-duty policemen — were paid more than the women employed by the Victorian Order of Nurses to care for the city's elderly. Instead of paying for playground supervisors, she recommended that the city replace them with "responsible fathers," who would volunteer their time looking after their neighbourhood parks at no expense to the city. With the money saved, she suggested setting up recreational centres for seniors, "where they can go to get out of the way of the young people and find the companionship where they can write, sew and play checkers and that sort of thing."

Charlotte took her battle with the ORC, then under the chairmanship of Marylu Thorburn, a leading member of the Local Council of Women and daughter-in-law of her longtime friend Ella Thorburn, to the board of control. After a long-running battle, she eventually had her way. The ORC was integrated into the parks and playgrounds committee, and therefore came under council's direct control.

The other major issue in her first month in office concerned the Civic Hospital, the city's main public health care facility for which approval had recently been granted to expand the number of beds from 840 to 1,100. It, too, came under Charlotte's social utilities portfolio, and as a civic agency whose funding directly affected the city's overall budget. Unlike the ORC, though, it was informally controlled by council, for the mayor and two councillors occupied three of the ten seats on the board of trustees, and council named six of the other trustees from the general public. The tenth seat was reserved for a representative of the hospital's medical staff.

The difficulty on the hospital board for Charlotte was that she faced two former civic politicians as stubborn as herself. One was the new chairman, Charles Everett Pickering, whose appointment Charlotte had seconded at the first city council meeting of the year. A millionaire industrialist who had been a city councillor since 1938, until he placed fifth among candidates for the four controller positions in the December election, Pickering's was a rags-to-riches story. As a young man, he had left a broken home in rural Blackstone, Massachusetts, to eke out an existence for a couple of years in the hobo jungles of New Jersey and New York City. Eventually he was introduced to the owner of Dustbane commercial cleaning products in Boston. He later bought the company and transferred its headquarters to Ottawa, from where it spread across North America and eventually to Europe.

The other was Dr. Gerry Geldert, an anaesthesiologist who had served on city council as either an alderman or a controller since 1927, and who had unsuccessfully contested the last two mayoralty elections in 1948 and 1950. Geldert had the distinction of receiving the first private radio station licence in Ottawa in 1924. Like Pickering, he was a man of independent means and considered his time on the hospital board as community service.

Charlotte's first clash with Pickering came at their January 17 meeting, when Pickering proposed that "no member of the medical profession shall be appointed chairman of the board." Charlotte protested, suggesting that the words "medical profession" be changed to "medical, healing and allied practitioners," so as to include people like chiropractors and osteopathic practitioners. Neither party would budge, and eventually Pickering, as chair, decided to postpone a decision so they could ask city council to suggest proper wording.

That dispute was a minor matter compared to Charlotte's explosion at an emergency meeting of the hospital board one month later. The meeting had been sought by the three council members on the board, because all three had been absent two days earlier when the board approved room rate increases, raising the daily patient room rate to ten dollars a day, up from the current nine dollars. Charlotte was opposed to the increases and charged that Pickering and Geldert, who chaired the hospital's board and finance committees respectively, had been underhanded in implementing the increases without the elected councillors present. No sooner had the emergency meeting begun, though, when Charlotte, "at first pale and then crimson with anger . . . turned away from the long board table, snapped shut her voluminous briefcase, picked up her purse and angrily walked from the room while the remaining trustees stared after her in astonishment," the *Ottawa Journal* reported.

Four days later, she submitted her resignation from the hospital board to Mayor Goodwin, citing "the repetition of experiences which had already made other efforts of mine futile on previous occasions in the few weeks in which I have been on the Board . . ." Not only had the February 22 meeting approved the rate increases that she questioned, it had also moved ahead with plans to build a hospital expansion even though the hospital's nursing school, an institution dear to her heart, did not have so much as a basement or a proper lecture room. Her resignation was not accepted — shades of her latter days at the Welfare Council — and Charlotte went on to battle Pickering and Geldert at the board over other matters in the following months.

Other issues which led to disagreements with many of her colleagues included a proposed increase in bus fares, a plan to redevelop Britannia Park, a sixty-acre playground in the far western corner of the municipality, and a motion to increase staff salaries by ten per cent. She opposed the bus fare increase and she wanted Britannia Park redeveloped as a large housing community, but she lost on both accounts. The decision on staff pay increases was postponed to a later date.

As her first month on council drew to a close, she involved herself in one other issue, property development. It was a simmering issue and would result in lengthy, well-publicized battles both inside and outside the council chamber for the next two decades.

On this occasion, it concerned a new subdivision, Manor Park, and the fact that a developer had successfully lobbied a previous city administration to expropriate a plot of land for its development. A smell rose from the deal when it was revealed that Warren Beament, who represented the developer, Alvin Enterprises, also acted as agent for the city in dealing with the owners of the land. Beament said those who had houses on the land were told their homes would be replaced by a new subdivision, but the owners of vacant lands were not informed about the subdivision plans, and therefore were not aware of their lands' potential value. The owners of the undeveloped land were offered $200 an acre, while the homeowners could get $1,200 an acre.

When veteran controller Dan McCann suggested that everything Beament had done was legal, Charlotte shot back: "It's justice we are after, and that outweighs legality."

At January's end, she could look back on a month during which she had proved herself a politician to be reckoned with, an indefatigable worker who, while most of her council colleagues were occupied with their regular day jobs, immersed herself in all the issues before council, and especially the complexities of the *Ontario Municipal Act*, which governed how the province's municipalities were to be run. While most of her colleagues spent their evenings at home with their families, the spinster churned out her regular six columns a week for Thomson Dailies and three columns a week for the *Citizen*. Her only respite came at the end of January when she stopped writing her weekly column for the Halifax *Herald-Chronicle*.

Journal reporter Bobbie Turcotte shadowed Charlotte on January 30, when the controller became acting mayor for an afternoon while Goodwin attended the opening of Parliament. Turcotte described the seventeen-hour adventure as "enough to make strong men controllers lose control." Turcotte reported that Charlotte had been working until 1:30 the previous night, arose at 7:30 a.m., and spoke to the cleaning woman who tended to her "bachelor girl" seven-room apartment at eight o'clock. Between eight and nine, she had breakfast, arranged to have her home phone repaired, and used a neighbour's phone to call the office and leave directions to her secretary for the day ahead. From nine to ten o'clock, she prepared a report for the Ontario Hospital Association, ordered groceries for her apartment, and packed a food parcel for friends in England. In the following hour, she wrote a memo calling on the province to provide a mental health hospital in Ottawa and received two male visitors at her office, one wanting her to find him a house and the other seeking part-time work. Between 11 a.m. and 2 p.m., she spoke to officials about an emergency housing shelter, met the leaders of a property owners association, dictated responses to some of her voluminous incoming mail, and read reports from the local social agencies.

After a hurried, twenty-minute lunch of beef stew at two o'clock at a drugstore counter, she got into her 1946 Plymouth and drove to a board of control meeting a few blocks away. However, the Plymouth stalled and she had to scurry across Confederation Square to make the meeting on time. It was a historic occasion locally — the first time a woman sat at the head of Ottawa's board of control. The meeting lasted until 6:30 p.m., at which time Charlotte returned to her car to find a ticket on the windshield because it had been parked illegally. Back home by 6:45, she spent about forty-five minutes reading eight different newspapers, and at 7:30 cooked herself a pork tenderloin dinner. This was followed until 9 p.m. by a coffee and chat with an unidentified friend, and then she turned to her personal financial affairs, her freelance columns, and made a number of telephone calls. Then to bed at 12:15.

That first month in office proved a prelude to future skirmishes in municipal affairs, for controversies abounded and Charlotte inevitably was in the middle of the fray.

In late March, "red faces and raised voices reigned supreme at board of control," the *Journal* reported, as councillors debated whether or not senior city staff should speak publicly on matters of interest to their departments. In this case, the city's medical officer of health had complained to the media about the lack of suitable office space for his department, but that matter was overshadowed by a general debate on who should speak for the city. As far as Charlotte was concerned, only the elected politicians should do the talking, while others on the board felt officials should be free to discuss openly their areas of responsibility, as they had always done.

In April, she attacked rampant nepotism and patronage at city hall, and threatened to resign from the Ottawa Recreation Commission board over the ORC's funding. She also voiced concern about the amount of sick leave city workers were taking. After visiting local quarries to see if the city was getting the proper sand for winter streets, she blasted her fellow board of control members for ignoring the fact that many public works contracts went untendered. "What is this board of control anyway?" she asked. "Why do we sit here buying material that the department heads say is the only and best material and equipment there is. We run into the same thing on [sewer] pipes — only a certain kind with a certain number of threads will suit — only the product of one special company. It's absurd!"

She believed that the city was being run in an inexcusably outdated and inefficient, if not occasionally fraudulent, manner and that her fellow controllers were either blind to the fact or else chose to ignore the situation. Summoning up the evangelistic fervour of her long-ago boss at the Social Service Council of Canada, Rev. John George Shearer, Charlotte waged a one-woman campaign to clean things up. She looked into the affairs of various departments, called for reports, voiced her concerns and opinions, and demanded action. Her activity was so fast and furious, in fact, that the mayor called her aside and warned her against "browbeating" staff and overstepping her authority.

"In recent weeks," the *Citizen* reported on May 4, "Controller Whitton has been increasingly critical of certain civic officials and has charged them with using 'pressure' tactics to secure higher appropriations for their departments . . . Some senior officials, red-faced and irate, have even talked of resigning. Mayor Goodwin, it is reported, has become incensed at what he feels is unwarranted interference with the city officers. He has received a number of complaints from senior men regarding the attitude of Controller Whitton has taken toward them . . ."

She was indeed fighting the city's bureaucracy, which was well entrenched. Starting with the secretary of the board of control, Charlotte observed that Edgar Pearce had worked at city hall since 1917, under eleven different mayors, and had been secretary of the board since 1918. If anyone knew how the bureaucracy worked, it was Pearce. Just down the hall was the mayor's secretary, Miss May Byers, who had also been working at city hall since 1917, and who knew where many a civic secret was stashed. Other mainstays (with their years of service) included city finance commissioner G.P. Gordon (21 years), water works commissioner W.E. MacDonald (20), city solicitor Gordon Medcalf (19), city clerk Nelson Ogilvie (15), assistant commissioner of assessments B. MacDonald (14), tourism commissioner and Civic Hospital trustee Dr. Gerry Geldert (9), and fire chief Gray Burnett (7).

Unperturbed by the bureaucrats' lengthy experience, Charlotte was determined that the politicians should regain the upper hand at city hall. Her numerous battles with bureaucrats and fellow councillors alike drew mixed reviews locally and headlines nationally. In May, the Vancouver *News-Herald* enthusiastically wished "this little package of dynamite" was on Vancouver city council to wield her cost-cutting broom, while in Ottawa, the *Journal* admitted that Charlotte had attracted a reputation as a Carrie Nation-type reformer branding an axe, "but that is not the Controller Whitton we know. Miss Whitton is no fire-eater, doesn't go about things that way . . . If there is anything terrifying about her it is her terrible industry, her concentration on the task to which she has set herself, and her strength rests in the public certainty of her integrity, her intelligence, her courage and competence . . . It is *The Journal's* opinion, in this fifth month of her service at City Hall, that Miss Whitton's election as controller was one of the finest things to happen to our municipal life in many years."

On the other hand, an editorial in the *Citizen* decried the growing animosity between senior staff and politicians, and the "outbursts of bad temper, personal discourtesies and insistence of having one's own way at all costs . . ." Finance commissioner Gordon was so displeased with Charlotte's "discourteous remarks" on one occasion that he let it be known that he eagerly looked forward to retirement that summer.

There was at least one other dispute at city hall before the summer recess in which Charlotte was involved, and once more it concerned a developer. The board of control, despite Charlotte's opposition, approved the rezoning of a piece of suburban farmland for a subdivision, and Charlotte, ever suspicious, demanded to know who owned the company. The company's lawyer refused to say, and the mayor and her fellow controllers showed no interest in finding out, which only infuriated Charlotte all the more. The row merely intensified the tension that marked the board meetings, but by the time the small-scale developer's name became public the following month, the matter had become a non-issue.

The only other civic event of note before the August recess was a July visit to Ottawa by the Lord Mayor of London, England. Charlotte, who in the spring had opposed a motion to include $5,000 in the city's budget for civic receptions, now wanted to spend $1,000 on a grand banquet for the British visitor. She once again got her way, but not without much grumbling by some councillors who recalled her earlier opposition to civic receptions and her claim that this was no time to pay for frivolous items when the country was at war in Korea.

Meanwhile, she continued writing her nine weekly newspaper columns for Thomson Dailies and the *Citizen*, which allowed her to expound on a broad range of subjects. It was her only outlet from local politics and she attacked it with her usual vim and vigour. In June 1951, for example, her Thomson columns covered, in part, divorce, home loans, national defence and the ongoing Korean War, education, inflation, nursing, the blandness of women's clubs' meetings, and women's clothing. Writing on the latter on June 30, she quipped: "Now, I'm short, and sort of cubical, solid and set you'd say. You can turn me almost any way; my bust, hip, waist-line and skirt length are almost exactly the same. Besides I'm muscular and so I need good seams, and a good broad-beamed base unless my skirts are going to be 'seat sprung' and look like a sack in rear-guard action. What do I find? I find that the '18 ½' which was my perfect fit seems

Elizabeth Langin Whitton, Charlotte's mother, 1915.

Charlotte Whitton Collection, Library and Archives Canada, PA-126398

to have gone the way of the 5-cent chocolate bar . . ."

The following day, her spirit darkened. She received word that her mother had died in Renfrew's Victoria Hospital. Aged eighty-one, Elizabeth Whitton had been ill since February, but had only entered the hospital four days earlier.

Just as she had done when her father had died, Charlotte rushed home and handled the funeral arrangements, although this time she was assisted by her siblings. She also shared her grief with her readers, for in her July 16 column in the Thomson papers, she recalled:

> My mother was really an amazing sort of person, who, from my first memory of her, simply pulsed with energy. Until her eightieth birthday, just over a year ago, she was as lively and vigorous as a bright bird on a tree. But there was nothing simply flitting and perky about Mother. She was one of the hardest working women I ever knew, as she was one of the most unselfish . . . My mother's life was not unshadowed; it was in fact a life of rather continuous struggle from her childhood and unrelenting through most of her married life. Yet she never flagged nor brooded

bitterness long. She had both physical and moral strength and a gift for getting fun out of almost any situation. She had a great courage of heart, as great as her kindness, and her warmth of spirit went out in a love of people and unfailing thoughtfulness for them. Everything she ever had she would give away as cheerily as most people would cast aside a burnt match. . . .

Indeed it had been a hard life. Born to Irish immigrants Michael and Elizabeth Langin in Rochester, New York, on June 27, 1870, Elizabeth emigrated with her family to Canada and eventually settled in Carleton Place, Ontario. In 1894, Elizabeth Langin, then twenty-three, and John Whitton, twenty-two, decided to marry. There was a serious problem, though, for Elizabeth was Roman Catholic and John was Methodist, and neither their families nor their churches would condone a mixed marriage. So they hopped into a horse and buggy and eloped to nearby Almonte, where they were wed in the local Anglican church.

It had been a reasonably happy marriage, although John often was away in distant Whitney, leaving Elizabeth to raise their four children with the help of her austere English mother-in-law, Matilda, and to operate a boarding house in Renfrew that took in, at various times, schoolgirls from county villages, teachers, lumbermen, bankers, accountants, lawyers, and the odd professional hockey player. It must have been a difficult time for Elizabeth, in more ways than one, for Matilda was an ardent anglophile who disdained most things Catholic or Irish, although, according to Charlotte, Matilda considered the hardworking Elizabeth "the only responsible Irishwoman whom she had ever met, and even qualified that, a little."

Nevertheless, Charlotte's mother went cheerily through life, donating baked goods to Protestant and Catholic charitable bazaars alike, serving on the boards of the Catholic Women's League, the Salvation Army and the Children's Aid Society, and she organized the Royal Canadian Legion's annual poppy drive in Renfrew for thirty years, for which the local branch made her an honourary member. To many of the children in town, she was known as "the lady with the cookies" due to her generous handouts of home-baked goods.

14 "Coronation" at City Hall

"Mayor Goodwin is dead." Word spread quickly across the city that the good-natured, hard-working Goodwin had been felled by a heart attack the previous day and had died several hours later at the Civic Hospital.

Like many an Ottawa resident, Goodwin and his family had fled to the lake so as to escape the city's heat and humidity. Goodwin, however, had returned from the family cottage at Patterson Lake in the Gatineau Hills, to purchase groceries.

Hyman Fine told the media that Goodwin had just bought baskets of peaches and tomatoes at his store, but soon returned complaining of severe weakness. One of Fine's employees was in the midst of driving him home when his condition worsened. He was taken to his doctor's office and then rushed to the Civic by ambulance. He died shortly after midnight. The date was Tuesday, August 28, 1951.

Charlotte, resting at McGregor Lake, was informed shortly after Goodwin had entered the hospital and quickly drove into the city; she said later that she had spent a few minutes speaking to him before he passed away, but did not disclose the details of the conversation.

As acting mayor, she called an emergency meeting of the board of control for 9 a.m. that day, during which they decided to hold a civic funeral at St. James United Church and declared August 30, to be a day of mourning for which city businesses were invited to close shop. The matter of naming a formal replacement was put off until September 4.

In the days immediately following Goodwin's death, the city was officially in mourning, but behind the scenes, political activity was bristling. At issue was the choice of Goodwin's successor. Many thought Charlotte was the obvious choice, considering her decisive victory at the polls and her "acting mayor" status, but after eight months on council she had alienated many councillors and outside interest groups, and these people, supported by a ruling from city solicitor Gordon Medcalf, argued that the "acting mayor" status was for temporary purposes only. Therefore, due to Goodwin's death, a new election was necessary. The *Ontario Municipal Act*, which regulated municipal affairs, was unclear on the matter.

Charlotte apparently remained above the fray, commenting, "It is as regrettable as unseemly that the appointment of a new mayor should be under discussion before the mayor who has served us is interred with honours," but several aldermen complained of being bombarded with women phone callers urging them to support Charlotte for mayor, while other aldermen said they were contacted by other interest groups. On the day after Goodwin's demise, the *Citizen* polled councillors and reported that of the eighteen of thirty-two councillors contacted, ten favoured Len Coulter for mayor, one preferred Charlotte, and one opted for Frank Plant, a sixty-seven-year-old businessman a former mayor (1921–23, 1930) and subsequent board member of the Ottawa Hydro-Electric Commission. The remaining six declined to divulge their choices, while the rest could not be reached.

In the days prior to the September 4 council meeting, the debate played out in the news and editorial pages of both English-language newspapers, with the *Journal* solidly on Charlotte's side and the *Citizen* equally favouring Coulter. The French-language *Le Droit*, as usual, paid little attention to Ottawa city hall and did not comment. The *Citizen* cited a straw poll of councillors as proving "overwhelming endorsation" of Coulter as mayor, but when council met, it postponed the issue for one month as a mark of respect for Goodwin and to better prepare for the imminent arrivals of the Lord Mayor of London followed by Princess Elizabeth and Prince Philip, the Duke of Edinburgh. This naturally left Charlotte, the acting mayor, with more time to show her mettle for the top council job.

According to a columnist in the *Journal*, the September 4 meeting proceeded with military briskness. "Chieftainess who ruled with such a firm hand was Madame Mayor, Dr. Charlottte Whitton . . . Women were in the majority in the audience, and attentive they were . . . The controllers sit facing the aldermen and public gallery, the mayor's chair behind them. One of the little mysteries the city cabinet keeps to itself is how a controller knows Dr. Whitton wants him to speak. She points a yellow pencil at the back of the controller who is to reply. And he rises, without looking around. It's a good trick . . . Everyone was as quiet as a lamb when the otherwise all-male council received its instructions about dress from Dr. Whitton. At the civic banquet for Princess Elizabeth and the Duke, there will be no formal dress, said the acting mayor, firmly . . . Dark suits will be in order. 'And that doesn't mean you can wear tennis shoes with a dark suit either,' said Dr. Whitton sharply. Council bowed its collective and obedient head and got back to the business in hand. Sewers, naturally."

Without anyone declaring it, it was obvious at that point who was running the city. It was Charlotte. Later in the week, a social utilities committee she chaired recommended a major slum clearance program and that the slum be replaced by a low-rent housing project. She also ordered that, henceforth, all of the city's vehicles should carry the city's crest and an identification number. When one juvenile court judge insisted on driving an unmarked city car, she snarled at the city clerk, "Mr. Ogilvie, you write Allan Fraser and tell him to GET THAT NUMBER on his car. Tell him to take his car to the Bayview Yard [city workshop] and have the crest and number put on AT ONCE." (The capitalization was included in the Citizen's report.) Then she advised council that from then on there would be no more secret, "in camera" meetings at city hall—a clear break from the past—and that the city's $31-million debenture debt was far too high and would have to be trimmed severely.

Her main opponent for the mayoralty, Len Coulter, told the media that he thought Charlotte deserved the mayoralty due to her strong finish at the December polls, but if pressured by enough councillors he would consider accepting the post. Thus, while he dithered, Charlotte seized the opportunity for all it was worth. Commands went out to various departments and city hall took on a new intensity, a new vivacity. Amidst it all, she nonchalantly took a day off to travel to Toronto to speak to that city's Inter-Club Council for Women, advising them that more women were needed in municipal politics: "Women have a finer sensitivity for ethical and moral

*Charlotte meant
business when she put
the mayoral chain of
office around her neck.*

Paul Horsdal photo, Paul Horsdal Estate, Library and Archives
Canada, PA-145691

values. Often they can draw to male attention something not previously expressed." Meanwhile, Ottawa was left without even an acting mayor in town in her absence.

The jockeying for the mayoralty continued during the month of September — even quiet Dan McCann was touted as a candidate — but when council sat down to vote on the matter on October 1, the result was anti-climatic. Election of the new mayor by council took just twelve minutes, and the choice of Charlotte, moved by Coulter, was unanimous. The rest of the meeting was taken up with talk of sewers and sidewalks, roads and railway crossings.

The following day, Charlotte was officially installed as Mayor of Ottawa. The ceremony was somewhat less than she could have hoped for — after all, her heroine Elizabeth Tudor had been borne on a royal barge along the Thames River and then in a gleaming, gold litter through the crowd-lined thoroughfares of London to her coronation in 1559. Charlotte had merely the city's black Cadillac for transportation through nearly deserted city streets — but she was in charge of the capital city of Canada, she was its chief magistrate, and she would henceforth be addressed formally as "Her Worship." The city was now hers and having anticipated the occasion, she had had a massive, throne-like, carved wooden chair resurrected. It had been commissioned in 1914 for a previous mayor, Taylor McVeity, and used by him and his successors until the city hall fire of 1931, since which time it had sat ignored and neglected in the attic of a local fire station. The mahogany woodwork and Spanish Moroccan leather gleamed after expert restoration, while the two-metre-high backrest towered impressively over the diminutive mayor.

Both local English-language newspapers welcomed Charlotte's elevation, and even *Le Droit* wished her well, but all three papers emphasized the need for co-operation with other councillors and with city staff if she was to succeed. The *Globe and Mail*, like papers across Canada, paid heed: "Life should be eventful in Ottawa, now that Dr. Charlotte Whitton has been appointed mayor . . . Dr. Whitton deserves luck, but she doesn't need it. She has something much better—pluck. During her richly varied career, she has shown courage and realism to a degree seldom equalled in Canada's public life. These qualities, coupled with her boundless energy, will see her through whatever problems she encounters. Would there were more people like her in the municipal governments of this nation—and in the other ones, too."

Among other preparations for her new position, she stopped writing her thrice-weekly columns in the *Citizen* and her six weekly columns for Thomson Dailies.

Ottawa, in 1951, was a growing community of nearly 200,000, an increase of almost one-third from a decade earlier. This was due in no small part to the growth of government during the war, followed by the postwar baby boom, and the city had annexed large sections of neighbouring Nepean and Gloucester townships two years earlier to help accommodate the growth. It was the sixth largest city in Canada in terms of population after Montreal, Toronto, Vancouver, Winnipeg and Hamilton, and new housing was going up rapidly. Within its forty-eight-square-mile area, there were 353 miles of streets, 255 miles of water mains, and 200 miles of sewers. The federal census of that year reported that approximately sixty-eight per cent of its residents had been born in Ontario, thirteen per cent in Quebec, seven per cent in the rest of Canada, five per cent in England, and the remaining seven per cent came from the rest of the world. Roman Catholics made up about half the population, while Protestants of various denominations made up the remainder, along with small pockets of Jews and those of other faiths. Females made up roughly one-third of its workforce, a clear reflection of the importance of the secretarial-rich public service jobs in the city.

The municipality had come a long way since its formation as Bytown in 1826 when Lt.-Col. John By of the Royal Engineers arrived from England to build the Rideau Canal, linking the Ottawa and St. Lawrence rivers. It had seen early prosperity during the heyday of the Ottawa Valley timber trade, and then received a much needed financial shot in the arm when, in 1857, Queen Victoria unexpectedly made this hard-scrabble village in the middle of nowhere the capital of Canada. Construction projects subsequently blossomed to accommodate Parliament and the arrival of thousands of public servants.

The city had its shortcomings certainly, but on the day she became mayor, Charlotte could muse only on the positives, such as a decent economy and, in its status as national capital, its frequent role as host to important international visitors. As for the latter, the recent visit of the Lord Mayor of London on September 8 and the upcoming arrival on October 10–11 of Princess Elizabeth and Prince Philip must have been uppermost in her mind.

The visit of the tall, elegant lord mayor, Sir Denys Lowson, and his glamourous wife, Patricia, would have been like eating the icing before the cake for Charlotte, for here she was hosting English nobility and a person whose office represented 1,900 years of English history.

Obviously wanting to make a good impression on her London counterpart, she wore the mayor's chain of office over her plain black dress when she formally presented him with the key to the city. However, she felt herself at a severe disadvantage standing next to the lord mayor who, in addition to his chain of office, was attired in full official regalia — an embroidered, knee-length jacket and a prominent jabot, a frilly lace "bib" worn in place of a necktie. He was also accompanied by the Sheriff of London, a swordbearer, and two footmen. As a further embarrassment, Charlotte had to explain to Sir Denys that the civic reception for him was being held at the Château Laurier Hotel rather than at city hall, simply because Ottawa had no city hall.

There was no need for any apologies during the Royal Visit, however, as it was organized by the federal government as part of a cross-country tour and the Ottawa stopover comprised a whirlwind of activities, leaving the royal visitors little time to catch their breaths. Nevertheless, Charlotte made her presence felt. She was among the welcoming party when the royals arrived by train from Montreal, she was there when they arrived at Lansdowne Park to the cheers of thousands of schoolchildren, she was there when the princess laid a wreath at the National War Memorial, and she was there at a state dinner at Rideau Hall, albeit all the time in the background, as federal officials remained in charge.

The second day was better. Charlotte and city council played host to the royals at a civic luncheon at the Château Laurier, and the future queen was amused as two youngsters chosen by Charlotte — Controller Paul Tardif's daughter Nicole and the late mayor's son Eric Goodwin — presented her with gifts for her children, a royal blue windbreaker with the city crest sewn on a pocket for two-year-old Charles and a baby blue blanket woven in the Ottawa Valley and embroidered with her name by Montreal nuns for his infant sister Anne, as well as a box of maple sugar cookies for both. For their mother, Charlotte presented the princess with a $1,000 cheque for the charity of her choosing.

Following the luncheon and a change of clothes all round, Charlotte led her visitors on an informal boat cruise on the Ottawa River, speaking eloquently about the river's boisterous past.

The royal stopover was successful by all accounts — pictures of a casually attired princess and prince square-dancing at Rideau Hall were featured in newspapers across Canada and the United Kingdom the next day — and as the royals continued on their tour westwards, Charlotte's thoughts turned back to city hall.

It was a mess. The veteran bureaucrats had been running the show and the part-time politicians had allowed inefficiency and disorder to thrive. Nepotism was rampant, as was patronage. If there were to be any improvements, a strong hand and a determined will were needed. There was bound to be opposition both from staff and from longtime politicians, and there was bound to be battles, but Charlotte was ready. Ready, aye ready, and keen to do battle!

On October 15, she delivered her inaugural address to council as mayor and laid out her platform for the remaining fifteen months of the council's term in office. Her wide-ranging speech filled thirteen pages of the official minutes and in it she dissected and analyzed the broad range of problems facing council. There was the unfinished business of the 1949 annexations of major portions of Nepean and Gloucester townships; there was the need to rein in the Ottawa Recreation Commission and the city's semi-autonomous bus and hydro services, and the need to change the property assessment system; city departments had to get their budget estimates in sooner than in the past; the federal government had to be persuaded to pay a greater share of the city's infrastructure requirements; low-cost housing was urgently needed; and a new city hall building had to be built.

Teamwork at the council table was essential, she intoned. "So we shall close our ranks, strike our tents and take up the march again. That journey will demand clarity of vision, stoutness of heart, firmness of will and a fearless, honest following of truth; for the civilization which has so long served us and our fathers is changing and we are changing with it." Major political changes were occurring in the world, and because those changes affected Canada, it "thus makes this city one of the world's vital centres."

That week, a feature on Charlotte in *Newsweek* magazine reflected international interest in Ottawa's doughty woman mayor. It was headlined: "Lady at the helm."

Later in the month, *Toronto Telegram* columnist Margaret Aitken spent a day in the mayor's office and found "a room of noble proportions and dignity with rich crimson drapes and carpet and a massive desk, also of battleship proportions, behind which Ottawa's diminutive mayor looks perky and cocky." Delegations were coming and going all day and "some day somebody should put Charlotte Whitton in a book, a book of fiction because only if you see her in action can you believe it." At one point Aitken counted four controllers, two secretaries, and three reporters in the office; she reported, "The picture of her sitting solemnly among these nine males calmly dominating the scene by sheer force of gregariousness enchanted me. If one of the controllers appeared to get a bit uppity or argumentative she would bring things back to their proper place with a rolling sweeping 'Now gentlemen'."

Council meetings were held on the first and third Mondays of each month in the public school board's headquarters and normally began at 7:30 p.m. and ended by 11. If they went past 11, then each half hour a councillor would move for a thirty-minute extension. The next regular meeting after Charlotte's inaugural, on November 5, continued until 2:10 a.m. Under Charlotte's rule, time was practically irrelevant. For one thing, she did not have to get up the next day like the others to go to a regular nine-to-five job, but more important, she was determined that all necessary council work would get done when it should be done, and not sloughed off to a later date as had been done in the past. Similarly, senior city staff were expected to be fully conversant with issues affecting their departments and to be prepared to do whatever had to be done at whatever the cost in time and effort. Charlotte was a workaholic, and she expected as much from everyone else.

At the November 5 meeting, for example, council wrestled at length with storm sewers, downtown parking, street lighting, a funding request by the recreation commission, personnel matters, the civic crest on civic cars, and "local improvements." Each topic was discussed with a new thoroughness by council, yet one rule stood out above all others — there must be greater efficiency. When it came to "local improvements," such as new roads, sidewalks or other infrastructure, Charlotte warned, "the alarming uncontrolled rate at which the debenture debt accrues through the routine filing of local improvement applications and their routine recommendation by the board of control and their routine adoption by council once the board of control and the [Ontario] Municipal Board have passed them" must cease. In the past, too many spending items had slipped by without proper study, she maintained, so henceforth all such items should be put into one package and delivered to the city finance commissioner, who in turn would see what was affordable and then inform the board of control and council of his recommendation. Only then would councillors vote on the individual improvements.

Further, she had issued a memorandum to all departmental heads ordering them to reduce the impending deficit by exercising "the most stringent economy . . . The practice of requesting transfers from accounts where there is an unencumbered balance to accounts where expenditure is contemplated above the amounts provided in the estimates is one of the procedures which defeats and discourages sincere efforts at economism since it can penalize those officials who keep within their appropriations." In future, she commanded, they would have to receive the finance commissioner's approval for such transfers, but they should only seek his approval after they had tried every cost-cutting measure possible.

It was by then obvious that Charlotte fully comprehended the broad workings of the city administration, and it also was becoming obvious that no detail was too small for her critical inspection. In November, for example, she called for a report on the cost-effectiveness of providing overalls for garbage collectors in the sanitation branch, and in December, she issued a lengthy report on the mayor's Cadillac in which she noted that despite having been driven only 18,000 miles, it got only nine miles to the gallon, had two bald tires, and needed new brake linings, valve reconditioning, and gaskets. It cost $1,350 each year to operate the car, as well as $2,550 for the chauffeur's salary, plus his cost of living bonus and $300 for his uniform, which was manufactured in the police department's Tailor Shop.

"There is need of an official car for official use and occasions, but for all ordinary driving I would prefer to use my own car, as I have always done," she informed police chief Duncan MacDonnell. Consequently, she told him to return the chauffeur to his former position with the sanitation department, park the Cadillac in the police garage instead of a private lot, and she would take taxis in emergencies when she could not drive her own vehicle. Further, her car was to be adorned with a civic crest "solely for quick passage through traffic when on official business but, otherwise, no official connection or cost to be associated with its operations — these costs to be mine personally."

One month later, she reconsidered and advised MacDonnell that there were times, such as formal occasions or when the weather was bad, that she would need a chauffeur and it would be best if that chauffeur was a policeman. If a policeman was not available on a particular occasion, she wrote, "one of the garage mechanics who could put on a uniform cap and a plain heavy coat" would suffice. For out-of-town trips, a uniformed police chauffeur was required "because of obvious advantages in traffic, etc." (Years later there would be many a tale about Charlotte and her police chauffeurs. One, told to the author by McGregor Lake cottager Dr. Jim Coupland, mentioned that when his daughter was married in Montreal in September 1953 and Mayor Charlotte was invited, she arrived with a police escort with sirens screaming their way through city traffic. Another time, in April 1952, she advised her hostess at Rochester University in New York State that she would be arriving with two female friends and "my Police Sergeant [who] will look after himself somewhere where he can garage the car." She was there to receive her fourth honorary doctorate and to speak on "Women in a Breaking World.")

One of the hallmarks of Charlotte's reputation as an effective mayor was her success in housing the poor. It had long been a concern of the former welfare administrator, for she believed society was based on the individual family and if that family were to survive and thrive, it had to be lodged in suitable housing. In a 1946 magazine article, she had argued that the federal and provincial governments should get involved in supporting low-cost housing, for "if the Dominion succeeds in providing decent, safe, accessible housing for the low market third of her people, under measures that are solely financial and highly centralized, she will indeed make social history as the first state in the world to do so." By 1951, the federal government had done just that, having introduced special loans for low-cost housing through the Central Mortgage and Housing Corporation. But it was up to the provinces and the municipalities to make the first moves, and thus far few had ventured into this field.

Charlotte charged in unafraid. The situation in the fall of 1951 in Ottawa was at crisis proportions, for some 4,000 families were housed in slum-like conditions. A number of them resided in run-down, temporary emergency shelters, mostly based at two local airports, and the federal government wanted them out of one of the airports in order to use the buildings for military purposes. In the meantime, Charlotte had heard about a local bakery owner's plan to house his own employees in affordable housing, so she set up a meeting with him to discuss the possibility of expanding the program, so long as it could be done cost-efficiently. The owner, Cecil

Morrison of Morrison-Lamothe Bakery, was eager to help. As he recalled in his memoir, *The Life and Times of G. Cecil Morrison*:

> Mayor Charlotte Whitton invited me to lunch and asked
> me to head a scheme for a low rental housing development
> for the city. I was a busy man with a company to look after
> and didn't want to be drawn into this time-consuming
> project, but Mayor Whitton was very persuasive. She told
> me how serious the city housing problem was. The Health
> Department had condemned 4,000 homes in Ottawa as
> unfit for human habitation. "But the city can't enforce the
> by-law and close down these homes because there is no
> place for these families to go. They can't live under a tree
> in this climate," said the Mayor. She was an old friend of
> the family, so at last I gave in. "All right, Charlotte, I'll build
> you fifty houses." I didn't like rental schemes, preferring
> that people owned their own houses, but she replied that
> there was a need for both kinds.

Thus was born the Ottawa Lowren Housing Corporation. Because CMHC ruled that its loans to such undertakings were limited to non-governmental, limited-dividend companies that could make no more than a five-per-cent profit, Charlotte talked Morrison into establishing the OLHC as a private company, with a board of directors consisting of himself and three other men and one woman. At the same time, the city purchased a ten-per-cent interest in the company, providing Charlotte with a say in its administration. She also emphasized that the new housing had to be located in built-up areas, rather than in the suburbs, so that the new residents would be close to work, school, and stores, and thus save on transportation costs. In effect, she was well ahead of her time, proposing infill construction in the city's core before it became popular.

Her efforts were successful, despite resistance from some community groups opposed to low-rent or low-cost housing in their neighbourhoods, and also at times from Morrison, who did not want to get involved in rental housing. He wanted to build houses for the less fortunate on the basis that they would pay ten per cent down on their mortgages at the time of the sale and the remainder in the following years. That was fine with Charlotte, but she also wanted him to build low-rent housing. She argued tooth-and-nail for rental housing and a rent-to-income policy in which the renter would pay one-quarter of his month's salary in rent. Also, the low-rent, three-bedroom units were confined to families earning between $2,000 and $3,500 a year (roughly $17,000 and $30,000 in 2010 terms) and who had at least two children under sixteen.

Not surprisingly, she got her way. On November 18, 1952, Mayor Charlotte Whitton tossed the first ceremonial shovelful of sand at a location on Presland Road in Overbrook adjacent to two short streets that were later named Whitton Crescent and Whitton Place. There would be many more such projects in Ottawa in the years ahead, and the scheme was copied in cities across Canada.

Other substantial achievements during her first term of office included concluding annexation agreements with Nepean and Gloucester townships, merging the Ottawa Recreation Commission and the playground department, reaching an agreement with the federal government to raise its "in lieu" payments covering part of the city's infrastructure costs, reducing the city's debt load, and getting the ball rolling for a new city hall. They did not come easily. There was opposition from other councillors, there was opposition from city staff, there was opposition from community groups, yet Charlotte had the stamina and the determination to succeed regardless.

Departmental heads complained of Charlotte's micromanaging of their domains, councillors were not always informed of her civic plans, and ordinary staffers feared her cost-cutting, job-elimination efforts. No matter. In July 1952, Edgar Pearce, the elderly secretary of the board of control, was miffed when she informed him that from then on he was to provide Charlotte with the minutes of each board meeting before distributing them to the controllers so she could "correct" any mistakes. In October, she upset her office staff, along with Pearce, when she called in the police to investigate the disappearance of a city document. The latter ruckus faded after she publicly apologized for overstating the seriousness of the situation when the police found no malicious intent on anyone's part; she admitted the document was rather inconsequential at any rate.

She also angered many Canadians when she avoided the installation of the first Canadian-born governor general, Vincent Massey, in February 1952. She denied that she had boycotted the ceremony, suggesting she had had a previous engagement, but her opinionated opposition to Massey's selection for the vice-regal post had been broadly reported the previous month. She had said that naming a Canadian to Rideau Hall meant "the fine, detached dignity of the Crown disappears . . . the appointment of a Canadian as governor general means that the office of governor general will come under criticism and comment and therefore will shortly disappear."

While squabbles, rows, and arguments were a prominent feature of her early mayoralty, Charlotte's sense of humour, her quick-wittedness, and her appreciation of the value of a friendly media image helped to leaven what often was a nasty, caustic persona. In August 1952, for example, most Ottawans smiled when they read that she had led a group of local women to inspect the propriety of the "girlie" shows at the Exhibition, and there was much merriment in October when the mayor mounted a Massey-Harris two-furrow plow to participate in a special, mayors-only plowing match at the nearby Carp Fair. (True to form, Charlotte practised plowing for two hours a day in the month preceding the match at Kilreen Farm, home of her sister Kay and brother-in-law Frank Ryan, located just outside Ottawa. When she lost the competition to Toronto mayor Allan Lamport, she demanded to see the judges' scoring sheet.)

Although she had retired from writing her newspaper columns since becoming mayor, she occasionally fitted in a freelance magazine article, such as one she wrote for *Maclean's* magazine in August 1952, entitled, "Will women ever run the country?" In it, she described the trials and tribulations of women politicians, and included the following observations:

> There is an instinctive unease on the part of the male against the female in sallying out from her customary settings and duties into the preserve he and his have long held undisputed and decisive sway. . . .
>
> The dinosaurs may be deep in their prehistoric graves but their spirits come out to range at night. The solid dead weight of tradition is still a mighty barrier to the progress of women in the business of government. . . .
>
> No, it's not easy for the man or woman who treads a

way not yet thronged — the path of the pioneer. None is
a stranger path than that of a woman ranging in a world
hitherto a male preserve. She must do all that would
become a man and yet nothing that would not become a
woman. She must kick off at the football game opening
and witness, unperturbed, the special program of the
Fire Fighters' Dinner. Yet she must also fulfill all the
functions of a female of the species — open bazaars, visit
the maternity floors, keep track of the golden wedding
anniversaries and indite [sic] recipes for the cookbook
of the Circle of Willing Helpers of the parish of her own
ward . . . And she must take as much interest in the new
baby clinic as in her neighbouring city's plans for a ten-
million-dollar bridge. And whatever she does — Oh!
Doesn't every woman know it! — she must do twice as well
as any man to be thought half as good.[4]

After fourteen months as mayor, it was time to face the music; the
voters would decide on December 1, if Charlotte was to carry on with
her ambitious program for two more years, or whether they would
opt for more peaceful, more predictable times at the council table.

"I have made mistakes," Charlotte told the Local Council of
Women in October. "I shall make others. I hope they have not been
and will not be major or many. Some of them cannot but be those
of such qualities as I possess. One cannot pass the half-century mark
of a life, not always easy and not be prone to battle as well as proven

---

4   This last sentence appears in most collections of quotable quotes and
     usually includes a further sentence: "Luckily it's not that difficult." The
     quotation is usually attributed to the 1963 edition of a short-lived
     newsmagazine, *Canada Monthly*, but its origin is the *Maclean's* article. As
     well, the last sentence appears to have been added by a copy editor at
     Canada Monthly in 1963, for it was not part of Charlotte's original piece.
     Further, her main quote was not quite as original as is usually thought. In
     the 1930s, for example, Agnes Macphail, Canada's first female member of
     Parliament, wrote that women had to be "twice as good [as men] for half
     as much pay," and in the same decade, journalist Mabel Burkholder wrote
     an article on pioneer newswoman Kathleen Blake "Kit" Coleman in which
     she stated: "Newspaper work was no sinecure for a woman in the days
     when Kit entered journalism. Women entered it on sufferance and had to
     do practically as much as two men to prove that they were half as good as
     one man."

in combat; it is not whether one fights that should be taken as the judgment of the day but why and for what one fights."

And fight she would. A pro-Whitton newspaper advertisement early in the campaign said as much: "Dr. Whitton is a fighter. She fights special privilege, and in so holy a war she neither asks nor gives quarter. Her enemies are greed, and sloth, and waste, and incompetence. She has trodden on many toes, but only when the public interest demanded that drastic treatment. She does not suffer fools gladly, and there is no tolerance in her for the idea that what always has been must be. Miss Whitton is as forward-looking as tomorrow's dawn." Although her only opponent in the mayoralty contest was Len Coulter, the affable druggist, it was a nasty campaign marked by innuendo and mud-slinging.

"Did Saint George sit and enjoy the roses . . . Did Saint Joan of Arc stay a peaceful woman among her father's sheep when she ran France?" she asked at a campaign meeting in November. At another meeting, she attacked city staff for participating "in what I think must be the most vicious case of organization to get a mayor out of office in all the long history of Ottawa and Bytown." The vitriol continued. Certain city contractors were determined to see that she lost, she complained three days before the election. "It is here that the nastiest, messiest set-up is out against me, pulling down my cards in space for which I have paid, ganging up and yowling like animals as I go to some of my meetings, planning — and I warn you — to create disorder and trouble in this city over this weekend and on election day. They hope I, as Police Commissioner, will call out the [police] force. I will not."

For his part, Coulter complained that he was unfairly branded as the man who arranged cheap tax assessments for his friends and the "Mr. Big" behind the group backing a yes-vote in a plebiscite on professional Sunday sports, which Charlotte opposed. He denied both claims, and he deplored the fact that opponents had called his home and insulted his wife and children when they answered the telephone calls.

The media loved the spectacle. *The Journal*, which usually forgave Charlotte her transgressions, wavered in its editorial support. "The fact is that Miss Charlotte Whitton has brought a new note and tone to our municipal life and it is her remarkable personality that dominates the present campaign. . . . Mr. Leonard Coulter . . .

is a cautious man, slow to come to positive conclusions, is not spectacular in his speech or his methods, but he would be a mayor to whom we could point with pride, a chief magistrate in the tradition of the high office at stake. . . . Miss Whitton has ideas (her mind works like 'instant' coffee) on everything, and it follows that sometimes she is wrong . . ." The *Citizen*, a frequent critic of its former columnist, backed Coulter: "However well-intentioned the present administration may be, it has been marked by a great deal of furious sound but little action. . . . Miss Whitton's manifest inability to work harmoniously with her colleagues and to refrain from interfering in departmental administration has led to endless wrangling and hostility between her and her colleagues in City Council and civic employees. . . . Judged by the record, Controller Coulter has shown sounder judgment on controversial issues and greater capacity to carry his colleagues with him on a course of action."

As the early results came in on election night, December 1, gloom permeated in Charlotte's campaign headquarters. Coulter took an early lead, and the mayor, reporters noted, was uncharacteristically quiet, burying herself among the banks of telephones as poll captains relayed the latest results. It was only in the later hours of the evening that the edge to Charlotte seemed evident, and it was not until after midnight that Coulter conceded defeat.

The final vote count: Whitton — 37,373; Coulter — 33,498. She had just snatched victory from what would have been a most embarrassing defeat. A *Journal* reporter asked her how it felt to have won, but "the mayor didn't answer. Only a slight smile around her lips showed the slackening of the night's strain."

As 1952 ended, Charlotte won another poll: She was selected Canadian Woman Newsmaker of the Year for the second time in a row.

15 "I've Been to London to Visit the Queen"

I t had been a close election in December, but that was ancient history come January. Len Coulter returned to his drugstore business, and Charlotte sat all-powerful at the head of the council table. On the five-person board of control, she could rely on her intellect and her sharp tongue to control re-elected veterans Dan McCann, Paul Tardif and John Powers, while Roy Donaldson, a man with previous aldermanic experience, would need some time to get up to speed on city-wide administration. At any rate, like the other three, he was no match for Charlotte in wit, wisdom, or tenacity. As for the aldermen, they could squabble among themselves over ward politics, so far as Charlotte's broader plans were concerned, and most city staff by now bowed before her every whim. She truly was queen of her realm, limited though it was.

Broad plans she had in spades. Now that she had whittled the debenture debt down to $12 million from the $31 million of two years earlier, it was time to assert more control over the city's planning, she advised council in her inaugural address. It would not be easy. Nine years before John F. Kennedy voiced a similar appeal to Americans, Charlotte asked council: "Is it too much to hope or to ask that all of us who work for this city should get together to see how we could do a little more for Ottawa rather than to do Ottawa for a little more?"

Developers were building subdivisions here, there, and everywhere both in the old city and the rural lands annexed from Nepean and Gloucester, and, due to its national capital status, there was much overlapping of federal and municipal jurisdictions when it came to planning. In fact, federal incursions into Ottawa's civic planning reached as far back as the end of the nineteenth century when Sir Wilfrid Laurier established the Ottawa Improvement Commission in an effort to beautify what then was an ugly lumber town that its own residents seemed unwilling to improve. Such had been the case, too, under Mackenzie King, who in the late 1920s ordered the razing of numerous buildings in the central core to make way for the National War Memorial and a proper ceremonial route for visiting dignitaries.[5]

Similarly, in 1950, Louis St. Laurent released a report by internationally prominent planner Jacques Gréber of France that called for the demolition of Union Station downtown, the removal of railway tracks from the city centre, and the establishment of a "green belt" arcing around the city's perimeter which would be reserved for agricultural or parkland uses.

Things had not changed much in the federal-municipal relationship by 1953, but they were about to under Charlotte. As she noted in her inaugural address, the locally run Ottawa Planning Area Board operated under provincial jurisdiction, but it was expected to co-operate with the federally run National Capital Planning Committee, an advisory body to the Federal District Commission, and the National Capital Planning Service, which was answerable to the Department of Public Works. Each had its own board and planning experts, and often their ideas did not coincide, although they adhered to Gréber's National Capital Plan. Charlotte's solution was to strengthen the city's Planning Area Board by including herself, one controller, one alderman, and other local officials — all city appointees — on the new twelve-member panel. She knew she would eventually be butting heads with the federal government over planning issues, for as mayor she also had a seat on the Federal District Commission, which was a successor to Laurier's Ottawa Improvement Commission.

Charlotte hoped to cut through all this red tape by strengthening the Ottawa Planning Area Board, but she would have a mighty challenge on her hands.

One thing she had going for her, as the *Globe and Mail* once mentioned, was pluck.

She was fearless when it came to senior levels of government, and if she had a problem, she'd take it to the top, whether it meant

---

5   Typical of King's disdain for the board of control was this diary entry on October 22, 1927, in which he wrote of summoning the city's mayor and controllers to his office for a half-hour, informing them that he intended to revitalize "the heart of the City . . . [and] they left delighted at 12:30."

contacting Premier Leslie Frost or Prime Minister St. Laurent. Days after her inaugural, for example, she complained to Frost that the Liquor Licence Board was allowing too many licensed outlets in Ottawa and that the city wanted a say in the distribution of the licences. The longtime temperance campaigner followed up with another letter in February, warning Frost that some licensed restaurants were linked to dance halls and "are becoming absolute dens of vice. The situation here is getting so bad that it is likely to break at any time with pretty serious repercussions . . . You are the best Premier, the most balanced and the most respected in my memory in the Province, and I do ask you again, personally, to go into this matter and to go into it quickly because it is going to break not only here but elsewhere."

Frost, as usual in his responses to Charlotte, was non-committal and passed the letters on to the relevant provincial ministries for further consideration.

In a separate letter to Frost dated the same day, Charlotte expressed concerns over her labour problems with Ottawa's police and fire departments. They wanted "quite unrealistic and exorbitant" pay increases. She disagreed with their demands, and she feared that as usual they would head for mediation and receive what she considered an overly generous settlement by the provincially appointed mediator, thus skewering her own cost-cutting efforts. She wanted to eliminate the mediator and let the city and police and fire personnel work out their own agreement. Again, Frost was non-committal, although he expressed some interest in the idea.

There were several other minor conflicts that Charlotte attended to in the early months of 1953, but what really enthused her during that period was the upcoming coronation of Queen Elizabeth II.

To say that Charlotte looked forward to the coronation on June 2 was like saying the buyer of a lottery ticket hoped to win the big prize; it was a given. Her involvement in the coronation was a labour of love that she had been working on privately since at least the previous September, when she wrote to some of London's leading boatbuilders inquiring if they could construct a "Queen's Shallop," or covered royal barge rowed by eight men, as a gift for the new queen from the City of Ottawa. At the same time, she wrote Canada's high commissioner in London, Norman Robertson, asking him to have his staff

Charlotte was proud of her official regalia and its connection to her British heritage.

City of Ottawa Archives, MG011/CA19128

find accommodation for her and a friend while they attended the coronation, even though she was unsure of winning, or even seeking, the mayoralty in December.

Sorry, replied the boatbuilders in November. Building a "Queen's Shallop," complete with traditional ornamentation and carving, would be far too costly. Robertson, on the other hand, had not replied by January, and Charlotte, having been re-elected mayor, was becoming concerned not only about where she would be staying in London, but what she would be wearing to the formal parties she planned to attend. What will the other women mayors be wearing, she questioned Robertson, noting that as Mayor of Ottawa, the only ceremonial attire she then had was the chain of office.

Finally, in early March, she was able to inform her friend Jack Pickersgill, clerk of the Privy Council, that Robertson and his staff not only had found accommodation in London for her and her friend, but had also arranged a car rental for their extended road trip to Scotland, as well as well as much sought after tickets for the Royal

Garden Party at Buckingham Palace. The friend accompanying her was Miss May Byers, her secretary and a strong supporter in her latest election campaign.

Meanwhile at city council, she had a surprise for her male colleagues. "Future Councils Berobed, Bewigged And Bewildered," read the front-page headline in the *Citizen* on February 27. The newspaper revealed how Charlotte, at a closed-door caucus two weeks earlier, had left the men agog when she announced plans that for future formal occasions, such as the start of council terms or the visits of Very Important Persons, they would be properly "robed." The formal attire, she informed them, would include the following:

> For the mayor: floor-length, red silk robe with miniver (white) fur trimming and cuffs, a black satin and gold lace trimmed tri-cornered hat, a lace jabot and chain of office.
>
> For the controllers: robes of maroon panama cloth trimmed with gold lace, with cockade hat with a gold-netted button.
>
> For the aldermen: robes of blue panama cloth with black velvet facings and cockade hat, with gold-netted button.
>
> For the city clerk: black corded silk robe (no hat).

The media were ecstatic — the story made headlines across the continent, and *Time* and *Life* magzines called to set up photo sessions — but the councillors seemed in shock. On March 2, at another closed-door caucus, they approved the new sartorial order, only to listen to another Whitton proposal to purchase a proper landau, or horse-drawn carriage, such as the one the Lord Mayor of London used when driven to Westminster, for the mayor and council. It, too, would be used only for special occasions, such as the opening of Parliament.

"Is Gilded Coach Next For Cinderella Mayor?" asked a front-page headline in the *Citizen* of March 3, over a news story and cartoon featuring Charlotte in a Ben Hur-type chariot. Even the *Journal*, though still supportive of the mayor, reported that the councillors "had been faced with a 'fait accompli' when it was pointed out to them that the robes were already on order." However, as the paper advised in an August editorial, "It would be easy to poke fun at the decision — easy, but perhaps short-sighted. It is the conviction of members of council that the wearing of formal robes on such occasions will enhance the prestige of that body of our elected representatives — that it will help develop in the mind of each individual a greater sense of dignity, of civic responsibility, and of dedication to the public interest. With that conviction we have no thought of expressing disagreement."

The media weren't the only ones chortling. In the House of Commons, British Columbia member of Parliament Alexander Cruickshank warned, "If the Mayor of Ottawa should become a member of this House, I would be a little worried . . . The Mayor of Ottawa may decide to clothe us in these 'Charlotte' gowns . . ." He added that it was unfair to the rest of the country that the federal government was spending heavily on beautifying Ottawa when that city's municipal council was wasting money on such costumes.

In addition to the formal clothes and the city's representation at the coronation by the mayor and her secretary, Charlotte also set up a special coronation committee that would organize suitable celebrations in Ottawa on June 2. These would include trooping of the colour and a massed band concert on Parliament Hill, religious services across town, fireworks, and — the highlight for some — a flotilla of boats on the Rideau Canal led by councillors bedecked in their fine, new robes of office.

Privately, she sought St. Laurent's approval to introduce a further touch of English heritage to local proceedings by having a suitably garbed mayor and city council greet the governor general at the gates of Rideau Hall whenever he left the vice-regal residence to open Parliament.

The mayor, Charlotte wrote to St. Laurent on March 23, would touch her hat and say, "Your Excellency, may I, in the name of the citizens of the Capital of Her Majesty's Dominion of Canada, present their allegiance and assure to you, Her Majesty's representative, free passage and safe conduct through the City of Ottawa to the Houses of Parliament?" Then, having assured the governor general of his "free passage," the mayor and councillors would board their landau, or landaus, and lead the governor general's procession to the Hill. St. Laurent replied that the councillors could greet the governor general at the gates of Rideau Hall if they wished, but the RCMP escort was quite adequate to ensure the Queen's representative's "safe conduct" to Parliament Hill.

Having completed the local arrangements, Charlotte had just a few more tasks to complete before leaving for London on May 14. There was her letter to the Lord Mayor of London advising him that his September 1952 visit to Ottawa had persuaded city councillors to accept their "robing"; her letter to old friend Elsie Lawson in London, seeking good seats for the running of the Epsom Derby; another letter to High Commissioner Robertson, asking him to arrange a good viewpoint for the coronation parade because she would be providing coverage for the *Ottawa Journal* and the Thomson papers; and her request to the deputy minister of health, asking him to use his influence with the immigration authorities so as to exempt her from having to take the mandatory smallpox vaccination. "My reactions have been so violent to inoculations that I have had to go into hospital on one occasion, and the other, to bed at home, with day and night nurses for some days," she wrote Dr. D.G.W. Cameron. There is no record in her files at the national archives of Cameron's response.

Finally, after so much preparation, she was set to celebrate.

How much did the coronation mean to Charlotte? Well, an excerpt from her January 9 note to recreation commissioner Alf Dulude opposing the naming of costumed queens and princesses at neighbourhood winter carnivals provided some indication: "'I think the Committee should give very serious attention to the fact that the Coronation of the Queen is a religious ceremony in which there is a dedication of her life to the service of the State and that this is part of a service in which the highest sacrament of the Christian Faith, the Eucharist, is part of the religious office. To desecrate this high office at any time, and particularly in the Capital City of Canada and in the year of Coronation, is an affront to the religious convictions and to the deepest sensibilities of the majority of the people and, I believe in fact, of most thinking people . . ."

Years later in a newspaper column, she would describe attending the coronation as "the thrill of my life."

Her visit began in London on May 15, and from there she and Byers drove north to Scotland with overnight stops at Bath, Warwick, and her ancestral hometown of East Witton, where she had herself photographed in full mayoral regalia outside the gates of the local school. She met the school principal, a Miss Whitton from West Witton, who gave her "a lucky stone" from the River Ure, which she vowed to keep always in the pocket of her mayoral gown. Then it was on to Edinburgh, where the *Evening Dispatch* reported on May 22 that she was thinking of running for a seat in the Canadian Parliament. It continued: "This was the woman whose luncheon speech at the City Chambers drew tremendous applause yesterday; this was the woman whose humour had the Councillors leaning back weakly with laughter, but whose eloquence later had them jerkily [*sic*] silent—'What a speaker!' they said admiringly."

Then the big day, Coronation Day, arrived. Charlotte, in her ceremonial regalia with Byers at her side, sat enthralled in her pew high in the east gallery of Westminster Abbey's south transept. "You could not believe that you were looking down upon the Queen clad in robes of state, crowned and seated on her throne," she wrote days later for the Thomson papers. "It was an experience to transport one from here and not into all the tides of all our story and all the hope of our future but, strangely enough, as humbly grateful and still unbelieving that this privilege was mine, I knelt and shared the homage offered by the peoples of her realm, my own heart filled with memory of my mother and grandmother and how hard they had worked that I might stay at school and how their hearts would have filled to know that I was in The Abbey for the crowning of the Queen." That and other similar recollections were contained in a 26-page pamphlet published later titled *By Command of the Queen*.

Following the coronation, she recounted:

> Those of us invited to Westminster Hall . . . had to make
> a 'run for it,' as one gorgeously accoutred potentate, I
> know not who, said to us, tossing his head like a child
> to shake the rain from the diamond cluster of his gold
> encrusted turban. The mantles of the knights in their
> dazzling hues clung to them, the judiciary shook dry their
> wigs, the military pranced as unperturbed as the women
> who had provided themselves with wraps against the
> Abbey's chill and therefore defied the drenching. It was a
> pageant—tiaras and turbans, evening gowns and evening

dress, brilliantly jewelled with the insignia of decorations, and, of course, Highland full dress stealing the show, none more dashing that Colonel Allan Chambers, DSO, D.V.A.'s [Department of Veteran Affairs] overseas administrator, in the full dress of the Canadian Scottish.

There were more social activities in the days ahead, such as attendance at Epsom Derby and a visit to the town of Frant in Sussex, where Ottawa founder Lt.-Col. John By once lived and where she planted an oak tree in his honour and had tea in the rectory with the parish council. Then, it was time to return to Ottawa and once more face discord and discontent over sewers, sidewalks, and the ongoing search for a new city hall.

The only negative note during this period was the death on February 12 of her eighteen-year-old cat Rustie. Rustie, she informed listeners of Ottawa radio station CFRA, had been her most faithful companion since the death of Margaret Grier five years earlier, and only recently had been staying with a friend because she was so tied up in her work. During summers, Rustie remained at the cottage at McGregor Lake, and when Charlotte arrived, Rustie "would leap in and out of the boat as it grated on the landing, and talk little cat chit-chat all the way up the rock flagging to the cabin doing her best to trip me, as she would roll in sheer joy in the grass and leaves along the path, or in the bank of thyme at the topmost slope." Upon her pet's death, "We wrapped the silky, soft, little body in a fine wool scarf and then in a tin box, and I drove her home, up to the garden she had loved at Renfrew. There she will lie just where stand the hollyhocks under which she would hide to scare the groundhog that lived in the gully. And because she would roll with glee when spring broke among the jonquils in the garden border, I put one of the first jonquils of the year with her and left her there, close to where those whom she had adored await, too, another day . . . And, then, I turned my car and drove back to your City and mine and the duty of the day."

Fortunately for Charlotte, the excitement of the coronation eased the passing of so close a companion.

By mid-June, Charlotte was back at city hall. But it was a calmer, mellower Charlotte. There were few outbursts from the mayor's office and council meetings remained brief—they lasted just over one hour in her absence, compared to the five or six hours under her chairmanship—as Ottawa's summer humidity descended on the town. Even reading the minutes of meetings held in her absence did not set off a verbal explosion, although she must have bitten her tongue when she noted that her colleagues had approved without argument a $6,372-plus-interest, court-ordered payment to the city's former finance commissioner for back wages, which Charlotte had fought, as well as approving a sweet deal for an up-and-coming property developer, a francophone housebuilder from the Sudbury area named Robert Campeau. Campeau was one of a number of small property developers in the national capital profiting from the postwar housing boom, but he had managed to avoid sharing infrastructure costs with the city on a new subdivision because he had registered the subdivision just prior to the fees going into effect. Charlotte said nothing, but undoubtedly kept his name in mind, for their sibling-like quarreling in the coming years would both disturb and titillate Ottawa residents, eventually become part of urban legend.

Dearer to her heart was a decision by the council in July to accept an invitation from the Central Canada Exhibition Association, which operated the summer "Ex", to wear their new ceremonial robes and cockade hats on the reviewing stand for the fair's opening parade.

Days later, though, her mood was sombre as she wrote a longtime friend, Miss Marcella Penzel of Little Rock, Arkansas, describing the loneliness she was feeling during one of her few trips to McGregor Lake. She had not invited anyone to her cottage that year and she did not even consider putting the dock in the water. There were no rowboat or canoe escapes on the gentle water, no bass fishing, only thoughts of friends and visitors who had died in recent years, such as Margaret Grier, Margaret Mackintosh, and the nursing superintendent at the Civic Hospital, Gertrude Bennett. "All are dead now and not even little Rustie following me at twilight."

October brought back signs of the testy, suspicious Charlotte, for it was then, as she noted in a confidential memorandum for her personal mayoral files, that she began questioning certain land dealings in the then largely undeveloped southern area of the city known as Alta Vista. The public school authority, which required city council approval to borrow money for new lands and buildings, was considering purchasing an undeveloped ninety-acre site along Smythe Road and, confidentially, informed the board of control of its intentions. The board, consequently, discussed building sewers and water mains in that direction. That was all done behind closed doors, but somehow, Charlotte learned, developer Robert Campeau had recently taken out an option to buy a substantial portion of the land for $470 an acre and now the school board was being asked to pay $1,500 an acre. To Charlotte, it seemed obvious: Campeau had a mole either on the board of control, or someone high up in the planning department, and her instinct pointed to a board member, Campeau's fellow francophone, Paul Tardif. However, all she could do was order the planning department to investigate further.

Meanwhile, she had many other matters on her agenda. For example, in the fall of 1953, the public library board hired a highly qualified francophone as its chief librarian, against her wishes; the federal government moved the National Film Board to Montreal from Ottawa, despite her opposition; she was involved in ongoing disagreements with the Federal District Commission over zoning for the move of Carleton College (later University) to a larger site; and a decision on the new city hall site was still pending. On a more positive note, she opened talks with the CNR aimed at developing an industrial park on their railway lands in the east end of the city.

The acrimony continued into 1954. It began in late January when Charlotte marched into a meeting of the CCEA's all-male executive meeting, "like Daniel into the lions' den," according to the *Journal*, and told them they were running their show "like so much eye-wash." She snapped at them, particularly at Len Coulter and longtime controller Gerry Geldert, for ignoring the six city councillors on their board and also for consuming too many cigarettes and too much alcohol at taxpayers' expense. Although the board members denied overspending on themselves and argued that the drinks were served at one luncheon only, Charlotte threatened to take their lease with the city for the Lansdowne Park grounds to the Ontario Municipal Board for investigation and possible cancellation. "Every mother's son of you knows you've gotten away with this way of doing things because it's almost political death to do otherwise or to come here as I have," the *Journal* quoted her.

The week-long "Ex" was next to sacrosanct in Ottawa. Established in 1877 by city council as an annual summer fair, which included a large agricultural component, it had from the start the support of a broad cross-section of the public and received considerable donations from the city's lumber barons. It was located at the city-owned Lansdowne Park, just south of Centretown, and received a regular grant from city council for operational expenses. Rarely a topic of controversy, in recent years it had seen attendance rise and the city's contribution decline from $34,000 in 1948 to $16,000 in 1952. Its popularity with many Ottawans and visitors from throughout the Ottawa Valley was reflected by previous councils' support. In 1946, Ottawa council gave it a ten-year lease to Lansdowne for a mere $1 a year, and in 1949 mayor Eddie Bourque's council extended the lease an extra three years, to 1959.

In Charlotte's eyes, that was like giving away the company store. Ever mindful of the public purse, she was keen to change that generous leasing arrangement, but in early 1954, there were still five years remaining on the contract. Her hands appeared to be tied in this case, but Charlotte would not be put off so easily.

She became aware that the CCEA board was using the buildings on the grounds, which were otherwise unused for 51 weeks of the year, as their personal warehouses, so she demanded to know what authorization they had for doing so. About the same time, she ordered a fire inspection, and in mid-February, the inspector's report confirmed her fears; the Coliseum building was a firetrap. The inspector found there were twenty-eight new cars parked on the first floor and eighty-six on the second; the 300 mattresses on the third were meant as beds for junior farmers when they attended the "Ex." In other buildings, there were used cars, electrical appliances, and sundry other items owned by people connected to the CCEA.

Meanwhile, another fire was kindling inside her. A junior staffer at the prestigious Ashbury College, a private school in Rockcliffe Park, where many diplomats and senior public servants enrolled their sons, had had the effrontery to complain in a letter to the editor of the *Journal* on February 9 that the newspaper was spending too much attention on the mayor's "immature political pranks, or quoting her hysterical outbursts . . . Miss Whitton is a comic opera type of civic official and should be dealt with as such . . ." The following day she threatened the letter-writer with a lawsuit, despite acknowledging that public officials had to accept criticism. "However this does not apply to defamation of character into which category, I believe you may legally assure yourself, certain of your statements fall." At the same time, she pressured Ashbury headmaster Ronald Perry to reprimand his staffer and write a public apology in the *Journal* "that you have read this letter with some surprise and regret that it should have been written by a junior member of Ashbury College staff, that you wish to dissociate yourself and the College entirely from any association therewith and that you feel that this letter should be printed . . ."

Replied Perry: "Naturally, I feel very badly that such a letter was ever written particularly by a member of the Ashbury College staff. I can only suggest that Mr. Locke did not realize the effect of such correspondence. I am glad that Mr. Locke has forwarded a letter of apology and I do hope that the matter has been cleared up to your satisfaction . . . On behalf of Ashbury College, I should like to add my own apologies and trust that in future members of my Staff will display a greater measure of common sense."

One year later, in March 1955, Charlotte had a similar joust with another Ashbury staffer, when Peter Falstrup-Fischer, an Englishman who recently had arrived at Ashbury after teaching in different European nations, wrote to the *Journal* complaining of potholes on one of the city's busiest thoroughfares. Charlotte again felt personally slighted, and immediately took her case to headmaster Perry, who had words with his new employee. She also wrote Falstrup-Fischer:

> I have ascertained that, though you write on Ashbury
> College paper, your letter has no authority whatsoever
> in respect to Ashbury College, or its Trustees and I think,
> therefore, it is in very poor part for you, a few months in
> Canada, to have associated the name of a school of fine
> traditions by the use of their letter head [*sic*] for a private
> communication . . . As a person of Yorkshire descent and
> who respects British and government traditions, I am
> surprised at the tone and circumstance of your letter.

But Falstrup-Fischer, a graduate of Cambridge University, refused to back down. He wrote back that it was "utterly fantastic" that she should write "such a discourteous and overbearing reply . . . British traditions, which you claim to respect, are greatly concerned with maintaining a liberal attitude and polite approach to people and problems in general, and I can only reiterate my amazement at your thunderous response to my first letter. I lived in Yorkshire for a few months during the last war, when I was flying in Bomber Command, and I can see no particular reason why your Yorkshire descent should produce surprise to my letter of 21 March, because I found Yorkshire people to be individualistic and understanding, even if a bit awkward at times."

Stung by such impertinence, Charlotte once more wrote headmaster Perry: "Mr. Falstrup-Fischer is the type, I should judge, who causes Canadians to put out the sign 'No English need apply.'"

Returning to February 1954, Charlotte made the headlines again near the end of the month when she stormed out of a closed-door board of control meeting, "white faced with anger," according to the *Citizen*, and charged that one company had a monopoly on the local cement business because certain controllers were blocking an out-of-town firm from developing a second quarry in the city. She did not name the controllers, but Tardif, who was becoming a regular irritant to her, acknowledged that he had voted against approval of the second quarry until he had more information on its plans. There were other mayoral outbursts during the year, such as those against the board of trade, the city's chief librarian and the Ontario Association of Mayor and Reeves, but they were overshadowed by a number of mayoral accomplishments as council headed towards a December 7 civic election.

Charlotte could point to progress towards finalizing a site for a new city hall, the signing of a hotly debated contract with the firemen, approval of a major shopping centre in the west end, the hiring of a new superintendent at the Civic Hospital, co-operation with the provincial government for a new bridge in the city that would be named after municipal affairs minister George Dunbar, and the hosting of the Queen Mother, who opened two reconstructed bridges on Sussex Street and received a pair of boxing gloves for her grandson, Prince Charles, a golden maple leaf for her granddaughter, Princess

Anne, and more maple sugar candies for both children. (Charlotte explained the gift of boxing gloves for the future king, "as becomes a Prince of our traditions, he may be well taught in the arts, both of defence and, if need be, of offence!").

While she was all civic business almost all of the time, she did find a little time for a few personal pursuits, such as asking the Speaker of the House of Commons to place a plaque outside the Commons' door honouring Agnes Macphail as the first female member of Parliament, welcoming the federal Progressive Conservative Party to its convention in Ottawa, having a Whitton family coat of arms designed for herself, and borrowing a .38-calibre pistol from the police department.

The coat of arms, arranged through Canadian heraldry expert Alan Beddoe, included a quill pen, an artist's brush, a few drops of blood and a teardrop, while over it all sat an inverted wastepaper basket and a black and blue wreath holding an ink pot and a lighter bearing the city's coat of arms. Inscribed on the shield was the motto, "Blood. Sweat. Tears."

As for the Iver Johnson nickel-plated, five-shot pistol, it was borrowed from an accommodating chief of police, Duncan MacDonnell, only after Charlotte had tried to buy it, but had been advised by the city solicitor that she could not since it was police property. She told MacDonnell that she wanted it for her personal protection at McGregor Lake (which was outside his jurisdiction in Quebec), because "I am alone a good deal of the time and we have had a good many refugees in the area in recent years." No problem, replied the ever accommodating MacDonnell. "I am enclosing with the pistol a few rounds of ammunition and can assure you that the application for registration [in Quebec] has been completed and forwarded and in a matter of a few days, when the official form is returned to me, I will forward it to yourself."

For a while, it appeared there might not be a mayoral election in December 1954, due to a lack of an opponent, or opponents, to Charlotte. Also, in late September, the *Citizen* published rumours that she was about to be named to the Ontario cabinet by Premier Frost, possibly as minister of municipal affairs when, as expected, George Dunbar retired.

By mid-November, however, two names were prominently mentioned as potential mayoral candidates and Dunbar announced his intention to stay put.

Her two opponents were David Burgess and Edouard "Eddie" Bourque. Burgess was a public servant and the low-profile chairman of the Civic Hospital board of trustees, while former mayor Bourque, who had lost to Grenville Goodwin in 1950, was last seen in the media after his defeat practising his longtime hobby — whittling traditional French-Canadian street scenes from blocks of wood. Neither seemed a serious threat to the incumbent.

Nevertheless, Charlotte plunged into her campaign with her usual intensity. But only after threatening to quit even before her campaign had officially begun. She demanded an all-out effort from her volunteer campaign team, and when word got out in mid-November that she might not run, her mailbox was besieged. This time, though, the pleaders were men as well as women, for now Charlotte was seen by many as an incorruptible force at a city hall that still retained vestiges of the bad old days when corruption and patronage seemed commonplace.

During the past year, a federal-provincial-municipal deal to build the cross-town multi-lane highway, which she named the Queensway, had been negotiated, 632 substandard dwellings and 227 slum units had been demolished, and residences had been found for the ousted tenants, and the federal and municipal governments had worked in harmony to improve traffic conditions in the city and on other projects.

In a series of radio broadcasts prior to this election, she reached out to those wanting to keep their property taxes low — "Don't you think the old mayor is still the best horse in the field? Keep her in harness"; to francophones — "I come to you, speaking my tongue, and hoping that you will bear with me while I attempt to say a few words in your tongue, though I am sure that when I am finished you will think that it is no tongue that has ever been on earth since the Tower of Babel"; and to the ordinary voter, explaining the municipal budget by showing that for every dollar spent by the city, thirteen cents came from the province, seven cents from the federal government, fifty-one cents from property taxes, and the remainder from service charges.

Heading into the polls, Bourque had the support of *Le Droît*, Burgess the *Citizen*, and Charlotte the *Journal*. The last, though, warned that she must "mend her ways and quit her seeming assumption that she is the source of all wisdom."

The outcome of the mayoral election was a foregone conclusion: Whitton — 32,687; Burgess — 22,590; Bourque — 13,546. For board of control, newcomer George Nelms topped the polls with 38,398 votes, followed by Paul Tardif, Roy Donaldson, and Ernie Jones.

"It's good that she is back in Ottawa," enthused an editorial in the *Montreal Gazette*. "There are unlikely to be many dull moments."

"We are sure most Canadians were pleased to hear that Charlotte Whitton is again mayor of Ottawa . . . Charlotte is the type of girl we all like, full of fire and brimstone," cheered the *Lethbridge Herald*.

16 Advantage Whitton

T he people had spoken. They wanted integrity in their politicians and they wanted action at the council table, and their support at the voting booth provided Charlotte with all the ammunition she needed to achieve this. If the wily woman mayor was exuberantly flamboyant at times, and if she could be accused and found guilty of outlandish behaviour and misbehaviour at times, so be it. She was certainly putting the dull, old public service town on the map, even if it meant occasionally dressing up her councillors as if they were attending a pirate costume party.

Her first target in 1955 was Robert Campeau, the equally zealous and short-tempered housebuilder-turned-property developer. As Charlotte complained to Ontario planning and development minister, W.K. Warrander, in a January 11 letter, Campeau appeared at a board of control meeting the morning after her re-election to urge the speedy approval of a housing subdivision on Smyth Road in Alta Vista, even though he had not provided detailed plans for the subdivision. At the same time, plans were afoot at the publicly owned Ottawa Hydro-Electric Commission, on which Charlotte sat as the city's representative, to buy land for a hydro substation in the neighbourhood to supply the proposed subdivision with power. There seemed to be an inordinate rush to satisfy Campeau, Charlotte warned Warrander, especially at the board of control where she had been outvoted on Campeau's bid, and she urged the minister to overrule the board's approval through his authority under the *Planning Act*.

She complained that even as Campeau awaited board approval, he went ahead with excavation on his subdivision and he had ignored federal government plans in the area for a possible parkway or public park. Furthermore, his subdivision was located well beyond other built-up subdivisions in the area, therefore requiring the city to pick up the full cost of extending roads, sewers, and sidewalks up to his property line, since the federal government, which owned much of the undeveloped property between the subdivisions, refused to share the infrastructure costs.

Warrander was won over. He ordered the Ontario Municipal Board to investigate, but unhappily for Charlotte, the OMB sided with Campeau, as had the Ottawa Planning Area Board and the city's technical advisory committee earlier.

Interestingly, when Tardif asked her for a copy of her letter to Warrander, Charlotte complied, but warned him pointedly that it was for his eyes only "and not for transmission to the Campeau Construction Company, or any representative of the said Company." It was an obvious warning to Tardif that she suspected him of being Campeau's mole on the board of control.

Once Campeau received OMB approval for his Elmdale Acres subdivision on Smyth Road in February, he wrote Charlotte in what seemed to be a tartly tongue-in-cheek greeting:

May It Please Your Worship:

It is with a great deal of pleasure and satisfaction that the officials of this company write you now to compliment you on your own personal endeavor in insisting on a proper operation of the Ottawa Area Planning Board and their Advisory Committee . . . We have very much appreciated the co-operation which we have received from yourself, the Technical Advisory Committee and the Ontario Municipal Board throughout our recent negotiations which have made it possible to arrive at a satisfactory conclusion.

Answered Charlotte, equally facetiously:

My dear Mr. Campeau

I want to thank you for your kind letter of February 24th and to say how gratified I am that you felt that you have received just and, I would take it, satisfactory treatment in our negotiations in this whole matter. I can assure you that at no time have I been swayed by any personal considerations in any of these procedures . . . What is

Robert Campeau and Charlotte exchange pleasantries at a social gathering.

Bill Olson, Dominion-Wide
Photographs Ltd., Library
and Archives Canada,
e016783839

good for the whole community cannot but be good for the responsible subdividing firm and, most important of all, for those who will live in the homes which you are building.

Advantage Campeau, one would have surmised. In fact, that's just what Campeau did surmise, because in early March, he advertised in local newspapers that construction on 225 homes would begin the following month with completion targeted for the fall. Also, his overall project in the area would eventually include 1,700 homes, a shopping centre, and space for schools.

Not so fast, read a press release from Charlotte the next day. "In view of certain press announcements and after consulting the officials of the City, I feel compelled, in the interests of the general public, to make it thoroughly clear that insofar as the City of Ottawa's best efforts and knowledge are concerned, the [start on] construction of houses in this area cannot be assured for April." Home buyers, therefore, could not be certain that their new homes would be ready by the fall as advertised, simply because Campeau still had not obtained his building permits from the city. Advantage Whitton.

Advantage, but not match, which would continue for years.

At the end of March, she contacted OMB chairman L.R. Cumming to say that not only was Campeau continuing to advertise his homes in the subdivision for sale, but was also promising to have them ready for occupancy on or before September 1. Furthermore, he advertised that electricians "have installed the finest in electric wiring and installations," although the city had not yet approved it. The OMB chairman, though, like the minister and the premier, steered clear of what was becoming an increasingly nasty bit of infighting in the national capital.

While Campeau was Charlotte's number one target in early 1955, another man was finding his way into her gunsight — George Nelms, her deputy mayor.

Nelms, forty-nine, was an optometrist, a businessman, a fundraiser for the Anglican church, a longtime schoolboard trustee and, as Charlotte was learning, an investor in Ottawa real estate. He operated Nelms Opticians in Centretown, lived on fashionable Sherwood Drive in the west end, and was a member of a handful of local service and private clubs. During his time on the public school board (1942–54), he had served as board chairman (1948–50) and chaired the board's property committee (1945–47, 1951–52). He was therefore quite conversant with property values in the city, and it was this interest in real estate that attracted Charlotte's attention.

The first mention in her archived files of Nelms's real estate dealings was a note dated January 30, 1954, from her secretary, May Byers: "A man who gave the name of David McDermot telephoned. He asked if there was a man by the name of Nelms on the Public School Board, and then said a good deal of property was being bought by the school board in the Alta Vista area and suggested it would be a good idea to look in the transfers of property prior to their purchase and see who was involved." At the bottom of the typed note was a handwritten note signed "C.W." that remarked, "Nobody knows who this man [McDermot] is. I think it might be well to have Mrs. M. Knight prepare a record of all public school and collegiate board purchases since annexation with the listings of owners, purchases and transfers. Then we could be properly informed."

She received a report from the city's planning and works director, Cecil Wight, in March, then apparently did not feel she had grounds to proceed further on the matter. However, her interest obviously was piqued, for the inference was that Nelms, who chaired the school board's property committee, might be using confidential information at the school board to buy undeveloped land in his own name for later resale to the school board at a profitable markup. This concerned Charlotte because city council was required by law to approve school board debentures for purchases, including new school properties.

In December, just prior to the municipal election, she received another note from another unknown man complaining that Nelms had been selling brooms to the school board through a company that Nelms co-owned with either Mr. or Mrs. Orian Low. Mr. Low, a lawyer, was also a school board trustee. At the same time, the complainant acknowledged that he, too, had bid on the brooms contract, but had lost. Again, Charlotte may have looked further into the allegation, but apparently found no grounds for further action. However, when the new board of control met for the first time on January 4, 1955, George Nelms was named to the planning and works portfolio, providing him an inside view of discussions concerning future land use, such as the new subdivisions that were springing up helter-skelter across the city.

In her inaugural speech to the new council on January 4, Charlotte did not mention Campeau, Nelms, nor any developer by name, but rather spoke of the need for efficiency, for cost-cutting measures, for city staff to lower their salary demands, and especially for the need of positive development in the city and its infrastructure. In connection with the last item, she introduced a $34-million, five-year public works program.

Four years earlier, the federal government had released the so-called Gréber Plan aimed at making over the face of Ottawa and her sister city Hull, across the Ottawa River in Quebec, by proposing broad thoroughfares, more parks, more bridges, relocation of the spiderweb-like railway tracks outside of the city's built-up areas, and improved town planning that was more in keeping with a national capital's image, but there was only so much the senior government could do. The rest was up to the two cities and the two provinces, and none of them was eager to spend the money required. Of most immediate interest to Ottawa was a new twenty-mile east-west, multi-lane highway through the city on the grounds recently vacated by the CNR. Although the highway was primarily a provincial concern, both federal and municipal governments contributed large amounts of land and monies towards it, and, according to Charlotte, she named it "The Queensway" in honour of the new queen when provincial officials debated whether to call it an expressway or a throughway.

While she was involved in Queensway planning, as well as the construction of four new bridges across the Rideau River and Rideau Canal, her mind was not far from an array of developments in other parts of the city. One in particular caught her special attention; a proposed high school in the Alta Vista area that, she informed Premier Frost in a confidential letter at the end of March, "will shock you as it shocked me." She told him that George Nelms had been handling the land purchase for the school board on behalf of council, but instead of taking the board's site recommendation to council for consideration as he was expected to do, he had allowed it to go straight to the OMB for approval.

"This is creating not only a condition of chaos but of resentment throughout the province and serious confusion within the different communities," she warned Frost. Sorry, education minister W.J. Dunlop replied from Queen's Park. Frost was on holidays and after discussing the issue with his own staff, Dunlop advised, "the Ottawa problem is one which must definitely be settled locally without interference from here."

Not to be put off so easily, she wrote Frost again days later: "May I urge you, if you think I have any political savvy at all, and any sense, really, of what is just, to give most serious consideration to this simple administrative clarification which will give realistic play to the grant limits on secondary schools?" Again there was no reply from the premier.

Nineteen fifty-five was becoming a most difficult year for Charlotte. Not only did she need to keep a close eye on Campeau and Nelms, but during the first three months alone she had confrontations with the Central Canada Exhibition Association executive over its tax-free status in the city, the Canadian Repertory Theatre after it had gone to the media about the noisy snow-clearing operations near its premises, the radiologists at the Civic Hospital over their after-hours private clinics, Ashbury College teacher Peter Falstrup-Fischer for his letter to the editor, and the Ottawa Gyro Club over its promotion of Little League baseball for youngsters. She even had a confrontation with a "little devil" she had caught tampering with a fire hydrant sign.

A public speaking tour of the Atlantic provinces at the end of April eased the tense situation at city hall temporarily, but by May there was another verbal explosion. It occurred behind closed doors at a board of control meeting on May 24, the upshot of which saw Charlotte announcing her resignation as mayor, Nelms following suit with his resignation as lead controller, and the other controllers seeking safety by avoiding the media.

The rain of resignations began with that of the city's treasurer, A.H. Ritchie. Ritchie's resignation, effective July 31, was announced at the closed-door meeting. He offered no reasons for quitting, but the local media reported rumours he was stepping aside because he could no longer handle the pressure at city hall. As word got out, the knives came out. Charlotte charged that there was a "power group" of controllers and aldermen, as well as some unnamed outsiders, who were intent on running city hall their way. She complained that the heads of most city departments were being pressured by this group to speed up the normal bureaucratic processes, particularly when it came to approving various subdivisions, and more resignations could be expected. Seemingly caught off guard, Nelms, who would have succeeded Charlotte as mayor upon her resignation, also announced after the closed-door meeting that he, too, would quit because he did not feel confident running the city without the city treasurer's support.

The next day, however, Nelms changed his mind and said he would stay. Charlotte, pressed to identify the opposition "power group," named controllers Tardif and Donaldson and aldermen Wilbert Hamilton, Howard Henry and R.J. Groves, but she did not identify the "outsiders" involved with them. She repeated her intention to resign and added that not only was Ritchie still quitting, but city solicitor Gordon Medcalf and planning and works commissioner L.W. Pillar were considering resigning as well. Until her resignation, though, she would stand her ground. "Only this weekend, two aldermen boasted they would first break the mayor and when she was out of the way they would get rid of the balky departmental heads. Well, my health is better than any of them and I intend to fight. I won't fight with knives in dark alleys either, but in the open with my broad axe," she told the *Citizen*.

Retorted Hamilton, the longest-serving alderman: "'I say it is a case of her resigning or several more departmental heads will leave within the next few months."

Added Tardif: "I have heard her at least 30 times threaten to resign and it hasn't happened yet. It's the same old smokescreen she used before the last elections."

The ruckus continued for days, and even the *Journal*, Charlotte's longtime supporter, advised in an editorial: "Mayor Whitton's tempers tend to follow a style, and this not the first time she has threatened to resign . . . It is the plain duty of the mayor to put the city's system of government back into quiet and efficient running order . . . The people have had quite enough of alarums and crises and mass resignations."

Inevitably, that particular furore blew away like snowflakes in a gale, but more fireworks were expected at the next council meeting on June 6 over spending on a new high school. On that date, however, Charlotte was far away in the United States receiving yet another honorary doctorate — her fifth — this time from Smith College, a prominent women's university in Northampton, Massachusetts.

There were other dust-ups at city hall during the summer involving various personalities, but Charlotte, who disregarded her earlier resignation threat, successfully worked with the federal government on infrastructure improvements and higher "in lieu" payments. She also looked after her own neighbourhood, in particular her own street, ordering the police chief to step up patrols for parking violators. At the same time, she copied the memo to the city's planning director, the chairman of the traffic committee, and to the board of control. In it, she blamed the increasing number of apartments on the street for the heavy traffic and suggested that "no parking" signs be introduced on one side of the road. The following day, police chief MacDonnell replied, "The parking on Rideau Terrace will be given immediate and vigorous attention."

On November 9, 1955, Charlotte's brother, Stephen, died at the age of forty-six. Charlotte's favourite, Stephen was thirteen years younger than his famous sister, and she had adopted an almost maternal concern for him throughout his often troubled life. When he dropped out of university at age twenty to find work in Saskatchewan for a few years, she convinced him to return to Queen's, and when he had difficulty finding a job after graduating with a bachelor of commerce degree in 1936, she wrote influential friends seeking job interviews for him. At one point she offered to pay his salary for his first few months with a company. That particular effort did not work out, but she was influential in finding him a temporary job in the accounting section of the A.J. Freiman department store in Ottawa.

He married Kathleen Cunningham in 1945 and they had one son, John Hezeltyne Whitton, but in 1949, Stephen suffered a stroke while working on the Thessalon tunnel in northern Ontario. He remained lame and had blurred speech for the rest of his life. In August 1955, Charlotte wrote Eileen Flanagan, director of nursing at the neurological institute of the Royal Victoria Hospital in Montreal and an occasional visitor at her McGregor Lake cottage, requesting Flanagan to use her influence to have Stephen admitted to the Montreal institution because his doctors in Ottawa were having little success in treating him. Stephen was admitted to the Royal Vic, where he died not long after. That left Charlotte with only two immediate surviving family members, her brother John, a project engineer on a construction site at Kitimat in northern British Columbia, and her sister Kay, the socialite wife of Ottawa radio station owner and prominent horse-breeder Frank Ryan.

On a more cheerful note, Charlotte finally received some good news in mid-November as a result of her long-running efforts to obtain a proper city hall building for Ottawa. It had been a prime objective of hers from the day she accepted nomination for the board of control in October 1950, and one she had worked on continually with the Federal District Commission in the intervening years. Now it appeared to be a giant step closer to closure.

Ottawa had been without a proper city hall building since the previous one, located on Confederation Square in the city's core, was razed by fire in 1931. Since then, successive city councils tried fruitlessly to agree on a new site, particularly because the federal government, and former prime minister Mackenzie King especially, wanted the old site and acres around it reserved for a grand public park reaching south from Parliament Hill to Laurier Avenue. In 1949, then mayor Edouard Bourque announced plans to locate on Nicholas Street, on the east side of the Rideau Canal just opposite Mackenzie King's proposed park; however, when that did not work out, council looked at twenty-two sites around the city, all of which proved inadequate or unavailable for one reason or another. Then, after swaying between choosing one site or another downtown, and after Charlotte established a new site committee in 1952, a new scheme went forth. It would place a small, formal city hall building of only four or five storeys for the councillors and a few key departmental managers on the old city hall site, despite King's dream and Jacques Gréber's official plan, and build a high-rise office block for most other city offices on the Nicholas Street site.

No, said the Federal District Commission. The Elgin Street site was reserved for parkland and there would be no city building of any type allowed there. But, Charlotte reminded FDC chairman Maj.-Gen. Howard Kennedy, the site had been donated to the city in perpetuity by Bytown pioneer Nicholas Sparks, only if it was used as either a town hall or a marketplace. Kennedy would not budge. Dismayed, the city site committee rethought its strategy and agreed to study two more sites well away from the city's core, but those, too, were deemed inadequate because of their location. The stand-off continued through 1953, 1954, and most of 1955, as other sites were suggested, studied, and dismissed.

Then a letter from Kennedy arrived in November 1955. "In order to assist in arriving at a choice amongst the possible sites, but with no desire to dictate in any manner which may be selected, I have been authorized by the Government to offer a site on Green Island between Sussex Street and the Minto Bridges," it read. In return, the city would have to give up the Confederation Square site. Charlotte was delighted. She knew she was never going to change the federal government's mind about Confederation Square and she had seen the site on Green Island, a seven-acre patch of land in the Rideau River about two-thirds along the ceremonial Sussex Street (later Drive) route between Parliament Hill and the governor general's residence at Rideau Hall, and had had it studied earlier in the year as a possible choice. Now it was on the table. Charlotte took it to the board of control that day, and was able to write Kennedy later in the day that the board had approved it promptly and she would take it to the next full council meeting. And by the way, she added, she presumed he knew that the Confederation Square site was worth eight or nine times the value of the Green Island site, because of its central location, and then there was the matter of Sparks's will. The bargaining was just beginning, but at last Charlotte was assured of her city hall site, which council approved on January 30, 1956.

The new building could not have come too soon for the city's staff, who were upset by Charlotte's cost-cutting methods, cramped by the lack of proper office space and facilities, and pressured by property developers who were throwing up housing subdivisions like Johnny Appleseed spreading his seeds across America.

Among the most prominent complainers was Robert Campeau. Born in Sudbury, Campeau had arrived in Ottawa in 1949, built a house and sold it quickly, built another house and sold it just as quickly, and then started building a group of houses and purchasing undeveloped land for still more houses until, in 1955, he was the largest housebuilder and subdivision developer in town. Campeau was an excellent builder — the author lives in a Campeau-built home and can attest to the company's workmanship — but when it came to finances, Campeau was driving by the seat of his pants. Often he sold his homes even before his subdivisions received council approval, and as far as bylaws were concerned, he did not spend an inordinate amount of time reading the fine print. He was a man on a mission, and his mission was to get rich quick. In order to achieve that, he had to build and sell homes quickly, and he could only do that if he received the required permits from city hall promptly and if he could encourage the city to build watermains, sewers, and roads to his subdivision in the quickest possible time. Unfortunately for him, city hall did not always move at the velocity of the man.

This was especially true in 1955, as he emphasized in a sharply worded letter to the board of control in November. "For the past few months your Department of Planning and Works has been hopelessly unable to cope with the demands made upon it for materials in the new subdivisions made necessary by sewer installations and road building and so forth. Such things as culverts for intersections and for individual driveways, manhole covers, even sewer piping, have been either in short supply or completely lacking. For some weeks now there have been no culverts," he complained. Furthermore, at least thirty-five residents of just one street in his Applewood Acres subdivision in Alta Vista — where he and Tardif lived two doors apart on Applewood Crescent — could not park their cars in their driveways because the city had not yet installed culverts, yet they were ticketed by police for parking illegally on the street. In another case, manholes were covered only by loose wooden planks that were subject to easy dislodging. "I can not help picturing a young child living on the project removing planks off a manhole and falling in; I am sure the City would find itself in a most embarrassing situation," he warned.

Thus chastised, L.W. Pillar, the city's works commissioner, wrote to advise him that construction of his new homes on Paugh Street in Applewood Acres had not been completed according to specifications and therefore a new inspection would be required when the proper work was done. Obviously miffed with Campeau's aggressiveness, Pillar directed a confidential memo to city council explaining that his stressed workers had laid twenty miles of sanitary sewers during the year and more than a quarter of them went to or were in new Campeau subdivisions. As well, they had worked overtime concentrating on roads to his Elmvale Acres properties resulting in delays in street construction elsewhere. Moreover, he informed city council, that while staff were on holidays, Campeau workers had broken into the city's sewer system and made their own connections between the new houses and the sewer system. "I informed them that the next time this was done I would prosecute," Pillar warned.

Campeau and other developers were not the only ones pressuring Pillar. Inside city hall, Charlotte was pressing him during the summer over delays in the construction of Dunbar Bridge over the Rideau River, which was named after the municipal affairs minister and Ottawa South member of the legislature, George Dunbar. She wanted it to be opened officially in mid-October by Princess Margaret, during her visit to the city, but Pillar said it was impossible because of a North American steel shortage, among other reasons. In the end, Margaret was invited to inspect completion of a second structure, the Hurdman Bridge, and Charlotte and other local officials set a plaque at the Dunbar Bridge site "to mark the initiation of the last portion of the works."

On the way to the latter ceremony, her car broke down due to a faulty carburetor, but Charlotte fixed the problem with a bobby pin and arrived on time.

As this tumultuous year concluded, Charlotte happily informed the editor of the *Citizen* that she had received 4,000 greeting cards at Christmas and George Nelms confirmed widespread rumours that he was involved, both legally and ethically, in the ownership of a real estate project in Alta Vista.

On the bitterly cold afternoon of January 1, 1956, the phone rang in Charlotte's warm Rideau Terrace apartment as she was emerging from a comfortable mustard bath meant to cure a miserable, lingering cold that had forced a brief stay at the Civic Hospital. Fire chief John Foote was on the line. The USSR embassy was on fire. Embassy staff refused to allow his men onto their gated grounds to fight the fire. Homes nearby were threatened, and if the wind changed direction, much of Sandy Hill, the prosperous neighbourhood where the embassy stood on a bluff overlooking the Rideau River, would be at risk. Charlotte raced to the scene on Charlotte Street—the name was coincidental and not related to the mayor—about a half-hour's drive from her apartment. She was not going to let those darned Russians burn down her town. As crowds lined the street outside the tall gates of the stately mansion, and as embassy staff hurriedly removed boxes of files amidst billowing smoke and dancing flames, Charlotte threatened to read the *Riot Act* so as to allow the firemen in, diplomatic immunity or not.

Fortunately for Charlotte, and the people of Canada, the acting secretary of state for external affairs, health and welfare minister Paul Martin, father of a future prime minister of the same name, arrived on the scene at about the same time and deterred her from tramping on international convention. The embassy and land within its gates were foreign soil, after all, and forcing firemen through the gates might be seen as a territorial invasion. At other times, that possibility might have seemed highly improbable, but the Cold War was nearing its peak. It had only been seven years since the Gouzenko

City controllers look on as Charlotte wields a hefty shovel full of dirt in turning the first sod for the future city hall on Green Island, September 25, 1956.

City of Ottawa Archives, MG393

Affair, when Soviet cipher clerk Igor Gouzenko fled this same embassy and disclosed an international Soviet spy ring operating from its confines.

Eventually, Soviet ambassador Dimitri Chuvanin went out to the street in front of the embassy, and diplomatic discussions ensued until, finally, Chuvanin allowed the firemen in. By then the building was nearly gutted. The blaze was extinguished by 11 p.m. and all homes in Sandy Hill were saved. No one was injured. The only physical altercation during the affair occurred when Fire Chief Foote tried to enter a second-floor room containing wireless and decoding instruments and was blocked by a Soviet staffer. Foote told reporters later, "I gave him my shoulder, because I had a job to do, and the Russian took a swing at me. I ducked." No harm was done to either man. The Soviets quickly moved to temporary quarters until a new, maximum-security granite building was constructed at the same location.

It was a busy, but not particularly difficult year. There were the usual disagreements with Campeau, but her inaugural address in

January was well received, as was her personal report in February to the federal commission on Canada's economic prospects. In April, Civic Hospital trustees accepted her $1,000 gift for a memorial chapel in Margaret Grier's name, and in August, after much haggling, the Privy Council approved a deal with the city whereby the city would obtain most of Green Island for its new city hall in exchange for the former city hall site on Confederation Square.

In turning the first sod on Green Island on September 25, a robed Charlotte could not help but reflect on a piece of local history: "It is doubtful whether even the Ark of the Covenant has wandered as frequently about as the municipal government of the community that is today the City of Ottawa. The building which we plan and hope will rise here will be the *seventh* edifice to house our municipal life." The eight-storey building would be completed in two years, but by then Charlotte would no longer be a member of city council.

Rumours had been circulating during much of 1956 that opposition to Charlotte's rule at council was becoming emboldened and there might be a good run in the upcoming civic election. No names were mentioned publicly, but as early as the first week of January, it was noted that far fewer local politicians attended Charlotte's annual "at home" party at Lansdowne Park, usually the highlight of the city hall social calendar. Again in early January, George Nelms and Paul Tardif voiced their annoyance at the mayor's decision to postpone two board of control meetings because she was ill — both men said the deferments caused them to make costly postponements in their personal businesses — and Nelms was reported as saying that the board could get along quite well without her.

In May, she issued a lengthy news release, beginning, "I have steadfastly refused to begin the civic election campaign until the autumn in the interest of carrying on the City's business. But when a statement is made, such as that attributed to Controller Nelms in respect to industrial and commercial development in Ottawa, I cannot ignore it as Mayor, in fairness to the Board of Control as a whole and in protection of the financial position of Ottawa and its people." Nelms apparently had leaked the fact that Charlotte was trying to organize a "citizens' corporation" to amass a land assembly in the city's southeast next to the CNR's industrial lands, and before she was able to set up her arm's-length corporation, a local developer, the so-called "Shenkman Interests," had purchased much of the proposed land that she was after. She did not claim that Nelms was in cahoots with Shenkman, but emphasized that he should not have given out "the team's signals to the possible grave disinterest of the city in its negotiations at the federal and provincial level and with the private interests with whom discussion was being arranged. It does not much matter what happens to me or to Controller Nelms but it does as to what happens to the city. May I ask the controller to play the game according to the rules."

By September, the rumours had turned into a constant drumbeat, and when a *Citizen* reporter asked if she would be running in the Ottawa West riding held by Liberal George McIlraith in the next federal election, which was expected within a year, she responded, "As a matter of fact, the member for Ottawa West and I have been working so effectively together for the last few months [on various federal-municipal projects] that I would like to see the Prime Minister give him a well merited appointment to the Senate and I would carry West Ottawa. Then you would really see the National Capital go places with me pushing it in the Commons, George McIlraith in the Senate, and Howard Kennedy riding along in the FDC."

At about the same time, Margaret Grier's elderly sister, Sister Dora of the Sisters of Saint John, wrote from the Toronto area, "So you may run for the [Progressive Conservative Party] leadership. If you do, I hope that you will attain it by a fine majority. In any case, you will make the Liberals fearful!"

Charlotte put the rumours to rest on October 31. On the sixth anniversary of her entry into local politics, she issued a press statement saying that she would not contest the next civic election.

So, while she was going, she was not gone. There were still sewers and similar sundry items to attend to, and Charlotte was not one to shuffle off with her work undone. Consequently, she was pleased to note in a letter to Premier Frost in November that the board of control had just approved a $43-million sewer construction program in which the federal and provincial governments had agreed to pay $11 million each, with the city picking up the remainder.

Even Robert Campeau was in a good mood that month, she mused while reading a personal note he sent, in which he enclosed a cheque for $100. It read:

Dear Mayor Whitton:

I am rather upset about the clumsy manner in which I tore your evening gown at the Fireman's Ball last night; please accept my sincere apologies. In view of the fact that I am convinced your dress is ruined, I would appreciate it very much if you accepted the enclosed cheque with which I trust you can purchase a suitable replacement.

Yours sincerely, Robert Campeau.

She replied:

My dear Mr. Campeau:

You will never credit, I am sure, that the Mayor of Ottawa would consider not depositing any cheque with the Campeau name on it, at once, and seeing whether it might not even be increased. Now do not worry about your "clumsiness," it was because you were stepping as lightly and gracefully as a modern cavalier that you got entangled in a skirt, that like too many of modern dresses — and like the Mayor herself — covers a lot of territory. The dress, like the Mayor also, will never be quite the same because of what it — and she — have been through but by running a new line through the "subdivided" portions I can still maintain adequate frontage for a few more promenades.

Further, she advised him, that in order to avoid any suggestion of conflict of interest, she was donating his cheque to the Grey Nuns towards the purchase of clothes for the residents of the nuns' retirement homes.

As the cold days of December 1956 arrived, Charlotte remained coy about her future, political or otherwise. However, she did place advertisements on the sides of city buses and streetcars showing her informally in slacks, snowboots, winter jacket, and curling tam, along with the message, "Hi Ottawa, good-bye for now. Au Revoir — Charlotte."

The rumours about her future continued to swirl. Some people said she would run for the provincial legislature upon George Dunbar's retirement, others were convinced that she would seek McIlraith's seat in the House of Commons. In the *Journal*, veteran reporter Richard Jackson said she had told friends she was considering four possibilities: a federal cabinet post, a provincial cabinet post, a position with the United Nations, or a position with a major American foundation. Charlotte, uncharacteristically, remained mum.

As the last days of December dawned and died, the local media said their farewells to their favourite newsmaker. The *Journal*, in an editorial headlined "Miss Whitton Bows Out," observed:

> Mayor Whitton never entertained the least doubt that she was head of the administration. She could use her women's wiles to gain a point but also she could be a hard and sometimes ruthless driver of her controllers and aldermen, her departmental heads and the bodies of which she was an ex-officio member. Where Charlotte sits is the head of the table. She knows so much about so many things, and has opinions on them all to express with voluble eloquence, that slower but perhaps not less competent minds appear at a disadvantage . . . Miss Whitton is not an easy person with whom to work, and perhaps her chief fault in the field of civic politics has been a sort of intellectual arrogance, a contempt for these lesser minds — an attitude which has made co-operation difficult and has cost her the support of some of those who did not fail to realize her outstanding qualities . . . This volatile and versatile lady will be heard from again, so Ottawa can say no more than good-bye for now, Charlotte, thanks and good luck.

Even the *Citizen* praised "This Truly Remarkable Woman:"

> Much was accomplished, a great deal was ventured and many plans were made for the future . . . Mayor Whitton was everywhere; did everything . . . the name "Charlotte" became synonymous with Ottawa. In Canadian cities from coast to coast — and, indeed, in the United States and other lands — the traveller from Ottawa would be greeted with the query, "How's Charlotte?" . . . She was interested

in practically everything . . . only a person blessed with some sort of a supercharger in the physical and nervous system could have weathered such a pace for so long . . . Even her opponents will admit she has changed things tremendously and the City Hall will never be the same again . . .

The last word in this chapter should go to the woman herself. The following is an excerpt from her valedictory speech to city council at its last meeting of the year, on December 17:

. . . The time has come for me to say good-bye. It will be strange not to be thinking always of "the City," to have Monday come without council and Tuesday without board of control; and Wednesday without the OTC [Ottawa Transportation Commission] and Thursday without the Civic Hospital and Friday without Hydro or the Library Board. It will be strange to look upon the snow softly and steadily falling and not be worrying about its clogging of the ways to church and school and work — or the cost of clearing them; or the uncertainty of the garbage collection, or what the spring freshets will do to the ditches, drains and storm sewers or the scorching summer sun to the water supply, the grass and gardens; or the thunderstorm to the hydro, or what will happen to the crowded beaches, or whether the firemen will opt for an arbitration or the Exhibition Association seek new concesssions . . .

For what a weariness it all can be — be the spirit ever so willing — to try to serve a great modern city in all its needs, the clock round, the week through, from year's end to year's end, and all the time to be about explaining and defending and trying to believe (and have others believe) that each and all of us are seeking but one end — the good of the City itself . . .

But now, I say, "Good-bye" — that word into which, in the centuries of our spoken English, we have shortened the old "God be with you." "Goodbye" and "to match the sorrow of each day's growing — so, too, Good-Morrow!"

17 The Diefenbaker Affair

Charlotte deserved a rest. Now sixty, this human dynamo had devoted twelve-hour days, sometimes longer, tending to the concerns of the national capital, shaking up its often lethargic municipal bureaucracy, battling the increasingly confrontational board of control, sparring with aggressive property developers, befriending provincial cabinet ministers, and twisting the arms of federal officials at all levels. Now she was out of it. The city was in the hands of George Nelms, who had been acclaimed mayor in December.

To escape the January cold, Charlotte wisely headed south to the warm welcome of longtime female friends in South Carolina, for rest, relaxation, and mental regeneration. There was much to look forward to on her return, however, for employment offers filled her mailbox during her absence. For example, the managing editor of the *Journal*, T.G. Lowrey, asked if she was interested in writing a weekly column; she turned him down, remarking that she had already received three similar offers and had chosen to return to her thrice-weekly column with the *Citizen* and to broadcast a weekly Sunday afternoon radio commentary on CFRA, the local radio station owned by her brother-in-law, Frank Ryan. As well, old friend and new leader of the federal Progressive Conservative Party, John Diefenbaker, was anxious to have her run in Renfrew South during the next federal election, which she seriously considered as she rested by "the mist-veiled marshes of South Carolina's 'east low country,' vibrant with the song of their hidden birds."

She returned to Ottawa in February, fully restored and her typewriter at the ready. The *Citizen* promoted her column, "On Thinking It Over," by advertising that "She has a sharp tongue, a sharper eye and a mind the sharpest of the three." She signed her column

"Charlotte," but below a head-and-shoulders photo of herself read the caption "Dr. Whitton."

The columns spilled out on a range of topics — on Israel and its rightful place in the Middle East, on the city's firemen and the need for a responsible fire commission to keep them in check, on the increasing threat from communism internationally, on pollution in the Ottawa River, on education in Ontario, on the good work the Catholic nuns in Ottawa were doing by forbidding their teenaged female charges from viewing "the primitive and suggestive distortions of [Elvis] Presley," when he appeared for a single performance at the Auditorium. She was back at her best, voicing her opinions on whatever came into her head, no matter how unpopular or odd those opinions might seem to certain segments of the population. As a columnist, she had free range, and it was an opportunity she unquestionably enjoyed.

Surprisingly for some, due to her perceived anti-Semitic attitude, which dated back to the late 1930s when she was accused of opposing the immigration of Jewish child refugees from Hitler's Germany[6], she vigorously supported Israel in its ongoing war with Egypt during the Suez Crisis. This was one year after Egypt's Gamal Abdel Nasser had seized the Suez Canal and Israel, Britain and France had attacked Egypt in an attempt to keep the canal open for international shipping.

In another column, she deplored the state of the world and the incompetence of the United Nations for its inability to curb Nasser, prevent the invasion of Hungary by the Soviet Union, or penalize India's Jawaharlal Nehru for cracking down on democracy in Kashmir. Further, allowing Nasser to get away with seizing the Suez Canal would have been like withdrawing the Allied forces from Europe in 1943 on a vague promise from Adolf Hitler that he would discuss his enemies' concerns sometime later. "It just is not good enough and Israel should not be added to the burnt offering of [ousted British prime minister Anthony] Eden, Britain and France. Economic sanctions mean Israel's destruction, for her people would prefer their own death to that of their state."

---

6   In fact, she lobbied for the acceptance of British children into Canada first, and recommended that the Jewish children and adults be sent to "areas and countries now but semi-settled and set apart for such purposes," such as Palestine.

The threat of communist world dominance continued to be Charlotte's prime target, but as the month progressed, her thoughts increasingly turned to federal politics. Prime Minister Louis St. Laurent was expected to call a federal election shortly, and John Diefenbaker was knocking on her door.

How could she resist? Theirs was a relationship that could be traced back to at least August 1944, when Diefenbaker, then an opposition backbencher addressed a letter to "Dr. Charlotte Whitton," suggesting that the Conservative Party should publish an article she had written on postwar security. The following year, Charlotte wrote "Dear J.D.", warning him that women were becoming turned off by the Tories and were either staying home from the polls or voting for the CCF. In 1948, he had supported her in the House of Commons with regards to the "Babies for Export" court case in Alberta, the same year she affectionately referred to him as "Johnny D" in *Molly Mugwump* and offered to support him in what became a failed attempt to secure the party leadership.

In 1949, he wrote to her while she was travelling in Britain, saying he was anxious to discuss party affairs when she returned, and that he regularly read her columns in the *Citizen* and passed them on to his mother, who enjoyed them immensely. "They were magnificent," he stressed. Similarly, he praised her radio commentary of February 16, 1952, when she had spoken in favour the Royal Family. It was "a wonderful and inspiring message. It combines rare scholarship coupled with an appreciation of the finest things for which Kingship stands."

Theirs was a platonic, political affair, but that did not stop Charlotte from inviting Diefenbaker, then a widower, to be her date to the National Press Club Ball in February 1953. It made the front page of the *Journal* when their private conversation, presumably leaked to the paper by Charlotte, was printed for all to read. As Diefenbaker recalled in his memoirs, *One Canada*, he was approached soon after by St. Laurent's wife, Jeanne, who warned, "Don't ever marry Charlotte Whitton. You are too much alike to ever get along." Mme. St. Laurent need not have worried; Diefenbaker married Olive Freeman Palmer later that year.

"What's a woman to do?" Charlotte asked readers in her February 22, 1957, column. All indications pointed to a federal election, she was tempted to run as a Conservative candidate, and besides, she added with a trace of sarcasm, "I am sure my sister [Kay], the president of the Ottawa Women's Liberal Association, is storing up energy in Havana for something more strenuous than just spring at the Ryans' Kilreen Farm."

Not only were Diefenbaker and his backroom advisers anxious to have her run in Renfrew South — the riding once held by Tom Low, for whom she worked in the 1920s — but they were also keen that she campaign nationally to attract the women's vote. If the Tories were successful in ousting the Liberals, there might well be an important cabinet post for her. But time was running out. She would have to decide immediately, for the Renfrew South nomination convention was to be held the next day. Still undecided, she informed her readers she would attend the convention, but "just to see old friends and find out what the issues are in that hard-headed, warm-hearted county."

That was not how Diefenbaker saw it, according to his memoirs. He recalled that his candidate recruitment campaign was going smoothly in general, but there were a few minor problems, such as the situation in Renfrew South.

> I wanted to get Charlotte Whitton to run . . . She could
> have won very easily; she was raised in that area. Typical
> of Charlotte, she wouldn't say yes and she wouldn't say
> no. I spent an hour with her in my office one morning
> discussing the question. That finished me; Gordon
> Churchill had to take over. When I went into the House at
> eleven o'clock, he was with her; when I came back at one,
> she was still saying the same thing over and over again.

The following day she phoned him to say that she decided to attend the Renfrew South nominating convention and wanted to drive to Renfrew with him. He disagreed, arguing that the other nominees would feel he was favouring her over them; she, however, reminded him that she had not yet decided on her candidacy. They drove separately to Renfrew. Once there, Diefenbaker waited patiently on the platform for more than three hours as the locals spoke, for he had been promised that his full speech would be broadcast by the local radio station.

No candidate was to speak for more than five or ten minutes. I don't know how long Charlotte spoke, but it was over an hour. And she ended up saying, "I will not run!" The result was that instead of having forty-five minutes on the radio, I had five minutes.

The *Citizen* reported that Charlotte "could have walked away with the Tory nomination for the asking." Instead, Jim Baskin, a local hotelier with a keen interest in horse racing, won the nod, as well as the election, and served in the House of Commons until 1963. In retrospect, Charlotte had just missed her big chance. In the short run, she most definitely would have received a cabinet post; in the long run, she might have become the first female prime minister of Canada. Ironically, the normally decisive politician was sidetracked by her own waffling.

That was February. In March, Charlotte contented herself with writing columns on topics ranging from her opposition to Medicare and evening shopping in Ottawa, to her growing despair for the Britain she had once known, and to attacking the Bank of Canada for suggesting lower interest rates. Come April, she was back in a political mode — more railing against Mayor Nelms and his pro-business board of control, more support for Israel, more complaints about pollution in the Ottawa River — but her main focus was the Conservative nomination in the local riding of Carleton. Despite her pronouncement in Renfrew, she had not given up the idea of federal politics.

It was a long shot, for the riding's executive favoured either of her two opponents, longtime Tories Dick Bell and Russell Boucher, to herself, but as she told the nominating meeting, "I seek your nomination tonight . . . because I believe that my country faces a crisis in democracy. I want to have a real and active part in the battle to make Parliament a place of real discussion and decision, where the Members are again subject and attentive to the votes and voice of the people . . . But even as I ask for your support, I know that I may be licked before I start. I'll likely go out on your first ballot." Which is exactly what happened. Bell won the nomination and was elected to Parliament, where he remained, off and on, until 1968.

Diefenbaker won the June 10 election, chasing the Liberals from power after twenty-two years in office, but only with a minority (Conservatives — 119 of the 265 seats in the House of Commons, Liberals — 104, CCF — 25, Social Credit — 19, Independent — 5).

Commented Charlotte in her June 19 column:

> Perhaps I should explain why I called Mr. Diefenbaker "Hurricane Johnny" in my Sunday broadcast . . . well, first I called Mr. Diefenbaker "Hurricane Johnny" because he started sweeping in from the Atlantic, with just a threatening storm at Newfoundland, but hitting Prince Edward Island and the mainland with the force of a tidal wave from Cape Breton almost to the Laurentian Shield. Across the Prairies he swept, shaking the grain elevators and the oil derricks. He rolled on down the Western Rockies to break with full impact from the Interior of B.C. right to the Pacific. John Diefenbaker, in the very force of his storming anger, convinced the people that government should be brought back under the control of Parliament.

One month later, writing from England where she was touring for five weeks, she reported to her *Citizen* readers that the British were happy to have a Canadian leader who favoured the Commonwealth, who toasted the Queen with a glass of milk, and who was a reformed heavy cigarette smoker.

Charlotte did not confine herself to newspaper work and politics in 1957. In May, she had the whole city chuckling when the newspapers pictured her in a duck's costume for her celebrity role in an Ottawa Philharmonic Orchestra pantomime. In June and July, her British tour included a stop at Westminster Abbey to pay her respects at the tomb of Elizabeth I, presentation to the current Queen Elizabeth at a Buckingham Palace garden party, and a return to her ancestral home in the Yorkshire Dales.

On a side note, in February, Rev. Lionel Bruce, rector of St. Alban the Martyr, assured her she could still use the front pew that Sir John A. Macdonald once graced, even though she was no longer mayor.

In one of her lighter moments, Charlotte performed the role of a duck in a charity pantomime put on by the Ottawa Philharmonic Orchestra, May 1957.

Duncan Cameron, Capital Press Ltd. Collection, Library and Archives Canada, PA-137870

The only stumbling block on the British tour, she recounted, was choosing to downgrade to economy class for the flight to London, in order to save $170. The problem was her seatmate, a spoiled nine-year-old travelling alone. En route, he claimed to have a swollen jaw, so the stewardess treated it with candy. Then he cut his finger, and it was suitably administered to. As Charlotte was trying to sleep, the boy "discovered that the special light brought the stewardess, [and] he set up a traffic system of his own. Both stewardesses . . . were courtesy itself and patience personified . . . So, when he had had a drink, a sandwich, a blanket, a picture book and a toy airplane, I took a hand about 11 p.m. (The same hour as one's endurance used to snap at Council). I said 'Now, lay off or I'll have to lay you off and have you put in the cockpit for the night.' He slid into his blanket and slept like a kitten till dawn. I'll admit it was not Institute of Child Study technique, but it worked!" Alas, the child welfare expert from days gone by never really had much empathy for children at the personal level.

One of the year's few sour notes occurred in October when the queen arrived in Ottawa for the opening of the Queensway, the cross-town expressway for which Charlotte had toiled such long hours at city hall, and she was ignored. Then, in November, she was ticketed for illegal parking on Wellington Street in front of Parliament Hill by Constable Eddie Paul, "my own familiar friend and aide all my years at the Mayor's New Year's Reception."

By early December, she returned to political mode. Diefenbaker's minority government was stumbling and there was little doubt that another federal election was in the offing. Charlotte looked at the local constituencies and opted for Ottawa West. The Liberal incumbent, George McIlraith, age forty-seven, was an uninspiring, soft-spoken lawyer, who had held the seat since 1940 and seemed "as safe as if he sat in the Senate," but she was confident she could defeat him. At any rate, she told her *Citizen* readers on December 2, McIlraith would be a good opponent, for he was "a decent, pleasant, hard-working chap, conscientious, responsible and respectable. He's just been unfortunate in the company he's kept," she added slyly, referring to her sister Kay, president of the Ottawa Women's Liberal Club, and Kay's husband Frank Ryan, a prominent McIlraith supporter. McIlraith was also her personal lawyer and, as the member of Parliament for Ottawa West, had proved helpful to her mayoralty on several occasions when she sought advantage with the Liberal government on federal-municipal issues.

On the other hand, as she advised her readers two days later, provincial politics looked tempting as well. After learning first-hand as mayor the constitutional control the provinces had over the municipalities, especially in areas like welfare, health and education, she mused that Queen's Park might not be so bad after all. Regardless, she was itching for a political fight, as she noted in recounting the following anecdote from her childhood. One day, when out cutting lilacs, she had dropped her "special" knife, which was picked up by a boy who walked off with it. She had given chase and "I claimed it and he refused to give it up. I grabbed it and he struck at me. I struck back. (Dad had taught us 'give and take' with a 'right guard' and a left 'upper.') He started to run, but as he fled his unhindered way, he kept running back and sticking out his tongue." Then the unfortunate urchin fell and "he was sprawling at my rather grim mercy when mother appeared. I had my knife back, so I was deterred from vengeance. And said mother: 'If you're running for a fair fight, keep your eyes and your fists both forward, and run straight ahead.'" This time, Charlotte indeed planned to run straight ahead, this time at quiet, balding, bespectacled George McIlraith.

First, however, she would have to win the Tory nomination. There was a heavy snowstorm in Ottawa on nomination day, but the meeting hall was filled with five women for every man, Judith Robinson of the *Toronto Telegram* reported next day. Charlotte's opponent, lawyer Ossie Howe, didn't have a chance, according to Greg Connolley in the *Citizen*: "Ossie Howe had just started talking when some of the ladies took out their knitting needles and started knitting — this was the tip-off that he was headed for the guillotine. It was certainly ladies' night at the West Ottawa Progressive Conservative nominating convention." Added Robinson, "When Charlotte was introduced, she was greeted with cheers, clapping and cowbells. To liven up an already excited crowd, she told a story about the Saturday night cockfights in Renfrew, which although illegal, were accepted because Saturday night was the policemen's night off and they enjoyed the fights as much as everyone else." The results: Whitton — 1,166; Howe — 350.

Having successfully passed that test, Charlotte was set to go after McIlraith. She was sure she could crush him in an open debate, so pressed him to join her in a public meeting. He wisely dodged the invitation. As Beatrice Ross, then a young McIlraith supporter, told the author, McIlraith was "a good Scot, a strong Presbyterian, a very honourable man in every way. The reason he didn't argue with her was because she was so quick with a comeback and had such a great sense of humour, and he wasn't able to match her there. He did it his own way, went quietly about his campaign; he had a wonderful organization, a good group of people around him."

For Charlotte, it was like boxing with a ghost.

When the ballots were counted on the evening of March 31, 1958, McIlraith had won, Charlotte had lost, one of the few Tories who did that night. Diefenbaker had grabbed the largest majority in Canadian history, with 209 seats out of a possible 265.

Charlotte was crushed. In a contest that was described as the most expensive in the Ottawa area — McIlraith had spent $11,989.48 and Charlotte $11,106.96 — she had lost to the longtime incumbent by just over 1,000 votes.

Her sister Kay was cheerful, but did not gloat. In her unpublished manuscript, Kay described how McIlraith visited Charlotte afterwards at the Civic Centre, where she had rented a room for a victory party:

> . . . and Charlotte, as emotionless in defeat as Grandmother Whitton, who would not tolerate self-pity, quipped brightly and passed under arches of upraised hands made by her supporters to join in what was to have been a victory party—but was a banquet hall deserted. Piles of sandwich boxes, coffee cups and services ordered for 2,000 were lined up on tables extending the whole length of the hall . . . all but 500 [supporters] departed . . . Afterward she went home to her empty apartment—all alone—and called me . . . You couldn't forgive her for trying to upset our riding, but you had to admire the way she battled.

Two days later, Charlotte used her newspaper column to describe her agony in defeat: "Yesterday was April Fool Day but I helped usher it in, just a few hours earlier. I certainly played April Fool to too many people in failing to redeem Ottawa West for the Conservative Party as it marched, with banners flying, from sea to sea."

She was downhearted, she admitted, but suggested that she might well return to civic politics to recover her crown, or tricorn hat, as mayor of Ottawa.

In response, George Nelms scoffed at the idea and offered this advice: "I served 13 years as a school trustee and it's not a bad idea to get the pulse of the people now and then. A wonderful place to start is as an alderman or a school trustee."

Snubbed again!

This time it was on the occasion of Princess Margaret's visit to Ottawa in August to open the new city hall on Green Island. Despite all the effort she had put into making this a reality, Charlotte was once more ignored by Nelms and his board of control, which included former Whitton antagonists Paul Tardif, Ernie Jones, and Wilbert Hamilton, and a new man on the civic scene, lawyer Sam Berger. It was the third time in the two years she had been out of office that her previous efforts had been overlooked by the current council, the two previous being the laying of the cornerstone for the new city hall and when the queen pressed the button setting off the first explosion in the construction of the Queensway. Her sister Kay attended the city hall opening as a reporter for CFRA and looked on as Charlotte arrived alone.

> [Charlotte] passed through the reception line as an ordinary citizen without any recognition that this City Hall was her prime accomplishment. She was ashen-faced as she came up to me, trying to make myself shrink into the background with my microphone. "Well, Mrs. Ryan, how did you get an invitation here?" I signalled "on air" and I put one hand by the "mike" to block out her remarks — then as I moved forward to cover the Princess' arrival, whispered, "I'm working only." However, I realized that Charlotte was reaping the harvest of insults and even injuries she had sown in her eight years of political activity.

Still, Charlotte had broader ambitions than attending ribbon-cutting ceremonies in the nation's capital. Now that "Johnny D." and his Tories were in power, she pictured herself as a Canadian ambassador in some far-off land. In a lengthy "private and confidential" letter to Diefenbaker in which she spelled out her experience and abilities, she proudly suggested that she would make a fine ambassador and although he had not asked, her preferences were Sweden, Mexico, and Switzerland, in that order. Or, if those positions were not available, she was willing to accept the top diplomatic posting to Chile.

Alas, Diefenbaker was unmoved by her pleading and as 1958 was nearing its end, Charlotte was involved in yet another big controversy. There were substantive rumours that Diefenbaker was going to name her chairman of the new National Capital Commission — basically the Federal District Commission under a new name — when she was approached by CBC television producer Ross McLean who wanted her to host a controversial new show he was launching called "Close-Up." Her first guest on October 8 would be the outspoken American social critic Elsa Maxwell. When Charlotte agreed to the part-time position, a delighted McLean wired her, "Elsa Maxwell accepts with delight our invitation to be interviewed . . . Urges that you ask realistic and tough questions . . . All here quite excited prospect your first assignment as TV journalist. Ross McLean CBC."

Unfortunately the interview did not go well. Although McLean had provided cue cards with dozens of questions for his novice interviewer, she ignored them and engaged a startled Maxwell in a non-stop argument, which she, Charlotte, dominated. Public reaction was immediate, and the CBC forwarded the more than sixty responses to Charlotte.

"If tonight's 'Close-Up' was Miss Whitton's first assignment please make it her last," wrote John Flinn of Sillery, Quebec.

"Well!!! You certainly scraped the bottom of the barrel with the programme for Wednesday, October 8th. It was a most disgusting exhibition of inanities, ill breeding and bad manners. There was nothing of interest, nothing elevating, nothing entertaining, unless one gets pleasure out of a good old 'Fish Wife' brawl over the back fence," added S. M. Parks of Lochaber Mines, Nova Scotia.

"Please, no more Charlotte Whitton. She was both rude and repulsive," wrote Mrs. G.H. Merrian of Sudbury.

"We actually viewed Miss Maxwell and heard Charlotte Whitton, for the rudeness with which Miss Whitton conducted herself on this occasion was obnoxious even to those who, heretofore, had credited here with having a brain. Apparently Miss Whitton is an avid reader but has never learned to listen," suggested Miss Esther Taylor of Ottawa.

"More Charlotte Whitton? Please!!! No! no! no! no! NO! NO! The interview was awful!!," grumbled K.L. Morrison of Cardinal, Ontario.

"Charlotte may not be quite as fat as Elsa, but she's far more fatuous. That raucous voice, that hideous heh-heh, that puritan priggishness — Lord save me from it all. What caused her? What's her cure?" asked David Levy of Richmond Hill, Ontario.

"After tonight's performance by Charlotte Whitton I feel I must write to try to prevent any further ghastly exposure to this woman on your otherwise excellent and stimulating programme . . . Please, oh please, never let us be subjected to her again," pleaded Mrs. Peter Landry of Montreal.

Of the five dozen responses, only one letter was positive.

"The interview between Charlotte Whitton and Elsa Maxwell was interesting—Miss Whitton was splendid. How about an interview between Miss Whitton and Mrs. [Eleanor] Roosevelt?" suggested Miss Ada Huguenin of Montreal.

Charlotte, who had earlier performed so well in occasional appearances on a CBC-TV panel show called "Fighting Words," was not asked back to "Close-Up". Her fledgling career as a television interviewer was finished. Column writing and public speaking would have to suffice for the time being, although she did manage to work in a one-week visit to Japan in early December as an observer at an international conference on social work.

Early 1959 was a relatively restful period, for Charlotte contented herself with her *Citizen* columns, her weekly radio talks, and her occasional public addresses. There was time for another winter visit to friends in South Carolina and more time in the spring and summer to sit by McGregor Lake and ponder her future. She loved her cottage, but it could be a challenge at times, she told her readers in late May. In fact, she had just gone with a friend to open the cottage after its winter hibernation and found "the small dainty 'spoon' oars of my new boat purloined," although the rowboat remained in place. After borrowing ill-fitting oars, she and the friend loaded their supplies and, with Charlotte rowing and the friend in the stern, they barely managed to make it across the lake to the cottage due to a heavy crosswind. Once there, they found invasive squirrels had eaten through the beds and blankets, and they found a family of young squirrels nestled in one of the beds, and "a flying squirrel missed me by one fur tail . . . Your hands are full of grime; you've broken every fingernail, and that with a dinner address Monday for the Hastings and Trenton air station teachers; and your hair's been caught on every branch and your head's hit every beam, to say nothing of the real wallop from the hanging lamp which almost fell you . . . [Does anyone want] to buy a summer place on McGregor Lake, garage, boathouse on each shore, well furnished cabin, woodshed, work-house on the hill, one well-wooded acre? Opened up for season and going cheap for anyone who seeks exhaustion."

There were no takers, for in July she described another cottage visit during which she arrived to find that she had been robbed again. As well, she was beset by a porcupine upsetting her garbage cans, a whip-poor-will's constant call, a swallow's nest in her boathouse, and a munching rabbit in her garden. Then there was the bottle of ginger ale that had exploded in her refrigerator and being attacked by wasps. Wisely, she returned home to Ottawa for a warm meal, a warm bath, a warm bed, and a really good night's sleep.

Perhaps she was getting bored with the relative inactivity, for in August she addressed a lengthy handwritten note to Diefenbaker from McGregor Lake advising him that she was "prepared to carry out any assignment as decided, at home or abroad. I only ask that it be really useful, engage me to the fullest of my capacity and that it be decided as soon as possible. Of course, I hope that it will afford an opportunity to add to the glory of John Diefenbaker, and, thus, of the Conservative Party in our life and tradition, which at least one of my Irish relatives would thereupon claim, could not but add to the glory of God Himself in the end." In fact, she was asking him to name her Canadian ambassador to Ireland. Despite her zealous regard for England, she now was summoning up long dormant Irish roots to win the appointment.

"P.S. Because I am no more ashamed of sentiment than you are, I confess to a real 'hankering' for this Irish possibility. I do believe in the 'closeness' of the dead and my Irish mother . . . would be the happiest where she dwells, were I to be entrusted with this mission."

Besides, she added in a five-page addendum, she was ready to proceed to the Irish posting "as quickly as desired," she was known across Canada "as characteristically Irish," some of her family members were Catholics, she had done a social welfare study for Montreal's Irish Catholic community in the 1930s, and her brother-in-law, Frank Ryan, had good relations with the horse-breeding community in Eire. Her final paragraph informed Diefenbaker that her appointment to Dublin would be a "whale of a good thing, at home and abroad." In the margin, she wrote "Please" with a double underline.

Her pleadings were for naught. Diefenbaker did not respond, although he did keep her in mind for future consideration.

Defeated at the federal level, temporarily ignored by Diefenbaker, no longer sought by the Ontario Tories, Charlotte returned her thoughts, and her columns, to local affairs. She criticized the women's press club's plan to serve wine at the reception prior to their triennial convention in Ottawa, she argued at length with police about a woman who had taken her downtown parking space one day, and she complained about the ill effects of bingo on its players. Her biggest complaint by far, though, concerned George Nelms and his work at city hall.

Although she may not have realized it at the time, though that is questionable, she was about to start her campaign to recapture the Ottawa mayoralty in the municipal election which was a full year away. In her CFRA broadcast of November 22, 1959, and in a similar commentary in her *Citizen* column the following day, Charlotte unloaded a bombshell. She inferred that Nelms had used his position as mayor to enrich himself.

Specifically, she said Nelms had arranged the city's purchase of forty acres of farmland in the Alta Vista area near two of his own undeveloped properties as the site of a future hospital. His properties, which he co-owned with lawyer and fellow former school board trustee Orian Low, measured 13.9 and five acres, respectively, and were about a quarter mile from the proposed hospital site. The benefit to Nelms was that once the hospital was built, it would have to be serviced with sewers and watermains, and those same sewers and watermains would be readily accessible to Nelms's properties.

Nelms was outraged. Yes, he owned the two pieces of property at Heron and Walkley Roads that she referred to, but it was unlikely that the hospital would be built for at least another decade, so services to his properties would be delayed as long as that. "She is not telling the truth. As usual they are only half-truths and propaganda for which she is well known," he responded on the same day as the column. He said he bought his share of the properties in 1951 and 1952, and the "purchase of this [hospital] property was in no way connected with the fact that I own land in the near vicinity," which he described as being about a mile away.

Charlotte claimed the situation "remains, from start to finish, a mysterious brain-child of His Worship the Mayor." She charged that the hospital board never asked city council to find a new site for a hospital and questioned how the $100,000 price tag, later increased to $185,000, made its way through the city's budget process and

approval by the Ontario Municipal Board. She said city finance commissioner J.H. Lowther, whom she had hired during her mayoralty,
"stands out in intelligence and integrity. Had he not been misin-
formed, he just would not have included this in the City's Capital
Budget, taken it before the OMB and put it in the sale of debentures.
He must have had instructions. He could not have included, certi-
fied and sold the debentures simply by word of mouth."

Nelms responded by saying that he pushed for the purchase of
the hospital site because of rising land values, the same reason he
had purchased his share of the two properties in the early 1950s, at a
time when he was not yet involved in municipal politics. He argued
that at that time, there were hospitals to the north of the city in Hull,
and in the eastern, western, and central parts of Ottawa, so it was
natural to expect a new hospital would eventually be built in the developing southern section. Besides, he grumbled, "Of what concern
is it of anybody where I own land?"

The debate continued for days. A map of the area in question
appeared in the *Citizen* on November 24 and included information
taken from registry records showing Nelms had bought the five-acre
property from Myrna Cochrane in 1951 for $7,750 and the 13.9-acre
property from Elsie Hamel in 1952 for $10,500. Therefore, he paid
approximately $1,550 an acre for the Cochrane property and $755
an acre to Hamel. By 1959, properties in the area were valued at
about $9,000 an acre.

Charlotte returned to the attack in her November 30 column.
"There is one clear-cut issue, one person pre-eminently involved."
She argued that it was "implicit" in the *Municipal Act* and "explicit"
in the Ottawa Procedural Bylaw that whenever an issue arose which
might benefit a councillor in the "least degree," that member must
declare his interest and abstain from voting. The penalty for not
doing so was forfeiture of his seat on council. Yet expropriation of
the forty-acre hospital site was carried out "on the Mayor's personal
responsibility without disclosure (unless in a closed meeting of the
board of control) of essential information which, in all its aspects,
only the Mayor would have in his quintuplet personality as Head
of Council, Chairman of the Board of Control, ex-officio member
of the Civic Hospital Board and of the Planning Board and owner
of one block of 13.9 acres of land in the immediate vicinity, and

another five acres two-thirds of a mile east."

Incidentally, an unaddressed memo in Charlotte's files at the national archives dated November 23, 1959 — the same date as her first column on the hospital issued appeared — showed that she had registry information on more of Nelms's real estate dealings. For example, in 1941, he had purchased three lots in the Alta Vista area for $5,000, and in 1950 sold part of them to the public high school board and to the Ontario government for a total $60,550. Her memo read: "Note — Profit in 9 years (4 of them war years) 1100%. Profited by 11 to 12 times (less negligible interest and taxes) purchase price and sold at this 'mark-up' ... This purchase was made on May 8, 1941, a day of grim memory for Canadians and the Allies for it marked the terrific stepping up of concentrated air attack on the ports and docks of the U.K. That day Liverpool received the worst attacks and casualties."

It was obvious she was waging a personal vendetta against the man who had replaced her as mayor, the same one she would probably face in the next civic election. Two days later, she sent a "personal and confidential" letter to the chairman of the OMB, Lorne Cumming, that began, "Because you and I were schooled in the same ethics and I think have both attempted at a good deal of cost still to honour them, I am sending you for your personal information some material which I think you may find of interest to read and have on file." She then recited Nelms's property dealings above and noted that Nelms was a trustee on the public elementary school board when he sold land to the high school board, and the fact that the elementary board had a representative on the high school board hinted at a conflict of interest. However, she shied short of claiming an actual conflict of interest on Nelms's part.

The case continued. On December 2, Nelms announced that he planned to divest himself of all land holdings in the city and instead direct his real estate interests to the suburban townships around Ottawa, as well as to the Brockville and Toronto areas.

On December 7, the hospital site issue went before city council. "I am here to be judged," Nelms told his fellow councillors. He asked them to clear his name in the face of "wild irresponsible statements" by unnamed persons, and said he could not understand how anyone could consider that he would profit from the new hospital site. "I have done no wrong intentionally or unintentionally. What is wrong with owning property? Is it something filthy in the eyes of the general public? Certainly it is in the eyes of some people." The council meeting lasted until 1:30 a.m., and in the end, the councillors decided to postpone a decision to a later date.

As Charlotte continued her remorseless attack in her thrice-weekly newspaper column, controller Berger moved, and it was approved by council on December 11, that the issue of the hospital site purchase be put on hold pending a wide-ranging conference on all city health issues, including a possible new hospital site.

(Almost a decade later, the Riverside Hospital — later to become part of the amalgamated Ottawa Hospital — was built on Smyth Road in Alta Vista, dozens of blocks east of the originally proposed hospital site on Heron Road.)

On February 5, 1960, the normally indomitable Charlotte was rushed to the Civic Hospital and operated on for a twisted bowel and appendicitis. She was hospitalized for one month and then ordered by her personal physician, Dr. Peter Burton, to take a holiday in South Carolina. While she willingly complied, Charlotte had no time to be sick. There were the newspaper columns to write, Premier Frost wanted her input for a study on government reform, and *Canadian Home Journal* editor Doris Anderson asked her to write a two- or three-part series on her life that could be turned into an autobiography. The magazine series did appear, but she had no time to write a full autobiography and she had not enough time to help Frost with his study. She did, however, find time for a months-long, "confidential" letter-writing campaign to Frost warning him against proposed legislation allowing the advertising of alcoholic products in the mass media.

The campaign began from her hospital bed on February 23, the first day her doctor allowed his impatient patient to use her dictation machine. "The more I think of the matter, the more I might myself be prepared to take a definite part with you, if you so desired, in trying to make some real progress in this complicated problem," she advised the Premier. Six days later she notified him that she would be passing through Toronto on March 7 and 8 on her way to the Carolinas, and if he wished, he could visit her at her cousin's house there.

Later in March, she acknowledged in a memorandum to Frost that Canadian media needed the advertising money and that it was impossible to stop alcohol advertisements in the American media from reaching Canada, so she proposed that he establish a regulatory agency, called The Supervisors of the Advertising of Alcoholic Beverages, which would have a "consultative panel" of overseers to police the ads. The panel would include one representative each from the Federated Women's Institutes, the Ontario Council of Women, the Catholic Women's League, the IODE, the Ontario Business and Professional Women's Clubs or the Federation of University Women, the Ontario Federation of Agriculture, the Ontario Labour Council, the Ontario Teachers Federation, as well as two representatives from temperance groups and two from the beverage industry. Further, the premier should provide some funding for the temperance groups in the province.

In late April, she addressed another "personal and confidential" letter to Frost admitting that her previous memorandum may have been too long and too time-consuming for him to read, but "I would urge you please to read again and thoroughly my memorandum. It is open to amendment, but . . . if, as up to this date, these suggestions of mine are of no worth, then I would appreciate your so advising me, in that I feel I have an obligation which I cannot longer beg in this whole field."

She wrote to him again in May and July, and finally at the end of July received this reply:

> May I say first of all that our conversations and your memorandum assisted me a great deal . . . As a matter of fact, arising out of it we have been able to bring about a very considerable degree of unanimity. Church, temperance and other organizations have been very complimentary and I think they will be pleased with the results which we are able to bring out of this matter . . . I may say the ramifications of my discussions in this matter with church and very many authorities have been great indeed. I do not think that any have been more helpful than my discussions with you.

But The Supervisors of the Advertising of Alcoholic Beverages remained a figment of her imagination.

Meanwhile, she continued to keep an eye on city hall. In her April 22 column in the *Citizen*, headlined, "The Incredible Case of Mr. Tardif," she drew attention to the particularly close relationship between Paul Tardif and Robert Campeau, the city's leading property developer. She remarked that Campeau always seemed to get preferential treatment when he sought council approvals for his new subdivisions, and in the previous year, while Nelms was visiting England and Tardif was acting mayor, as well as chairman of the city's planning board, the board allowed Campeau to locate a service station in his subdivision, which city planners had opposed due its location next to a prestigious apartment block. When the matter went before city council, it was rejected by a majority of councillors, so Campeau took it to the OMB. Tardif, although acting mayor, appeared at the OMB to argue Campeau's case against his (Tardif's) own council.

Charlotte's reaction: "Throughout, Controller Tardif has behaved incredibly. An elected representative of the people, he has used his office to oppose Council's repeated decision. He has acted directly as the advocate of Mr. Campeau at the OMB, yet he could appear there only by reason of his civic office." Council must call Tardif to account publicly, she urged, "for he has placed Council in contempt."

She mentioned that Tardif and Campeau were neighbours on Applewood Crescent, but what she did not mention, and perhaps did not know, was that the two also had cottages next to each other on Lake Deschênes, Quebec, and that Campeau was such a familiar visitor to the Tardif home and cottage that he was known as "Uncle Bob" to the Tardif children.

Incidentally, Tardif was elected as the Liberal member of Parliament for Russell, east of Ottawa in a fall 1959 by-election. He continued to serve on city council and in the House of Commons at the same time.

This was definitely not the last dispute between Charlotte and either Campeau or Tardif.

On June 22, 1960, for example, Campeau sued Charlotte for $190 in damages after she physically, but only temporarily, stopped a workcrew from cutting down trees on one of his properties just a few doors west of her own three-storey apartment block on Rideau Terrace. Campeau's intention was to build a twelve-storey apartment block on his site, but Charlotte, other nearby residents, and controller Berger tried to delay it, arguing that sewers and watermains in the area were inadequate to service it. Nevertheless, Campeau continued with construction thanks to the approval of Mayor Nelms and his board of control. In a letter published in the *Citizen*, he mused, "We are wondering if Miss Whitton now realizes that the scene she made in front of our property . . . was a ridiculous waste of time and effort. However, we will be sure to extend an invitation to Miss Whitton to attend the formal opening of our building."

Charlotte had one other feisty battle in 1960 prior to running in the upcoming civic election, and it once more involved CBC producer Ross McLean and his program, "Close-Up". Referred to by many critics at the time as "the Shady Lady Affair," it concerned a television documentary on divorce that aired on May 26. What raised the dander of Charlotte and many others was the inclusion of an interview with an unidentified secretary who claimed that she supplemented her regular $70-a-week salary by working as a $100-a-night co-respondent, or professional "other woman," in divorce cases. (At the time, divorce proceedings in Canada required Senate approval, and divorces were normally granted only if one of the parties was found to have been unfaithful.) The woman said that she sometimes worked four or five nights a week and regularly earned at least $300 a week. At the latter rate, she might have earned $15,600 a year, or well above the $12,000 salary earned by the mayor of Ottawa or an ordinary member of Parliament.

When Charlotte learned in advance of the show's contents, she wrote a scathing column, complaining about its "vicarious wallowing" in sin, and suggested instead that it should have featured learned religious leaders discussing "the dignity, decency and decorum, characteristic of the overwhelming percentage of hearings in divorce or marital causes in this country." She then mailed copies of her column to numerous influential persons across Canada, among them the chairman of the Board of Broadcast Governors, which oversaw the CBC, and Bishop Ernest Reed of Ottawa of the Anglican

*Charlotte at the podium,
November 1960.*

Ottawa Journal,
City of Ottawa Archives, MG 011

church. The bishop informed her that he had asked the CBC to cancel the program, but the program went to air nevertheless.

When the chairman of the Board of Broadcast Governors, Dr. Andrew Stewart, replied on May 31, he said the program had not "broadcast any obscene, indecent or profane language." Therefore, no further action was required on the board's part; anyhow, the board did not act on complaints just because some people might be offended by a particular program.

Unsatisfied, Charlotte took her complaint to Governor General Vincent Massey. In a "confidential" letter, she implored, "There are few Canadians, held in higher regard than you, and few, who have striven more consistently to uphold reverence for the Crown in our life. I am therefore making bold to appeal to you, as the one person, now, who can intervene to protect the Crown from the devastating disparagement, in respect to which considerable harm has already been done and particularly among the Roman Catholic community, whose loyal affection has so centred about the high example of family life of the Royal Family itself." She damned the program as "so sordid a presentation of the experience of a commercial divorce co-respondent's collusion to defeat the Courts, as has ever disgraced a screen."

Meanwhile, Charlotte received an offer from Diefenbaker to set up and run a national nursing program. "What you suggested offers an opening in a field I know well," she replied, but she was ready for a more important role. "This would be to take over and throw together at once a concise and practical memo of suggestions for what would become *your* national welfare programme . . . the most effective memorial you could have associated with your name and Government, looking to Confederation Centennial, 1967." He did not bite. So Charlotte turned once more to thoughts of wearing the mayor of Ottawa's splendid red robes of office and the black tricorn hat.

George Nelms had had enough. Wealthy due to his real estate holdings, his downtown optical store and his partnership in other local businesses, he did not contest the 1960 mayoralty election. He was through with local politics; or so he thought. Thus the door was open to Charlotte and anyone else who might wish to call herself or himself "Mayor of Ottawa." As usual, there were numerous potential candidates rumoured ready to contest the December 5 election.

Charlotte, like the others, played her cards close to her chest. On November 7, she wrote in her final column for the *Citizen*—her 552nd in four years—"I have no illusions as to the problems that immediately face Ottawa. In fact, other than the Finance Commissioner and the Mayor himself, I doubt whether there is a person in this city more fully aware of them than I." She once again slammed the current council, especially for what she termed its last-minute spending spree, and concluded, "And so, where I had been ready, 'the conditions precedent' being met, to announce my candidature today for the office of Mayor, I am instead simply going on some leave, and wishing you—Good Luck, Good Government and Goodbye for now."

In other words, she was relying on the same tactic that served her so well in 1950 when running for controller; she would run only if she was assured of the wholehearted support of numerous volunteers.

Obviously the tactic worked again, for just three days later she announced privately to her draft committee that she had received such overwhelming backing that she felt forced to run. The official announcement of her candidacy was sent out on November 25, eleven days before the election. Meanwhile, her opponents also had announced their intentions, revealing a four-way race: Charlotte, controllers Sam Berger and Ernie Jones, and an also-ran, A.L. (Achille Lucien) Dubé. In reality, though, it was a duel between

Charlotte and Berger, the suave, wealthy lawyer-controller who was the city's first Jewish candidate for mayor and a co-owner of the Ottawa Rough Riders football team for which he had been a director and legal counsel since the 1930s.

In Charlotte's eyes, Berger and Jones epitomized the old style of civic politics, where a backroom meeting or a furtive handshake was as good as a formal motion in an open council meeting. Although both men would have strongly disagreed with that characterization, and with good reason, Charlotte saw herself as a veritable Joan of Arc, an underdog against the vested interests in town.

Her "new deal" platform included plans to streamline city council and municipal procedures; limit borrowing as much as possible; establish a new position of public utilities commissioner to oversee water, sewer and hydro facilities; hire a housing commissioner; modernize city fire services; improve zoning provisions; build a new courthouse; create a city research and promotion bureau; and open a theatre/concert hall. Moreover, her first priority would be a new sewerage program aimed at handling waste from the city's ever-growing suburbs. But, the cost-conscious candidate concluded, "every item, and the entire program, [is] to be determined and effected within a proper balance of assessment, debt, loans and taxation."

Berger, on the other hand, campaigned as "the man of experience, the man of action," while Jones suggested his fourteen years on council as both alderman and controller were enough to make him a deserving mayor. Dubé, a retired schoolteacher who enjoyed quoting the classics in his campaign speeches, called for more funding for Catholic schools, better opportunities for francophones, and bilingual street signs. Neither Berger nor Jones offered constructive platforms, preferring instead just to run on their record.

All-candidates meetings were a mismatch, for not only could Charlotte outspeak and outwit her opponents, but they often were stacked with Whitton supporters. The author's brother attended a typical meeting and recalled that while Berger was speaking, a number of female Whitton supporters trouped in and marched to the empty front rows, causing a minor ruckus moving chairs and finding their seats. Then, as they settled down, Charlotte walked in and the women turned away from speaker Berger to direct their attention to their plucky candidate as she made her way regally across the hall to a seat in the front row. By the time she sat down, Berger's speaking time was almost up.

The women loved it, but the press was not impressed. The *Citizen* turned its back on its former columnist, as did *Le Droit*. Even the *Journal*, Charlotte's longtime friend and admirer, felt Berger, who got along well with people and had shown leadership at the board of control and in his co-ownership of the Rough Riders, deserved the mayoralty. Charlotte, on the other hand, had lots of talent and was renowned for her integrity, but she was not a team player and so could not accomplish what needed to be done, the *Journal* concluded.

The people disagreed. When the polls closed on the night of December 5, 1960, Charlotte was returned as mayor. The results: Whitton — 35,532; Berger — 33,825; Jones — 9,317; Dubé — 2,675.

The second, more uproarious, Whitton era at city hall was about to begin.

18 Blushing and Flushing

Charlotte came out swinging. After the pleasantries of her official reinvestiture had been dispensed with at the start of council's first meeting on January 3, 1961, she left no doubt about who was in charge at city hall.

She discarded most of the items on the agenda set by the previous administration and immediately took aim at the city's tendering process. She demanded that in future there be a review of all contracts where the lowest bidder did not get the contract. Furthermore, on hearing that two city officials from the same department planned to attend a conference in Washington, she ordered that henceforth no more than one person from a city department could attend any out-of-town conference. She also gave warning that she would be closely inspecting city workers' overtime sheets to make sure the taxpayer was not being gouged.

She was just warming up.

She warned that "throughout Canada, all our major cities are caught in the vortex of a rapidly changing social era," but Ottawa was in a worse condition than most because of the profligate spending of the previous administration. Of the $14 million the city was allowed to borrow during the current fiscal year, according to provincially set limits, the city had already borrowed $13 million, so there was little left to support the previous council's broad public works program that included further hospital services and major road, bridge, and sewer construction projects as well as a river pollution cleanup plan.

At her first post-election news conference, she had told reporters, "A lot of important things have to come out of the mothballs down here." While she declined to elaborate, she left the clear impression that she had some very damaging information about some very influential people in the city, which would come out only in due course. This time in office she would focus on city business alone, around the clock, and across the weeks and months ahead. There would be fewer out-of-town speeches, little time for relaxing at McGregor Lake, less time spent on advising Diefenbaker's federal government or Frost's provincial cabinet.

Thus it was in the first days of January. But if she was to accomplish much, she would need the full support of council and, especially, her four colleagues on the board of control.

At first glance, the latter seemed a more accommodating group than during her previous terms as mayor, for the lead controller, Lloyd Francis, was a soft-spoken, former federal government economist whose council experience was limited to one term as alderman. Joining him on the board was another newcomer, Don Reid, a furniture store owner who had been a low-key alderman for six years, as well as veterans Paul Tardif and Wilbert Hamilton. It was inevitable, based on past history, that there would be friction with Tardif and possibly Hamilton, but Francis and Reid must have seemed like pushovers for the strong-willed Charlotte.

The controllers' first meeting with the new mayor went smoothly as they arranged their "portfolios" for the coming year. Francis would be acting mayor in Charlotte's absence and would oversee health, welfare, and fire and police retirement fund issues and serve as the board's link to the school boards. Reid would look after planning and development, urban renewal, sewage, and river pollution. Hamilton would handle personnel, civic reorganization, and the Central Canada Exhibition Association. Tardif, meanwhile, requested no special duties, due to his having been elected as a member of Parliament in October 1959. Charlotte seized the city's purse strings by taking on the finance portfolio in addition to handling the mayor's statutory memberships on the police, hydro, and transportation commissions; the hospital, library, and health boards; the CCEA; and her ex-officio role on all council committees, as well as chairing the board of control and council meetings.

In an interview two years before his death in 2007, Francis recalled his first meeting with Charlotte: "Here was a diminutive person talking all the time, dominating the conversation, dominating the agenda, a little overwhelming. I'd never held public office before and veteran councillors told me to be careful with her, don't trust any report, read all the fine print."

Civic affairs received front-page coverage late in January after four years of relative peace when Charlotte decided it was time to bring certain election campaign rumours "out of the mothballs" and put them before the general public.

The rumours concerned three civic politicians and their alleged involvement with land developers. Named were George Nelms, Sam Berger, and Paul Tardif. Days earlier she had mentioned that she soon would release information that "will shake the city to its very foundations." Therefore, on January 30, just one day after Lloyd Francis released a statement allegedly linking Tardif with the ownership of Urbandale Realty Corporation Limited, she announced to council that she, too, had been checking rumours concerning not only Urbandale, but other local land developers as well, and was deeply concerned that some civic politicians had failed "to disclose interest" in private companies doing business with the city while they held office.

"I would have preferred to avoid the necessity of submitting the undernoted information in advocacy of the adoption of the policies and procedures prefacing the 1961 Capital Budget, did it not appear imperative that council should realize how vital these are to the assurance of rights and priorities to all the property-owners and taxpayers of Ottawa, and, indeed, the protection and conservation of their resources in actual tax revenue and borrowing powers," she suggested piously. "Relevant evidence, which dictates these policies and procedures as necessary for the equitable, just and honourable use of this city's resources and credit, I am compelled — and as I intimated publicly earlier I might be required to do — under the obligations of my oath of office, now to transmit to council." Distasteful as it was, she suggested, she would have to name names and say just which politicians had failed to disclose their interests.

First she turned on Tardif. In March 1956, while she was still mayor and Tardif unknowingly to her was a partner in Urbandale Realty, the company had applied for a subdivision permit. The permit was denied the following month on the advice of the city's technical advisory committee, because it was beyond reach of the city's sewer network. The company applied again in September and October, with similar results. Likewise, a year later, the technical committee ruled the subdivision was premature, only to learn within days that the city planning board, with Tardif in the chairman's seat due to Mayor Nelms's absence, approved the 150-lot subdivision. The approval was ratified by the board of control one month later and put to council on December 2 by none other than controller Tardif.

"Thus within a matter of some six weeks, a project which had been continuously rejected was picked up and carried through the Ottawa planning area board, the board of control and city council," she commented tartly. "Throughout these entire proceedings it will be noted that neither in the Ottawa planning area board nor in the board of control, nor in council did Controller Tardif declare interest . . . I submit this information to council, raising at this time no question in relation to the significance thereof, other than its conclusive evidence, that the policies and controls, submitted by the majority of the board of control for the protection of the people of this city and their resources and credit and all applicants and developers who follow regular procedures, should be adopted."

Then she directed her spotlight on Nelms. She recalled that everything was above board in March 1960, when the question was discussed of extending a watermain to the Walkley-Heron roads area, for he had declared his interest in two properties there and had left the mayor's chair. But in October of that year, he made no such declaration when council approved construction of the watermain as part of a provincially assisted winter works program. She noted the surprising speed with which the project passed through the various approval stages: the OMB approved it on October 18, the board of control called tenders on October 25, and the lowest bid was accepted on November 21, just nine days before the civic election and Nelms's intended departure from the political scene.

"It is my submission that had interest been declared this quick priority and unusually expeditious handling of this extensive work at this share of cost to the general rates, would have been more thoroughly examined by council and the electorate in those immediate days." She then referred to a second proposed watermain near the Walkley-Heron intersection that would affect the properties Nelms shared with Orian Low. She charged that there was "no declaration in any of these proceedings" by Nelms until November 28, the day his application went before the board of control. She suggested that it, too, had received special attention at the municipal level and therefore had jumped the queue of upcoming watermain constructions.

Third on her list of targets that day was Sam Berger, lawyer, property developer, former controller, football club president, and the man she recently had defeated for the mayoralty. Again it involved sewer construction for a new subdivision. In this case, she claimed Berger had failed to disclose his interest in the Armstrong subdivision in the city's west end, where a new $104,500 storm sewer had been approved by council on October 3, 1960, just two months before the civic election. She had learned later that Berger had held a second mortgage on the subdivision since 1955. "From January 1, 1957," she remarked, "Samuel Berger was a controller of the City of Ottawa, and continued in office, through all the transactions affecting this subdivision, agreements and works beneficial thereto, from registration on July 22, 1959. Particularly was this undisclosed interest significant in the period from October 3, 1960, when this $104,500 item was placed in the special priority winter works budget before council, right through to the award of contract and approval by council on December 19, 1960. Declarations of interest were withheld throughout all this period, and particularly of the conditions attached to the mortgage of $64,520, held by Samuel Berger."

Reactions were immediate. "Character assassination," scoffed Nelms. "I note Miss Whitton is again enjoying her indoor sport of character assassination. As a former mayor and now a taxpayer, I deplore that this capital city is becoming a circus with Miss Whitton as ringmaster." He said his interest in the Walkley-Heron area was well known, and that Charlotte should spend more time at her desk and less time snooping through archival records. Berger was equally indignant, adding that he was considering legal action. Tardif laughed it off. He said Charlotte was using the threat of a scandal simply to make him more amenable to support her own projects at city hall.

Charlotte did not consider it a laughing matter. She sought the city solicitor's advice about the possibility of a provincial inquiry, but was advised that civil court was the place to take the issue further if she wished. Apparently, she did not wish, especially after receiving a note early in February from L.J. Armstrong of the Armstrong subdivision informing her that while he had taken out a second mortgage with Berger in 1956, he had paid it off in September 1959, well before the sewer construction issue went to council; therefore, there was no conflict of interest. Similarly, she was advised in April by lawyer John C. Clarke, who had been her financial agent in the 1960 election campaign, "that in my opinion no direct charge of financial interest can be attributed to Mr. Berger subsequent to September 11th, 1959."

In late April, lawyer Gordon McMichael advised her that if Nelms, Berger, or Tardif had not sued her within sixty days of the publication of her allegations, she was in the clear. Happily for Charlotte, no lawsuit arrived. Once more, her allegations remained unproven and the storm she had raised had passed over. Other storms, however, loomed on the horizon.

For a while, the board of control and council meetings proceeded with proper decorum, but the arrival of summer and its accompanying heat and humidity tested everyone's patience, causing tempers to flare to the point that by mid-July Charlotte felt forced to issue a three-page "statement of privilege" reminding councillors about proper council decorum:

> Regardless of the individual merits or efforts of any
> members of council, including the mayor and board of
> control, public respect for council turns upon the sense
> of responsibility, and of conscientious and expeditious
> discharge of public business and duties by council,
> as a body; proceeding under the statutes and bylaws,
> wherefrom it receives its authority; and with at least some
> modicum of observance of proper parliamentary procedure
> and the ordinary dictates of courtesy and good manners,
> from which really all such rules of order flow, and upon
> which they are based, among free members of free and
> responsible assemblies, conducting free and responsible
> government.

Like a harried schoolteacher scolding her unruly pupils, she continued:

> I deem it my responsibility, as head of this council,
> seriously to advise you, my fellow members that, in my
> considered opinion and judgment, and due in definite
> degree to disregard, or indeed deliberate ignoring of
> statutory or bylaw requirements, this council, because
> of obvious waste of time in trivia and certain individual
> bickering and irresponsibility, is suffering a deterioration
> in public respect, and consequently in public confidence in
> council as a whole . . .

And one other thing, she added before concluding, a city bylaw required all councillors to remain in their seats until the mayor had left hers.

By September, the lecture had been forgotten. On the 26th, for example, she was back on the front pages after stomping out of a board of control meeting only to then shout at board members from the second-floor public gallery. Francis, who had replaced her as chairman, threatened to have the ever-present police constable eject her from the hall for interfering with board business. But, as the *Journal* reported, "It flared up out of nowhere like a Summer storm, raged and died with no apparent conclusion or decision. It was by far the wildest board performance this year — ranging from bitter anger to rib-tickling belly laughing." Before the meeting concluded, however, Charlotte had quietly resumed the chair and pleaded for "decency and dignity" at the table. The city's business was conducted then in fairly orderly fashion.

Yet within two days, there was more of the same. At one point during the meeting, Francis and Tardif, both known Liberals, were privately arguing over one issue, Reid and Hamilton, both Tories, were debating another, while Charlotte appeared to be talking to herself. Later she called Francis "a blackguard" for trying to appeal a recently approved amendment to the emergency measures bylaw, and at another point she refused to tell Francis and Tardif the value of properties involved in a land trade between the city and the National Capital Commission involving a proposed new hospital in Alta Vista. Tardif subsequently complained that the mayor was editing the minutes of board discussions without the board's approval, and Francis charged that Charlotte had a private vendetta against him.

In his interview with the author, Francis mentioned one incident that reflected the general state of affairs at board meetings. He had made a motion to cover the ditches along Woodroffe Avenue, a north-south thoroughfare in the west end, for safety reasons, but Charlotte had tried to block the motion because she thought he was doing a favour for Robert Campeau, who was building a subdivision nearby. The controllers disagreed with the mayor and outvoted her, four to one. However, when the minutes were read at the next board meeting, there was no mention of the motion. Francis said he questioned the clerk about the motion's absence, but the elderly man, Edgar Pearce, who was about to retire after forty-three years on the job, said he had included it in the minutes; presumably Charlotte had deleted it. Francis placed the motion before the board again and it was approved again, "but she fought it all the way."

Fortunately for her sanity, Charlotte often recovered her sense of humour after troubling times. She had the ability to laugh at some of her more eccentric actions and at her volatile temper. She rarely held a grudge for a long time, a virtue often shared by her combatants, especially politicians such as Paul Tardif.

One colourful event occurred in July when she became the adopted daughter of Chief Yellow Horn of the Peigan tribe of the Blackfoot Confederacy at Fort McLeod, Alberta, and was named "Princess Ma-Chee-Wa-Kee" (Princess Pretty Woman). It's uncertain exactly why she was chosen by the Peigans, but it may have had something to do with her national reputation as an outspoken speaker and a woman unafraid of standing out in the crowd. Certainly she stood out in the crowd that day as she smoked the peace pipe with Chief Yellow Horn and participated in the Owl Dance with the chief and his "braves." In return, she received a beaded jacket and moccasins, which she presented years later to the McDougall Mill Museum in Renfrew, where they remain in a special display case of Whitton artifacts. Later that year, the photo of an anguished-looking Charlotte sprawled on her rear at a curling rink she helped open at Lansdowne Park made newspapers world-wide. Hovering above her with a huge smile on his face was George Hees, trade and commerce minister in John Diefenbaker's cabinet.

That same November, as she was being harried and pilloried by the press and her council colleagues, she surprised reporters by

Chief Yellow Horn of the Peigan tribe of Fort McLeod, Alberta, adopted Charlotte, or "Princess Pretty Woman," as his daughter in 1961.

Charlotte Whitton Collection, Library and Archives Canada, e016783840

confidently forecasting a snowfall before the 22nd, because she had just seen earthworms on the banks of the Rideau River. The worms knew there was going to be snow, she explained, because otherwise there would be frost and the worms would have been at least six inches underground. The first snow of the season fell on November 20. Once again, Charlotte was right.

Her sense of humour stood her in good stead that month. The director of the city's emergency measures organization announced on November 1 that he was quitting because of Charlotte's interference in his group's affairs. "I intend to take a damn good rest and forget all about Charlotte," forty-one-year-old retired army major R.F. Walker told the media. He suggested council had two options: "Accept the ineffective and confused pattern already established by Mayor Whitton," or replace her as chair of the EMO. Goodbye, Walker, replied Charlotte, and for once council supported her by accepting Walker's resignation.

The following day at the board of control, however, Charlotte complained that the male controllers were orchestrating a witch

Trade and commerce minister George Hees thought it a riot when Charlotte lost her balance while throwing the first stone at a new Ottawa curling rink in 1961.

Gordon Karam, Citizen-UPI photo, courtesy of the **Ottawa Citizen**

hunt against her, Francis accused her of trying to block his access to civic operations, and the remaining three controllers stalked out of the meeting, complaining that she was deliberately delaying debate on a slum clearance project. A few days later, she angered the city's federal public servants when she suggested that their private club, the 27,000-member Recreation Association, could do without the city's tax exemption if they each paid a little extra in dues.

One week later, she once more tangled with the ever-irascible Tardif. In an effort to rush through a rezoning bylaw to allow a new gas station, she cited Section 211C, an obscure clause in the *Ontario Municipal Act*; Tardif remarked, "This is the speediest bylaw I've ever seen. I don't know how she can make 211C do so many illegal things for her."

When Charlotte arose from her chair, Tardif told her to sit down and, according to press reports, she screamed, "I will not sit down while you give out with lying words."

Tardif stood up and Charlotte sat, silently clapping her hands in time with each word he said. Perturbed, he turned to her and said,

"Your worship, would you like me to sit down and you could sit right on my lap?" Glowering, she remained silent as alderman Cecile O'Regan was heard to remark, "Oh God, not again," and another alderman gently sang the hymn "Tell Me the Old, Old Story."

After this and earlier noisy rows involving the mayor at the Civic Hospital board and the Ottawa Transportation Commission, the media benches at council were crammed full — the public galleries always were packed — and on November 16, even the *Journal*'s Parliamentary columnist, Richard Jackson, joined in the fun. No one was bored. There was the usual verbal sparring during the board of control meeting, but afterwards Charlotte let loose on the media in what Jackson termed "a breathless 75-minute monologue . . . It was like three board of control meetings, the EMO [Emergency Measures Organization] committee and the Congo debate of the United Nations rolled into one." He reported that her complaints were widespread, but basically boiled down to her plight as a sixty-five-year-old woman being ostracized by insignificant aldermen and an irresponsible press. He said she talked so fast that it was hard to keep proper notes, and it all began when a reporter merely asked for her reaction to negative comments about her chairing of the emergency measures committee, which work she had likened to "stirring the maggots in a dead horse." Nearing the end of her "monologue," she argued that she still was working sixteen to eighteen hours a day on city business and chastised reporters for limiting her lunch time to a cup of coffee.

Fortunately, December was better. She was forgiven a $1.25 parking ticket in Toronto after arguing the point, and at the South Renfrew Progressive Conservative convention highways minister W.A. Goodfellow described her as "the most intelligent woman in Canada." At the end of the month, she was named Canada's Woman Newsmaker of the Year for the fifth time since 1950.

That was the Charlotte the public saw, the erratic, flamboyant, combative little woman with a smile one minute and a whiplash putdown the next, always looking for a fight, always hogging the headlines. What the public did not see was the co-operative Charlotte, the cajoling Charlotte, the careful, cautious, hard-working, tight-fisted Charlotte who refused to pay a dime of taxpayers' money if she could avoid it. What the public saw little of was the successful Charlotte.

Certainly her first year back in the mayor's chair had been a turbulent time. Certainly there had been distemper, disrespect, and disorder, but she could, and did, point out that there had been significant progress behind the scenes at city hall, as most departments functioned as they were expected to do, and committee work, for the most part, went smoothly.

In her "state of the city" report to council on January 2, 1962, she noted that the number of building permits had increased almost fifty per cent over 1960 and the city's debt was lowered by $7.2 million. Many more roads and sidewalks had been built and several bridges across the Ottawa and Rideau rivers and the Rideau Canal were under construction or restoration. City hall had been reorganized so that the overly burdensome workload of department heads was eased, and council had approved bylaws concerning downtown parking, the handling of dangerous goods, and a building code, among many other matters.

Meanwhile, council had been working on a new official plan for the city's future, and efforts were made towards a new housing program that would be announced in 1962. Also a 250-bed geriatric centre, later to be named after her late friend and former colleague Marjorie Bradford, was opened thanks to a fifty-fifty cost-sharing agreement with the provincial government.

As well, she noted in her ninety-minute address, council, at her strong urging, had passed a bylaw that charged subdivision developers a special fee for sewer construction if they wanted to jump the queue of developers in obtaining new sewers, and a water treatment plant had been built in the west end to limit the amount of city sewage entering the Ottawa River. As an aside, she quipped, "Possibly 1961 may rank in Ottawa's history as the Great Sewer Year. After all, one could be remembered by one's city for worse things than the modernization of sewage disposal and the ending of the pollution of the majestic Ottawa."

She need not have worried, for she was well known in and beyond Ottawa as much more than Our Lady of the Sewers. At any rate, she must have felt that city affairs were in check, for in mid-April she left for another month-long holiday in the British Isles which included, as usual, London, the Yorkshires, and Scotland. The difference this time was that she included on her itinerary Ireland, the location of her sought-after ambassadorship three years earlier, with stops in Dublin, County Wexford, County Limerick, and County Clare. It appeared she had not altogether abandoned the idea of diplomatic duty there.

Returning to Ottawa, she was in fine form in June when the Queen Mother arrived for a brief visit—a wonderful occasion for Charlotte to shake out the mayoral robes and tricorn hat—and she delighted photographers again when she used a woodsman's heavy broadaxe to down a puny pine tree to open the city's fifth tourist office on the western outskirts. Days later, she enlivened a photo opportunity when she took five swings before cracking open a bottle of champagne on a new $20-million sewer, remarking, "I've seen champagne put to better uses."

June was also the month she announced a controversial, three-year, $7-million housing program that was intended to clear the backlog of families needing adequate housing. She called it "urban renewal" while others termed it "slum clearance," but the upshot was that she recommended the low-rental housing be spotted around the city, rather than clustered in familiar poor districts, such as Overbrook, the scene of her first low-rent project a decade earlier. Not surprisingly, middle-class communities such as Riverview Park and Ridgeview Park, where she intended to locate the 374 new units, were more than mildly upset. The proposed units would lower property values, the homeowners complained, but Charlotte toughed it out at public meetings and in the media and eventually had her way. The program also included the establishment of a five-person housing commission, and the hiring of housing inspectors to ensure that the new homes were properly maintained.

It was not a new Charlotte that returned from the British Isles, however. For example, just fifteen minutes after the Queen Mother had left city hall, she and Tardif were once more slinging sour shots at each other.

"You are a pathological liar . . . a cheap Tory trickster," Tardif charged during an argument over the reasons a board of control meeting had lacked quorum.

"You, Tardif, are beneath the capacity of the House of Commons because you are so cheap . . . you are so low that a snail would have to dig a trench to get under you," she shot back.

Three days later, in the general election that saw Diefenbaker's Conservatives reduced to minority government status, Tardif was returned in Russell with an 80,000-vote majority over his Tory opponent. Controller Lloyd Francis, meanwhile, lost in Carleton to Dick Bell. The two local results were a mixed blessing for Charlotte, for she would still have to work with Francis for the foreseeable future, but Tardif said he would not seek re-election to council at the end of the current term in December.

Meanwhile, she had been fighting a losing battle to ban a harness racing track in Gloucester Township, just south of Ottawa. The township wanted the racetrack, but Charlotte, who had long opposed gambling of any sort, hinted in separate letters — all marked "personal and confidential" — to municipal affairs minister Fred Cass, attorney general Kelso Roberts, treasurer James Allen, newly installed premier John Robarts and Prime Minister Diefenbaker that American gangsters might well be behind the track's ownership. Besides, the track would probably require water and other services from Ottawa that were badly needed in the capital. Eventually it was learned that the people behind the proposed track included, among others, James Baskin, the member of Parliament for Renfrew South since 1957, and her brother-in-law, Frank Ryan. As well, Ryan's wife Kay said the track's board members included some of Charlotte's election campaign supporters, such as paving contractors and a leading Ottawa lawyer. "The whole thing did not concern Ottawa or Charlotte, nor did she ever mention it to me, although she must have heard or read about the Frank Ryan Memorial at Rideau-Carleton [Raceway] being the most prestigious race in Eastern Ontario, and that I've paraded the race horses with my beautiful hackneys every year."

Only Cass responded to her letters: "I would appreciate it if in future when you are writing to me you would do me the courtesy of allowing the letter addressed to me by you to reach me before you release it to the local newspapers, or discuss it with the press." Besides, he added, his department was not responsible for horse racing in the province. In the end, her efforts were in vain. In what she termed "one of the most blatantly irregular proceedings right through," the racetrack received a licence to run seventy races the following year, and the Frank Ryan Memorial Trot continues today as one of the top two events in the track's season.

Two months later, she lost another long-running personal battle when the OMB ruled in favour of a Renfrew dairy that sought to expand its operations next to the house she had bought for her mother, and which she had kept after her mother's death for her own retirement in the Valley town.

It was business as usual in Ottawa, however, and once more Charlotte was front-page news in early November when she hinted that the federal government was about to announce a major redevelopment of the city's core around Confederation Square, from the former train station east of the Rideau Canal past the National War Memorial to the west side of Elgin Street. Although the government said the plan had been in the works for years, the "leak" sparked widespread rumours that Diefenbaker was about to appoint her to a prominent federal position.

"Judge Whitton? [Civil Service] Chairman Whitton? Senator Whitton? Even Ambassador Whitton? Whitton something-or-other for sure . . . although only Prime Minister Diefenbaker probably knows what," wrote the Tory-friendly *Journal*'s parliamentary columnist, Richard Jackson, on November 8. It appeared that Charlotte's days in civic politics were numbered. It appeared that she was headed for a larger, more important role, a role in which she could exercise her intelligence, her drive, and her high spirits to maximum advantage. It appeared that Charlotte's star was about to shine as it had never shone before.

Then came the slugfest.

"Mayor Swings Her Fists At Tardif," shouted the *Journal*'s front page.

"Whitton-Tardif bout makes fight history," roared the *Citizen*.

"She was absolutely berserk," a trembling Paul Tardif told reporters afterwards.

"It's the worst display I've ever seen," remarked Lloyd Francis. "We've had many rough sessions but this time was the first time fists were actually used."

The action took place on November 13 at a closed-door meeting of the board of control in controller Don Reid's office. The purpose of the meeting was not disclosed, possibly because it concerned personnel matters, but the ruckus between Charlotte, standing 5′ 1″ and 130 pounds, and Tardif, 5′ 8″ and 165 pounds, began when, according to Francis, he grumbled that Charlotte had not let him speak the previous day at the opening of a local hockey arena.

One thing led to another and, in the midst of the argument, Charlotte complained that she was getting only four hours' sleep at night and that she had no family to follow in her footsteps — an obvious dig at Tardif whose son Serge had announced his candidacy to replace his father on the board of control in the upcoming civic election. Tardif retorted that he "told her it was no fault of mine that you have no children. You could, if you were not so busy and had time for other things. Then she went absolutely berserk,

Paul Tardif's battles with Charlotte at city council were legendary, but they became friends in later years.
City of Ottawa Archives, MG011/CA3952

and swung at me four or five times." He said he backed off and none of her blows landed, although Francis, in his 2005 interview, said Charlotte also kicked Tardif in the shins.

Charlotte was not available for comment that day, but gave this account to reporters the next: It was triggered by "one of the filthiest . . . most obscene remarks that a person can say to a woman and there wasn't a man there to defend me . . . I gave it to him. No respectable woman could stand there and take what he said . . . I wish my brother didn't have a silver plate in his head [from an occupational injury] or I'd have him down here to give Tardif what he deserves. He ran for all he was worth. So did Controller Francis. The only one to stay behind and apologize for Tardif's dirty, obscene remark was Controller Reid." Reid, a passive giant of a man at 6′ 4″, refused to discuss the scuffle in his office.

Two days later, at another board of control meeting, this time in Charlotte's office, she had the men momentarily concerned for their lives when she pulled a gun out of her desk drawer during yet another verbal tussle with Tardif. They recovered quickly, for it was obviously a toy pistol, and not the real pistol she had received years earlier from the police. "It ended on a hilarious note though," *Journal* reporter Tom Kerr noted, with Tardif pleading theatrically, "Don't shoot!" According to the *Toronto Telegram*, Tardif asked, "Is it loaded?" and Charlotte snapped back, "No, I wouldn't waste a three-cent cap on you."

John Diefenbaker failed to see the humour in the situation. As he recalled in a CBC interview after Charlotte's death:

> I recommended her to the Queen for appointment as Ambassador to Eire and the prime minister of the North Ireland and de Valera, the president of Eire, they spoke so highly of her, so I recommended her appointment when there was a vacancy, as Ambassador to Eire, and the Queen accepted it, the powers of plenipotentiary were given by her signature and that night at council she got very annoyed with a controller with whom she had frequent verbal combat, she struck him. It was too bad, in my opinion, I didn't think that Ireland would want the import of any fighters so that ended Charlotte's career as a representative for Canada. She never got over that, but nonetheless, our friendship remained.

A rather lackluster, mean-spirited mayoral campaign ensued, in which her two opponents, controller Sam Berger and alderman Jim Groves, touted their experience and their ability to get along with others. Charlotte, meanwhile, battled with opponents of her housing plan and the local media who supported Berger again. The main issue remained the mayor's personality.

The people favoured Charlotte's eccentric personality and the election results were conclusive: Whitton — 40,062 votes; Berger — 34,044; Groves — 18,245. Lloyd Francis topped the balloting for controller, followed in order by Don Reid, former alderman Ellen Webber, and former controller Ernie Jones.

A confident Charlotte gives the "V" for victory sign as she casts her ballot in the 1962 municipal election.

City of Ottawa Archives, MG011/CA18293

Berger, incidentally, retired from civic politics, saying he was not bitter at the results, but that Groves, in splitting the anti-Whitton vote, was "foolish, a beggar, a whiner, ignorant, stupid, dishonourable, indecent, undemocratic, a bigot, prejudiced, ordinary, a meddler, selfish." Berger served as president of the CFL between 1964 and 1971. In 1969, he sold his shares in the Ottawa Rough Riders and moved to Montreal, where he bought the struggling Montreal Alouettes.

At the end of 1962, Charlotte was named Canadian Woman Newsmaker of the Year for the sixth time.

A new year meant a new game, a new council. Wilbert Hamilton had retired at the end of his last term and was named a commissioner on the city bus company board, and Paul Tardif had bowed out, concentrating his energy on his parliamentary duties. Concerning Tardif, she remarked wistfully, "If, in truth, the Mayor hopes now for a degree more of 'peace in our time' to the right of the chair, this anticipation must, in no wise, be interpreted as detracting from full recognition of the lively mind, sharp energy, business acumen, and, when he so chose, very real and valuable, practical help and sound reasoning which Controller Tardif brought to the dispatch of civic business." (Tardif continued as a member of Parliament until 1968 when he was named a citizenship court judge, a position he held for eleven years. He died in 1998 at the age of ninety. For the rest of their days, he and Charlotte remained on good terms and frequently wrote one another friendly greetings on special occasions. Tardif's son Serge gave up his aspirations of succeeding his father on council after his unsuccessful bid in the 1962 municipal election.)

The new council had to deal with the usual myriad of minor issues, as well as major items, such as the continuing growth of the city and the accompanying demands of developers. Charlotte rarely met a developer she did not dislike and distrust, and while some developers played loosely with the legalities, Charlotte could meet them at their own game.

One instance occurred in early 1963 when Elgin Cooper Realties battled to save its plans for a three-and-a-half storey apartment block in New Edinburgh, less than a kilometre from her own apartment. Elgin Cooper had received the building permit the previous August, but in September, city officials had decided that it was not in line with a proposed bylaw, so had cancelled it. Not surprisingly, Elgin Cooper challenged the cancellation, and in January, city solicitor Donald Hambling advised Charlotte that the developer had a good case, but that he was prepared to fight the case in court if she wished. She did want to fight it, and although she found only mixed support in council, she was determined to press the issue. However, after much private discussion with her councillors, she ordered Hambling the following April "to take whatever procedure is necessary to obtain the deferment of the court hearing." In other words, delay it as long as possible.

The dispute dragged on until January 1965, when the new board of control authorized Hambling to drop the case and let the construction proceed.

London, Dusseldorf, Copenhagen, Moscow, Kiev, Leningrad — Charlotte was in the air again. She left Ottawa on April 8, 1963, and returned on May 4. Her itinerary included twelve days in the Soviet

Charlotte's desk was always piled high and her calendar full
when she was in office.
City of Ottawa Archives, MG011/CA6672

Union, a country she had so often warned about in her newspaper columns and speeches as a threat to world peace and civilization itself.

It was a marvelous holiday, and she was particularly impressed by her Moscow visit, as she informed her counterpart in the Russian capital:

Never have I had more cordial, generous and thoughtful treatment than the privilege of being the guest of your Soviet and of the Soviets of Leningrad and Kiev . . . From a small child, my imagination was fascinated by Moscow and Nijni-Novgorod [sic] even as we studied about these great cities and the history of Russia . . . So, against this background and admiration, I went to the great Capital of your great State, and I went, I quite admit, with considerable misgiving, and not a little prejudice, but, I hope, with my mind open. I am grateful for the magnificent opportunity and the cordial reception which you accorded me, and I have left with only wonder and

admiration for the tremendous achievements, particularly
of your City, when one thinks that in less than 50 years
you have been the centre of a revolution and of two wars,
in which great destruction was wrought . . . [and] how
very much there is still to do, throughout the U.S.S.R. and
throughout your own great Soviet of Moscow itself.

It must have been a most enjoyable visit, for months later, in
writing to a friend, she admitted gaining nine pounds.

When she returned to Ottawa, she learned that on the day that she
had left, Lloyd Francis, the senior controller, had been elected as
member of Parliament for Carleton and had resigned from city
council.[7] His place as acting mayor in Charlotte's absence was taken
by Don Reid, the gentle giant who avoided confrontation whenever
possible; filling the fourth spot on the board of control was a francophone alderman and member of the legislature, Jules Morin.

Although far from docile, the four controllers were not her main
source of concern in the months after her return. That, for the time
being, was alderman David Dehler, a lawyer and champion of bilingualism and human rights. Charlotte, who spoke French to a
limited degree, had always opposed bilingualism at city hall. She
considered "the French fact" an irritant in Canadian history — she
once described the expulsion of the Acadians as "neither hastily nor
ruthlessly executed: it was a twice deferred act of military necessity."
As Marion Dewar, mayor of Ottawa in the 1970s and '80s, told the
author, Charlotte always made sure that there were no francophones
among her senior city staff.

So she was more than a little upset in May 1963 when Dehler,
a first-term alderman, moved to establish a committee that would
work towards making Ottawa "a truly bilingual national capital" in
time for the centennial of Confederation in four years' time. She immediately ruled that out of order. Defeated but undaunted, Dehler

---

7   Francis, a Liberal, and Dick Bell, a Tory, represented Carleton in the
    Commons for the next twenty-one years, with each man succeeding the
    other in seven federal elections, up until 1984. Francis also served as
    Speaker of the House of Commons and was later appointed ambassador to
    Portugal by Prime Minister Brian Mulroney. He died of stomach cancer in
    January 2007 at the age of eighty-six.

was back with another motion in mid-July. This time he moved that the letterhead on all municipal stationery and all city traffic signs be bilingual, as well as all assessment notices and other information going out to residents from city hall.

Blocked again, he turned his attention to human rights at city hall. He recalled that, in March, he had moved for a revision of the city's employment form so that candidates for city jobs would no longer have to indicate their creed, nationality, or place of origin. He acknowledged that while his motion had been soundly defeated by his fellow councillors, because staff were already working on a revised form, no progress had been made on the matter. He blamed the delay on "Her Worship's catch-us-if-you-can attitude."

> It seems incredible that, because of the dictates of one person, council as a whole, including board of control, should refuse to own up to its responsibility to ensure that the provincial legislation is implemented . . . Let us put an end to the psychological reign of terror which exists at city hall at the expense of the dignity of each elected representative and the dollar of each taxpayer. Must all beg and bow to the whims of a dictatorial demagogue?

Two days after making that comment, the city's director of personnel, R.J. Wilson, advised board of control that since Dehler's original motion had been defeated, nothing further was done on the issue, aside from discussing it with the Human Rights Commission and the Minister of Labour. However, since January 1, the city had hired fifty-two Roman Catholics, fifty Protestants, and one "Hebrew." All spoke English, while thirty-six spoke French; other languages spoken included Chinese, Greek, Polish, Italian, German, and Dutch.

August seemed to be the preferred month for British visitors to Ottawa. On August 26, the Lord Mayor of London — this time it was Sir Ralph Perring filling the honorary, one-year post — arrived in full style, packing five mayoral robes, lacy jabot and chain of office, and accompanied by his official sword bearer, his mace bearer, his city marshall, his chief high commoner, and two sheriffs. *Journal* columnist Richard Jackson described him as "an urbane, pleasantly sociable and immaculately groomed English gentleman with a shiny silver-grey pompadour."

Although she had only one mayoral robe and no official aides with which to greet the distinguished visitor, Charlotte put on a fine show by arranging for him to travel to Lansdowne Park in the governor general's landau. Once there he officially opened the annual Ex to the delight of thousands of children, especially after he gave away 10,000 balloons carrying the message "Buy British for Value." He was then transported in a thirty-four-boat flotilla along the Rideau Canal to downtown and on to city hall, where Charlotte played the gracious hostess at a lavish banquet.

At one point during the banquet, after they had toasted the Queen with apple juice and had exchanged gifts — Charlotte presented her guest with two Inuit soapstone carvings and in return received a set of 1773 Georgian vases — the suave Lord Mayor leaned over to Charlotte. Eyeing her corsage, he whispered, "If I smell your rose, will you blush?"

To which Charlotte replied, "If I pull your chain, will you flush?"

(That anecdote is part of urban legend in the national capital, and as the author has been unable to track its source, he believes it was probably Charlotte herself who first spread it.)

There was time for pleasure, and there was time for work, or, in Charlotte's case, time for combat. As the fall progressed, she angered the firemen by describing the thirty-five-cent-an-hour pay increase they were awarded in arbitration as "rather sickening"; she continued her jousting with Campeau and other developers; and she was involved in a shouting match with the only other woman on the board of control, Ellen Webber, over the presentation of reports on welfare administration. Webber, whose portfolio included the welfare department, suggested that Charlotte's report on welfare finances could be included in her report. Charlotte, however, suspected Webber of undermining her authority and rejected the suggestion. As tempers escalated, both women rose from their desks. Charlotte warned, "You can't tell me . . ." but was stopped short by Webber.

"No one tells you anything. All you do is scream, rant, rave and carry on like . . ." at which point Charlotte left the boardroom, only to return once tempers had cooled.

In December, Charlotte upset both the Jewish community and the francophone community, the latter comprising about one-third of the city's population.

Nine months earlier, local businessman and philanthropist Bertram Loeb privately offered the city $450,000 to build and equip a cancer research centre at the Civic Hospital as a memorial for his parents and a brother. The only conditions were that the family name be associated with the centre and that the offer be approved unanimously by council. Loeb was a prominent food retailer in Canada, with business interests in Israel, and he was a distinguished member and supporter of the tight-knit local Jewish community. His offer was welcomed by the hospital's board of trustees and by city council with one exception, Charlotte. After she had been informed of the offer in March, she had done some number-crunching, and while the centre might be a welcome addition to the hospital, she figured it would cost the city in additional operating funds. This would mean an increase in property taxes, which frightened her. A council decision on the offer was put off until the following March, and pressure was put on Charlotte to change her mind.

She did not, and the outcome was twenty-to-one in favour of accepting the offer, which had since been raised to $500,000. Consequently, Loeb offered the money to Carleton University instead, whose officials accepted with alacrity and delight. Charlotte had angered not only Loeb and the Jewish community, Civic Hospital trustees and her council colleagues, but even the city solicitor. He was enraged when she accused him of double-crossing her in advising the board of control that a municipal plebiscite was not required on the issue, as Charlotte had suggested. "It was absolutely cooked up," she said of solicitor Hambling's advice. "It is without precedent in the history of Ottawa."

Hambling, unlike most city staff, answered back. "I will not prostitute my ability, integrity or training as a lawyer to satisfy the whim or caprice of any single individual or person."

While the Loeb issue was simmering in the background, other controversies were receiving larger headlines. Bilingualism at city hall became an especially hot topic, as once more alderman Dehler pushed for bilingual traffic signs and bilingual letterhead on municipal stationery. By now he was receiving additional support from the five francophone members of council as well as some anglophones, especially controller Webber. Furthermore, this coincided with the newly launched Royal Commission on Bilingualism and Bicultural-ism; bilingualism was taking on a national dimension.

December had gotten off to a bad start for Charlotte, for there was a move in council on the second to allow the French word "*Cédez*" to be added to the English "Yield" on traffic signs in the largely francophone By Ward in Lowertown. On the third day, the four controllers refused to attend a closed-door meeting in her office to discuss a proposed city-wide zoning bylaw, one that would have far-reaching consequences for the city's skyline for years to come. Also on that day, her brother J.B. died in Renfrew; he was sixty-four.

The zoning issue could be set aside until the new year, but the wrangle over a bilingualism policy was not so easily postponed. The matter came up again at the December 10 council meeting, and once again Charlotte ruled Dehler's bilingualism motion out of order. She ruled that there was nothing in provincial legislation allowing the city to adopt bilingualism, so therefore as chairman of the coun-cil she could not allow a vote on the issue. When it was pointed out that Hawkesbury and Eastview, immediately to the east of Ottawa, had bilingual traffic signs, she replied that was none of her business as mayor of Ottawa, that it was the responsibility of the provincial government to change the legislation if it wished. Despite protests from councillors, the matter was dropped and the city's signs and letterhead remained unilingual.

Reaction was swift from the francophone community, especially from its younger members, some 200 of whom marched peacefully on city hall on December 13. Similarly, *Le Droit* and all the area's francophone politicians at all levels campaigned vociferously in fa-vour of bilingual signs and were encouraged by a number of an-glophone politicians. Their protests fell on deaf ears, however, for Charlotte was in Renfrew attending to her brother's estate. On her return to Ottawa, she simply ignored the issue.

At the end of December, she was named runner-up to national health and welfare minister Judy LaMarsh, another outspoken femi-nist, as Canadian Woman Newsmaker of the Year.

Although she was particularly tight-fisted when it came to spending taxpayers' money, Charlotte did have fond dreams for her city and a vision of it as a great capital of the world. She just did not want to spend Ottawa taxpayers' money on those dreams, especially when she could cajole friends in high places, such as Diefenbaker or Frost, to carry much of the financial load. However, by February 1964, those old friends were no longer in power. Diefenbaker, now in Opposition, was busy defending his party leadership from disgruntled rebels. Frost had retired in 1961 to be replaced by John Robarts, a more forward-looking leader and one who did not always appreciate Charlotte's contrary views on current topics such as bilingualism.

Nevertheless, she was a politician to the core, and she knew when and how to pull strings behind the scenes. Thus it was that she privately reached a deal with Prime Minister Lester Pearson in which the city would provide a prominent site on Confederation Square opposite the National War Memorial free of charge to the federal government so long as Pearson agreed to build and operate a prestigious performing arts centre upon it. It was one of the most prominent sites in the city, wedged between the square and the Rideau Canal, and it had been donated to the city in 1848 by the original owner, Bytown pioneer Nicholas Sparks. It had been the site of the former city hall, with a combined police-fire station in the rear, until it burned down in 1931.

There was just one difficulty in handing over the land to the federal government. Sparks had donated the land to the city only if it was used for either a town hall or a marketplace, and the arts building, later named the National Arts Centre, was neither. If not used for either purpose, the land was to revert back to Sparks's heirs, according to the pioneer's bequest. To solve that dilemma, Charlotte suggested that since the site had been used for a city hall until 1931, that fulfilled the terms of the will. She further proposed that the current heirs might accept a plaque on the building acknowledging their ancestor's donation as compensation. When Pearson remained uncertain about the legality of that proposal, Charlotte came up with another scheme: The government could include a gift or flower shop in the building and consider it a market.

Pearson, keen to have a major showpiece in time for centennial celebrations just three years away, accepted the proposal and thanked Charlotte in writing for her "constructive and imaginative attitude . . . The contribution of the City of Ottawa of the site for it is an action that will be much appreciated by all Canadians."

Curiously, when the NAC was opened officially in 1969, Charlotte's name did not appear on the official guest list.

Although her personal negotiations with Pearson on this issue had served her well, she was not quite as successful when the National Capital Commission moved on its plans to improve the appearance of Confederation Square and the buildings surrounding it, as well as the government's major properties in other parts of the city. As NCC chairman Lt.-Gen. Findlay Clark advised her in early April, the city's new zoning bylaw, which restricted the height of buildings to 150 feet, "would unduly restrict" his commission's plans. Preoccupied with other personal and civic matters, Charlotte waited until the end of August to appeal to Pearson directly.

Pearson was unmoved. The federal government was the senior government according to the *British North America Act*, and "if this fundamental legal point is understood and appreciated, then there should be no grounds for disagreement between the City of Ottawa and the Federal Government on this point." In other words, the federal government and its NCC were not bound by the limits of the city's zoning bylaw and could do as it pleased. Regardless, the NCC made few changes around the square in the next few years that contravened the bylaw's guidelines.

Charlotte's preoccupation during this period included another extended overseas trip and yet another dispute with yet another developer. The three-week journey began on April 10 and included Rome, Beirut, Cairo, Jerusalem, Ammam, Tel Aviv, Athens, and London. More than a personal junket, it was practically a diplomatic mission, for prior to leaving she had coaxed Arnold Smith, under-secretary of state at External Affairs, not only to arrange the various visas and a dispensation from having to take the normal inoculations, but also to provide introductions to senior Canadian diplomats at stops along the way. Consequently, she travelled in style, managing to meet the Pope at the Vatican as well as other foreign dignitaries.

In Israel, thanks to arrangements made by the Israeli ambassador in Ottawa, she had lunch with the mayor of Jerusalem and dinner with Israeli foreign minister Golda Meir. She visited a kibbutz before spending a night at the Canadian ambassador's residence in

Tel Aviv. On her return via London, she was guest of honour at the prestigious Forum Club at the invitation of Canadian justice minister Lionel Chevrier and a future prime minister, John Turner.

Back in Ottawa in mid-May, the Ottawa supplement of the *Canadian Jewish News* featured a full-page advertisement from Charlotte in which she enthused about her Israeli visit and wrote of visiting "Israel's ancient Holy City where today I saw women of Israel weeping and 'would not be comforted' at King David's tomb and climbed the way of pilgrimage to Mount Zion." She remarked how Ottawa's Jewish community was then into its third generation and was comprised of "outstanding citizens of the Hebrew faith and race [who] have made a contribution beyond easy recording to every phase of our community's life."

Coincidentally, it was a Jewish developer who made her return to the capital somewhat less than welcoming. Irving Greenberg, who had started Minto Construction with his brothers Gilbert and Lorry in 1955, was, like Campeau and other developers, frustrated by what he saw as Charlotte's delaying tactics. In his case, Minto planned to build a 483-apartment complex in Alta Vista, but the board of control refused to grant a building permit because of the lack of sewer capacity. Greenberg, however, said he had confirmation from a private firm of consulting engineers that sewer capacity was adequate for servicing his apartment complex. To support his claim, he announced plans for a demonstration at city hall on June 1 of about 1,000 labourers involved in the project, and whom he would have to lay off if it did not go through.

And that is exactly what he did. And Charlotte was prepared.

She called in an extra half dozen policemen, and when the workers arrived in the foyer at city hall, she stood guard at the top of the staircase next to the second-floor council chamber, warning the crowd below not to mount the curved, marble stairway or she would read the *Riot Act*, which, incidentally, she had had the city solicitor bring out the previous year when she thought it might be needed during demonstrations over the bilingualism issue. None of the men approached, but when they loudly jeered her, she threatened again to read the *Riot Act* and to have the police chase them from the building. According to reporters there, she threatened once more to read the *Riot Act* before allowing Greenberg to reach the second floor and speak to the only councillor who would speak to him, alderman Charlie St. Germain. The rest of council went into a closed-door session and only came out after the workers had dispersed. In all, the demonstration only lasted about fifteen minutes, and a short time afterwards, a fashionably attired Charlotte left for a formal dinner at Rideau Hall in honour of the visiting Irish president, Eamon de Valera.

Greenberg, through Minto, which would become the largest housebuilder and landlord in the city, waited more than a month before he struck back. In mid-July, he offered council $5,000 of his own money to fund a public inquiry into the city administration's "gross negligence and incompetence," especially the sewers, water, and roads branches of the Works Department. Although his offer was refused, he made his point, for council agreed to fund its own inquiry; it would become a minor issue in the forthcoming municipal election campaign. Also, Greenberg decided to run for controller.

The 1964 election campaign would be Charlotte's last hurrah. Even the visit of Queen Elizabeth in October seemed of secondary interest to her, for this time the opposition seemed ominous and dissatisfaction with her dictatorial rule and irrepressible shenanigans was widespread. Don Reid was wooed by a committee comprising a cross-section of the population, including former civic politicians, businessmen, doctors, lawyers, and community groups, to seek the mayoralty and bring peace to city hall. Their intent was not so much to get Reid elected as it was to get rid of Charlotte.

Timid Reid, who was not anxious to run against the fiery Charlotte, nevertheless accepted the challenge, but ran a low-key campaign. About the only colour was provided by his "Dolls for Don," female supporters who were meant to balance Charlotte's "Petticoat Brigade." Interest in the campaign was finally sparked when Frank Ryan, CFRA radio station owner and Charlotte's brother-in-law, joined the race about one month before election day. Two other candidates, retired boilermaker Louis Paradis and truck-rental operator Alfred Lapointe, entered the contest as well, but were given no chance of winning.

Charlotte, obstinately, relied on "More of the same" as her campaign message, while Reid advertised himself as "A big man for a big job." Ryan, running as "A man of action," counted on his

Despite her diminutive size, Charlotte thought nothing of attacking the much larger Don Reid.

Citizen-UPI photo, courtesy of the **Ottawa Citizen**

experience as a successful businessman and farmer to win the job, while sneering at his opponents' campaign symbols — a broom for Charlotte, a vacuum cleaner for Reid — as regrettably childish. He also advertised himself as "the only candidate who can step dance, play the fiddle, show prize horses and heifers, speak French and the Ottawa Valley lingo." Not surprisingly, his wife Kay campaigned for her husband, to the chagrin of her sister.

In typical style, on November 17, Charlotte opened her campaign with a twenty-two-page dissertation on the city's need to retain her at the helm. There were many reasons, she argued, but among the main ones was that she alone would successfully battle the federal forces which were considering the amalgamation of the city into a nationally run "federal district," much like Washington, D.C., a district that would include neighbouring municipalities on both sides of the Ottawa River. She also called for three-year terms for council instead of the then two years, and she suggested that if the board of control failed to be more co-operative, council should replace the four controllers with "permanent appointed executive officials" who would do most of the controllers' work at the mayor's direction, thus ensuring the mayor much more power at city hall.

Various issues were discussed at all-candidates meetings, but the campaign boiled down to one question: Whether or not the people of Ottawa wanted Charlotte back. The newspapers were solidly behind Reid, but would the public follow?

Charlotte was well aware of the strong tide of opposition to her rule, and as election day neared, she repositioned herself as the poor underdog fighting against the wealthy "high-powered campaigning" of her opponents. "It is the eve of Saint Catherine's Day," she told viewers at an all-candidates television debate on November 24. "Most of you probably know that Saint Catherine is the patron saint of spinsters. What you may not know is that because of her skill in debate, she is also the patron saint of philosophers. Exasperated by her logic, power and influence, her persecutors in Alexandria, some 1,650 years ago, put her to death by grinding her in an engine, with a spiked wheel. However, death proved glory to her. Her body was ultimately buried high on Mount Sinai in a shrine of veneration to this day . . . How fitting therefore that I should get into my first election debate [of 1964] for the mayor's chair on Saint Catherine's Eve."

She was pulling out all the stops. On November 29, she addressed a telegraph to CBOT, the local CBC television station, demanding "the filmed interviews made November 24th are not to be shown without my written permission." That same week, she limped into an all-candidates meeting wearing a regular shoe on her left foot and a moccasin on her right, explaining that her cat, Felix Ferdinand, had bitten her on the ankle as she was kneeling by her bed saying her evening prayers. However, she was outdone days earlier by Frank Ryan when he fell backwards off a two-foot-high platform at CBOT prior to a televised panel discussion, landing on his back and head on the concrete floor. He was rushed to hospital, but soon returned to the campaign with what seemed like minor bruising.

Media opposition to the mayor was unrelenting. Both the *Journal* and the *Citizen* had offered their editorial support for Reid, and *Le Droit* was expected to follow suit.

All-candidates meetings in the final weeks of the campaign were packed, often split between Charlotte's "petticoat brigade" and by her opponents. The meetings were held in local schools, and all were awash in rising animosity. Some three dozen candidates for mayor, controller, alderman, and school board trustees vied for listeners' attention. Mayoralty candidates spoke for ten minutes, the rest had five minutes each. Speaking order was based on a first-come, first-talk basis.

Heckling and noisemaking ruled the first two meetings, but the third, on December 2, outdid them all. An estimated 300 people were packed tightly into the Woodroffe Public School auditorium to hear twenty-seven candidates state their cases, and they were not disappointed as far as entertainment value was concerned. It was one of the wildest campaign meetings in the history of Ottawa.

"Whitton Threatens To Read Riot Act," read the front-page headline of the *Citizen* the next day.

"Mayor Jeered, Shouted Down At Noisy Rally," echoed the *Journal*.

It began badly for Charlotte, my brother Hugh, a spectator, told me much later:

> . . . but as she spoke, she got more and more [of the audience] on her side and she got a strong ovation when she was finished . . . She then went down into the audience and as was her custom, sat in the front row, at which point, Irving Greenberg, who was waiting to speak, grabbed the microphone and accused her of having talked out of sequence.
>
> Well, of course, he's got the microphone and he's drowning her out, [so] she jumped to her feet . . . trying to defend herself, but she's getting this noise from the stage. She then stormed the stage, grabbed the microphone from him and she started to say that she had swapped places with some other candidate and the crowd had now become unruly, and they obviously were stirred up by Greenberg and she threatened to read the *Riot Act*.

Indeed she had spoken out of turn, for she had been the twenty-fourth candidate to arrive, yet had spoken in fourteenth position after switching places with school board candidate Roy Bushfield.

She tried to explain amidst the furore that she had sought the switch because she had a television interview arranged that evening, but the explanation was overpowered by the ensuing pandemonium. The jeering, clapping, and chanting escalated as Charlotte conferred with the chairwoman of the meeting, Mrs. F.D. Richardson, hoping to restore order, and when that effort failed, Charlotte tried twice to read the *Riot Act*, but was drowned out. Overcome by the increasingly angry dissent, she walked out in a huff, her authority as mayor dissolving in a sea of catcalls and taunts.

The following evening's meeting at Elgin Street Public School, attended by another 300 persons, was mild by comparison. Ryan charged that Charlotte was "a clever, designing hothead whose single-handed dictatorship has brought her to her present situation." She retorted that Reid's campaign was run like a Tammany Hall operation, referring to the notoriously corrupt organization that once controlled New York City politics on behalf of the Democratic Party. She also quipped that Ryan "has been second place to one Whitton for 35 years and I see no reason for him to take after this one."

Reached later, Reid reacted, "People keep asking why I don't hit back at my opponents, but I was always taught not to hit my elders."

The war of attrition having exhausted itself, the final meeting at Connaught Public School was "by far the quietest audience of the campaign," the press reported. Reid promised peace at the council table if he was elected; Ryan vowed to improve Ottawa's image in the world; and Charlotte warned, "You don't change pitchers in the last inning with an overwhelming victory in sight . . . and the City of Ottawa under the Whitton administration is well on its way to becoming one of the most beautiful cities in the world."

Then the public spoke. On December 7, the election results for mayor were as follows: Reid — 43,991; Ryan — 26,996; Whitton — 25,608; Paradis — 706; Lapointe — 395.

There was little doubt what the public wanted. It wanted peace in the council chamber, which was one thing that Charlotte found impossible to provide.

"A swan song for a tough old bird," read the headline over the Hamilton *Spectator* editorial two days later, and that was as good a summation as any of the views offered up by editorialists and commentators from one end of the country to the other.

The Ottawa Journal, in an editorial entitled, "A 'Thank You' to the Lady," observed that:

> Charlotte Whitton has done a great deal for the City of Ottawa and for its people. Her defeat is not a denial of that but a feeling that it was time for a change, a feeling that the Mayor had worked herself into a nervous exhaustion that imperilled her own welfare as well as the city's.
>
> Miss Whitton has given to our public life a kind of dash and verve that was a happy change from the other extreme of stuffiness that had been our habit. Her dash and verve led her and the people of Ottawa into too mad a chase of late, even into confusion, but it was for all that a likable trait.

The *Citizen's* editorial concluded that:

> While Mr. Reid deserves the congratulations and co-operation of the community, the community owes a debt of gratitude to Mayor Whitton and Mr. Frank Ryan. This newspaper has, more often than not, considered Miss Whitton's judgment mistaken. Nevertheless, she has always given everything she had to the community she loved. After so many years in office, her defeat was perhaps inevitable — it is a law of politics that no politician can stay too long in office without courting defeat.

Seemingly untouched by all the media attention and the greetings of hundreds of well-wishers, Charlotte remarked that she planned to write a book that would make a lot of people "break out in a nervous rash."

She was not through with civic politics just yet, she hinted slyly.

19 Sex, Drugs, and Rock 'n' Roll

Charlotte was bitter in defeat. "For the first time in 14 years my life is my own. I do love this city, but it does not love me or want my services anymore," she told reporters on election night. She railed at Kay, the kid sister she had helped put through university and who had campaigned for her husband, Frank Ryan, and she blamed Fran Baldwin, the freelance journalist who had voluntarily taken on the difficult task of campaign organizer in 1962 and 1964, for her loss. When controllers Jules Morin and Ernie Jones tried to console her by telling her she had achieved much for the city, she snapped back, "I have been beaten again by the same combination that caused my only defeat before. At that time, my sister worked against me too and I was beaten in the West Ottawa general election by George McIlraith. What, I suppose, is the use of having a York-shire and Irish family if you can't have murderous difference?" And now Kay had done it again, she complained.

When she visited Don Reid's campaign headquarters that night to offer the perfunctory congratulations, she came face to face with Robert Campeau, the increasingly wealthy and powerful developer.

"Shake hands," Campeau said, extending his right hand.

"I won't, I won't," a *Journal* reporter quoted her as saying. He continued, "She shivered with rage, and her forefinger began puncturing the air in the direction of the builder. 'Bob Campeau, I . . .,' she couldn't finish her sentence."

"All I want to do is shake hands," Campeau told her, but two women who accompanied Charlotte quickly led her away.

One thing about Charlotte, though, she went down fighting. Her mayoralty did not end until the new year, three weeks after the election, and for much of that time she remained in familiar form, battling fellow councillors over budgetary issues, angering community groups who did not want her low-rent projects in their neighbourhoods, and frustrating child-care groups by her ongoing opposition to a dedicated hospital for sick children. But she could satisfy herself that both Irving Greenberg, who had kicked up such a fuss about her alleged interference with his proposed subdivisions, and Serge Tardif, Paul's son, had been unsuccessful in seeking seats on the board of control.

As the final days in her mayoralty counted down, some attitudes softened. Even Campeau buried the hatchet, to a certain extent. "Mayor Whitton worked hard for the city in her own way. It just wasn't effective. She's earned her retirement and I wish her well," he remarked as he announced more large-scale projects, which, he hinted, would meet little opposition from the new, more accommodating council under Reid.

At the final meeting of the old council on December 21, Charlotte was given a three-minute standing ovation by the estimated 200 people attending after she had delivered a sombre farewell. Decidedly sentimental, she reminded her colleagues wistfully that she was leaving only because one of them, Reid, had defeated her and because a family member, Frank Ryan, had tried to do the same. Speaking to some sixty high school students in the public gallery, she advised them to further their education and serve their country. "There have been kind words spoken here about what my country may owe me, but it is not that which is in my heart at the moment, it is what I owe my country." As the gallery rose to its feet, *Journal* reporter Tom Kerr observed, "The mayor sank into her chair and slowly began removing the chain of office for the last time for at least two years."

A mini-avalanche of job offers began filling her mailbox, many from Canada's leading book publishers and newspaper editors. Prentice-Hall of Canada reminded her that its previous offer of a book contract — perhaps an autobiography, perhaps something else of her choosing — was still on the table. McClelland & Stewart heard that she was working on a manuscript about the Ottawa Valley and was anxious to publish "that book, or indeed any other, [that] would be of interest to us." McGraw-Hill, Charles Scribner, and Ryerson Press were interested in her autobiography, as was *Maclean's* magazine and the *Toronto Star*. Toronto radio station CHFI-FM wanted her to do a series of three-and-a-half-minute talks, and a Carleton University student sought an interview and, for some inexplicable reason, promised not to bring a camera or a tape recorder to the session. Surprisingly, the *Citizen*, for whom she had written more than 500 columns in the past, showed no interest in having her back as a writer.

Scores of public speaking requests arrived from service clubs, church groups, and professional associations across the country, only a few of which she found time to accept.

The lone private television station in Ottawa at the time, CJOH, offered her a contract to do five fifteen-minute shows a week, which she accepted. Entitled "Dear Charlotte," it was a freewheeling program, with host Bill Luxton supplying readers' questions and Charlotte replying off the cuff in her inimitable, rambling style. In the first week, for example, she dealt with the following: "Are you afraid of death?" "What did the Pope say to you?" "Why is God so slow in conquering the forces of evil?" "Do you think that it's possible for anyone to really and truly love their enemies?" "How do you think a Christian should view communism?" "Are you ever afraid?" "Do you ever have trouble sleeping?" "To be a successful career woman, does a woman have to remain a spinster?" "Is it still a man's world?"

Occasionally she would introduce her own topics, such as local politics or the need for more women in politics, or a perspective on the death of Frank Ryan. Ryan, sixty-three, died on March 2, less than three months after the civic election, in Del Ray Beach, Florida. He had just returned to his winter home there after a one-month trip to South America with his wife Kay, a journey that was part-holiday and part-business. They had been selling off their prized collection of award-winning hackney horses, Angus cattle, and Suffolk and North Country Cheviot sheep, when he had suffered a fatal heart attack on his return to Del Ray.

Later that day, Charlotte told viewers that despite her sorrow at his passing, Ryan, president of a radio station, "more than most, would appreciate that . . . the show must go on. Nor would Frank Ryan, more than I, wish me to ignore the severance in our usually good relations, occasioned by his candidature in the 1964 mayoralty contest. Frank Ryan, boy and man, was known to and of our family, for half a century now. He was all Irish, of the Ryans of Carlow and the Barony of Idorne — merry and generous of heart, keen of mind, inflexible of will, firm — indeed to a certain fierceness — in his convictions and loyalties. What he deemed right, he would pursue, despite all consequences . . . If the heart-deep sorrow of so many of his fellow men today be any testimony, he has now acquitted himself well indeed as an honourable Christian gentleman."

The pre-taped show was a solid success, and numerous letters of support arrived at the station. It continued until the middle of 1966, and was also broadcast on television stations in Montreal, Toronto, and Kitchener.

"People used to say," Bill Luxton remarked in a 2009 interview, "'I don't know how you can stand working with that woman,' and I used to say, 'It's not that bad, I look forward to the challenge of doing it.'

"The thing was, once she was asked one question, you were pretty set for fifteen minutes, you didn't ask very many more. The big problem was trying to shut her up, because we had fifteen minutes and that was it, there were no commercial breaks." Luxton had worked out a system to warn her when her deadline was near, by drawing circles on their desk, but she frequently ignored him. "So I'd say, 'I'm sorry, Dr Whitton, we're out of time,' to which she usually replied in her screechy voice, 'I was just getting started.'"

Pre-taping the program allowed Charlotte plenty of time for other activities, especially personal correspondence with a broad range of friends and acquaintances, ranging from Mrs. Mary York of Ottawa, who was celebrating her ninetieth birthday, and former governor general Vincent Massey, to the Anglican primate, the Most Rev. H.H. Clark, and Prime Minister Lester B. Pearson. Many of her letters to influential persons offered unsolicited advice — she complained to Clark about declining Christian values in the church and she advised Pearson that he should name the new External Affairs building after O.D. Skelton, Canada's first external affairs minister and her history professor at Queen's — but were duly noted. Pearson replied that it was "an admirable suggestion and one which will certainly be considered by the Government; I am indeed grateful to you for writing to me about it." (The structure was eventually named the Lester B. Pearson Building, a title it retains today.)

Her future financial stability was an increasing concern, and in August, as she was returning by plane from a one-month sojourn in England, she became most attentive when a councillor from suburban Nepean, Grant Carman, suggested that she might be interested in selling her McGregor Lake retreat. However, after having enjoyed it for some three decades, she was not prepared to give it up just yet, although her visits had become limited to a few times each year.

As the fall of 1965 arrived, influential Conservatives, such as former Ontario premier Leslie Frost, prodded her to seek a seat in the House of Commons in the upcoming election; however, after some thought she issued a press release, entitled, "'I know what I want for my country but not where to find it." It began:

> I shall not be a candidate in this 1965 federal general election. I would have liked to be a member of the House of Commons in this next Parliament . . . because I believe that only on the floor of the House of Commons can the rapidly encroaching Fascism in the governing — I do not say Government — of Canada be effectively faced, rejected and defeated.

The times were passing her by and she was feeling increasingly out of touch with both current politics and current lifestyles, such as the new feminism advanced in the United States by Betty Friedan and others, as well as young people's growing inclination for sex, drugs, and rock and roll. For her, "flower power" was something you enjoyed in the garden.

She spoke little about municipal politics, then in May 1966, she moved out of her apartment on Rideau Terrace in New Edinburgh and into a small, two-storey, A-frame, Tudor-style house at 1 Renfrew Avenue in the Glebe, a fashionable area just south of Centretown and home to senior public servants, academics, lawyers, and doctors. The house was on a cul-de-sac and backed onto Central Park, a green space administered by the NCC. It was here that she would call home for the rest of her days.

Charlotte spent much of the summer arranging the September 30 move — for example, she paid Frank Flesher Upholstering $356 to refinish her antique sofa, her antique rocker, her antique gentleman's chair, her short-arm sofa and to clean her rug and polish her bookcase and small table — and also arranging the October 7 sale of her beloved cottage to Grant Carman. It was undoubtedly difficult to part with two properties so close to her heart, but even Charlotte could see her energy waning and her time on earth winding down.

In November, however, the old fire flickered again. She announced her candidacy for alderman in Capital ward, representing the Glebe.

"I am impelled primarily by a sense of obligation and responsibility to the community of which I have been resident now for well over two score years," she emphasized in a prepared statement. "I do not feel that I can ignore or escape the responsibility of seeking active and influential participation in the ordering of the municipal life of my city, insofar and as long as may be vouchsafed me."

The city faced new challenges, such as the setting up of a regional government, the downloading of some health services and growing municipal debt, yet city council seemed more concerned with establishing more recreational facilities for the young and ignoring the poor and the elderly, she charged. Outdoor swimming pools and rinks were nice, but what about better housing, she asked.

> Whether my remaining years be few or many, I ask the
> privilege of representing this fine, old ward in the capital,
> and of giving back some of what life has given me, to the
> continuing betterment of the capital of my country, Canada.
> I offer you really a bargain — a thoroughbred mayor, placed
> first in five of six starts, courageous of spirit and firm of will,
> going as a bargain for the price of an alderman.

It was a four-way battle for the two seats on council for Capital ward, pitting Charlotte against incumbent alderman Claude Bennett and two newcomers to the political scene, university professor Paul Baril and investment dealer Wilfrid Marshall, but the outcome was never in doubt. Bennett, who also was Charlotte's insurance agent, retained his position as senior alderman for the ward with a first-place finish, while Charlotte earned junior alderman status by finishing second ahead of Marshall and Baril respectively.

"The old grey mare is still what she used to be," she had told a campaign meeting. She promised to put "a lot of ants in some people's pants" on council.

Don Reid, who championed recreation, professional sports facilities and a children's hospital, was returned as mayor, along with all four incumbent board of control members, Kenneth Fogarty, Ellen Webber, Murray Heit and Ernie Jones. As usual, there was a brief sense of post-election comradeship among the victors. Even Paul Tardif, Charlotte's pet foe from past councils, wrote to congratulate her on her election:

> It is now evident that the administrative body of the City Council will have a fully experienced Alderman. On several occasions you publicly stated that one of your ambitions was to have a Civic Funeral and your present standing makes you eligible for that privilege. However I hope that the citizens of Ottawa will not be called upon to make this expenditure, during the present term, as most agree with me that there is no special rush for this ceremony to be held. Yours truly, Paul.

Indeed, Charlotte had expressed her hopes for a civic funeral several times to different people, and had even promised to leave money in her will to pay for it. For the moment, though, it was not necessary. The old urge to get out there and shake things up, the urge that had inspired her to take those first steps into the political wars in 1950, surged again. She may have been seventy, but she had the spirit of a thirty-year-old.

That fighting spirit was easily aroused. By February 1967, city hall reporters began counting and timing her contributions in council. The *Journal* reported on the 7th that she had spoken about fifty times during the previous night's six-hour session; on the 22nd, the *Globe and Mail* noted that she had spoken twenty-nine times on eighteen subjects for a total of fifty-six minutes and fifty-eight seconds during a five-hour meeting the night before.

Among her pet peeves was the Central Canada Exhibition Association, the private, broad-based group that operated the annual summer Ex on the city-owned Lansdowne Park in Capital ward, the same group that she had battled as mayor in the mid-1950s. This time, the CCEA was in the news because the board of control had approved a ten-year extension of its lease on the park, but two aldermen, Pierre Benoit and Don Kay, questioned the wisdom of providing the group with what they saw as an overly generous agreement. Charlotte could not have agreed more, and before long it was she who was leading the battle against the extension and in favour of city council retaining control of the park, where, during her absence from council, a combined indoor rink and conference hall called the Civic Centre had been erected to add to the facilities already there. Among the latter was the football stadium used by the Ottawa Rough Riders of the CFL.

As well, she was furious that the board of control, including the mayor who also sat on the CCEA board, released a copy of the complex, nineteen-clause contract to aldermen after business hours on a Friday night, and expected council to approve it at its next regular meeting the following Monday night. She was outraged that the "the practically implicit sleight of hand" by the board would be allowed to rush the lease through so quickly. After much debate, Reid and the controllers backed down and postponed the lease extension pending further review.

The dispute might have ended there, with an amicable compromise eventually arranged, but Charlotte was not one to let an advantage go for naught. She was aware that the issue was in the public's mind and that the controllers were fearing a backlash, so she pressed on during the rest of the year. But once more her delaying action proved ineffective. Council eventually approved the lease extension by a sixteen-to-three vote.

Undaunted, she consulted Ottawa lawyer Donald Diplock, and they discussed taking the issue to the OMB. Diplock advised that she could be disqualified as an alderman if she lost, but Charlotte was adamant about proceeding. That was in March 1967. By April, she was feeling less certain, particularly when Diplock told her that she had already run up a legal bill in excess of $2,000, and work on the case was ongoing. On the other hand, the city probably would have to pay his bill if she won.

By August, the dispute had escalated to the point where Sam McLean, an aldermanic candidate in the past election, charged in

Ontario Supreme Court that Charlotte should be removed from council for waging her battle against the council of which she was a member, in contradiction of the *Ontario Municipal Act*. Also, Diplock told her that he and his associates had spent 294 hours so far on the issue, and if they were to charge her at their regular rates, she'd be on the hook for about $9,000, although he had no intention of charging her that much if she lost. If she won, then his office would accept whatever costs the court awarded her, up to the amount that he normally would charge her.

She prepared a thirteen-page memorandum in which she spelled out the situation and which she was prepared to make public. Diplock advised caution, stating that her explanation of the complicated issue would only confuse the public, which he suggested was already on her side. In the meantime, to confuse matters further, McLean's case was dismissed by Ontario Supreme Court Judge Peter Macdonald, only to have McLean appeal the dismissal and have the appeal put over until the following October.

In October, the legal gavel slammed down on her. Mr. Justice R.I. Ferguson of the Ontario Supreme Court ruled that, as a city councillor, "She cannot settle her disagreement outside council and remain on council too." She therefore forfeited her right to sit on council and should be removed, Ferguson ordered. Consequently, Charlotte was ejected from council and Reid ordered a by-election for December 16. After further legal dispute between Charlotte and Reid, acting mayor Ken Fogarty and city clerk Alf Hastey over the setting of the date, the by-election went ahead as planned and Charlotte was returned in a landslide. She received more than twice the number of votes of her three opponents combined.

Although the CCEA controversy occupied much of Charlotte's time, she managed in her usual fashion to squeeze in a myriad other commitments — a dispute with the city's parking authority in February, a speaking tour in Western Canada and a row with the provincial government in May, and public addresses sprinkled across the continent throughout the year. In September, she was one of the few vocal supporters for John Diefenbaker at the Progressive Conservative Party's leadership convention when he went down in defeat to Robert Stanfield. In October, she gave serious thought to running in the provincial election in either Ottawa South or Ottawa Centre — even so far as taking out nomination papers — but changed her mind at the last minute and did not file in either riding. She also upset many Canadians when she was widely quoted as referring to Expo 67, the highly popular world's fair held that year in Montreal, as "a cheap but costly commercial show."

While her re-election demonstrated that she had won her case against the CCEA in the court of public opinion, the lease issue itself remained in limbo before the OMB. When the OMB finally released its decision on March 28, 1968, Charlotte was elated. "The lease cannot be approved," OMB chairman R.M. McGuire ruled, and any future lease with the CCEA should not extend beyond the life of the city council approving it, i.e. two years. As well, the city was ordered to pay the cost of all proceedings. She could hardly have expected a more favourable decision and only added to the pleasure she had received when, the previous November a different court had ruled in her favour against Reid, Fogarty, and Hastey, and had awarded her $791.85 in legal costs.

But nothing came easily when Charlotte and her lawyers were involved. She challenged the bill charged by Louis Assaly, her lawyer in the Whitton-vs-Reid-Hastey-Fogarty case, and she had ongoing disputes with other lawyers concerning a cottage her father had left his children and the sale of her McGregor Lake property.

Other matters that concerned her in 1968 included a complaint in January from a neighbour in the Glebe that Charlotte's cul-de-sac was cleared of snow before all other streets in the neighbourhood, closure of her beloved Elizabeth Tudor chapter of the IODE due to loss of membership, and resignation from the city's tourist and convention bureau after less than two months on its executive board because the bureau had printed more tourist maps of Ottawa than she thought were needed.

On a more positive note, she was invested into the Order of Canada as a member in April. Other inductees included Olympic skier Nancy Greene, golf star Marlene Stewart Streit, and musician Bobby Gimby.

Above all, Charlotte spent considerable energy fighting various proposed changes to the city's zoning bylaw, some of which included rezoning in portions of her ward and others involving high-rise buildings that developers, including Robert Campeau, were constructing. As an alderman, however, her influence was greatly reduced from what it had been during her time as mayor. Consequently, when she did not get her way on council, as was frequently the case, she took her argument to a higher authority, the OMB.

Once more, Campeau and other developers were stretching the bounds of the city's planning bylaw. In 1954, with Charlotte in charge, council had passed Bylaw AZ-64, which had set out zoning plans for the entire city. Among its most prominent clauses was one that raised the maximum building height limit to 150 feet from 110 feet, the latter having been in effect since 1914 in order to protect the primacy of the Parliament Buildings, and the Peace Tower in particular, on the city's landscape. Unfortunately for Charlotte and the many who supported her on this issue, council under Reid had allowed numerous exceptions to the height limit. Therefore, by the time she returned to council as an alderman in 1967, Campeau had begun work on his twenty-two-storey (i.e. 250 feet) Place de Ville office complex in Centretown, while other developers had similar plans in the works.

Moreover, Campeau shocked most Ottawans on January 22, 1968, by announcing plans for a high-rise that would tower some 450 feet high on the block bounded by Sparks, Kent, Queen and Lyon streets, just a few blocks southwest of Parliament Hill. It would include twin towers, thirty-nine storeys high, that would house offices, a 200-room hotel, a 700-seat theatre, a large department store, underground parking for 1,700 cars, and indoor and outdoor restaurants. Valued at $60 million, it would generate $850,000 in annual property taxes, Campeau claimed. He named it Place de Ville II, and since it would be across Queen Street from his original Place de Ville complex, he proposed turning that block-long part of Queen Street into a pedestrian mall.

"Whitton Against Campeau Plans," read the front-page headline in the *Citizen*, and indeed Charlotte was among the more outspoken of the project's opponents. "Don't let us prostitute our great city for such a small fee," she argued plaintively, suggesting the project was totally out of proportion to the rest of the city core. A local citizens' groups also was outraged, and George McIlraith, member of Parliament for Ottawa West and minister of public works, as well as Prime

Minister Lester B. Pearson, voiced their reservations. For Pearson, it was one of his last public statements before handing over the reins to Pierre Elliott Trudeau. The project's opponents saw this as the developers' wedge to transform the low-rise skyline of Centretown into a high-rise office jungle, thus overriding Parliament Hill's pre-eminence on the cityscape.

"Your decision may have a fundamental long-term impact on the national capital," Pearson warned city council. "It is of the greatest importance to the future development of the area." But city council barely blinked. It allowed for a federal-municipal study on Centretown building heights, but eventually approved a scaled back version that led the way for future office towers in the area.

For her part, there was little Charlotte could do beyond speaking from a minority position. She fought against other high-rise developments in the city during 1968 and 1969, with mixed results.

For Charlotte, Place de Ville II was her last major confrontation with Campeau, a man she had battled in the council chamber, at the OMB and even on her own street, Rideau Terrace, for more than two decades. In the end, she simply gave up and turned to other issues.

For Campeau, Place de Ville II was yet another achievement in a career that would see his billion-dollar business empire expand to include major construction projects along Toronto's waterfront and ownership of some of the most prominent American department stores, and his personal wealth manifest itself through luxurious homes in Canada, the United States and Austria, before it all came crashing down in personal bankruptcy, an ugly divorce, and retirement to Ottawa in near anonymity. (When the author phoned him at home in January 2009 to seek an interview for this biography, he replied gruffly, "I don't want to get involved with that, thank you very much," and hung up. When called again fifteen minutes later, he delivered a similar reception.)

With the arrival of her seventy-second birthday on March 8, 1968, Charlotte began paying more attention to her physical condition. She had put on weight, her face was puffy, and she required frequent medical attention. There were almost monthly visits to her general practitioner, Dr. Peter Burton, appointments every three or four months with her podiatrist, Dr. Leo Bishop, and regular eye examinations by Dr. Keith Edwards. Dr. Alvin Cameron cared for her teeth, including a lower denture. Grenville Goodwin Optometrists, once owned and operated by the mayor she replaced, charged her $21 for a pair of glasses, and in October 1969, Burton charged her $10 for an electrocardiogram and $6 for an X-ray.

Overall, she was adopting an increasingly grouchy attitude towards life in general, as evidenced by her views on the Royal Commission on the Status of Women ("I wouldn't appear before it if you pointed the noon-day gun at me"), the "autocratic" and "arrogant" CBC producers and their "montebanking interviewers," and magazine and newspaper editors who asked for snapshot reviews of her life.

"How I could cover now more than 50 years of very active going in 150 words is beyond me," she replied sharply to an editor at the Montreal-based *Weekend Magazine* who asked her to summarize her political career. In Ottawa, she complained bitterly to city staff and the police because a driving school was using her cul-de-sac as a practice zone for three-point turns and, accidentally, running over her bushes.

Marguerite Barclay, eighty-seven years old when I interviewed her in 2007, was a neighbour of Charlotte's when she moved onto Renfrew Avenue and recalled a woman who was friendly but generally kept to herself and her cat, except when she felt the neighbourhood children were getting out of hand. One time, when one of Mrs. Barclay's four children was in his teens, he was playing ball with his friends in front of Charlotte's house when Charlotte came along and ordered them off the street, so that taxpaying adults could drive on the dead-end patch of pavement. When the youth protested, suggesting that he had a right to play there because his father was a taxpayer, Charlotte threatened to have her lawyer speak to "his" lawyer about the matter.

On the other hand, "Sharl" generally got on well with her four children, especially when they were little. At Halloween, "She never opened her doors to children . . . but after everything was over, she'd phone me and say send your kids over," and provided them with lots of goodies. On another occasion, Charlotte found a stray pup in the park behind her home, took it in and cared for it for a few days, and then turned it over to the Barclays because, in her words, "Every family should have a dog."

Charlotte was a confirmed cat person, however, and each Christmas she would arrive at the Barclay house with a card and a present from her cat to the Barclay cat. Ever since the 1930s, Charlotte had kept one or more cats, and for years she presented the Rustie Whitton Memorial Trophy annually to the National Capital Cat Club, of which she was a member. Claude Bennett, who was her fellow Capital Ward alderman for almost a decade, suggested that it was not surprising that Charlotte worked long hours at city hall, for her social life seemed limited to her books and her cats.

And the telephone. Her telephone was Charlotte's prized possession, a tool for catching up on old friendships and a weapon to wield in the political wars. As mayor, she thought nothing of calling city clerk Alf Hastey and other senior staff at home after midnight as she toiled into the early morning hours. As alderman, and even in retirement, she was often on the phone to one and all.

"I had an uncle who was in the assessment department and he got calls at 4 a.m., and that's why a number of senior personnel in the city [administration] delisted their home phone numbers," Bennett said in an interview. He recalled that when he joined council in the early 1960s, veteran alderman Jim McAuley offered the following advice for receiving Charlotte's phone call: "Just put the phone down, come back fifteen minutes later and you haven't missed a thing."

Gilles Tardif, one of Paul's sons, recalled that when Paul was a controller on Charlotte's board of control, she used to phone him regularly on Sunday mornings before the next day's council meetings to discuss agenda items. Despite their constant and often bitter bickering at the council table, the lengthy telephone conversations "were quite pleasant and civil," Gilles said. "Many people thought my father and Charlotte were like fire and water and that if they had any communication, it wasn't pleasant, but that wasn't the case."

The late Marion Dewar, who was mayor of Ottawa between 1978 and 1985, said that when she decided to run for board of control in 1974, Charlotte was on the phone to her every day with advice. Unfortunately, Dewar ruefully recalled in an interview before her death in 2008, most of the calls came just as Dewar was preparing or serving the evening meal for her husband and four children.

"She called to ask how organized I was and whether I had all the workers in all of the beauty parlours. I said 'Well, no,' and she said 'Well, you should; that's where you get all your information,' so I said, 'Well, I'll look into it, Charlotte.' 'Never mind looking into it, get them in there because that's where you'll find who's having an affair with whom.' And she said, 'It's just amazing how you can disarm them, just before you go up to speak, you say, "Hello Mr. Smith, and how is Connie Brown today?"' So I said, 'I'll consider it.'"

Dewar, originally a public health nurse and later president of the New Democratic Party, a member of Parliament, and chair of Oxfam Canada, went back to the kitchen table that night and told her family what the former mayor had just advised. They were shocked. "I said I had no intention of doing it," Dewar added, "but it really threw me."

At about this same time, Charlotte was becoming increasingly disillusioned and even ill-tempered with the women's movement. When a researcher from the Status of Women Commission sought her responses to a questionnaire on women in politics, she replied, "I have written just thousands of words on this topic over the years and just haven't the time or inclination to offer myself for an inquest now," and suggested that the researcher or her "diggers" should check out the many articles she had penned on the topic for both *Chatelaine* and *Maclean's* magazines. Had they done so, they would have found a stack of references, and if they had had the opportunity to delve through Charlotte's files at the national archives years later, they would have found that she had been preaching "women power" regularly since at least 1909, when at the age of thirteen in Renfrew, she had argued in favour of female suffrage during a debate at the Anglican Young People's Association in St. Paul's Church.

Also, they would have found that in 1919, writing under the pseudonym "Kit in the Kitchen," she had advised readers of *Social Welfare*, in an article entitled, "Woman's Right To Power," that out of the debris of the First World War, "new worlds are to be created, and creation is woman's primal right and power." Or, they would have found similar thoughts and phrases in the hundreds of speeches she had given to women's and church groups and social welfare conventions around North America during the ensuing years, and among her hundreds of newspaper columns in the 1940s and 1950s.

In 1951, she told a British reporter covering the Royal Tour in Canada, "I've been called the last of the battling suffragettes. It isn't so. I just believe women shouldn't be pushed around." Months later, she told a Canadian journalist that she would not be surprised to see a woman elected president of the United States within ten years.

As her years in civic politics progressed, however, her disillusionment increased. Women were quick to help out when it came to organizing political campaigns, she noted, but few were ready to risk running for office. She was particularly scornful of women's auxiliaries in the churches, service clubs and political parties, suggesting they were leaving control of the organizations to men while the women were content to "cut sandwiches."

She might have pointed out that while some women had succeeded in Canadian politics — in 1921, Agnes Macphail was the first women elected to the House of Commons; in 1957, Ellen Fairclough became the first woman cabinet minister at the federal level — their numbers were well short of the roughly fifty per cent of the population that they represented. On Ottawa's city council, for example, women were still a rarity in the 1960s and would remain so for at least another decade.

Charlotte remained committed to the feminist cause, but her definition of feminist did not fit well with the more aggressive attitudes of women like Betty Friedan and Gloria Steinem in the United States, or Toronto newspaper columnist Laura Sabia, who founded the National Action Committee on the Status of Women in Canada. "The discussion of women's rights per se is somewhat out of date — that we women must insist that it is ALL human beings now, the humanity of us, the essence of the spirit of each, male and female, that is paramount," Charlotte told the Business and Professional Women's Association at their 1967 convention in Montreal. She repeated that message the following year to a standing-room-only audience of the Women's Canadian Club of Toronto, urging women to stop fighting for women's rights and instead join men in the fight for human rights. "We must crusade together for the sanctity and decency of human life," she stressed.

Charlotte had one more "crusade" to engage her declining energy before retirement from public life — "Oldster Power."

"Oldsters," or those over sixty-five, were becoming a forgotten segment of the population as "a youth cult" was being established, "and the people and governments, at all levels, bow low in adulation before youth," she wrote in preparation for a cross-country speaking tour in the fall of 1969. It seemed that Canadians had better yield to youth:

> . . . or have their rural routes crammed with roaring traffic; their fences smashed, their fields fouled; their poultry run down in bloody pulp or their humble shopfronts broken; their tobacco and news stands sacked; their coffee shops and snack bars raided; their cars "swiped," or, at best, "side-swiped;" their tires slashed; their seats of learning "sat-in" or "squatted in" or just plain "bust-up." All this is youth? And youth is heaven? Or is each of smashed-up, overrun communities to be youth's heaven on earth, as of right? [sic] A simple, bald, loudly blown statement that practically half the population of Canada (some 10,200,000) is under 25 years of age can put the fear of youth — and the contempt of maturity and age — into more than the national convention of a political party. But, while the statement is factually correct, in practical terms it can be fallacious. It demands examination — or the yaw swings hopelessly off course.

The "oldsters" deserved much better, she argued. Although they comprised only eight per cent of the population, they deserved improved housing conditions and improved health care. She called for a Central Application Registry where seniors could seek information and assistance, such as out-patient care, and she called for more private boarding houses and small nursing homes for the elderly. Quoting from a talk she gave in Ottawa almost two decades earlier, she said there was no field of social work which called for so much understanding, patience, and imagination as care for the aged. "The nation which abandons consideration and care for its aged and broken loses its soul," she warned.

Her tour, which she entitled, "The Angry, the Anxious, and the Aging," was sponsored by the Association of Canadian Clubs and began on October 7, with stops in Halifax, Charlottetown, Moncton and Saint John, before returning to Ottawa on October 10. Nine days later, she left for engagements in Victoria, Vancouver, New Westminster, Edmonton, Calgary, Regina, and Winnipeg, and returned to Ottawa one October 31 in time to seek re-election as the alderman for Capital ward.

"What a tremendous success your tours were," Eric Morse, the national director of the Association of Canadian Clubs, wrote in November. "You weren't just a star: you were a bomb! We appreciate, too, that you are a real 'trouper'." Although she gave virtually the same talk in each city, with the usual unscripted asides for which she was renowned, her addresses received broad media coverage in each of the cities visited and attracted much positive feedback.

Compared to the exhausting "A.A.A. tour," her re-election for alderman in December 1969 was a breeze. She easily cruised to a first-place finish in Capital ward after Claude Bennett, the sitting senior alderman, moved up to the board of control. She received 4,254 votes compared to 2,620 for runner-up Garry Guzzo, 2,013 for David Gourlie, 1,511 for Ed Henry, 1,149 for George Hynna, and 404 for Leo Morency. Meanwhile, Don Reid, who did not seek re-election as mayor, was replaced by controller Ken Fogarty.

By finishing first in her ward, Charlotte automatically earned a seat on the new, thirty-one-member regional council, which would manage the new metropolitan-style Regional Municipality of Ottawa-Carleton. That body was introduced by the provincial government in 1968 in order to provide certain region-wide services for the City of Ottawa and a number of suburban and rural communities in Carleton County. Among those services were property assessment, welfare, regional planning, regional roads, water distribution, sewage collection and treatment, and issuing debentures. The city, on the other hand, retained control of police and fire services, local roads, hospitals, building inspections, industrial development, and recreation. For the citizens of Ottawa and the region, the little woman with the powerful voice was back in the public eye for another two years to rock the boat at city hall, and at regional council to boot.

Once more into the fray went Charlotte. If she had been a frontier cowgirl, she would have had two guns blazing. But she would have been firing mostly blanks by this time. At the first city council meeting of 1970, she sought in vain to be elected one of eight council representatives on the CCEA's board, then was generally ignored when she threatened to use the *Ontario Municipal Act* to have the CCEA board election declared void because it had been held behind closed doors.

Similarly, when council's self-described "old woman" attended her first regional council meeting one week later, her desire to sit on the homes for the aged committee was rejected by her fellow councillors, although they did grant her a seat on the separate social welfare committee and allowed her "honourary member" status on the seniors' homes panel.

It was an auspicious meeting for Charlotte, however, for as the *Journal* reported, "in typical city council form, she was on her feet countless times, questioning innumerable items." She was the lone dissenter against the first motion of the new council, which concerned who would sit on the region's executive council — a sort of board of control for the region — and she and Gale Kerwin, also an Ottawa alderman, opposed the second motion concerning council seating. Charlotte and Kerwin, who sat to her immediate right, were located in the bottom left corner far from the chairman's table at the top of the U-shaped council table. She argued that the seats around the council table should be reconfigured so that rural and urban councillors were interspersed with one another, rather than in separate rural and urban clusters, as was the case. Again her request found little support.

Perhaps it was only coincidence, but during this term on both city and regional councils, Charlotte was the only woman. "It's been twenty years since I was the first woman elected to city council and it's a disgrace to the women of Ottawa that the same poor old hen is still the only one here," she remarked caustically to her municipal colleagues.

Garry Guzzo, a twenty-eight-year-old lawyer and the junior alderman for Capital ward at the time, said in an interview that despite the animosity shown her by some councillors, Charlotte remained a powerful voice on city council, questioning municipal staff just as ferociously as she attacked her council opponents.

"No mayor, no politician could get away with what she got away with some of the staff, sometimes in closed meetings but sometimes in board meetings or council meetings; she'd tee off on a staffer and crucify him. She had her favourites and even they felt a rough going over from time to time. It was not good form, no question about it." He said she was able to score debating points because "nobody expected any woman to be as rough or as forceful as she was . . . in debate and in argument; there were times when she could match any sailor [for foul language], but only when she would be exasperated, when someone wouldn't see things her way or when some alderman who was making an argument that had been kicked around and found faulty three or four times in the last ten years, she'd lose patience and run off at the mouth."

Guzzo, though more than three decades younger that his accomplished colleague, was close to Charlotte at the time, for not only was he learning lessons in local politics at the hands of an expert, but often he drove her home from late-night council meetings, as she no longer liked driving after dark because of diminishing eyesight. He recalled that often after council meetings, a number of the councillors stopped off for drinks at a nearby hotel, but Charlotte wisely refused to join them for fear of extending the verbal slugfests she so enjoyed at the council table. So "when I drove her home, she always wanted me to come in for a drink. I was a beer drinker, and she wouldn't have beer, and she'd have whisky and she didn't believe in mix."

She liked hard liquor when he knew her in the early1970s, but "she could hold it." She always took her drinks straight — "no mix, no ice, just the way God intended you to drink it. If He wanted you to put Coke in it, He'd have put Coke in it," she had told him. He recalled one occasion when he drove her home and returned the following morning at 8:30 to take her to another city meeting. He found her working at her typewriter in the same clothes she had worn the previous evening. She had apparently worked through the night, possibly on one of the books she had promised but never published. Nearby was a whisky bottle, "and I can remember how much the bottle had gone down; I don't think she had any breakfast, but she said 'Let's go,'" and she carried on almost as usual at the meeting, although a little less outspoken than her norm.

She had always enjoyed a glass of wine or a modest nip of gin or brandy, but in her later years, the former temperance campaigner obviously increased her alcoholic intake. Claude Bennett, her former colleague as Capital ward alderman and later city controller and a provincial cabinet minister, said he never saw her drunk, but there were social occasions where "she'd have more to drink than she thought she was drinking . . . Others would fill her glass to keep her going . . . She reminded me of [former controller] Wilbert Hamilton, who always had a white drink in hand 'for ulcers.'"

As for her occasionally indelicate language, Bennett said, "She could do it pretty good, but I'm not sure she could do as well as her sister." He recalled visiting Kay at her Kilreen Farm one day and she was berating a farmhand, "and I've never, I mean *never*, heard such language from a woman."

Bennett mentioned another anecdote that is part of urban legend in the city. It concerned Ottawa Rough Rider great Bob Simpson, who served briefly as a city councillor in the early 1960s, but who was better known as a colourful raconteur after his retirement from professional football. Simpson had the floor in council and, in his inimitable locker room style, asked, "Do you know what goes on in a [locker room] shower?"

"The place went quiet," Bennett recalled, "and we all figured we should be under our desks," expecting some obscene response to blurt from Simpson's mouth.

"Yes, I do," Charlotte quipped immediately, to the astonishment of her fellow councillors.

"What?" Simpson demanded.

"The taps go on in the shower," Charlotte retorted with presumed innocence, and the normally loquacious ex-footballer was struck speechless.

Another time, when the two were arguing, Charlotte cut Simpson short by telling him, "One thing's for sure, Bob, they'll never find your shoes under my bed in the morning."

A more affectionate perspective of Charlotte was made by *Toronto Star* columnist Lotta Dempsey. In an April 21, 1970, column, Dempsey told of visiting Charlotte and finding her in fine form. "For more years than Dr. Whitton or I would willingly record, we have foregathered spasmodically for a relaxed (?) twosome of chat over food. That takes in territory anywhere from Victoria, B.C., to London, England, when we would happen to find ourselves in the same spot at the same time . . . Well, the other day just about everybody in sight stopped by the secluded table she had chosen in an alcove of the [Château Laurier Hotel] Grill. Charlotte always knows exactly where she wants to sit or stand . . . but this particular alcove to which the maître d' immediately let us have [had] fond associations from her days as mayor. 'I could observe any aldermen going by to fancy meals with promoters, without being seen,' she chuckled."

Almost ignored by "the boys" on council and in the media during her last term of office, Charlotte concentrated less on city and regional business and more on outside pursuits, such as her public speaking career. In February 1970, she spoke to Canadian Club assemblies in Hamilton and London, Ontario, and in March, she gave fifteen-minute Lenten lectures daily at St. Paul's Anglican Cathedral in London, Ontario, over a period of five days. In the fall, she resumed her profitable "Angry, Anxious and Aging" tour, speaking to receptive audiences in ten cities across Western Canada, and she spoke to the Gerontology Society in Toronto on death, "the last and final faring forth."

The "AAA" talks were much the same as those of the previous year, chastising society for ignoring the elderly and lavishing too much attention on youth.

The Lenten talks, on the other hand, were a mix of philosophy and theology. Lent for Charlotte was a time for reflecting on where life began and where society was going. The Spirit of God gave meaning to Lent, she told parishioners, "forever making all things new, heralded with the springing of Earth itself to new life, and of new and enduring vitality within venerable and proven resources." Pessimistically, she saw the increase in drug use as "the resort of anguished, bewildered human beings without any firm belief or faith, seeking any escape from reality."

Further, she warned, "We face the possible decline and disappearance of [Western Christian Society], in large part because we have failed to keep vital the deep inner wisdom and truths which would afford stability as human life and the social order attempt to adapt to change." It was becoming an alien world, a world for which the term "sin" meant nothing. The only solution, she offered, was an abiding faith in God.

Life on the periphery of politics did not suit Charlotte well in her final term of office, for although her voice was often heard, her influence rarely was felt. She made few true friends on either the city or regional councils, with the exception of Andy Haydon. Haydon, who represented Nepean Township on regional council and who later succeeded Denis Coolican as council chairman, was the grandson of Senator Andrew Haydon, the man who had financially supported Charlotte's campaign in the 1920s when she was raising funds for a new women's residence at Queen's University. In an interview, Andy Haydon stated he was unaware of that connection, but thought that she had treated him — then in his late thirties — with motherly attention, always softly addressing him formally as "Andrew," because both she and his grandfather were keenly interested in Ottawa Valley history.

"I had a great respect for Charlotte, and it was a strange relationship, because you know Charlotte, she was very outspoken." He said former mayor Reid also sat on the regional council as an Ottawa alderman, and she and Reid "were the bitterest of enemies, and anything that Don Reid supported, she would stand up and scathingly denounce the project. It had nothing to do with the project, it had to do with Don Reid. But she would never take a strip off me and I wondered why."

Another regional councillor she could not stand was realtor and former professional boxer Gale Kerwin, who unfortunately sat to her immediate right,. They often voted differently on regional council issues, but on May 12, 1971, Charlotte erupted when Kerwin was so bold as to second her motion to disband the council itself. The councillors were a bunch of "political eunuchs," she had raged, and "we give a monthly demonstration of the futility of this council" because it merely rubber-stamped the executive committee's motions. As for Kerwin, who spoke against the motion even though he had seconded it, she continued, "There is no one I less wanted to second [the motion] or speak on it." Then, according to the next day's *Journal*, there followed "the most ludicrous, unbelievable circus act" seen by council. "Swinging her arms as if she was boxing, Miss Whitton continued to tongue-lash alderman Kerwin," until she withdrew the motion and council was hastily adjourned.

That tempest was Charlotte's last full-blown outburst in local politics.

Celebrity had its rewards, however, as Charlotte was pleased to realize that year. On her seventy-fifth birthday, for example, some 300 people turned out in Renfrew to hear her recount a long life lively lived, and, in a prepared speech, Ottawa Valley historian and *Ottawa Journal* columnist Harry Walker praised her as "one whom I and most Canadians regard as the most outstanding Canadian woman of our time." Walker, who had known her since 1914 when as a cub reporter he had interviewed her about her scholarship to Queen's, also delighted the audience when he quoted a description of Charlotte by the *Citizen's* Phyllis Wilson: "a feminist to the core, she is also intensely feminine — grouses about her waistline, loves pretty clothes, perfume and flowers, worries about her hairdo, is vain about her tiny feet and slim ankles which a former prime minister once described as the most attractive in the country."

Similar pleasantries were pronounced when Charlotte hosted "At Home for a Cup of Tea" at city hall on October 1 to celebrate the twentieth anniversary of her election as mayor, and again on October 17 when hers was one of five portraits of former mayors hung on the walls of the municipal headquarters. On October 14, she proudly participated in the laying of the foundation stone for Bradford House on Porter's Island, a home for the aged that she did much to establish in honour of her former welfare council and city hall aide, the late Marjorie Bradford. In paying tribute to her long-time friend, Charlotte described Bradford as "one of the most useful people of her generation of Canadians."

A gentler, less obstreperous Charlotte was emerging in 1972. It's true there were some minor disputes at city council — her motion to refuse an extension to the Central Canada Exhibition Association lease was rejected, and she raised the hackles of the capital's sports-loving population when she voted to limit spending on the winter carnival and to require cyclists to buy licences for their bicycles — but overall, her demeanor was more tactful, more co-operative. It was practically a new Charlotte, and some wondered whether the new image was a sign that she planned to contest the December 2 municipal election, and if so, whether it would be for mayor, controller or alderman.

Whatever speculation might have occurred, Charlotte's plans came crashing down with a painful thud on the afternoon of October 20.

20 Hell on Wheels

T he telephone rang. Charlotte, napping on her living room couch, rose to answer it. However, her crepe-soled shoe caught on the rug and down she went, landing on her hip, unable to move. She lay there for nineteen long, lonely hours until her housekeeper of more than twenty years, Frieda Boehmer, arrived the following day. For once in her life, Charlotte was totally helpless. The woman who had portaged her own canoe through the Algonquin Park wilderness in her youth, who had travelled across the country and around the world by car, bus, truck, airplane and ocean liner, and who had jostled her way through countless political rallies could not move. She could call out and scream, but the woman whose high-pitched, screechy voice could quiet a rowdy political gathering or a pack of unruly councillors went unheard. Her front door was locked, her double windows closed. All evening, all night, and all the next morning she lay on the living room floor, unable to move and suffering unbearable pain, comforted only by Felix Ferdinand, the stray cat who had wandered into her campaign headquarters eleven years before and who had rarely left her side since. The irony of the situation, Charlotte said later, was that the telephone normally would have been within easy reach.

"Miss Whitton is thoroughly annoyed with herself for what happened that day," Shirley Foley, women's editor of the *Citizen*, reported five days later. "She blames the incident on the fact that she lay down for an afternoon nap without removing her shoes."

"I said to myself as a lay down, your mother would turn over in her grave if she could see you lying on this light [coloured] couch with your walking shoes on," Charlotte told Foley. Then, she explained, the phone rang, she sprang forward to answer it and tripped on the rug. She continued, "Luckily, I'm an old hockey player or the police would have been busy the next day trying to figure out who'd robbed and beaten me . . . but we hockey players were trained how to fall. I wrenched my body to avoid hitting my head . . . and landed on my hip."

Foley continued: "She can chuckle as she recalls the irony of having finally cleared her desk that day, leaving no papers hanging over the edge, the phone atop them, so that a tug on the papers would bring the phone tumbling down."

She may have chuckled at the irony, but the prognosis for her health was not good. At seventy-six, Charlotte faced greatly reduced mobility and an uncertain future. Certainly her political career was ended and there remained the question of what care she would need. Yet Foley found her in relatively good spirits as she sat up in the bed of her fifth-floor room at the Civic Hospital. Already she was taking tentative steps with the aid of a walker and, during Foley's visit, she was talking politics with another visitor.

"To a stranger on the set," Foley wrote, "it would have been a routine hospital scene: A concerned son standing at his mother's bedside. It was instead Garry Guzzo, now a city controller, mulling over matters of concern to their people [in Capital ward]. Immobility has in no way slowed down the flow, the torrent has not dried to a trickle. The breadth of Charlotte Whitton's ruminations, recollections and rhetoric is as timeless as ever."

Charlotte spoke of the future: "I'm 76 and have to prepare to meet my Maker . . . He's given me a couple of good warnings lately." And she spoke of the present: "If I run this time, it will be from my bed . . . but I can tell you one thing: I'll be at the last meeting of City Council in 1972. I made a commitment to the people of Capital ward to fill my term and I'll do it if it has to be in a wheelchair."

Already she was planning improvements to the hospital's administration and she was working on a nurses' manual based on her experience with the ward nurses. Jean Milligan, a former director of nursing at the Civic and principal of its nursing school, said in an interview, "She was nice to me, but she scared people and was a testy patient." Milligan recalled one time when walking down the corridor on the fifth floor she met a young woman who was delivering Charlotte's supper. She feared going into her room alone and asked Milligan to join her. "[Charlotte] would tell anyone what she thought," Milligan added. "She didn't care what people thought of her."

Guzzo, who visited Charlotte at the Civic on several occasions in late 1972, recalled, "I remember going up there with Claude Bennett, and she had the staff running in circles. She didn't think they were running the hospital the way she would run it and, therefore, they should probably do it her way. One time she told me, 'When you go back to the office, you sit down and phone him [Civic Hospital executive director Douglas Peart] and tell him I'm in here and this is wrong and that is wrong. If we don't do it, who's going to do it and get this thing operating right?'"

He brought her files from city hall, and although he was senior to her in the council pecking order, as a controller compared to an alderman, she nevertheless instructed him how to vote on different issues.

Charlotte's sister Kay, who had been in Massachusetts showing off her prized hackneys at the time of Charlotte's fall, recounted the hospital scene she saw upon her return. The ward was filled with flowers, mostly chrysanthemums, and the nurses were paying special attention to their special patient. Charlotte complained of a pain at the side of her neck and near her shoulders, but Kay did not pay much attention because "she complained about everything—the view of the brick wall from her bed with a small bit of sky. If she threw something and broke the window, she reasoned, the hospital would put her out. The nurses changed too often—everything, everything, was wrong. And where was Felix? Who was looking after her cat?" Kay reassured her that Frieda Boehmer was caring for Felix and was in good hands. A little later, Kay learned that Charlotte had also fractured her collarbone in the fall.

They discussed Charlotte's future. Given her reduced mobility, moving back to Renfrew Avenue in the immediate future was out of the question, so Kay invited her to stay at the bungalow in Alta Vista that she recently had purchased. The offer was accepted, and women caretakers were hired to tend to Charlotte; however, it did not work out.

"Her reaction to everything was negative, negative . . . She yelled and fought with everyone . . . it was apparent that we couldn't keep staff who would please her," Kay wrote. "She didn't like French; she didn't like Spanish; she just didn't like . . . We did get her into the dining room for dinner, even had dinner parties for her friends. She thoroughly enjoyed them and talked incessantly, so I never served soufflé after the first party; they always collapsed while Charlotte expounded on this and that."

Charlotte grew increasingly bitter as the months passed. She was especially displeased with the fact that city council had not improved the niggardly $35.21 annual pension she received as a former mayor, even though, as Kay pointed out, she had sufficient means from other sources to support herself. And the pain was not abating. She was downing Librium and Seconal tablets, and when Kay left the house, Charlotte would call the local drug store to order refills on old prescriptions for the sedatives. One morning when she was about to have X-rays on her hip and neck at the Civic, she began haemorrhaging; she required three blood transfusions.

Eventually, she agreed to move into a private room at Bradford House, the geriatric centre where less than two years earlier she had accompanied Premier Bill Davis in laying the commemorative stone. But "before she was there an hour," Kay wrote, "Charlotte wanted to leave because the nurses took away her Seconal and Librium! However, a pill or two was left with her for the sake of peace, and for another few months Charlotte stayed in her room, taking therapy and looking out the window."

Charlotte was unable to attend the final city council meeting of 1972, and when *Toronto Star* columnist Lotta Demspey visited her on November 14, the celebrity journalist whose career Charlotte had kick-started in Edmonton in the late 1920s noted, "She was too tired to talk. She even had the phone in her hospital room disconnected.

Charlotte was gone from city council, but definitely not forgotten. At its regular meeting on November 20, council unanimously approved Alderman Don Kay's motion to name its chamber Whitton Hall. In introducing his motion, Kay said, "The presence of Charlotte Whitton, C.B.E., M.A., D.C.L., LL.D., as alderman, controller and mayor has brought honour and distinction to this council chamber . . . This and former councils would wish to show their appreciation of the warm comradeship and unfailing sense of justice which pervaded all her actions, albeit often dispensed with caustic and biting tongue." He said the city hall and its "magnificent site" on Green Island were themselves a tribute to her vision and leadership, and his motion was meant to perpetuate for future councils her dedication to the public good.

On May 31, 1973, Whitton Hall was officially dedicated in a ceremony fit for a queen. As some 800 people looked on in admiration, and with a touch of sympathy, Charlotte, attired in a light-coloured dress topping black shoes with gold buckles, limped slowly into the hall with an aluminum cane in her left hand and the supporting arm of her personal therapist, Pamela Ross, on her right. She sat for much of the ceremony, but rose on unsteady legs as Mayor Pierre Benoit recited the dedication decree. The media reported that she reacted to the audience's standing ovation with a child's glee, and was pleased to see old political friends and foes, including John Diefenbaker and George McIlraith, cheering as much as the others. Mayor Benoit hailed her as "one of the greatest municipal politicians Ottawa has ever had," and county court judge and former mayor Kenneth Fogarty joked that "she was never at a loss for words; usually the right words and very often the last." Congratulatory telegrams from Queen Elizabeth, Governor General Roland Michener, Prime Minister Pierre Trudeau and Premier Bill Davis were read, but as usual Charlotte had the last word.

She hinted that she just might run for office again.

"Charlotte's immortal," read the headline over an editorial in the *Citizen* days later:

> No, Ottawa will never say goodbye to Dr. Charlotte
> Whitton . . . without Charlotte — who injected spice as
> well as pageantry into Ottawa politics, whose uniquely
> uninhibited style, and ferocious tongue transformed minor
> political bickerings into epic confrontations — Ottawa's
> stock of folklore would in fact be small indeed. But she has
> been absent too long, recuperating from that hip accident
> last fall. It was good to have her back the other day in
> the City Hall she built, in the council chamber that now
> carries her name, accepting salutes from a fond city and the
> mighty of our land.

The *Journal*, meanwhile, suggested "Charlotte's Hall" was a more appropriate name for the council chamber, for "no one has ever held higher the concept of the role of alderman, controller or mayor. Miss Whitton's sense of history identifies these offices with the first forms

Mayor Pierre Benoit and Charlotte at the naming of Whitton Hall,
May 1973.

City of Ottawa Archives, MG011/CA17664

of responsible government as they emerged in Medieval England. She always lived with a sense of the continuity and the essential dignity of offices which have sometimes seemed less important than other titles in a capital city."

A couple of weeks later, a column appeared in a community newspaper written by Grant Carman, Nepean and regional councillor and the purchaser of Charlotte's McGregor Lake cottage. He told how he had known Charlotte since he was a child—his mother and Charlotte were schoolmates at Queen's University—and how she had treated him so gently one time he and Nepean reeve Aubrey Moodie visited her mayoral office to seek her permission to hook up their suburb's sewage system to that of Ottawa's:

> I had not seen her since I had left my home some years
> before, but she had known me as a small boy, and I don't
> think had ever quite accepted the fact that I had grown up.
> Be that as it may, when we came into the council chamber,
> she turned to [Ottawa controller] Ernie Jones who was
> sitting next to her and said 'Ernie, get up and let young

Carman sit down.' Then she patted the chair alongside her, and started talking family reminiscences.

I can still see the stunned look of surprise on the faces of Ernie Jones and Aubrey Moodie, and my own feelings resembled those of a small boy caught with his hand in the cookie jar! But ten minutes later, when we got into the nitty-gritty of agreements, she carved me up along with the rest of them, and then with a look of shocked dismay on her face recoiled when I retaliated in kind.

And that is the way with Charlotte Whitton. She asked no quarter, she gave no quarter, and she enjoyed every minute of it. She could be the grand lady — as she exhibited in London once when I was there at a garden party with the Queen — or she could be the Renfrew comet, spitting sparks and gun powder in all directions . . . Her brain is as encyclopedic in its capacities as her tongue is with invective. She is a conundrum, a mixture, a delight, and a terror, and the city and this country, and perhaps the world is a better place because she has spent her years working for all of us here.

By this time, she had returned to the grey stucco house with the bright red front door on Renfrew Avenue and was regularly visited by Frieda Boehmer and friends who dropped by to chat or stroll with her on the little cul-de-sac. Other visitors, according to Kay, were her clergyman, her lawyer, and archivists from Queen's University and the national archives who later would accept much of her massive collection. She was indeed preparing to meet her Maker, but she also was keeping tabs on more mundane concerns as well, such as the $15.53 bill from Badali Brothers, the neighbourhood grocery, on May 16, for the delivery of potatoes, asparagus, grapefruit, chicken, bacon, and catfood. (The bill is one of many such effects she left with the national and city archives.)

She remained house-ridden at 1 Renfrew Avenue through much of 1973 and 1974. Although she seldom ventured beyond the cul-de-sac or her small backyard overlooking the park, she stayed in contact with friends and political associates thanks to two telephones in her home, one upstairs and one down, and the services of a visiting stenographer. Occasionally a former subordinate, such as Douglas

Peart, from the Civic Hospital, would seek her view on a topic, or she would be advised of yet another honour bestowed upon her, such as a life membership in the Canadian Federation of Professional and Business Women. And, on a rare occasion, as August 1, 1973, she returned to Whitton Hall to attend a civic luncheon for Queen Elizabeth and Prince Philip who were on another visit to Canada. This time, however, instead of hosting the Royal Couple, she was merely one of numerous guests in the hall.

By the end of 1974, her condition had worsened to the point that even she realized she needed full-time care, and accordingly returned to Bradford House. Although the thought of actively participating in the December 2 municipal election was out of the question, she was the first to sign Lorry Greenberg's nomination papers for mayor. Her spirits brightened considerably on election night when the city's first Jewish mayor made a detour to Charlotte's room on the way to his victory celebration.

Shortly after Greenberg's visit, Kay had her last long conversation with her sister. Kay did not relate the specifics, except to say that Charlotte still voiced guilt over the loss of her long-time partner, Margaret Grier.

On January 5, 1975, Charlotte's heart seized up. She was rushed to the Civic Hospital from Bradford House, and Kay, who was wintering at her Florida home at the time, hurried back to Ottawa to be with Charlotte at the end and to handle the funeral arrangements, which Charlotte had already planned down to the finest detail. Charlotte had always wanted a formal civic funeral with all the trappings, and Kay, unaware of her sister's exact finances, agreed to pick up the estimated $20,000 cost if the city would not. No problem, said Mayor Greenberg, the city would pay.

Once again, however, Charlotte's fighting spirit kicked in and she showed signs of recovery, in part thanks to round-the-clock care from private nurses. One of those nurses, Phyllis Swaren, clearly recalled in an interview the first few days after Charlotte had returned to the Civic. Charlotte was conscious and aware that death was nearby, but cheerfully discussing her funeral and singing the hymns that would be played. Swaren said she got on "beautifully" with Charlotte and the former mayor had a new joke for her every day. One of those jokes, Swaren remembered, concerned three young women who were visiting Mexico when one of them, Ana, fell seriously ill. The other two wanted to send a telegraph to Ana's parents to explain the situation, but they had only enough money to send six words. With thrifty ingenuity, they wired the following message:

ANACIN HOSPITAL ADAMANT BITTER ASININE PLACES.

Charlotte also spoke with glee of the famous newspaper photograph of her falling on her backside at the opening of a local curling rink, while federal cabinet minister George Hees guffawed off to the side. "She was actually quite pleased with it because it was on the same day the Queen was in the newspapers and she was on the front pages, and not the Queen."

In a more serious vein, Charlotte told the nurse that her proudest achievement was her success in drawing national attention in 1947 to the Alberta government's controversial adoptions policy.

When Kay arrived, the nurses warned her, "Don't be hurt if she doesn't recognize you. She's been terribly confused lately, but every day asks 'When is that sister of mine coming back?'" Entering Charlotte's room, Kay observed her sleeping sister propped up on her bed by pillows, with an oxygen tube in her nose and an intravenous tube on a bruised arm. When Charlotte awoke, she said drowsily, "Oh, imminent domain, imminent domain . . .Well, Kay, you got here at last. Did you know I was hell on wheels? Imminent domain." Kay could not explain the "imminent domain" remark, but "hell on wheels" was a term used by an Ottawa resident in a letter to the editor many years earlier during Charlotte's mayoralty complaining about driving over the city's many potholes in spring. It was also the term Kay planned to use for the title of her biography of her sister.

Two days before she died, a dazed Charlotte admired Kay's "new" hat, but Kay reminded her that she had had it for fifteen years. Their conversation, according to Kay, went as follows:

Charlotte: "I'm not . . . I'm a mess, but you look nice. I think this is the end, don't you? It is the end, isn't it?"

Kay: "I don't know; you've been like a Shetland pony all your life, so you'll probably prance again."

Charlotte: "Oh, no."

Charlotte then "slowly fell back again as the nurse adjusted the tubes, and she mumbled 'Hell on wheels.' I never heard her speak again."

That conversation occurred on a Thursday. On Friday, the hospital phoned Kay at home to inform her that Charlotte had only hours to live. She, in turn, phoned Rev. Serson Clarke, an Anglican priest, and they went to the Civic where he performed the last rites in the presence of Gwen Sellars, a friend of Charlotte's since their days at Queen's. Outside the private room, women hospital volunteers anxiously awaited word on Charlotte's condition. "She was still the heroine of women's new place in the world," Kay remarked.

At 3:30 a.m. on Saturday, January 25, 1975 — the International Year of the Woman — Charlotte Elizabeth Whitton died of congestive heart failure at the Ottawa Civic Hospital. Death came during a snowstorm outside, just as one had marked her birth nearly seventy-nine years earlier.

The flags at Ottawa city hall were lowered to half-mast that day on Mayor Greenberg's orders. Whitton Hall was cleared of all furniture except for Charlotte's desk and chair, the former draped with her colourful scarlet mayoral robe.

On Sunday, just as she had so carefully planned, her plain oak casket was wheeled into the centre of the chamber and the top half was opened. Charlotte's remains rested in silence, the *Book of Prayers* snuggled under her crossed hands. Atop the closed bottom half of the casket was the city flag; upon it rested her mayoral tricorn hat. A large bouquet from family stood before the coffin, while off to the side was a lectern with a black cushion holding her many medals of honour A four-man honour guard, including representatives of the municipal police and fire departments, the Governor General's Footguards and a local militia unit, the Bytown Gunners, stood at attention behind the coffin. A small area in front was roped off, and hundreds of Ottawans from all walks of life paraded past in solemn respect for the woman who had given so much of herself for her city.

On Monday, at 10 a.m., Charlotte Whitton's body left city hall for the last time, escorted by twelve honorary pallbearers: former prime minister John Diefenbaker; Mayor Lorry Greenberg; former

The graves of Charlotte and her companion, Margaret Grier, side-by-side at the Thompsonville Cemetery in Renfrew.

Photo by author

mayors Kenneth Fogarty, Pierre Benoit, George Nelms, and Don Reid; Ontario tourism minister Claude Bennett; Senator George McIlraith; Regional Chairman Denis Coolican; Nepean Reeve Andy Haydon; former Nepean reeve Aubrey Moodie; and deputy Nepean reeve Grant Carman.

A twenty-car motorcade followed the hearse to St. Alban the Martyr Church, a dozen or more blocks from city hall, along streets lined with people standing respectfully in the -15F cold. The Rt. Rev. William Robinson, bishop of Ottawa, spoke briefly in praise of Charlotte before a crowd of 400, as a woman of many personalities and an interesting combination of talents. The thirty-minute service was conducted by St. Alban's rector, Rev. Llewellyn Graham, and assisted by Charlottte's long-time pastor, Canon C.L.G. Bruce, and Canon Serson Clarke. Her body was then transported to Pinecrest Cemetery in suburban Nepean for storage in a vault until it could be properly buried in Thompsonville Cemetery, Renfrew, in the spring.

On May 17, a small cortege of cars containing civic and federal politicians and family friends, left Ottawa following a hearse driven by Charlotte's longtime civic chauffeur, Donat Lafond. At the cemetery, they were joined by the entire Renfrew town council and dozens of local residents. On the hillside overlooking the Ottawa Valley community, Canon Clarke conducted the burial service and Charlotte's remains were lowered into the plot next to Margaret Grier's, as a piper played the mournful "Flowers of the Forest." Immediately adjacent to the Whitton-Grier plot was that of Charlotte's parents, John and Elizabeth.

Later, a black tombstone was erected with the simple inscription: "Dr. Charlotte E. Whitton 1896–1975."

Immediately to its right is a grey stone marked:

IHS
Rose Margaret Grier
1892 – 1947
Beloved daughter of
Robert and Rose Grier
and dear friend to
Charlotte Whitton
1896 – 1975

Epilogue

On April 10, 1975, Charlotte's last will and testament was read in surrogate court. She had left an estate worth $318,242.33, composed of stocks, bonds, personal effects, and the house on Renfrew Avenue, which was valued at $49,500. Signed by Charlotte on May 14, 1974, in uncharacteristically small handwriting, it set out in forty-two clauses exactly how her effects were to be parcelled out. With customary thoroughness, she thought of everything and everyone. Her files, draft manuscripts, and research papers were to go to Public Archives of Canada, now Library and Archives Canada, and her university-related material to the archives at Queen's University. Many of the books in her extensive library were assigned to the library of the Sisters of St. John the Divine in Willowdale, Ontario, while others were given to her nephew, John Bartholomew Whitton (one of her three executors, along with George McIlraith and Margaret Whitton Mills, Charlotte's niece), or to the Queen's University library.

The money from the sale of her house was to be split between the daughters of John B. Whitton and Margaret Mills, and $500 each was dictated for a niece of Margaret Grier; for Mrs. Jamesina Shields, the woman who helped with the housekeeping at her mother's home in Renfrew; for Frieda Boehmer, her own housekeeper; and for Mrs. Isabel Read, her stenographer. Also, $1,000 was given to the Civic Hospital for a memorial to Margaret Grier.

The remainder of her estate was to be split into twenty-three equal shares and distributed among several Anglican parishes, to Queen's and Acadian universities and King's College in Halifax and Smith College in Massachusetts, to her next of kin, and to her godsons and goddaughters.

Nowhere was her only surviving sibling, Kay, specifically mentioned. Kay did not need the money, however, for she had inherited

This photo of a World War I soldier rested on Charlotte's desk. Although certain comments made by Charlotte hint he was her childhood chum, Clarence Sibary, no one seems to know for sure.

Photo courtesy of John B. Whitton

her husband's considerable wealth; in fact, she later donated such a sizeable contribution to Queen's University that the institution named the archives building, where Charlotte's collection is maintained, Kay Ryan Hall.

Despite the thoroughness of her estate planning, Charlotte left only an enigmatic clue as to what may well have been hidden in her heart since her teenage years in Renfrew. When her nephew John arrived at her home to arrange distribution of her effects, he came across a black and white photo of a young soldier on the desk in her study.

There was nothing on the photo to identify the soldier, but on the back was printed, "Missing Zillibeke June 1916."

Was this the man of Charlotte's dreams, the young man so many other men could not replace? Only Charlotte would know for sure, but John Whitton is convinced that that was the case. He recalled a talk Charlotte gave to a nurses' graduation ceremony in Renfrew in the 1950s. After mentioning each nurse's name she would make a personal comment. When she came to Marilyn Briscoe, she said, "One day, if it hadn't been for a sad day in 1916, this name might have been mine." John Whitton therefore suggested that the man in the photo was Clifford Briscoe, a schoolmate of Charlotte's at Renfrew Collegiate Institute and the young man who asked her out on her first date, a visit to the Renfrew Fair. But Briscoe died in June 1917 near Lens, outside Vimy, France, while the printed note on the back of the photo, presumably pencilled in by Charlotte, suggests the soldier in the picture was killed at Zillibeke, a ridge near Ypres (now Ieper) in Belgium in June 1916.

Without explanation, Kay Whitton identified the soldier as James Sibary, another schoolmate of Charlotte's at RCI. According to Veterans Affairs records, Clarence James Sibary was listed as missing after an enemy attack at Ypres in June 1916 and his remains were never found. A photo of Sibary in the *Renfrew Mercury* of March 23, 1917, depicts a young man identical to the soldier in the photo.

Another insight into the photograph was provided in a May 1973 issue of the *Toronto Star*, when columnist Lotta Dempsey wrote of visiting her friend, who was then convalescing at 1 Renfrew Avenue. Dempsey said she had been chatting with Charlotte for three hours and just before she left, she asked Charlotte the question she had been wanting to ask for thirty years: Had there been someone special among the Queen's University students killed in the First World War?

"Look on the desk, behind the lamp," Charlotte told her.

"I had seen the desk, its family and memorabilia pictures many times," Dempsey wrote. "But never the one behind the lamp. It was a picture of a handsome young man, a fine-looking boy, in uniform."

Charlotte told her:

I had come home for my first summer holidays from
Queen's, and so had he. I stayed working late as a cashier
in a store the night he came over to tell me he had enlisted,
and say goodbye. He sat on the veranda with my mother
and grandmother for a long while, and finally left. His
mother told me later, when he said he hadn't seen me, that
she said it was too bad he hadn't a chance to tell me, and
to say goodbye.

"Oh well," he said to his mother, "you know Lottie. She
would probably have done all the talking anyway."

Dempsey did not identify the young soldier in the photograph, nor did she indicate whether Charlotte had identified him. However, the fact that Sibary signed up for military service on July 30, 1915 — during Charlotte's first summer vacation from Queen's — while Briscoe signed up on November 24, 1915, points to the fact that it likely is a photograph of Clarence Sibary, who, as Charlotte related in a 1944 talk in Renfrew, was the young man "whose cradle I shared, beside whom I knelt at confirmation in St. Paul's."

One further note on the photo was provided by Frieda Boehmer's son Bill, who as a young man used to deliver his mother's home-cooked chicken dinners to Charlotte at 1 Renfrew while she was recuperating from her fall. Now an Ottawa restaurateur, Boehmer said he often noticed the soldier's picture on Charlotte's desk, but while he never asked Charlotte about it, his mother had told him it was a boy to whom Charlotte "was betrothed . . . and they made this little pact . . . and like the Canada Goose, it was for life."

Another item of interest is the story of "Charlotte's ghost." Diane McIntyre, current owner of 1 Renfrew Avenue and incidentally a one-time candidate for mayor of Ottawa, recalled in an interview seeing the ghost in 1979, the same year that she and her former husband, Graham Etherington, moved from Montreal and bought the house. She and Etherington were sitting late at night in the finished basement that Charlotte had used as an office, and while Etherington was concentrating on his work, McIntyre was reading. She happened to look up from her book to the doorway to the next room "and saw a woman come out of the wall, float across the room and go into the other wall, and I thought, 'I'm tired, I'm seeing things, like what was that?' I told Graham I'm going to bed, and he said why, and I said I'm starting to see things."

Etherington asked what she saw and she said she saw a woman float across the room.

"Well what did she look like?" Etherington continued, and she described the phantom as being a short and stocky woman attired in a sort of white dress and a hat. McIntyre, who had heard of Charlotte while living in Montreal but was not familiar with her appearance, said that the next day she and Etherington visited the public library where they viewed the library's photo collection of Charlotte. Sure enough, the phantom looked like the redoubtable Charlotte Whitton.

Then, Thanksgiving that year, we had company over, and we were all sitting around the living room talking and there was a campaign table, you know those skinny tables that sit behind a couch, at couch level . . . a campaign table behind a love seat . . . and it had plants all along the top of it and it fell over and none of the plants spilled, none of them smashed, they all landed upright and there wasn't a speck of dirt on the ground. And everybody said, "How did that happen?" And Graham said, "Oh, it must be just Charlotte," and it panicked everyone in the room. We all ended up going for a big, long walk and nobody wanted to come back into the house. We were all spooked by it. Meanwhile, by the way, the cat — we had a Siamese cat at the time — he was racing around like a mad thing, which wasn't his normal manner, he was usually a stately cat, but he was quite possessed . . .

Anyway, at New Year's Eve that year, we had people in again, and sitting around the living room after dinner, fire going, and this clock above this mantel that never worked and sitting there and looking like two o'clock and as midnight approached it started to chime. And it chimed midnight. And Graham and I looked at each other as if to say "The clock's never worked, did you fix it?" sort of thing, and sure enough it was saying two o'clock [while] it was striking twelve and once more we accepted it was Charlotte.

But what was strange about her presence is she seemed to appear only when there were men in the house. So I don't know, I put it down to she was discomforted by some man's presence and after my husband and I broke up, and I bought the house a second time, she didn't really come back. But I was told stories by neighbours and I have a stepson and whenever I have babysitters in . . . apparently the babysitters were quite spooked in the house quite often; they would find doors were opening and closing, something that happened to us several times and we said, "Oh, it must have been Charlotte," because there was no explanation.

Sources

Many of the details in this biography were obtained from the 134 boxes of personal files Charlotte Whitton left with Public Archives of Canada, now Library and Archives Canada. These files (MG30 E256), measuring eighty-four metres, or almost the length of a football field, contain a treasure trove of personal and professional information, ranging from ongoing correspondence with prime ministers Richard B. Bennett and John Diefenbaker, to more commonplace items such as grocery receipts and 25-cent tickets to a canoe club dance. Also included are hundreds of Whitton's files from her social welfare, consulting, and political careers, along with hundreds of greeting cards and letters from the famous, such as former prime ministers Louis St. Laurent and Lester B. Pearson, to the ordinary (mostly women), from across Canada and occasionally the United States and Great Britain.

Also, I accessed more Whitton files at the City of Ottawa Archives and the Queen's University Archives, scrolled through extensive newspaper clippings from *The Ottawa Citizen* and *The Ottawa Journal*, and conducted interviews with some four dozen people who were acquainted with Charlotte at different stages in her life. An unfinished biography of Charlotte by her sister Kathleen, on file at the city archives, provided intimate details about Whitton family life.

Most of my sources were mentioned in the text, but the following additions should be noted:

Bennett, Carol. *The Story of Renfrew, Volume II.* Juniper Books, 1984.

Clarkson, Adrienne. *Heart Matters: A Memoir.* Penguin, 2006.

Cosentino, Frank. *The Renfrew Millionaires: The Valley Boys of Winter 1910.* General Store Publishing House, 1994.

Hamlet, Elizabeth. *Charlotte Whitton and the Growth of the Canadian Council on Child Welfare, 1926–41, A Study of the Role of Social Reformers in Social Policy Making in Canada.* Master's thesis, Carleton University, 1979.

Moffat, Ken. *A Poetics of Social Work: Personal Agency and Social Transformation in Canada, 1920–1939.* University of Toronto Press, 2001.

Pigeon, Father L.P. *Le Lac McGregor Lake: Some Beginnings, Quelques Commencements.* (Self-published)

Rooke, P.T. and R.L Schnell. *No Bleeding Heart: Charlotte Whitton, A Feminist on the Right.* University of British Columbia Press, 1987.

Smallfield, W.E. and Rev. Robert Campbell. *The Story of Renfrew.* Smallfield & Son, 1919.

Splane, Dr. Richard. *75 Years of Community Service in Canada: Canadian Council on Social Development 1920–1995.* Canadian Council on Social Development, 1996.

Valverde, Mariana. *The Age of Light, Soap and Water: Moral Reform in English Canada, 1885–1925.* McClelland & Stewart, 1991.

Young, Scott and Astrid. *O'Brien: From Water Boy to One Million a Year.* Ryerson Press, 1967.

—Canadian Council on Social Development fonds at Library and Archives Canada, MG28 I10.

Index